Ernest George Ravenstein

**The Russians on the Amur**

Its discovery, conquest, and colonization, with a description of the country, its inhabitants, productions, and commercial capabilities

Ernest George Ravenstein

**The Russians on the Amur**
*Its discovery, conquest, and colonization, with a description of the country, its inhabitants, productions, and commercial capabilities*

ISBN/EAN: 9783337298982

Printed in Europe, USA, Canada, Australia, Japan

Cover: Foto ©ninafisch / pixelio.de

More available books at **www.hansebooks.com**

# THE
# RUSSIANS ON THE AMUR;

ITS

## DISCOVERY, CONQUEST, AND COLONISATION,

WITH

A DESCRIPTION OF THE COUNTRY, ITS INHABITANTS, PRODUCTIONS, AND COMMERCIAL CAPABILITIES;

AND

PERSONAL ACCOUNTS OF RUSSIAN TRAVELLERS.

BY

E. G. RAVENSTEIN, F.R.G.S.

CORRESPONDING FELLOW OF THE GEOGRAPHICAL SOCIETY OF FRANKFURT.

ILLUSTRATED BY

Three Maps, Four Plates & Fifty-Eight Wood Engravings.

LONDON:
TRÜBNER AND CO., PATERNOSTER ROW.
1861.

TO

COLONEL SIR HENRY JAMES, R.E.,

F.R.S., M.R.I.A., F.R.G.S.

DIRECTOR OF THE TOPOGRAPHICAL AND STATISTICAL DEPARTMENT
OF THE WAR OFFICE,

ETC., ETC., ETC.

THIS WORK IS INSCRIBED,

IN RESPECTFUL APPRECIATION OF HIS VALUABLE LABOURS

IN THE CAUSE OF

TOPOGRAPHICAL AND GEOGRAPHICAL SCIENCE.

# PREFACE.

THE progress of Russia in Asia, her rapid strides in the direction of India, and the acquisition from China of provinces far exceeding the British Islands in extent, cannot fail of being important to a nation with such vast interests at stake in China and the East as England has. In presenting therefore a work on Russian advance on the Amur, within the confines of the Celestial Empire, we feel that we are laying before the public a subject well worthy of their attention. It has been our endeavour to convey a correct idea of the past and present condition of the countries we treat of, their productions, inhabitants, and germs of future development,— information of value not only to the geographer, politician, or merchant, but also attractive to that daily-increasing portion of the public who find a pleasure in studying the state and prospects of distant countries.

This volume has not been written in a hasty manner, for the mere purpose of meeting publishing demands, but is the result of the progressive labour of several years. We have not only availed ourselves of all accessible publications, a list of which will be found in the Appendix, but have had the advantage of personal communications with Russian officers who themselves took an active share in the operations on the Amur. Mr. Lühdorf, established at Nikolayevsk since 1856, imparted to us a great deal of information on the commercial prospects of the country; and Captain Prütz

* In June 1857, we published a paper on the "Russians on the Amur," in Bentley's Miscellany.

allowed us to share his experience of a five months' residence at Nikolayevsk. To those gentlemen we beg to tender our hearty thanks.

Anxious as we have been to make the book as complete as possible, there will doubtless be shortcomings almost inseparable from a work of this description, and the reader may now and then desire more detailed information than we are able to afford. In all such cases we throw ourselves upon his kind indulgence.

Our illustrations are from authentic sources, and may be relied upon as true delineations of the scenery and the inhabitants.

The maps have been drawn expressly for this book, and will be found to present many new features, though we frankly admit them to be deficient in some minor particulars. For the orthography of proper names we have adopted the system recommended by the Royal Geographical Society, and employed in the Hydrographical Office. The letters *a* and *i* are always to be pronounced as in r*a*v*i*ne, the *o* as in g*o*, the *e* as in there, and the *u* as in fl*u*te. The diphthong *ai* or *ei* as the *i* in h*i*de. The consonants are pronounced as in English, but *kh* expresses a guttural.

We have avoided the use of foreign names, and terms of weights and measures, as much as possible, and the few which occur are explained in the glossary at the end of the volume. The dates are according to the Gregorian Calendar, which is twelve days in advance of that still in use in Russia.

With these brief observations we submit our work to the kind consideration of the Public.

37, SOUTHAMPTON TERRACE, WATERLOO ROAD,
*October*, 1861.

# LIST OF ILLUSTRATIONS.

### PLATES.

#### LITHOGRAPHED BY MR. J. JURY.

| NO. | | | PAGE |
|---|---|---|---|
| 1. Mangun Tomb | R. Maack, | to face Title. | |
| 2. View of Bureya Mountains | ” | to face | 179 |
| 3. View of Dyrki | ” | ” | 182 |
| 4. A Mangun Village | ” | ” | 378 |

### WOODCUTS.

#### ENGRAVED BY MR. W. BREWER, WITH THE EXCEPTION OF NOS. 19, 20, 25, 29, 32, AND 54, WHICH ARE BY MR. JOHN SWAIN.

| | | |
|---|---|---|
| 1. Arms of Albazin, from Description | | 45 |
| 2. Goldi Sledge | R. Maack | 96 |
| 3. Portrait of General Count Muravief-Amursky | ” | 115 |
| 4. View of Aigun, and reception of General Muravief by the Chinese in 1854 | Sverbéef | 118 |
| 5. View of Mariinsk, 1854 | ” | 120 |
| 6. View on the Shilka | R. Maack | 165 |
| 7. View below the Bureya Mountains | ” | 181 |
| 8. Goldi in a Boat | ” | 183 |
| 9. View of Dere, Lower Amur | ” | 188 |
| 10. ⎫ | | 194 |
| 11. ⎬ Tatar Monuments at Tyr . . . Permikin | | 195 |
| 12. ⎭ | | 196 |
| 13. Nikolayevsk, 1859, from an original sketch by Capt. Prütz | | 197 |
| 14. Manchu Mill | R. Maack | 256 |
| 15. Goldi Spindle | ” | 312 |
| 16. Birch-bark Basket | ” | 305 |
| 17. Sleeping Tent | ” | 335 |
| 18. Goldi Summer Hut near the Sungari | ” | 338 |
| 19. Oronchon | Sverbéef | 343 |
| 20. Manyargs, Woman, Girl, and Man | R. Maack and Sverbéef | 345 |
| 21. Manyarg Harpoon | R. Maack | 349 |
| 22. Oronchon Fishing Apparatus, from Description | | 349 |

| NO. | | | PAGE |
|---|---|---|---|
| 23. Manchu Matchlock | | R. Maack | 350 |
| 24. Manyarg Horn | | " | 356 |
| 25. Manchu | | " | 358 |
| 26. Manchu Cart | | " | 359 |
| 27. Manchu Barge | | " | 363 |
| 28. Fishing Apparatus near Aigun | | " | 363 |
| 29. Goldi | | " | 366 |
| 30. Orochis, from Castries Bay | | La Pérouse | 367 |
| 31. Mangun Belt | | R. Maack | 369 |
| 32. Mangun | | " | 370 |
| 33. Goldi Idol | | " | 370 |
| 34. Goldi Ear-ring | | " | 371 |
| 35. Summer Hut at the Usuri Mouth | | " | 372 |
| 36. Birch-Bark Canoe | | " | 372 |
| 37. Mangun Harpoon | | " | 373 |
| 38. Anvil | | " | 374 |
| 39. Bellows | | " | 374 |
| 40. Spear Head | | " | 374 |
| 41. Interior of a Mangun House | | " | 376 |
| 42. Goldi Idol Poles | | " | 377 |
| 43. Mangun Spear | | " | 379 |
| 44. Goldi Spear | | " | 381 |
| 45. Snare | | " | 382 |
| 46. Mangun Idol | | " | 383 |
| 47. The God Panya | | " | 384 |
| 48. Shaman Tomb | | " | 385 |
| 49. Cradle | | " | 386 |
| 50. Mangun Knife for cutting out Fish-skin Ornaments | | " | 388 |
| 51. No. 1, Mangun Pocket for Tinder | | " | 388 |
| 52.    2, Mangun Birch-bark Box | | " | 388 |
| 53.    3, Fish-skin Ornament | | " | 388 |
| 54. Gilyaks | | R. Maack and Sverbéef | 389 |
| 55. Aino Elder | | La Pérouse | 395 |
| 56. Aino Tomb | | v. Siebold | 397 |
| 57. Aino Burial-place | | " | 398 |
| 58. Orotskos with Reindeer | | " | 398 |

MAPS.

The Regions of the Amur to illustrate Events of the 17th Century, p. 1
The Regions of the Amur in 1861 . . . . (at the end)
The Lower Amur . . . . . . . p. 193

# CONTENTS.

## PART I.—HISTORICAL.

I.—MANCHURIA AND THE AMUR PREVIOUS TO THE APPEARANCE OF
THE RUSSIANS . . . . . . . . . 3

Manchuria 1100 B.C. is inhabited by Tunguzian tribes known to the Chinese as Suchi. The conquests of the Koreans first introduce a certain degree of civilization, and in the seventh century is founded the empire of Phuhai, which in 925 A.D. falls under the sway of the Kidans, also of Tunguzian origin. The Kidans in turn succumb to the Gin, who reign in China until 1234, when they are overthrown by the Mongol Yuen, who had been called into the country by the Chinese. On the expulsion of the Mongols, a native dynasty, the Ming, ascends the throne of China and subjugates Manchuria; but they are expelled from Manchuria in 1621 by Nukhatzi, a lineal descendant of the ancient Gin, and who becomes founder of the Manchu dynasty still reigning in China.

II.—FIRST NEWS OF THE AMUR, 1636; POYARKOF'S EXPEDITION,
1643 TO 1646 . . . . . . . . . 9

The Russian Cossacks steadily advancing through Siberia, hear for the first time of the Amur, when they stand by the Sea of Okhotsk in 1636. Further information is obtained by Perfirief on the Vitim; and Poyarkof, in 1643, leaves Yakutsk on an expedition to the Amur. He ascends the Aldan, crosses the Stanovoi Mountains, and winters in a Daurian village on the Dzeya. His extortionate conduct causes hostilities with the natives, and his officer, Petrof, meets with a repulse at Moldikichid. Having lost forty men by famine, Poyarkof descends the Dzeya and Amur, and winters in the country of the Gilyaks, whence he returns to Yakutsk by way of the Sea of Okhotsk.

III.—KHABAROF, 1647—1652 . . . . . . . . 14

A shorter route to the Amur is discovered by some Cossacks, and Khabarof avails himself of it on his first expedition in 1649. Arrived on the Upper Amur he leaves a small detachment at one of Lavkai's Forts, and goes back to Yakutsk for reinforcements. On his return to the Amur, 1650, he descends that river with men, storms a triple fortification, surprizes Tolga's village, and builds Achanskoi gorod, where he winters. He is attacked there by the natives, and subsequently by the Manchu. In the ensuing spring he re-ascends the Amur, and at the Bureya Mountains meets with one hundred and eighteen Cossacks, commanded by Chechigin and Philipof. Nagiba had been sent in advance with twenty men to announce the arrival of these reinforcements, but he missed Khabarof, and descended the whole of the Amur, returning by way of the Sea of Okhotsk to Yakutsk. Khabarof continues the ascent of the Amur, and, on his arriving at the Dzeya, part of his men mutiny, and one hundred and thirty-six out of a total of three hundred and forty-eight desert him. He winters at the Komar.

IV.—STEPANOF, 1652—1661 . . . . . . . . 26

The events on the Amur attract the attention of the Government at Moscow, and Simoviof is sent to make preparations for the arrival of a large military force. Exaggerated reports of the riches of the country cause it to be looked upon as the Eldorado of Siberia, and all sorts of adventurers make their way thither. Khabarof is recalled to be rewarded for his services, and Stepanof appointed his successor. Stepanof is not able to carry out the instructions of the Government in founding permanent settlements, but continues roving along the Amur and the Sungari. At Kamarskoi ostrog he is besieged in the spring of 1655 by a large Manchu force. Pushkin, who had been sent to the Argun, prefers joining Stepanof on the Lower Amur; both winter in 1655-6 at Kosogorsky, in the country of the Gilyaks. Stepanof continues his predatory expedition until 1658, when he falls at the mouth of the Dzeya in an encounter with the Chinese. The few remaining Russians evacuate the Amur in 1661.

V.—DISCOVERY AND OCCUPATION OF THE SHILKA, 1652-69 . . 34

The Cossacks of Yeniseisk push across Lake Baikal, and their reports induce the Voivod, Pashkof, to send Beketof to explore these territories (1652). Beketof crosses the Yablonnoi Mountains, and in 1654 founds Neludskoi ostrog, but want of provisions induces him to join his compatriots on the Amur. Pashkof having been appointed Commander-in-Chief of the Russian settlements on the Amur, leaves Yeniseisk in 1656, and following the footsteps of Beketof, founds Nerchinsk in 1658. In 1662 he returns to Yeniseisk, being succeeded by Tolbusin. The Amur itself had been forsaken at that time.

VI.—RENEWED ENTERPRIZES ON THE AMUR. ALBAZIN. 1666 TO 1682 . . . . . . . . . . 38

Chernigovsky, having slain the Governor of Ilimsk, flies to the Amur where he builds Albazin, 1666. He is joined there by others; villages are founded near the fort, and Albazin becomes a place of importance. The Chinese complain of the encroachments of the Russians, and Milovanof goes on a conciliatory embassy to Peking in 1670, and Spafarik in 1675. In spite of orders to the contrary, the Russians at Albazin again navigate the Lower Amur. They found settlements on the Dzeya, 1676-8. Milovanof in 1681 is appointed governor of these, and builds a fort on the Silimji. A proposed expedition into the country of the Gilyaks, does not take place, but Frolof with sixty-one Cossacks goes to the Amgun, where he constructs a fort. At the close of 1682 the Russians have settlements at Albazin, on the Dzeya, the Silimji, and the Amgun.

VII.—WAR WITH CHINA, 1683 TO 1687 . . . . . . 45

The Chinese make large preparations to expel the Russians

from the Amur. They intercept a detachment of sixty-seven Cossacks, under Mylnikof, above the Dzeya, and then destroy the settlements on the Dzeya and Amgun, taking the garrisons of Ust Zeisk and Tugursk prisoners. They then advance upon Albazin, where they arrive on the 4th June, 1685, and after a blockade of eighteen days the garrison agrees to evacuate the fort, and retire to Nerchinsk. The Chinese having destroyed the fort withdraw to Aigun, where they leave a strong garrison. The Russians return almost in the wake of the Chinese and rebuild Albazin. In the spring, 1686, Beiton is sent on a reconnoitring expedition to the Komar, and gathers information from a prisoner about the rumoured approach of a large Chinese army. He at once returns to Albazin, where the advanced-guard of the Chinese arrives on the 7th July. The Russians are surrounded in their fort, and offer a vigorous resistance until November, when the siege is raised in consequence of the expected conclusion of a treaty of peace.

VIII.—THE TREATY OF NERCHINSK, 1689 . . . . . 54

Venukof goes on a mission to Peking to arrange preliminaries for concluding a treaty of peace. Count Golovin is appointed Russian plenipotentiary, and leaves Moscow with a large retinue on the 20th June, 1686. On his arrival at Udinsk (28th Sept., 1687), he sends a messenger to Peking to ask the Chinese to fix upon a place for the conference. Selenginsk is chosen, but owing to the disturbed state of the Mongol country, the Chinese are not able to proceed to it, and the place of conference is removed to Nerchinsk, where they arrive on the 11th July, 1689, with a large force by land and water. Golovin reaches the place on the 18th August, and after several conferences the treaty of peace is signed on the 29th. By it Albazin and the whole of the Amur are ceded to China.

IX. - THE AMUR SINCE THE TREATY OF NERCHINSK, 1689 TO 1848 . 65

*a.* THE RUSSO-CHINESE FRONTIER . . . . . . . 65

Chinese Frontier Monuments — Arbitrary extension of the Boundary at the Gorbitza—Punishment of Persons crossing the Frontiers—Shobelzin and Shetilof's Expedition—Escape of Exiles across the Frontiers—Inspection of the Boundary by the Chinese.

*b.* THE RUSSIAN MISSION AT PEKING . . . . . . 71

The Russians taken Prisoners on the Amur are settled at Peking — The Russian Clerical Mission instituted by the Treaty of 1727—Present Position of the Mission (*See* also p. 449).

*c.* THE AMUR AND SAKHALIN UNDER THE DOMINION OF CHINA . 73

Government and Military Forces—Tribute—Sakhalin—Trade —Chinese Immigration.

X.—THE ROMISH MISSIONARIES IN MANCHURIA . . . . 78

M. Verolles is appointed Vicar Apostolic of Manchuria in 1838, and with his sanction M. de la Brunière undertakes a journey to the country of the Shang-mao-tze on the Amur. In May, 1845 he leaves Kai-cheu in Leaotong, and passing the newly-founded town of Asheho, proceeds to Sansin on the Sungari, whence he makes an excursion to Susu, a Goldi village lower down. He describes the Goldi "Fish-skins" living there, and the mode in which the Manchu collect their tribute. The arrival of some Manchu officials induces him to return to Sansin, whence he proceeds to the Usuri, and lodges in the hut of some ginseng-seekers. His stay during the winter enables him to become acquainted with the Chinese colonists and the natives. In the spring of 1846, he descends the Usuri and Amur, but is murdered by the Gilyaks. In the mean time the mission in Southern Manchuria makes progress, and M. Venault establishes himself at Asheho. The Christians are persecuted, but peace is restored in 1850, and M. Venault resolves to clear up the fate of his late fellow-labourer. By way of Sansin he proceeds to Imma on the Usuri, descends that river and the Amur to beyond Pul, and near Hutong concludes an act of reconciliation with the murderers. He hears here for the first time of the appearance of Russians. His return journey is attended by considerable hardships.

CONTENTS—PART I.

XI.—RECENT HISTORY OF THE AMUR . . . . . . 113

Proposals for re-occupying the Amur are made soon after the conclusion of the Treaty of Nerchinsk, but not until 1847, when Count Muravief is appointed Governor-General of Eastern Siberia, are steps taken towards it. Vaganof is sent to explore the Amur, and a naval "Amur Expedition" commanded by Admiral Nevilskoi is sent to the mouth of the river. Petrovsk, Nikolayevsk, Mariinsk, Alexandrovsk and Constantinovsk are founded between 1850 and 1854.

1854—5. . . . . . . . . . . . 117

Count Muravief conducts the first Russian Expedition down the river chiefly to supply the Russian squadron in the Pacific with provisions. The Chinese do not offer resistance. Muravief meets Admiral Putiatin in Port Imperial, and returns by way of Ayan to Irkutsk. War is declared against Russia by England and France. The results of the *naval campaign* of the latter are insignificant. The attack upon Petropavlovsk is unsuccessful, and the Russians effect their retreat to Castries Bay.

1855—6. . . . . . . . . . . 125

Three military expeditions descend the Amur, and colonists are settled between Mariinsk and Nikolayevsk. The allied squadrons are commanded in that year by Admirals Bruce and Sir James Stirling. The former enters the harbour of Petropavlovsk, and then sends three vessels to Ayan. Commodore Elliot in May sails up the Channel of Tatary and finds the Russians in Castries Bay, but they escape during a fog. At Cape Crillon he joins Sir J. Stirling, and the whole squadron then proceed to the Sea of Okhotsk, where they capture a Russian brig, and the Greta. The fleet returns to the south, and Commodore Elliot a second time sails up the Channel of Tatary. Urup is taken possession of in the name of the Allies. (A battalion of infantry starved to death, 449).

1856—7 . . . . . . . . . . . 136

News of the conclusion of peace arrive in July, and the Russians are left unfettered to carry on their plans. Count Muravief secures large means at St. Petersburg. Four stations are formed along the Amur, a postal service is arranged, and two small steamers arrive from America.

1857—8 . . . . . . . . . . 139
   Count Muravief returns to the Amur. Large bodies of troops descend the river and form stations along its banks. Captain Furruhelm avails himself of the newly-opened communications to convey provisions to the Russian settlements in the Pacific, and the United States send a commercial agent. Count Putiatin sets out on a mission to Japan and China, but is not successful in concluding a boundary treaty with the latter. The Amur regions are erected into the "Maritime Province of Eastern Siberia," and another squadron leaves Kronstadt for the Pacific. (*See* also p. 450).

1858 . . . . . . . . . . . 143
   Count Muravief concludes the Treaty of Aigun, 28th May, and Count Putiatin that of Tientsin on the 13th June. Blagovesh'chensk, Khabarovka and Sofyevsk are founded. The Amur Province is separated from the Maritime Province and the Cossacks are organised. The naval force in the Pacific is still further increased. The Amur Company founded.

1859—60 . . . . . . . . . . 147
   Colonisation is encouraged. Stations are formed along the Usuri and Sungachan and a surveying corps is sent there. German colonists leave European Russia for the Amur. Count Muravief for the fifth time descends the Amur. The Chinese, after the affair of the Peiho, assume a hostile attitude, but after the occupation of Peking by the Allies they are glad to sign a treaty, 14th November, by which the Amur and the coast of Manchuria are ceded to Russia. (*See* also p. 450).

The Regions of the Amur in 1861 . . . . . . . . 154
   Political Divisions. Population. Military strength. Naval force in the Pacific. Telegraphs.

# PART II.

## GEOGRAPHICAL, STATISTICAL AND COMMERCIAL.

XII.—GEOGRAPHICAL DESCRIPTION OF THE RIVER AMUR . . 161
   Introductory; the Amur from Ust Strelka to Albazin, 166; Albazin to the Dzeya, 168; Blagovesh'chensk to the Bureya Mountains, 175; The Bureya Mountains, 179; Prairie Region

of the Lower Amur, 181; From the Usuri to the Bokki Mountains, 184; Bokki Mountains to Mariinsk, 187; Sofyevsk to Castries Bay, 190; Mariinsk to Nikolayevsk, 192; Liman of the Amur, 200.

XIII.—THE COUNTRY NORTH OF THE AMUR . . . . . 202
Middendorf's Journey from the Sea of Okhotsk to Ust Strelka, 203; Usoltzof's Journey to the Source of the Gilui and to the Dzeya, 212.

XIV.—THE COUNTRY SOUTH OF THE AMUR.
The Coast of Manchuria . . . . . . . . . 224
Port St. Vladimir—Port Imperial—Ternay Bay—Bullock Bay—Sybille Bay—Port St. Vladimir—Port Sir Michael Seymour or Olga Bay—Victoria Bay—Tumen river. (*See* also p. 451).
The Coast Range . . . . . . . . . . . 232
The Usuri . . . . . . . . . . . . . 233
Source—Sungacha—Lake Kingka—Veniukof's exploration.
The Sungari . . . . . . . . . . . . 259
Source—Basin—Girin—Nonni—Maximowicz's attempted exploration.

XV.—SAKHALIN . . . . . . . . . . . 265
Extent—Interior—Aniva Bay—East Coast—West Coast—Schrenck's Journey.

XVI.—CLIMATE . . . . . . . . . . . 275
General Considerations—Dauria—The Upper Amur, Blagovesh'chensk—The Usuri. (*See* also p. 451)—Mariinsk and Nikolayevsk—The Channel of Tatary—Sakhalin.

XVII.—MINERAL PRODUCTIONS. . . . . . . 285

XVIII.—PLANTS . . . . . . . . . . . 288
Statistics of Plants, 288; Physiognomy of Vegetation, 292; Food Plants, 294; Trees, 299; Medicinal Plants, 308; Miscellaneous, 311.

XIX.—ANIMALS . . . . . . . . . . . 315
Mammals, 310, 452; Domestic animals, 317; Game and Fur-bearing animals, 320; Birds, 324; Fish and Reptiles, 334; Insects, etc.

CONTENTS—PART II. xix

                       PAGE

XX.—NATIVE INHABITANTS . . . . . . . 388
 Language—Manner of Life—Chinese names of tribes—Population.
 The Tunguzians of the Upper Amur, Oronchons and Manyargs . 343
  Territory, 343; Reindeer and Horses, 343; Chinese influences, 344; Features, 345; Dress, 346; Manner of Life, 347; Habitations, 348; Fishing, 348; Hunting, 350; Religion, 351; Nomadic Tunguzians of the Angara, and how they spend each month throughout the year, 351; Soloń, 357.
 Manchu, Daurians and Chinese . . . . . . 358
  Territory, 358; Appearance, 359; Dress, 360; Houses, 360; Idols, 361; Temples, 362; Fishing, 363; The Daurians on the Nonni, 364; Targachins, 365.
 Tunguzians of the Lower Amur, Goldi, Manguns, Orochi . . 366
  Territory, 366; Appearance, 367; Dress, 368; Fishing and Summer habitations, 371; Winter habitations, 376; Idols, 377; Bear cages and Bear hunts, 379; Snares, 380; Religious notions and Idols, 383; Artistic Instincts, 388.
 The Gilyaks . . . . . . . 389
 The Aino . . . . . . . 392
 The Oroke, or Orotskos of Sakhalin . . 398

XXI.—COMMERCIAL RESOURCES AND GERMS FOR THEIR DEVELOPMENT . . . . . . . . . . 400
 Productions: vegetable, mineral and animal—Manufactures—Commerce with neighbouring countries—Transbaikal and Siberia, 404; Kiakhta, 410; Japan, 412; Communications, 412; Government, its Merits and Shortcomings, 415; Amur Company, 421; Imports, 425; Exports, 428.

## APPENDIX.

HISTORICAL AUTHORITIES . . . . . . . . 431
HISTORICAL SKETCH OF RECENT GEOGRAPHICAL EXPLORATIONS . 434
 Middendorf—L. A. Schwarz—Vaganof—Muravief's First Expedition, Permikin, Sverbéef, Anosof—Admiral Putiatin and Lieutenant Peshchurof—Shenurin, Raebsky and Chikachef—Leop. von Schrenck—C. J. Maximowicz—Maack's Expedition with Kochetof, Gerstfeldt, Sondhagen and Fuhrmann—East Siberian Expedition of the Russian Geographical Society, L. A. Schwarz, Roshkof, Smirägin, Usoltzof, Radde, E. E. Meier

—Romanof—Maximowicz up the Sungari—Schmidt, Glehn and Brylkin—Veniukof's Exploration of the Usuri—Colonel Budogorsky, Lieutenant Dariyetarof, Captain Gamof—Richard Maack's Exploration of the Usuri—Perry Mc D. Collins—Pargachevsky—Esche and Jacoby—Lühdorf—Nazimof, Savalakhin—Naval Surveys, *Russian*, Admiral Nevilskoi, Boshnak, Rimsky-Korsakof, Putiatin; *English;* *French* — Atkinson's works on Siberia.

NOTES ON THE NAVIGATION OF THE CHANNEL OF TATARY, CASTRIES BAY AND THE GULF OF THE AMUR. By Captain Prütz . 445

ADDENDA AND ERRATA . . . . . . . 448

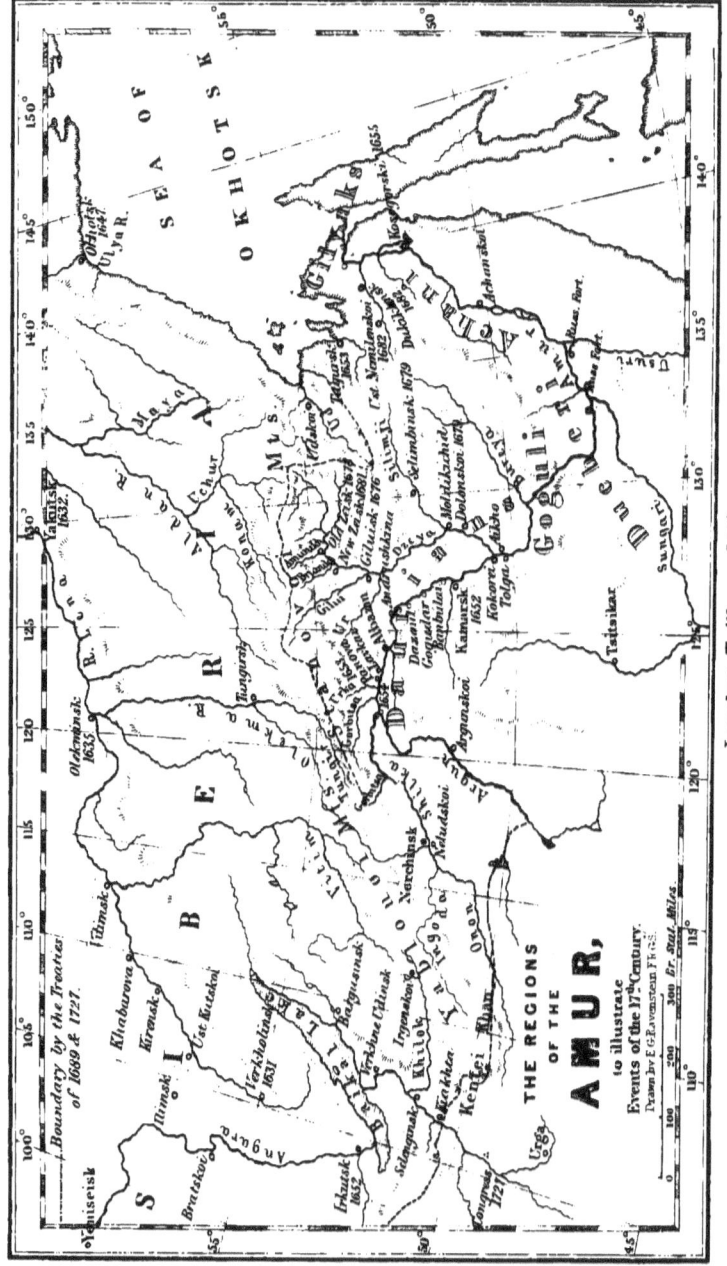

# THE RUSSIANS ON THE AMUR.

PART I.—HISTORICAL.

# THE RUSSIANS ON THE AMUR.

## PART I.—HISTORICAL.

### I.

### MANCHURIA AND THE AMUR PREVIOUS TO THE APPEARANCE OF THE RUSSIANS.

The Amur has not yet played that part in the world's history, which from its size we might deem its due. Although flowing, in its middle course, through regions which in fertility rival those of central Europe, it enters a sea ice-bound during half the year or more. The establishment of a commercial emporium at its mouth, could be of importance only to a power which, possessing territories in the centre of Northern Asia, sought by means of it to establish communication with transmarine countries. The nomadic and semi-civilised tribes, who from time immemorial occupy the basin of the Amur and its tributaries, never felt the want of such communication; and, moreover, inclination led these tribes to prefer conquests in the south, rather than to rely upon their own strength, and to found an independent empire in Manchuria. Thus we find the destinies of Manchuria almost uninterruptedly connected with those of China.

It was reserved to Russia, first to appreciate the importance of the Amur; but, before relating the events which led thither the forces of the Colossus of the North, we will give a short account of the tribes inhabiting the basin of the

Amur, prior to the first discovery of the river by the Cossacks in the seventeenth century.[a]

The tribes inhabiting these regions are mentioned for the first time in the Annals of China, 1100 B.C. They were then known as Suchi, or Zucheu. Gorski supposes their original seats to have been on the Steppes of Mongolia, whence they retreated before the advancing Mongols to the forests of Girin, north of the sacred Shan-alin mountains. From Girin they spread over the whole of present Manchuria, and colonies of them proceeded northward far into Siberia. The Chinese applied the name of Dun-khu to the eastern Mongols, and hence the name of Tunguzians.[b]

The manners and customs of the Tunguzians progressed with their political development. The ancient Tunguz learned from childhood to bend the bow and to tame the horse. His arrow-head was of stone, dipped in a deadly poison. Life was deemed of little value; the dead were buried in the open field, and a few pigs sacrificed on the grave, which was screened from sun and rain by a wooden roof. Age was but little respected; and to shed tears at the death of a relative was considered weakness in men or women.

---

[a] Gorski, "Origin and first Deeds of the Manchu Dynasty;" "On the Origin of the Manchu Dynasty of the Tsin, in 'Labours of the Russian Mission at Pekin.'" German Translation. Berlin, 1858—9. Plath, "The Peoples of Manchuria." Göttingen, 1838.

[b] According to Strahlenberg, the Arinians, a poor tribe on the Yenisei, called the Tunguzians, *Tonge-kze, i.e.*, people of three tribes, which Bulichef (Travels in East Siberia, vol. i.) refers to the Reindeer Tunguzians or Orochon (*Orocha*=reindeer); the Tunguzian fishermen of the sea-coast or Namki (Lamutes; *Nam*=sea), and the Daurians or Tunguzians, rearing horned cattle and tilling the soil. The Tunguzians, of whom the Manchu form a mere subdivision, are of the Turanian race of man, to which belong also the Mongols (Tatars), and Turks. Nevertheless, the name "Tatar" has been applied in a much more extended sense. The dynasty at present reigning in China, is for instance frequently called Tatar, though of Manchu (Tunguzian) origin.

During winter these savages lived in subterraneous dwellings, smeared their bodies with pig's fat to protect themselves against the cold, and wore garments made of hides or fish-skins. The women wore a dress of coarse linen. In summer they built huts at the fringe of the forest. Dogs, pigs, and horses, were their only domestic animals; the chase and fishing their only occupation. Each village acknowledged a hereditary chief, but was independent of all else.

The first amelioration in the condition of the inhabitants is due to the conquests made by the Koreans. Agriculture was introduced; villages combined, and, under common chiefs, formed small confederacies. In the fifth century, the Moho, whose lands extended to the Amur, paid tribute to China in arrows, bows, fur-clothing, and sables. Korea, in her wars with China, found powerful allies in these Moho, who sent to her aid an army of 150,000 men; but when Korea fell under the sway of the Chinese, in 677, the tribe of Tunguzians, subsequently known as the Manchu, retired to the Shan-Alin Mountains, and having been joined there by many Koreans, they founded the Empire of *Phu-hai*, or *Bokhai*, which at the height of its power reached from the middle of Korea to beyond the Amur, and from the Eastern Ocean to the Great Khingan. This empire was inhabited by 1,000,000 families, and maintained an army of 20,000 well-trained troops. The villages became towns, and the arts and sciences were cultivated by Chinese and Koreans invited into the country. The Emperor of China hastened to acknowledge his powerful neighbour as the "Most Sacred Emperor of Bokhai," and the country had become one of the most flourishing kingdoms on the Eastern Sea.

This kingdom in 925 fell under the sway of the *Kidans* or Liao, a dynasty also founded by a Tunguzian tribe, the Shygoey or She-wei, who inhabited the country stretching from Liao (Leao-tung or Shinking) to the Amur. The empire of the Kidans had been founded in 907 by Apaokhi, and existed until 1125. It included the whole of Mongolia and Manchuria, and extended from the eastern ocean to Kashgar, and from the Altai mountains to the wall of China. China itself was tributary from 1012 to 1101. The Kidans extended this power to the kindred tribes of the Mohos on the Sungari and Amur, who in the seventh century had again assumed the ancient name of Suchi. Part of these Suchi were entered in the books of the Kidans as civilised, others were described as "wild Suchi," but they kept cattle and horses. The dynasty destined to supplant that of the Kidan, we allude to the *Gin* (Aishin, Sushin or Niuchzen), arose among these wild Suchi. The founder of this family was Hian-phu of the tribe of the Wan-yan, who after a sojourn in Korea returned to his native country, introduced agriculture, and replaced the birch-bark huts by houses. His successors extended their power by policy, and the fifth of the line was appointed governor over the wild Suchi. He died in 1021. Agutha, the seventh of the line, whose birth in 1068 had been announced by the appearance of a five-coloured cloud, threw off the yoke of the Kidans, fortified in 1114 the passes leading into Manchuria, and assembled a small force of 2500 men on the Lai-leu river. Emissaries were sent to the kindred tribes of the Suchi, and the force at his disposal soon amounted to 100,000 men, most of them cavalry. Before invading China, he publicly enumerated the crimes of the Kidans, and called upon heaven and earth to second his undertaking. Large rewards were held out to the soldiers in case of victory, ignominious punishment in case of defeat. On marching out, the arrows were discharged to keep off misfortune, flames burst forth from the earth, and repeatedly settled on the points of the lance—a sign that the Gods were propitious. The army was divided into troops of 50 men, 20 of whom in the front rank wore heavy coats of mail, and were armed with lances and swords. The others in the rear-ranks had light armour, with bows and javelins. On approaching the enemy two men were sent in advance to reconnoitre, and the attack was made simultaneously from four sides. They advanced, trotting, to within a hundred paces of the enemy, and approaching the hostile lines at full speed discharged their arrows and javelins, wheeled round suddenly, and renewed this attack, until the enemy began to waver, and only then resorted to the use of the sword.

In 1115 Agutha assumed the name of Tai-tzu and the title of Emperor. His dynasty he called Gin, or the Golden, with reference probably to its stability. His successors reigned in northern China from 1115 to 1234, and southern China paid tribute from 1141 to 1213. Constant wars with the Koreans, Chinese, and Mongols, whose assistance had been solicited by the Chinese, broke the power of the Gin. The Mongols established themselves in China, and reigned as the *Yuen* until 1368. The population of Manchuria was decimated during this period, the towns were burnt, and ruins alone attested the former flourishing state of the country. One of the emperors of the Yuen dynasty went by sea to the mouth of the Amur, where he built in commemoration the Monastery of Eternal Repose, on the site of which may still be seen several columns with inscriptions recording the fact. (*See* chap. xii.)

The Yuen were overthrown in 1368 by a revolution headed by a common Chinese, who founded the dynasty of the *Ming*. At that time Manchuria was divided into Tsyan-chzu, Khai-zi and Ye-shen. The first of these, to the north of the Shan-alin, was the most important. In 1403 the Ming made Ye-shen tributary, and soon after the other districts also.

At Odoli however, in Tsyan-chzu, there appeared, about 1360, Aishin-gioro, a lineal descendant of the ancient Gin, and several villages acknowledged in him their chief. About the latter part of the sixteenth century one of his descendants, Nurkhatzi, enlarged the frontiers of the territory. In 1599 he introduced a Manchu alphabet; and the Mongol language, which hitherto had been employed in all written communications, was supplanted by the Manchu. The prisoners of war were settled in villages, and their prosperous condition attracted others. The Chinese who had invested Nurkhatzi with a fine sounding title, and a salary of 800 lan of silver a year, were first roused to the danger of having so powerful a vassal in 1616, when he assumed the name of Tyan-min, and title of Emperor. By his compatriots he is called Tai-tzu, *i.e.* "the first of his race." War was declared against him, but Tai-tzu repeatedly defeated the Chinese; and in 1621 settled at Mugden in Leaotong, which he made his capital. He died in 1626.

In China a revolution had broken out, and Li, a common Chinese, defeated the Emperor, who committed suicide in 1643. The opponents of Li called to their aid the Manchu, whose emperor expelled Li from Peking (1644), but died soon after; and the conquest was completed under Shunchi, then a child of six years of age.

It was about this time the Russians first appeared on the Amur. The tribes living there partly acknowledged Manchu sovereignty; but the Manchu, still occupied in the consolidation of their power in China, were not at first in a position to protect their subjects against the ravages committed by the Cossacks, and only in 1651 we find them actively engaged in the wars against the Russians. It was reserved to the great Emperor Kang-hi to expel the enemy, and force him, in the treaty of Nerchinsk, to evacuate the regions of the Amur.

## II.

## FIRST NEWS OF THE AMUR, 1636; POYARKOF'S EXPEDITION, 1643-46.

THE Russians made the first settlement at the foot of the Ural, towards the end of the 15th century. In 1587 they founded Tobolsk, whence with surprising rapidity they spread over the whole of Siberia. Tomsk was founded in 1604; Yeniseisk, in 1619; Yakutsk, 1632; and Okhotsk, in 1638.

The Russians received the first accounts of the existence of the river Amur from a party of Cossacks, who had been sent in 1636 from Tomsk to the Aldan river to make the Tunguzians living there tributary. Some of these, under the leadership of Ivan Moskvitin, kept steadily advancing towards the East, and in 1639 stood upon the shores of the Sea of Okhotsk, where they built a winter station, near the mouth of the Ulya river, for the collection of tribute. Here they met with Tunguzians from the river Ud, further south, who spoke of tribes dwelling along the Dzeya (Si) and Shilkar, who cultivated the soil, and with whom they bartered sables for corn. Another tribe near the mouth of the Amur, called the Natkani, carried on commerce in glass beads, copper vessels, silver ornaments, silk and cotton stuffs, evidently received from Japan and China.

In the same year (1639), another party of Cossacks, commanded by Max Perfirief, who had been sent from Yeniseisk to the Vitim, heard confirmatory reports with respect to the Shilka (or upper Amur). They heard about a prince of the

Daurians, Lavkai, who inhabited a stronghold at the mouth of the Urka rivulet; his people kept cattle and tilled the soil; silver, copper and lead ores were said to be found in his territories, and an active bartering trade was being carried on with the lower part of the river, whence silks, cotton stuffs, and other merchandise of Chinese origin were imported.[a]

These various reports did not fail to attract attention in Siberia, but particularly in the rising town of Yakutsk, which was just then becoming important through the fur trade. Its first Voivod, Peter Petrovich *Golovin*, resolved to have the river explored. One expedition was sent by way of the Vitim, but proved unsuccessful; a second, however, up the Aldan, succeeded.

Vasilei *Poyarkof* was placed at the head of 132 men, most of whom were Promyshleni, who previous to joining had been made to undergo some drill as Cossacks. He took with him a small half-pounder iron gun, with ample supplies of provisions and ammunition. On the 15th of July, 1643, the expedition left Yakutsk. For eleven weeks he ascended the Aldan and its tributaries, the Uchur and Gonoma, but being considerably retarded by numerous rapids and shallows on the latter river, he found himself obliged at the end of September to build winter quarters. Poyarkof left forty men here to guard the stores, and himself with the remaining ninety-two continued the journey by land, dragging their provisions on hand sledges. After travelling four weeks under great hardships, he came to the Brianda rivulet, a tributary of the Dzeya. After two days' descent of the Dzeya, he met the first Reindeer Tunguzians, at the mouth of the lower Brianda. Proceeding still further down the river, and passing the mouths of the Gilui and Ur, at the last of which he found Tunguzians with horned cattle, Poyarkof,

[a] Perfirief was not able to advance far along the Vitim; and a second party of seventy Cossacks, sent soon after him, returned also without having made any progress.

eleven days from his departure from the upper Brianda, came to a Daurian village at the mouth of the Umlekan, the inhabitants of which tilled the soil and kept cattle. His reception was most friendly; he was presented with ten oxen and forty baskets of oatmeal, a very acceptable gift to our famishing adventurers, who, in the vain hope of coming into rich and fertile regions, had left their winter quarters at the Gonoma with an insufficient supply of provisions. The Daurians were not at all reticent about giving information with respect to the country beyond. A Khan, *Borboi*, dwelled in a fortified town, about six weeks' journey from the Umlekan. He had not yet succeeded in making tributary all the tribes dwelling on the Amur, and occasionally sent out two or three thousand men, armed with spears, bows or fire-arms, to collect tribute from all who offered resistance. At his residence a considerable bartering trade was carried on, especially in silks and cottons imported from China. Manchu traders visited the dwelling places of the Tunguzians and Daurians regularly. The reports concerning Lavkai were confirmed.

The accession of ninety-two men to a small Daurian village soon caused provisions to run short. Poyarkof therefore sent Yushkof Petrof, one of his officers, to Moldikichid, a fortified Daurian village at the mouth of the Selimda, where provisions were said to abound. Petrof had received orders to entice the chiefs from the village, and keep them as hostages, so as to be able to dictate his own terms to the inhabitants of the place. No such stratagem, however, was required. The unsuspecting native chiefs, Dozi and Kolpa, went of their own accord to meet the Russians as friends, and offered their services. Petrof, instead of taking advantage of this favourable reception, detained the chiefs, and demanded instant admission into the village. This the Daurians would not grant; Petrof threatened to torture the hostages, and by his overbearing conduct provoked the inhabitants to an attack. They sallied from their village, several on horseback, and vigorously attacked the Russians, who had ten men made prisoners dangerously wounded and were obliged to retire with the remainder, many of whom were also wounded, to the forest, where the Daurians soon surrounded them. Kolpa was shot by mistake by his own people, Dozi escaped. After four days the vigilance of the Daurians relaxed, and Petrof was enabled to make good his retreat to the Umlekan.

His chief was naturally highly incensed at the ill success of the expedition. He refused to share the small stock of provisions yet remaining with Petrof's people; and they had to subsist on the bark of trees mixed with a little oatmeal and the roots of herbs. Poyarkof's own conduct had however scarcely been more judicious. The hostages whom he had taken escaped; and the natives, rendered desperate by his continued exactions, attacked his encampment, but were beaten off. It is said that Poyarkof offered the bodies of those slain in the contest to the companions of Petrof for food. Famine gradually thinned the ranks of the Russians; and ere the forty Cossacks left at the Gonoma arrived with provisions, nearly fifty men had succumbed to the pangs of hunger.

On their arrival the journey was continued without loss of time. After three days he came to a Daurian village at the mouth of the Gogul Kurgu; two days subsequently to the village Baldachin; and, on the fifth day, to the mouth of the Dzeya. The Daurian population was numerous, and all of them tilled the soil. After three weeks Poyarkof reached the mouth of the Sungari (Shingal), when he sent on a reconnoitring party of twenty-five men, all of whom, two excepted, were slain by the Ducheri, who at that time inhabited the banks of the Amur, from the Dzeya to four days beyond the Usuri. Nearly six weeks more were spent in reaching the mouth of the Amur, four weeks of which among the Natki, a tribe inhabiting the lower course of the river, and, like the Gilyaks, not yet tributary to any foreign power. Among the latter Poyarkof fixed his winter quarters, and collected as tribute twenty-eight zorok of sable.

On his return, in 1645, he took with him one of the chiefs as a hostage. He came in a boat to the mouth of the Ulya river, where he wintered, and early in the following year continued his journey to Yakutsk, and arrived there on the 12th June, 1646. A few men, whom he had left at the Ulya to collect tribute, did not stay there very long; for Nagiba, who passed that way in 1652, found no trace of them. In Poyarkof's opinion, 300 men would suffice to subject the whole of the territories visited by him. Three forts, with a garrison of fifty men each, should be erected in the country of the Daurians and Ducheri, and the remaining 150 men kept in hand in case the collection of tribute was opposed. Provisions abounded, and no serious resistance was to be apprehended.

We cannot deny to Poyarkof the merit of having been the first to explore the course of the Amur. At the same time his treacherous and cruel behaviour towards the natives, who had received him with open arms, makes him suffer greatly in our estimation; whilst his want of foresight, in entering an unknown region, in the middle of winter, without a sufficient supply of provisions, proves him to have been a man scarcely fit for the command of an expedition of this kind.

## III.

## KHABAROF, NAGIBA, CHECHEGIN AND PHILIPPOF. 1647 TO 1652.

THE accounts of Poyarkof kept alive the interest taken in the exploration and conquest of the countries of the Amur; and when some Promyshleni, who had been hunting on the Olekma, received information, in 1647, of a shorter and more commodious route to the Amur, measures were at once taken to render it available. Cossacks were sent to construct an Ostrog at the confluence of the Tugir and Olekma, and some of the men crossed the dividing range in 1648. At a Simovie of some Promyshleni they left the Olekma, and in two days arrived at the Urka river, a tributary of the Amur. They advanced cautiously, avoiding all villages, and came upon the Amur at a place half a day's journey below the mouth of the Urka. Here they saw a raft upon the river, and were told by their Tunguzian guide that his countrymen on the Shilka descended the river every autumn with their horses, to buy corn from Prince Lavkai. At the beginning of winter they returned by land to their own country. Lavkai's town was said to be a day's journey lower down; but owing to their small number the Cossacks preferred returning to the Olekma, notching the trees however on their route, to guide any future expedition.

In the year following this preparatory exploration, Yerofei Khabarof,[a] a wealthy Promyshleni, proposed the sub-

[a] Khabarof was born at Sol Vuichegodsk, in the government of Vologda. In 1636 we find him settled on a farm on the Yenisei, in Siberia. In 1639 he established the saltworks of Kutskoi, on a tributary of the Lena, which two years afterwards were declared crown property, without granting him an indemnity.

jugation of the newly discovered territories to Dmitri Andrev Zin Transbekof, the newly appointed Voivod of Yakutsk, who in that year had wintered at Ilimsk. Khabarof offered to bear the expenses attending the outfit of such an expedition himself, and promised to send the tribute collected to Yakutsk. The Voivod at once gave his consent. A few Cossacks were placed at the disposal of Khabarof, and rather late in the season he left Ilimsk with about seventy men. He wintered at Tugirsk, and on the 18th January 1650 continued his journey to the Amur on sledges. The bad conduct of Poyarkof and his Cossacks had already become known among the native populations, and on Khabarof's approach they deserted their dwellings. Instead of the one fort of Lavkai, Khabarof found five, from one to one and a half day's journey from each other, all belonging to the prince and his relations. The fortifications consisted of wooden walls, with four or five turrets for archers, the whole surrounded by a ditch and high earthwalls. Small, covered gates, for sorties, were placed beneath the towers, and secret passages led down to the river. Within the enclosure stood large wooden houses, with paper windows, each affording accommodation to fifty or sixty persons.

The first and second of these forts Khabarof found deserted; but on approaching the third, he saw five horsemen advancing towards him. These were Lavkai himself, two of his brothers, his son-in-law, and a servant. They halted at speaking distance, and conversation was carried on through a Tunguzian interpreter. Lavkai desired to know the object of the Russians in visiting his country. When told they merely came for the sake of trade, he proved incredulous: he had heard from a Cossack that the Russians intended to conquer and enslave the country. Khabarof replied, that he might possibly require a small tribute; but that, in return, the Tzar would take them under his powerful protection!

Lavkai's brothers seemed to hesitate; but the prince's opinion prevailed, and the conference was broken off abruptly by the Daurians, who rode away. An attempt to overtake them proved futile.

The fourth fort had also been evacuated; and at the fifth, an old woman only, who claimed to be Lavkai's sister, had been left behind. She had once been a prisoner at the town of Bogdoi, the governor of Manchuria, and spoke with raptures of the fine merchandize and fire-arms found in his capital on the river Nonn.

Khabarof now returned to the first of Lavkai's forts, which was not only the strongest, but also offered the greatest advantages for communicating with Tugirsk. The other forts he appears to have burned; at all events no further mention is made of them. He discovered here large pits filled with corn, which the Daurians had left behind. The river contained plenty of excellent fish; the forests sheltered valuable animals; and the surrounding country seemed well adapted for settlement. Well satisfied with his preliminary journey, Khabarof, with a few men, returned to Yakutsk, where he arrived on the 26th March, 1650. Those remaining behind collected tribute from the neighbouring tribes, which, together with some samples of wheat grown on the Amur, were forwarded by way of Yakutsk to Moscow.

Khabarof was most favourably received by the Voivod, who placed twenty-one Cossacks under his orders, and gave permission to enlist any number of Promyshleni. One hundred and seventeen of the latter joined, and Khabarof hastened back to the Amur, with the intention of exploring that river to its mouth. Lavkai's fort was destroyed and abandoned. On the 2nd June, 1651, Khabarof left on a number of large and small barges. Two days later the Russians passed the site of the Daurian village of a Prince Dazaul. On the third day two Daurian villages were passed, the inhabitants of which took to flight on the approach of the Russians.

In the evening they came in sight of a triple fortification recently built by the Daurian Princes Gugudar, Olgamza and Lotodim, with a view of checking the progress of the Russians. The forts were built of wood and earth and surrounded by a ditch about two yards deep, and into which led covered gateways. The Daurian garrison had been reinforced by fifty Manchu horsemen whom the Emperor Shun-chi had sent to collect tribute, and who, it was fondly hoped, would prove formidable champions in the coming conflict. Trusting to their superior numbers, the Daurians attempted to prevent the landing of the Russians, but on the first discharge of fire-arms, by which twenty of them were laid low, they retired precipitately into their fortress. The Manchu warriors fled inland. A demand to surrender was answered by a defiant discharge of arrows from the turrets of the forts. The Russians sucessfully replied with their fire-arms, and during the night, with the aid of three small cannons, effected a breach beneath one of the towers, and by sunrise they entered the first of the forts. The enemy, after a hand-to-hand fight, retired to the two remaining divisions of the fortress. At noon the first of these was entered by the Russians, and soon afterwards the third and last was taken by storm. No quarter was given to any offering resistance. Only a few Daurians made their escape; the others were slain without mercy. Two hundred and fourteen bodies were found in the first and second divisions of the fort, and four hundred and twenty-seven in the third. If we add to these the twenty men said to have been killed at the place of landing, the loss of the Daurians would amount to six hundred and sixty-one males. Two hundred and forty-three women and young girls, and one hundred and eighteen children, were made prisoners. The booty included two hundred and thirty-seven horses, one hundred and thirteen head of cattle, and rich stores of grain. The loss of the Russians was trifling in comparison: four killed, and forty-five slightly wounded. No quarter appears to have been granted, and the whole proceeding of Khabarof evinces unwarrantable cruelty and short-sighted policy.

Khabarof resolved to stay here for some time. On the day following this victory, the Manchu who had fled at the beginning of the battle, returned in the company of a Chinese Mandarin, wearing a silk gown and a cap of sable, who expressed a desire to live on friendly terms with the Russians.

Some of the prisoners were sent as messengers to the neighbouring Princes Dazaul, Banbulai, Shilginei and Albaza, requiring these to send in their submission to the Tsar. However, none of them returned; and on the 20th July Khabarof continued his journey, taking with him the best horses.[b] On the following day he passed Banbulai's village, which had been deserted by the inhabitants. Some scouts were sent in advance, and took a few prisoners, who mentioned a village belonging to Prince Kokorei, opposite the Dzeya; other Daurian villages were to be found lower down the river, the chief one of which had been built recently, and strongly fortified; it belonged to the Princes Tolga, Turuncha and Omutei. After two days and a half Khabarof passed the mouth of the Dzeya, but found the village deserted. He then sent a party in advance, who took the fort of Tolga (Tolgin gorod) by surprise, while the Daurians, unaware of the proximity of the Russians, were enjoying themselves at the village, a few hundred yards lower down on the river. When the main body of the Russians arrived the horses and cannon were landed, and the village was surrounded. All those offering resistance were cut down, and the three princes with one hundred of the most respectable inhabitants taken prisoners to the fort. Here they were made to swear allegiance to the Tzar, and they promised to pay tribute for

[b] The women and children, it would seem, had been liberated.

a thousand men subject to their authority. Turuncha and Tolga remained as hostages, and the others were permitted to return to their village.

Both parties appear to have lived peaceably together at first. The burthen of supporting two hundred Russians for a length of time was too much for the friendship of the Daurians, and one fine morning, the 3rd September, the whole village was found deserted. Khabarof was thus obliged to give up his intention of staying here during the winter. The fort and village was burnt, Princes Turuncha and Tolga were taken on board one of the barges, and on the 7th September the expedition sailed for the lower Amur. Tolga committed suicide by drowning on the following day, in consequence of the barbarous tortures to which he had been subjected.[c] Four days brought our adventurers to the defile of the Bureya mountains, two more were spent in the passage through them, and on the eighth day they arrived at the mouth of the Sungari. The country above and below the mountains was inhabited by the Goguli, whose villages contained but ten huts each. Below the mouth of the Sungari lived the Ducheri in larger villages of from sixty to eighty huts. Both tribes cultivated the soil and kept cattle. Seven days' journey below the Sungari commences the country of the Achani — Poyarkof's Natki — who depended mainly upon the produce of fishing for their sustenance.

On the 29th September Khabarof came to a large village of the Achani, ten days' journey above the Gilyaks, where he resolved to winter, and built a fort Achanskoi Gorod.[d]

[c] Khabarof himself admits having tortured and burnt his hostages. The memory of this treatment by the early Russians still lives among the natives of the Amur, and Middendorf was told in 1845 by a Nigidal (Natki), that the early Russians were devils, who made gridirons of the parents to roast the children. (Middendorf, iv. p. 174.)

[d] Maack discovered the remains of an extensive Russian fortification, on an eminence, a short distance above the mouth of the Usuri, which

The addition of two hundred persons to the population of a small Achani village, especially as these were in no mood to pay for provisions, formed a sufficient reason for hostilities on the part of the natives. When therefore a hundred men in two barges left on the 5th of October on a foraging expedition to the Upper Amur, the Achani and some Ducheri confederates, altogether perhaps 1000 men strong, attacked the fort from the land side. They were just preparing to set fire to its wooden walls, when Khabarof, with seventy men, made a sortie; thirty-six remained behind, working the three guns with great effect. The natives retreated after a fight which lasted two hours, and left on the field one hundred and seventeen killed, or one man out of nine. The Russians lost only one man. Two days after this affair the foraging party returned, their barges deeply laden, and a heavy tribute was exacted from the unfortunate Achani.

Khabarof, in anticipation of a second attack by a still larger force, put his fort into a better state of defence, a precaution which proved well timed. The Ducheri and Achani had sought protection against their foreign oppressors from the Manchu governor Uchurva, who resided at Nadimni. Orders had been given by him to Izinei, the

---

he considers to be identical with Achanskoi Gorod. This is evidently a mistake. Khabarof, in his account, does not mention the Usuri at all, but Poyarkof tells us that Ducheri dwelled for the space of four days' journey below it, and only then commenced the country of the Achani, amongst whom Khabarof took up his winter quarters. A glance at the map will show the satisfactory manner in which the reports of both explorers tally. Khabarof having passed the Sungari, remained for seven days in the country of the Ducheri. On the 23rd September he entered that of the Achani, and four days subsequently arrived at his winter quarters, which we are inclined to believe were somewhere about the mouth of the Khungar. The account of Achanskoi Gorod in Atkinson's Travels appears to us a mere elaboration of Maack.

governor of Niulgut, on the Sungari (Ninguta), to assemble an army, march against the Russians, and take them, if possible, alive! Izenei, full of confidence, gathered about him 2020 horsemen, armed with bows or matchlocks, several of which latter had three or four barrels. His artillery consisted of six iron cannons. Twelve shells of potter's earth, filled each with forty pounds of gunpowder, were to be used for blasting.

At daybreak on the 24th March, 1652, the Manchu made their appearance before the fort of the Russians. These latter were still asleep; and had it not been for the firing off of matchlocks by the Manchu, possibly with a view to intimidate their enemies, Khabarof might never have returned to tell the tale of his adventures. Fortunately he was thus roused, and prepared for defence. The Manchu placed their guns in position, battered the fort, and soon effected a breach, through which they prepared to take the place by assault. The Russians hastened to place one of their cannons behind the breach, and opened a most destructive fire upon the assailing column. Having repulsed them, one hundred and fifty Russians made a sortie, and took two of the Manchu guns which had been brought too close to the fort. Most of the matchlockmen having been disabled, the Russians were left masters of the field. Their trophies, in addition to the two cannons, consisted of seventeen matchlocks, eight standards, eight hundred and thirty horses and a few prisoners. The loss of the Manchu is said to have been six hundred and seventy-six killed left upon the field; the Russians had only ten killed and seventy-eight wounded.

The country surrounding Achanskoi was by no means fertile; and Khabarof, tired of living upon fish alone, and also apprehensive of renewed attacks by the Manchu, when, owing to the distance from Yakutsk, he could not reckon upon any reinforcements, resolved to reascend the Amur. Six barges (Doshchaniks) were prepared for that purpose; and, on the 22nd April, 1652, he left his winter-quarters.

At the mouth of the Sungari, an army of 6,000 Manchu and Ducheri had been assembled to prevent the Russians from landing at that part of the river; the wind, fortunately, was favourable, and enabled the Russians to pass without molestation. On the boats arriving at the upper end of the defile of the Bureya mountains, Khabarof unexpectedly met a party of one hundred and eighteen Cossacks and Promyshleni, who had been sent from Yakutsk to reinforce him, and were commanded by Tretiak Yermolaef *Chechigin* and Artemei Philippof *Petrillovskoi*.[a]

These men had left Yakutsk in the summer of 1651, soon after Khabarof's departure on his second journey. They were provided with thirty puds of lead and thirty of powder, most of which was left at Tugirsk to be forwarded in the ensuing spring. On the 21st of September they arrived at the Amur, built boats without loss of time, and descended the river as far as Banbulai's village, when the approach of winter stopped their further progress, and induced them to stay near the Kamara. As soon as the ice began to move (4th May), Nagiba, with twenty-six men, was sent in advance to apprise Khabarof of the approach of reinforcements. The main body followed, after the ammunition had been received from Tugirsk, on the 24th of May, and met Khabarof as stated above.

Nagiba however had missed him, probably in the labyrinth of islands above the mouth of the Sungari, where the presence of a large Manchu force rendered it dangerous to separate his small band. Scarcely below the Dzeya, on the fourth day since his departure, Nagiba had been surrounded by Daurian boats, but forced a passage. Slowly he descended the river, leaving papers notifying the fact of his

[a] Petrillovskoi was to go as ambassador to China, accompanied by a baptised Tatar, Anania Uruslanof, a serf of the Voivod of Yakutsk. The former never reached his destination, and the latter, in 1653, deserted to the Chinese, who heaped benefits upon him.

having passed, and, after four weeks of unsuccessful search, met a Natki, who told him Khabarof was staying lower down; a piece of information which proved erroneous. Three more weeks elapsed; Nagiba found himself surrounded by numerous Gilyak boats; to retreat or to advance was impossible. Nine days he remained in this precarious position, when hunger made him desperate; he effected a landing, killed thirty men who offered resistance, and took away the fish hanging in one of the store-houses near a village. After this feat he was permitted to continue his journey unmolested, and, after three days, on the 26th of July, he reached the mouth of the Amur. It was not considered feasible to return by the same route, and Nagiba resolved to build a larger boat, and, like Poyarkof, return by the sea of Okhotsk.

Just as he was putting to sea, a large Gilyak boat, with a crew of forty men, approached with hostile intentions; the Russians, however, slew every one of their assailants. At last they left. Violent storms raged for ten days, the boat was crushed between icebergs, provisions and ammunition were lost; but the crew reached the land in safety. For five days they continued travelling along the coast, subsisting on herbs, roots, and some seals thrown up by the sea. They then built another boat, and skirting the coast for a fortnight, came to the Uchalda river, where they found a plentiful supply of dried fish among the Tunguzians and Gilyaks living there. Nagiba stayed here until the middle of September, and then crossed by land to the Tugur river, where he remained till the summer of 1653 collecting tribute. At his departure he left behind Ivan Uvarof and twenty men, to complete the subjugation of the neighbouring tribes, whilst himself, with four men, again went to sea, and after four weeks reached the Nangtara river, whence he crossed the mountains to the Aldan. On the 15th of September, 1653, he arrived at Yakutsk. Reinforcements were subsequently sent to Uvarof, but the fort was finally destroyed by the Manchu in 1683.

We now return to Khabarof, whom we left at the defile of the Bureya Mountains. That commander considered his forces sufficient to maintain himself on the Amur. He ascended the river, collected tribute from the Ducheri, and was just about to build a fort opposite the Dzeya, when the outbreak of a mutiny among his men put a sudden termination to his plans. Out of three hundred and forty-eight[f] men, one hundred and thirty-six, led on by Polyækof, Ivanof, and Vazilief, deserted on the 1st August, at the mouth of the Dzeya, with three barges, and sailed down the Amur. Subsequently some of these appear to have returned to their allegiance; others may have gone over to the Chinese, or were slain by the natives.

The embassy which it had been proposed to send from the Tolga's village to Peking, did not depart, because no guide could be found. The proposed building of a fort at Kokorei's village, opposite the Dzeya, did not take place for want of a larger force. Messengers were sent on the 9th August to Yakutsk, to ask for reinforcements. For fear of the Daurians they mostly travelled by night, and spent nearly five weeks on the journey. Khabarof considered 6,000 men a sufficient force to resist 40,000 Manchu. Of course no such force was available at that time in Siberia, and the Voivod therefore sent the messengers on to Moscow, where the conquest of the Amur had already been under consideration for some time.

---

[f] From the number of men stated to be with Khabarof, thirty-eight, in addition to one hundred and eighteen brought by Chechigin, must have arrived from Siberia. They were probably brought to the Amur by Nikita Prokopief, who left Yakutsk on the 30th June, with orders to report on the country, and bring back the tribute which might have been collected. He was told to seek out Khabarof, either at Chipin Ostrog, or Albazin, on the upper Amur.

Khabarof, in the same year (1652), appears to have ascended the Amur to the mouth of the Kamara, where he built Kamarskoi Ostrog on an island opposite the mouth of the river, subsequently known as one of the chief positions of the Russians on the Amur.

Looking back at what had been done during the first nine years of Russian adventure on the Amur, we must acknowledge the perseverance of some of the leaders, but at the same time deplore that enterprises of this kind were left in the hands of private adventurers, who sought rather their own immediate benefit than the permanent advantage of the state. The natives appear to have been exposed to all sorts of extortion: tribute was levied to an unlimited extent, without any commensurate good being conferred upon the natives. No settlements of peasants, or tillers of the soil, were founded; the resources of the country were soon exhausted by perpetual foraging expeditions of Russian adventurers. When the Russians first arrived on the Amur, the natives cultivated fields and kept cattle. Ten years afterwards these fields had become deserts; and a country, which formerly exported grain, could not even support its own reduced population. There is no doubt that, had these expeditions been carried out upon a more sensible plan, Russia might have enjoyed these resources of the Amur two centuries before our times.

Five hundred and thirty-two Russians in all had left Siberia for the Amur. Of these, two hundred and ten remained with Khabarof, twenty occupied a small fort on the Tugur river, on the sea of Okhotsk, sixty-nine returned to Yakutsk, and two hundred and thirty-three were lost in the combats with the natives and Manchu, by famine, or desertion. The loss of the natives and Manchu, in killed, amounted, as far as can be ascertained, to about 1,600 men.

## IV.

### STEPANOF. 1652—1661.

REPORTS of the excesses committed by the adventurers on the Amur had reached Moscow, and it was resolved to send an army of 3,000 men to occupy the newly-explored territories in a more efficient manner. The Okelnichei and Voivod, Prince Ivan Ivanovich Lobanof Rostovskoi, was chosen to command this expedition; and Dimitri Ivanof Zin Simoviof, with a small body of troops, was sent in advance to prepare the way. He left Moscow in March 1652, reached the Lena late in the autumn of the same year, wintered at Chechwiskoi Volok, and continued his journey to the Olekma in the spring of 1653. He thence sent his men up to the Tugur river to rebuild the fort which had formerly stood there, and himself hastened to Yakutsk to consult the Voivod and ensure the success of the expedition.

Whilst Simoviof wintered at the Lena (1652—3), the two Cossacks whom Khabarof had sent for succour passed on their way to Moscow, spreading everywhere the most exaggerated reports about the riches to be found on the Amur, and the prosperous condition of their chief's settlement. They spoke of abundance of gold, silver, cattle, sables. The natives were said to wear satin dresses and gold ornaments. As might have been expected, these unfounded reports caused an immense sensation among the adventure-loving population of Ilimsk and Werkholinsk. Hundreds hastened to seek their fortune on the Amur. The Cossacks of Werkholinsk were the first to start for the Eldorado of Eastern Asia. They were followed by the carpenters engaged to build the boats for Rostovskoi's expedition; by fur-hunters, peasants, and convicts. Cossacks sent to bring back the fugitives, met with resistance. All along the Lena, lawless bands plundered the villages and devastated the fields. These disorders continued for several years; and as late as 1655, the brothers Michael and Yakof Zorokin headed a band of three hundred adventurers, and, plundering all along the road, advanced to the Amur, where they met with a miserable death. After that time, however, measures were taken to check these lawless proceedings. A fort was built at the mouth of the Olekma, and no one allowed to proceed to the Amur without a passport.

Simoviof, when he came back to the Olekma, met one hundred of these adventurers, but his orders to them to return were not heeded. Without delay, he continued his journey to the Amur, and in August 1653, he met Khabarof and three hundred and twenty[a] men at the mouth of the Dzeya. Small golden medals were presented to Khabarof and his companions in the name of the Emperor, as an acknowledgment for the services they had rendered. Simoviof at once communicated the instructions he had received. Khabarof was to go to Moscow, to report personally on the capabilities of the newly discovered territories. The command of the whole forces of the Amur was to devolve upon Onufrei Stepanof. Tretiak Chechegin, with four men, was to proceed upon an embassy to Peking. Three forts were to be constructed: one at the mouth of the Dzeya, a second on the site of Albaza's village, and a third at the mouth of the Argun. The soil was to be cultivated, and one year's provisions for an army of 6,000

[a] Khabarof, in the earlier part of the year, must have been reinforced, for we left him with two hundred and ten men in his winter quarters at Kamarsk.

men were to be collected. Previous to Simoviof's return forty-eight Promyshleni arrived on the Amur, and offered their services. They were placed under the command of Kashenitz and ordered to the upper Amur, to collect tribute. They built an Ostrog at the river Urka, where they wintered, but having expended their ammunition, they preferred rejoining Stepanof, on the lower part of the river. The embassy for Peking actually departed, but Chechegin and his companions were slain on the road by their Ducheri guides.

Simoviof departed with Khabarof, and took with him some Daurians, Ducheri, and Gilyaks, males and females, whom he presented to the Tzar; they were, however, restored to their families in 1655. At Tugirsk, where he wintered, he ordered forty puds of powder and forty of lead, with many iron agricultural implements, to be buried, instead of forwarding them to Stepanof, who sadly wanted ammunition. Khabarof, as a reward for his services, was created Synboyarskoi; and the villages on the Lena, extending from Ustkut to Chinskoi Volok, were placed under his superintendence. At the present time, his memory still lives in the name of the village of Khabarova, near Kirensk.

Unfortunately, none of the orders of Simoviof were carried out. After Khabarof's departure Stepanof descended the Amur to the mouth of the Sungari, where he obtained provisions. He then wintered in the country of the Ducheri.[b] In the spring of 1654 a second visit was paid to the Sungari; but after having gone up that river for three days, he met a hostile flotilla, and an army of 3,000 Manchu, besides Daurians and Ducheri. Stepanof courageously attacked the boats and put them to flight, but as Simoviof's sage arrangements had left him without powder and shot, he could not hope to make head against the land troops, and was obliged to retire. On

---

[b] Very likely a short distance above the mouth of the Usuri, where remains of an old fort have been discovered by Mr. Maack.

the 4th July he surprised a Daurian village, made some
prisoners, but found scarcely any provisions. This want of
provisions and ammunition is pleaded by him as an excuse
for not building the three forts. He ought, however, to have
carried out these orders during the previous year.

On again ascending the Amur, Stepanof met thirty
Yeniseisk Cossacks, who had left their chief, Beketof, in
search of other service; and soon afterwards he came upon
Beketof himself, with the remainder of the men (twenty-
four) entrusted to his command. In order not to interrupt
our narrative, we will not stop here to explain how these
Yeniseisk Cossacks came to the Amur, but reserve this for
the next chapter.

Stepanof resolved to winter at the mouth of the Kamara.
The old fort, built by Khabarof, had been destroyed; and it
was necessary, therefore, to build a new one. The new fort
was surrounded by an earth wall, with four bulwarks, surmounted by a double row of palisades, and was enclosed by a
ditch six feet deep and twelve wide. The approaches were
defended by iron spikes and spike traps. The guns were
mounted on a raised platform in the centre of the forts, and
pipes laid from a well to all parts of the fort, in case the
enemy should succeed in setting fire to it. A church consecrated to "Saviour of the World" was built here, and contained a miracle-working painting. Two Chinese prisoners
were baptised in this church subsequently, and sent to
Yakutsk. The Russian garrison numbered five hundred men.
The winter passed quietly; but on the approach of spring, a
Chinese army of 10,000 men, with fifteen cannons, numerous
matchlocks, and storming apparatus, appeared before the
place. The storming apparatus was carried on two-wheel
cars, and consisted of large shields covered with leather and
felt, behind which the marksmen might advance with safety
close to the fort; storming ladders, with wheels and iron
hooks; wood, pitch, straw, and other combustible materials.

Twenty Russians, who had gone to the forest to fell wood, were surprised by the enemy and taken prisoners. A number of Russians made a sortie; but they ventured too far, were surrounded and cut to pieces. The Chinese at once proceeded to the erection of batteries. One of these was placed on a cliff on the opposite bank of the river, two hundred feet high,[c] and at a distance of four hundred and seventy yards. The distance of two other batteries was one hundred and sixty and two hundred and thirty yards respectively. A continuous fire was kept up day and night, from the 20th March, but without producing any effect upon the earthen walls. The Chinese, at last, resolved to take the place by assault. Storming parties advanced from four sides simultaneously, but met with the most determined resistance. The hand-to-hand fight lasted through the whole of the night, from the 24th to 25th March; and at dawn the Russians made a sortie, compelled the enemy to retire, and several prisoners, two matchlocks, many cannon balls, and plenty of ammunition fell into their hands. Thenceforth the Chinese fired off their guns at long intervals, and scarcely ventured from their camp, which was pitched at eight hundred yards from the fort. After three weeks' siege they retired, having previously destroyed the boats of the Russians. During the siege the garrison prayed and fasted, seeking thus strength to undergo the hardships and privations their position entailed.

And most nobly did they hold their own against an enemy so far superior in numbers and well provided with ammunition, of which the Russians were almost entirely destitute. After the withdrawal of the Chinese, seven hundred and thirty cannon balls were picked off the field; but none weighed above two pounds.

Before leaving his winter quarters, Stepanof sent the

---

[c] Cape Bibikof (Long-tor) where traces of these batteries may yet be seen. See Index.

tribute he had collected direct to Moscow, instead of previously allowing it to pass through the hands of the Voivod of Yakutsk. This was by no means a wise proceeding, for he had mainly to rely upon the latter for a fresh supply of ammunition.

In the meantime Feodor Pushchin, with fifty Cossacks, had been sent from Yakutsk to the Argun (spring, 1654), at the mouth of which he built a Simovie. He ascended the river for three weeks without meeting any inhabitants, and resolved, therefore, to join his fortunes with those of Stepanof. He fell in with the latter at the mouth of the Sungari, and together they ascended that river and collected provisions to last for one year. They then sailed down the Amur, and built an Ostrog, in the country of the Gilyaks, which they called Kossogorski,[d] from its position on the slope of a hill. They were told here of thirty Cossacks under Anika Loginof, who had come by land from the north, but had been murdered. The supposed murderers were punished. During the winter above one hundred and twenty sorok of sable, eight black, and fifty-six red fox-skins were collected as tribute; and in the spring (1656), our adventurers re-ascended the Amur. Pushchin speaks of the country of the Gilyaks as the only place where tribute might yet be collected advantageously. He recommended to send annually some Cossacks, by way of Okhotsk, to collect it; and saw in this the means of preserving the lower part of the river for Russia, even should its upper part be lost.

On again ascending the river, the villages of the Ducheri were found to have been deserted. The burnt remains of Russian barges were found; and subsequently they heard that forty Russians, who had come down in them, had been killed by the Ducheri. These men, no doubt, formed part of

---

[d] The position of Kossogorski has been satisfactorily identified. It was situated on the island of Suchi, opposite Mariinsk.

Zorokin's band of three hundred adventurers.[e] And Pushchin found the corpses of the remainder, who had been starved to death, higher up the river.

On arriving at the Sungari, Stepanof, with a few men, ascended that river to reconnoitre, but found the villages deserted. He was told by a few solitary individuals whom he met, that the inhabitants had been conveyed by the Chinese up the Sungari, and been settled down on the Kurga River.

The future of Stepanof's small army did not appear in the brightest light. Provisions were running short, and it became more difficult from day to day to procure a fresh supply. On the 22nd July, he sent away Pushchin and Beketof, with twenty Cossacks, to take the tribute to Moscow. In their desire to find out a shorter route, this party lost their way, and before reaching Tugirsk forty-one of them had died of hunger. Fortunately they met here with a convoy of provisions intended for Pashkof, who was then just about to start for the Shilka.

Simoviof, in the meantime, had arrived at Moscow, and though the proposed expedition under Rostovskoi, as originally projected, had been given up on account of the disturbances which had taken place in Siberia, the central government showed its solicitude for the future of the Amur country by sending a letter to Stepanof (dated 15th March, 1655), assuring him of the Tzar's special favour and encouraging him to new enterprises. At the same time he was recommended to treat the native inhabitants with leniency, not to levy any excessive tribute, and to avoid unnecessary collision with the Chinese. These instructions, however well meant, did not prove of benefit in the state of affairs then subsisting on the river.

Stepanof appears to have remained at Kamarskoi during

[e] See p. 27.

the winter, 1657-8. When he again descended the Amur, in the spring, he met a fleet of forty-five Manchu boats below the Sungari, well armed with large and small guns. Stepanof had with him five hundred men; but of these one hundred and eighty abandoned him before the commencement of the fight, and others deserted to the Chinese. Stepanof soon found himself surrounded by the enemy; and his heroic resistance proved of no avail. Himself and two hundred and seventy men were either slain or made prisoners, and only forty-seven made their escape; fifty soroks of sable fell into the hands of the conquerors.

The one hundred and eighty deserters on ascending the Amur, met Potapof, who, with thirty men, had been sent from Nerchinsk to seek Stepanof. But instead of placing themselves under his orders, they robbed him of his provisions, and again descended to the mouth of the Amur, where they wintered amongst the Gilyaks. Having collected eighteen soroks of sable as tribute, they returned in the ensuing spring (1658) to Kamarskoi. On the way thither they were joined by the forty-seven Cossacks who had escaped at the Battle of the Sungari. At Kamarskoi the adventurers separated. One party of one hundred and seven took the tribute to the Lena; the others (one hundred and twenty men) returned in the summer to the Dzeya, where the Tunguzians had remained faithful. The former party did not again return to the Amur, and the latter took no further trouble about the collection of tribute. Most of them returned to Yakutsk in 1660, and a few (seventeen) joined Pashkof on the Shilka in 1661.

V.

## DISCOVERY AND OCCUPATION OF THE SHILKA.
## 1652—68.

WE will now go a few years back, to glance at the discovery of the Shilka river, which the Russians look upon as the chief arm of the Amur. Cossacks from Yeniseisk had pushed their exploratory excursions beyond Lake Baikal, across the Yablonoi Khrebet to the Shilka. One of these parties returned in 1652, and Pashkof the Voivod, a man of energy and enterprise, having gained from the men all information he could, resolved to send an exploratory party in that direction, without losing any time in applying at Moscow for an authorisation. The command of the expedition was entrusted to Beketof. On the 2nd June, 1652, the latter left Yeniseisk with one hundred Cossacks on boats. On his arrival at the Bratskoi Ostrog, he sent Maximof, with twenty men, in advance to the Irgen Lake, where he was to remain during the winter, to collect tribute and make preparations for crossing the mountains in the ensuing summer. Beketof himself, with the bulk of the expedition, wintered at the mouth of the Selinga river. In the spring (1653), the Cossacks made various excursions against the neighbouring Buriates; and on the 2nd June, the journey up the Selinga was continued on large barges (Doshchaniks). After twenty-seven days' travelling they were met by Maximof on the Khilok river; smaller boats were built and the navigation continued to the Ilgen Lake, which at that period still communicated with the Khilok. An Ostrog was erected there, and tribute in sables collected from the neighbouring Tunguzians. In addition to six soroks of sable, previously collected by Maximof, nineteen more were sent to Yeniseisk. In the spring of 1654, Maximof was again sent forward to reconnoitre; Beketof soon followed, and on reaching the Ingoda, constructed rafts, and descended that river and the Shilka to the mouth of the Nercha rivulet, opposite to which he built an Ostrog. He collected tribute, and at once began to cultivate some fields. For a time all went well; but Gantimur, a Tunguzian chief, who was dissatisfied at being subject to Russia, withdrew with his people to the right bank of the Argun, whence no persuasion could bring him back. The Tunguzians who had remained behind, also began to show signs of disaffection. After a time they surrounded Beketof in his fort, took away some of his horses, and laid waste the fields. The Russians suffered a great deal from want of provisions. Thirty men left Beketof to try their fortunes on the Lower Amur; and Beketof, with the remainder, followed soon afterwards, and joined Stepanof, as stated above (p. 29).

Other parties were sent out from Yeniseisk, in the years 1654 and 1655, to explore the country beyond Lake Baikal. Pashkof, not discouraged by the ill success of Beketof's expedition to the Shilka, proposed to the government at Moscow, to found a town upon the Shilka (Upper Amur), whence the surrounding territories might be subjugated with greater facility. His proposals were approved. He was entrusted with their execution; and appointed commander-in-chief of the whole of the Russian forces on the Amur. Ammunition was to be supplied from Tobolsk, and provisions from Ilimsk.

On the 18th July, 1656, Pashkof left Yeniseisk with five hundred and sixty-six men, and continued his journey to Bratskoi on the Angara, where he wintered. Part of his provisions had been sent on to the Tugir, but fell into the hands of the famishing Cossacks of Stepanof (see p. 32). He, therefore, sent the remainder—two hundred and twenty-five chetverts of flour, and five hundred puds of seed corn—to Ilimsk. In the summer of 1657, Pashkof got as far as Irgen Lake, where he wintered; and, in the ensuing spring, continued his journey to the Shilka, where he founded Nerchinsk (first called Neludskoi Ostrog, after a Tunguzian chief), at the mouth of the Nercha rivulet. His provisions soon began to fail; and the Russians, for a time, had recourse to fallen horses, to dogs, and any other animals they could procure, until a fresh supply of flour arrived, by way of Tugirsk, in 1659. Ammunition also was wanting. The supplies buried by Simoviof at Tugirsk in 1654, were thought of; but on search being made for the treasure, a wooden cross merely was found, and an inscription upon it stated that Zorokin and his companions had appropriated these supplies in 1655 to their own private use.

Whilst Pashkof was yet engaged in building Nerchinsk, he sent Potapof, with thirty men, down to the Amur (summer, 1658), to look for Stepanof, to acquaint him with his (Pashkof's) appointment to the chief command of all Russian forces on the Amur; to order him to send one hundred men to Nerchinsk, and to establish himself with the remainder at Albazin. These orders however came too late. Potapof was met on his road by the one hundred and eighty deserters from the battle near the Sungari, who robbed him of his provisions; and he was obliged to return, the object of his mission being unattained.

Only seventeen of Stepanof's men subsequently (1661) joined Pashkof; and at that time the Russians had no force whatever on the Amur. Pashkof removed his head-quarters to Irgenskoi, and left a small garrison merely at Nerchinsk. From this place he sent in 1661 a party of Cossacks against the neighbouring Tunguzians. Amongst these were fifteen men who had formerly been on the Lower Amur; and regretting the license they enjoyed there, they deserted. They built a raft; descended the river to Nerchinsk, where they intimidated the few men left to guard the fort (most had gone fishing), and took away their boats. Their intention had been to leave the Amur altogether, and seek their fortunes on the Lena, or elsewhere. Fate however had otherwise ordained. They were met and taken on the road by Larion Tolbusin, Pashkof's successor. Pashkof himself returned to Yeniscisk (1662).

Under the direction of Tolbusin and Daniel Arshinski (from 1669), Nerchinsk gradually rose into a place of importance.

## VI.
## RENEWED ENTERPRISES ON THE AMUR.
## ALBAZIN FOUNDED.
## 1669—82.

SINCE the year 1661 the whole of the Amur had been abandoned by the Russians; but Chernigovsky inaugurated a new era of enterprise, by establishing himself at Albazin in 1669. Nikitor Chernigovsky, a native of Poland, had been exiled to Siberia in 1638. In the year 1650 we find him "headman" of the agricultural colony at Chechinskoi Volok, and two years afterwards superintending the Ust Kutskoi saltworks. At that time a large fair was held annually at Kirensk on the Lena; and the Voivod of Ilimsk used to go there to settle disputes and collect dues. In 1665 the fair passed off as usual; but on his return the Voivod Lawrence Obukhof was surprised by one of the lawless bands then prowling about the country, and murdered. The leader of this band was Chernigovsky. Witsen in his "Noord en Oost Tartarije" tells us a somewhat more romantic tale. The Voivod was said to have dishonoured one of Chernigovsky's sisters, and was killed from a feeling of fraternal revenge. However that may be, the murderer and his companions sought to evade the consequences of this deed, by flying to the wilds of the Amur. At Kirensk Chernigovsky forcibly took the Hieromonakh Yermoghen (Hermogenes), who three years before (1663) had founded the Troitsk monastery; and on arriving at the Tugir river his band mustered eighty-four men. Fifteen of these, while on a plundering expedition, were slain by the Tunguzians. In the winter our adventurers crossed the mountains, and settled upon the site of Albaza's village, one of the old forts of Lavkai. The position was well chosen; the mountain ranges towards the north kept off the cold winds, and European cereals and plants could be cultivated with advantage. The fort was made of wood. It formed a parallelogram of one hundred and twenty-six feet by ninety. Two towers faced the water, and one stood towards the land; beneath the latter the entrance gate led into the fort. The whole was surrounded by a ditch, and further protected by chevaux-de-frise and foot-traps. The stores stood within the enclosure, but the ordinary dwelling houses of the garrison lay beyond. Yermoghen founded here the church of the Resurrection of Christ (Voskresenie Khristof).

In China, where Kang-hi, the greatest of the Manchu emperors, had ascended the throne in 1662, the re-appearance of the Russians on the Amur at once attracted notice, and a letter arrived at Nerchinsk in 1670, complaining of the encroachments of the Cossacks at Albazin, without, however, requiring that station itself to be evacuated. *Milovanof* was sent to Peking with a reply; he was presented to the emperor, laden with rich gifts, and returned to Nerchinsk accompanied by a mandarin and sixty-five Chinese soldiers.

The fugitives at Albazin were reinforced by other parties; and after some time, the tribute taken from the natives was regularly sent to Nerchinsk.[a] In 1671 Ivan Okolkof was sent from Nerchinsk, to assume the chief command. At his instigation the Hieromonakh Yermoghen built a monastery dedicated to "Our Saviour" (Spas Vsemilostivi), at a place called Brusyænoi Kamen, a short distance above the settlement. It was proposed subsequently to build a cathedral

---

[a] In 1672, the tribute collected amounted to four soroks of sables.

dedicated to the Archangel Michael, and a chapel of "Our Lady of Vladimir," projects never carried out. In the same year, and in that following, 1672, peasants arrived to till the soil. They built several villages, amongst which Pokrovskaya Sloboda, a few versts below Albazin, was the most important. The other villages were Panova, Soldatovo, and Andrushkina, the latter at the mouth of the Burinda. The government at Moscow, just then engaged in a war with Poland and Turkey, could pay but slight attention to the affairs of the Amur. The Cossacks sought to attract its attention by spreading a false report, in 1671, about a large Chinese force having crossed the dividing range and built a fortress on the Tugir. At Yakutsk, there were, at that time, but two serviceable guns, and the rumoured invasion was reported to Moscow. Simultaneously with this false intelligence a petition arrived at Moscow, signed by one hundred and one of the garrison at Albazin, and praying for a pardon for Chernigovski, in consideration of the services rendered by him subsequent to his offence. A couple of days however before the arrival of this petition at the capital, judgment had been recorded against him (15th March, 1672). Himself, his sons, and several others were found guilty: in all, seven persons were condemned to death; forty-seven were to undergo various sentences. Out of regard, however, to the critical state of affairs on the Amur, this decision was reversed, and the bearers of the petition returned with 2000 rubles (£300) as a present to the garrison of Albazin.

Many Tunguzians in the neighbourhood of Albazin, who had formerly been tributary, were again subjected, and this, it was feared at Moscow, might lead to fresh difficulties with the Chinese. To prevent it, an envoy was to be sent to China. Nicolas Spafarik, a Greek, was selected for this office. He left Moscow in 1675, accompanied by a large retinue. On his arrival at Tsitsikar he is said to have admitted to a Chinese functionary, that the Russians had no legal claim whatever to the Dzeya. At Peking, Spafarik made a favourable impression upon the Jesuit fathers by his learning. At first he insisted upon delivering his letters into the Emperor's own hand; but fearing his mission might prove a failure, he allowed himself to be persuaded that such was not the custom of the country. The letters were then received by a Chinese official at the foot of the Emperor's throne, and opened in the ambassador's presence. On his return journey (1676) Spafarik sent word to the Russians at Albazin, both from Tsitsikar and Nerchinsk, not any longer to navigate the lower Amur and the Dzeya, nor to collect tribute from the Tunguzians dwelling along the latter.

These orders however were not heeded. In that very year (1676), a Yashnoi Simovie had been built at the mouth of the Gilui, whence parties started on foot for the upper Dzeya to collect tribute. But owing to the difficulties which such journeys on foot offered, it was resolved to detach a party of seventy-one Cossacks and Promyshleni, commanded by Fedka Ostafeva, to built a fort on the upper Dzeya. They selected the mouth of the Numisha (Amumish) rivulet as a suitable spot, and built Zeisko Ostrog in 1678. In the same year, one hundred and eighty-one sables were sent thence as tribute to Albazin, and the tribes of the Ailagir, Tonki and Kautagen made their submission; their example being followed by the Uligari and Magiri. The chief of the latter gave permission to build a fort on the Selimba river (Selimbinskoi Ostrog). This was done in 1679; and a second fort, Dolonskoi Ostrog, at the mouth of the Dolonza rivulet, was established in the same year.

The Russian settlements on the Dzeya had hitherto been merely small stations for facilitating the collection of tribute. In 1681, however, the Voivod of Nerchinsk, Fedor Demenshevitz Voikof, entrusted to the Boyar Zin Ignatius Milovanof the task of exploring the Dzeya and Selimba rivers, with a view to the formation of some settlements on a larger scale. Milovanof describes the country around Dolonsk as highly fertile and productive. Rich pastures extended along the Dzeya as far as the Brianda river. The old fort of Zeisk (Verkhe Zeisk) had been washed away by the river, but at the request of the Ulagiri Tunguzians, Milovanof rebuilt it at a site a little below the Brianda. A small place Kaja was situated at the mouth of the Dzeya, and half a day's ride down the Amur stood the small town of Aigun (Gaigun), which formerly occupied only 2·70 acres, but had lately been increased to 13·5. It was defended by a square fort of 2·70 acres in the centre, the walls of which were twelve to eighteen feet high.[b] The surrounding land was fertile, and a considerable traffic was carried on with the Manchu, who ascended the Amur in boats, but landed about half a day's journey lower down. The inhabitants were not able to afford any information regarding the origin of the place. There was a road, passable for horses, from Dolonsk to the mouth of the Dzeya, which could be travelled over in four days. Thence, following the course of the Amur, Albazin could be reached on foot in three weeks.

In 1682 Milovanof sent in a report of his exploration, accompanied by a map. He proposed therein to found a town, either at the mouth of the Dzeya or in the neighbourhood of Aigun, positions very favourably situated for carrying on commerce with China. The government did not, however, enter upon any new undertaking; but resolved merely to strengthen the old settlements. Milovanof was ordered to establish himself at Selimbinsk, and reinforcements were sent to him from Albazin to fortify that place. He was to collect tribute in the name of the emperor. The trade in furs was forbidden to him; but as a special mark

[b] The remains of the earthen walls may still be seen; the outer enceinte encloses, however, thirty-three acres, and the square in the centre five acres English.

of favour he was permitted to deal in brandy, beer, bread, and tobacco. The settlements on the Dzeya and Silimja were declared independent of Albazin, and Milovanof reported direct to Nerchinsk. Strangers were to be received hospitably, and every protection was to be afforded to their enterprises, and so forth.

A proposed expedition to the Gilyaks at the mouth of the Amur, entrusted by the Voivod of Nerchinsk to Senotrussof, was not carried out, owing to disputes at Albazin, to which place Voykof had sent his son Andrei, as governor, in the spring of 1682. The garrison of two hundred men asked for their pay; and as there was no money in the public treasury, they insisted upon sables belonging to government being sold. Voykof went himself to quell these disturbances. Whilst there, Gavrilo Frolof requested permission to go with a party of Cossacks and Promyshleni to the rivers Bureya (Bystra) and Amgun (Khamun), which had just then become known, and the tribes along which were independent alike of Chinese and Russians. The Voivod granted the desired permission; but relented on his return to Nershinsk, fearing a collision with the Chinese. He sent counter-orders to Albazin; but the governor there, who had been chosen by the Cossacks, either would not, or could not, carry them out; and Frolof departed with sixty-one men.[c] He made his way to the Amgun, and built a Yasoshnoi Simovie at the mouth of the Duka or Dukika rivulet, which he called Ust Dukikanskoi. Shortly before him a party of Cossacks and Promyshleni had come from Tugursk, and built a Simovie at the mouth of the Nemilen rivulet. Both parties joined, took a few hostages from amongst the natives,

---

[c] According to Witsen, p. 3, Gavrilo Frolof and sixty men mutinied at Ilimsk. They slew the governor and fled for safety to the Amur. Information of this outrage may partly account for Voykof's reluctance to allow Frolof to depart.

and repulsed with little loss to themselves a body of three hundred Natki and Gilyaks, who were on the road to Tugursk to destroy that fort, probably at the instigation of the Chinese.

At the close of 1682 the Russian settlements on the Amur and its tributaries were as follow :—

Albazin, and a number of villages in its vicinity, on the Upper Amur.

Novo Seisk, Selimbinskoi Ostrog, and Dolonskoi on the Dzeya.

Dukikanskoi on the Amgun ; Tugursk and Udsk at rivulets falling into the sea of Okhotsk.

## VII.

## WAR WITH CHINA.

## 1683—1688.

ARMS OF ALBAZIN.

THE successful re-occupation of the northern tributaries of the Amur, and the prosperous condition of Albazin, where about 2,700 acres of land had been brought into cultivation, roused the attention of the Chinese. In the summer of 1683, preparatory to undertaking military operations on a large scale, they threw a strong garrison into Aigun, and fortified an Island of the Amur, two miles above that town.

A detachment of sixty-seven Cossacks, commanded by Gregory Mylnikof and intended for the reinforcement of Frolof, on the Amgun, left Albazin on the 17th July, 1683; but were intercepted at the Dzeya by a large Chinese force in five hundred and sixty small boats (busses) each of which carried twenty men, supported by several thousand horsemen on land.[a] The Russians landed on the northern bank of the river, and Mylnikof by invitation of the Chinese general crossed over to the other bank to have a conference.

[a] Witsen, p. 96, says 15,000.

He was, however, treacherously made prisoner. His men in presence of such superior numbers lost heart; some of them voluntarily surrendered to the Chinese and were sent prisoners to Peking; others fled to the Russian settlements on the Dzeya and Selimba, where they spread the report of a large Chinese army; and a few only returned to Albazin, arriving at the beginning of August. The Chinese, without loss of time, ascended the Dzeya; the settlements of Dolonskoi and Selimbinskoi Ostrog they found deserted, and they had nothing to do but burn down the houses. The garrison of Novo Zeisk however, not having been warned of their approach, were surprised and made prisoners. The Russians of the Amgun also abandoned their settlement, retired down the Amur, and reached Udskoi by sea; but the garrison at Tugursk fell into the hands of the Chinese.

In fact, at the close of 1683, the whole of the Russian settlements on the lower Amur and its tributaries had been destroyed, and Albazin alone remained.

Early in 1684, two Russian prisoners were sent back from Peking, with a letter to the governor of Albazin. This letter on its arrival at Aigun had been translated by some Russian deserters. In it promises and threats were held out to induce the garrison to surrender, but failed in their effect. On its receipt, Ivan Voilochnikof, a common Cossack then governor, assembled the garrison, and read the letter; but all declared in favour of defending the place. Aid and ammunition were solicited from Siberia. A new governor, Alexei Tolbusin arrived in June; and then Albazin, at the height of its prosperity, and on the eve of its fall, received a coat of arms, representing a spread eagle holding a bow and arrow in its talons.

Early in 1685 the Manchu advanced towards Albazin. Tolbusin on their approach ordered the neighbouring villages to be evacuated, and the forty dwelling houses standing beyond the fort to be burnt down. The garrison, including

Cossacks, merchants, Promyshleni and peasants, numbered four hundred and fifty men; their arms consisted of three hundred muskets and three small cannons. Reinforcements were however expected almost daily. Large supplies of ammunition and other warlike stores were known to have left Yeniseisk. Afanei Beiton, a Prussian nobleman formerly in the Polish service, and who had been made prisoner and exiled to Siberia, had organised a regiment of Cossacks at Tobolsk, six hundred men strong, and was expected to arrive in the early part of the year. The resources left at the disposal of Tolbusin were, however, evidently insufficient to resist a prolonged siege.

The Chinese forces ascended the Amur in one hundred large boats. They were in all about 18,000 men, including those who came by land. Their arms consisted of bows and sabres, and they brought with them fifteen guns, from five to eight-pounders, of European manufacture, besides some long tubes, weighing about fifteen pounds, with a touch-hole at the side, and which were carried on horseback.[b]

On the 4th of June the advanced guard of the Chinese arrived and seized some cattle. The first boats arrived at the first village below Albazin on the 10th; and on the ensuing day, the Chinese general sent in a demand for surrender, written in Manchu, Russian and Polish, and promising the greatest leniency if his demand were complied with. No attention was paid to this summons; and the bombardment commenced on the 12th. During the first few days the Russians lost one hundred men. Yermoghen, with crucifix in hand, encouraged the Cossacks by word and deed.[c]

[b] Witsen, p. 65. Müller, ii. p. 386, speaks of one hundred and fifty pieces of field-artillery, and forty to fifty siege-guns!

[c] After the destruction of Albazin Yermoghen retired to Kirensk, where he died; and in 1788 a stone monument was erected to his memory in the Monastery of Troitzk, which he had founded there.

The wooden walls and towers of the fort had sustained considerable damage, and ammunition began to fail. There appeared no chance of carrying the defence to a successful issue; and the inhabitants, headed by Yermoghen, the founder and superintendent of the Spaskoi Monastery, which had been but just completed, and the priest of the church of the "Resurrection" petitioned the governor on the 22nd, to make terms with the Chinese for a free retreat to Nerchinsk. Tolbusin saw himself compelled to accede to this request; a deputation was sent to the Chinese general, and the terms of surrender arranged. The garrison were permitted to leave with their arms and baggage; but twenty-five of them preferred going over to the Chinese.

Scarcely a day's journey above Albazin, the retreating garrisons met the long-expected reinforcements: one hundred men, with two brass and three iron cannons, three hundred muskets, and plenty of ammunition. They had left Nerchinsk on the 23rd June; Beiton's regiment had just arrived at Nerchinsk, and several of his men were amongst them. Had they come twenty-four hours sooner, the fall of Albazin might have been averted; as it was, all returned to Nerchinsk.

The Chinese followed the retreating Russians at a distance, as far as the river Argun. On their return to Albazin they burnt the fort and dwelling houses, but left the fields untouched. They then retired down the Amur, evacuated Aigun, which was situated on the left bank of the river, and removed the town to the right bank, three miles lower down to the site of Tolga's village. The new town was surrounded by a double row of palisades, eighteen feet high, and twelve feet distant from each other. The space between the two rows was filled up with earth to the height of six feet. The circumference of the whole was 1,200 yards. A well was in the centre. Two thousand or 2,500 men, with thirty cannons, were left as a garrison, and five hundred men to till the soil; the bulk of the army withdrew up the Sungari. Female settlers were expected in the summer of 1686.

We will now return to the Russians on the Upper Amur. Ivan Vlassof had been appointed Voivod of Nerchinsk in 1684; he was not a man to lose courage through a catastrophe, such as the surrender of Albazin. The arrival of Beiton's regiment had placed at his disposal a force larger than any Voivod possessed before him, and he was fully resolved not to surrender the Amur without another struggle. Five days after Tolbusin had returned with the garrison of Albazin, he sent down the river seventy men to reconnoitre the vicinity of the deserted fortress. They came back on the 7th August, after an absence of seventeen days. On the ruins of Albazin they found a solitary Chinaman, who owing to some mishap had been compelled to fly the companionship of his own countrymen. According to his account the Chinese had retired to Aigun.

Without loss of time, Beiton with two hundred men was despatched to Albazin. He was followed by Tolbusin, who at the request of the former inhabitants was again appointed governor. The whole of the forces then at his disposal amounted to six hundred and seventy-one men, with five brass and three iron cannons, and ample military stores. Further reinforcements followed.

They at once set about gathering in the harvest, but all of it could not be secured, as many hands were required to rebuild the fort, and erect habitations for the winter. The enclosure of the fort was formed by a wall, cleverly constructed of loam, grass, and the roots of trees. At the foot, this wall was twenty-eight feet thick, and on the 11th of October it had been raised to the height of ten feet. The approach of winter put a stop to the progress of the works, but in spring they were resumed with renewed vigour. The wall was raised to twenty feet. A house for the governor had been built inside the enclosure, and ten others for the garrison outside, but owing to the want of building materials more could not be done at the time. The fields were attended to, but not with that care, which a less fertile soil would have required. In the spring of 1686, rye and oats fetched nine copecks the pud; wheat, twelve copecks; peas and hempseed, thirty copecks; barley grits, twenty-five copecks.[d]

During the autumn, the settlers were kept in a state of inquietude by hostile parties lurking about the place. Tunguzians, who voluntarily brought in their tribute, were suspected of acting as spies of the Chinese. Several attempts to take one of the Manchu prisoner failed, and Tolbusin, desirous to be informed of the movements of the Chinese, sent Beiton with three hundred men to the Kamara (March, 1686), to gain some information regarding their whereabouts. Beiton encamped at the mouth of the Kamara on the 12th. On the 17th he espied a troop of forty Manchu horsemen in the direction of Tsitsikar, and at once gave orders to pursue them. After a hot chase of thirty versts, he came up with them; in the skirmish, which ensued, he lost seven men, but killed thirty Manchu, and took one of them, Kevutei or Govodeiko, prisoner. Through him Beiton learned that the Chinese governor at Tsitsikar had heard of the reconstruction of Albazin from some Targachins, who had been molested by Albazinian Cossacks whilst on the chase. The governor then sent out some people, who succeeded in kidnapping a Russian peasant, who confirmed the statements made by the Targachins. At that very time a Manchu army was marching upon Albazin.

Beiton at once returned to Albazin. The fort was put in a state of defence. The garrison numbered seven hundred and thirty-six men — a large force to be lodged for a long

---

[d] At Nerchinsk, rye-flour 3½ guilders a pud; wheat 4 guilders a pud, and meat about 48 stuivers a pud.

period in the mud-houses of the small fort. Their *material* consisted of eight cannons, one mortar, thirty large shells, four hundred and forty hand-grenades and an ample supply of powder and shot.

The Chinese forces advanced by land and water. About 3,000 horsemen approached along the left bank of the river; and being well acquainted with the country, they came upon the Albazinians quite unexpectedly (7th July). They surprised some horseherds on the fields, and out of thirty they killed or made prisoners twenty-two. Those who escaped were not able to reach the fort, but fortunately met with a detachment of seventy Cossacks who had been sent to watch the siege, and with whom they returned to Nerchinsk. Another party of twenty Russians were similarly surprised. The fort was soon surrounded; the fields were laid waste, and the crops destroyed. On the river the Chinese came on in one hundred and fifty barges, each carrying from twenty to forty men. Six of these barges were laden with ammunition and two with arrows. The Chinese had forty cannons, and twenty Europeans in the guise of Chinamen assisted in working them. Many Tunguzians from the neighbourhood joined the forces of the Chinese, and proved formidable bowmen.

The Chinese immediately seized upon the Russian boats. One general fixed his head-quarters on the island opposite Albazin, and in front of the mouth of the river Albazikha; another on the right bank of the river above the fort; and the third on the left bank below it. The branch of the Amur protected by the island served as a harbour. The Chinese encampments were at a distance of four hundred yards only, and the batteries at sixty yards. The wooden *abattis*, with which the Chinese sought to protect themselves, took fire, and was subsequently replaced by earthworks and ditches surrounding the whole of the fort, and forming regular parallels. On the 1st of September the Chinese attempted to carry the place by assault, but were beaten back with great slaughter, and in five sorties which the garrison subsequently made many Chinese were killed and several taken prisoners. Tolbusin was mortally wounded towards the end of September whilst reconnoitring the Chinese forces from one of the towers, and the command devolved upon Beiton. The garrison had not however suffered hitherto any heavy loss, but owing to the dampness of their underground habitations and other privations, diseases broke out, amongst the most destructive of which was the scurvy. By the end of November the garrison was reduced to one hundred and fifteen men. Ample provisions for another year remained, but only four hundred and eighty pounds of powder. Notwithstanding this sad state of affairs, the offers by the Chinese of a free retreat, in case of a surrender, and promotion to deserters, conveyed into the fort by means of letters affixed to arrows were rejected. Two messengers had been sent in October to Nerchinsk for relief, but the boat was unfortunately broken by the ice, and they arrived only after great difficulty at their place of destination. No aid could however be afforded at that time.

At the end of November the interference of diplomacy made itself felt at Albazin. The Chinese, on the last day of that month, received orders to retire three versts from the fortress—orders which they hailed with pleasure, as they, as well as the Russians, had suffered a great deal from infectious diseases. On the 6th May 1687 the Chinese withdrew another verst. During this truce the beleaguered were at liberty to leave the fort, to buy provisions and other necessaries, to send to Nerchinsk, and even to admit reinforcements. The Chinese offered to send surgeons to the fort; but Beiton, who had only sixty-six men with him, assured them everything was going on well; and to convince the Chinese general that he did not suffer, at all events, from want of provisions, he had a large pie made, weighing a pud, and sent it him as a present.

On the 30th August, 1687, the Chinese left Albazin altogether, and returned to their former quarters at Tsitsikar and Aigun. The Russians rebuilt their villages, and cultivated their fields anew. They were not however permitted to hunt, as the Chinese looked upon this as an infringement of their rights of sovereignty.

We will now turn to the diplomatic transactions which brought about the peace of 1689.

## VIII.

## THE TREATY OF NERCHINSK. 1689.

THE daily increasing complications with the Chinese, made it appear desirable at Moscow to come to some arrangement regarding the frontiers of the two empires. The Chancellor Nikifor Venukof, accompanied by Ivan Fafarof, was sent to arrange preliminaries. He left Moscow on the 11th December 1685, arrived at Peking in 1686, and brought back with him a letter for the two emperors. At Peking he also succeeded in inducing the Emperor to send a few Chinese officials and Ivan Fafarof to Albazin, to stay the siege. This, as stated above, actually took place on the 30th November, 1686. The original of the letter was written in Chinese, Manchu, and Mongol, and translated into Latin by the Romish Missionaries at Peking. Though addressed to the "Great white Lords, Brethren, Tsars, and Autocrats," its contents were first to be communicated to the Governor of Siberia.

As this letter conveys a good idea of the Chinese manner of thinking with regard to Russian operations on the Amur, we reproduce it here *in extenso*. It is dated 20th November, 1686—

"The officers to whom I have entrusted the supervision of the sable-hunt, have frequently complained of the injury which the people of Siberia (Sokha) do to our hunters on the Amur, and particularly to the Ducheri. My subjects have never provoked yours, nor done them any injury; yet the people at Albazin, armed with cannons, guns, and other fire-arms, have frequently attacked my people, who had no firearms, and were peaceably hunting. Moreover, they gave shelter to our deserters; and when my Superintendent of the Chase followed some deserters of Kandagan to Albazin, and demanded their surrender, Alexei, Ivan, and others, responded, that they could not do this, but must first apply to the Changa Khan for instructions. As yet, no answer has been vouchsafed to our inquiries, nor have the deserters been given up.

"In the mean time, my officers on the frontier have informed me of your Russians having carried off some peaceable hunters as prisoners; for instance, Kelera, Solona, and others.

"They also roved about the Lower Amur, and troubled and injured the small town of Genquen, and other places. As soon as I heard of this, I ordered my officers to take up arms, and act as occasion might require. They, accordingly, made prisoners of the Russians who were roving about the Lower Amur; no one was put to death, but all were provided with food. When our people arrived before Albazin and called upon it to surrender, Alexei and others, without deigning a reply, treated us in a hostile manner, and fired off muskets and cannons. We therefore took possession of Albazin by force; but even then we did not put any one to death. We liberated our prisoners; but more than forty Russians, of their own free choice, preferred remaining amongst my people. The others we exhorted earnestly to return to their own side of the frontier, where they might hunt at pleasure. My officers however had scarcely left, when four hundred and sixty Russians returned, rebuilt Albazin, killed our hunters, and laid waste their fields, thus compelling my officers to have recourse to arms again.

" Albazin consequently was beleaguered a second time; but orders were nevertheless given to spare the prisoners, and restore them to their own country. Since then, Venukof and others have arrived at Pekin, to announce the approach of an ambassador, and to propose a friendly conference to settle the boundary question, and induce the Chinese to raise the siege of Albazin. On this, a courier was sent at once to Albazin, to put a stop to further hostilities."

Fedor Alexevitch Golovin, the envoy extraordinary, left Moscow on the 20th of January, 1686, accompanied by Ivan Zin Vlasof, and the secretary Semön Kornitski. His escort was formed by a regiment of Regular Militia (Strelzi), 1500 strong and commanded by Colonel Fedor Skripizin. The Colonels Paul Grabof and Anton von Smalenberg were to command two other regiments to be raised in Siberia. A Stolnik, Alexei Sinyavin, and five attachés increased the splendour of the embassy. Ivan Loginof was sent forward to announce at Peking the actual departure of the embassy; on this, the Chinese army before Albazin received orders to retire to Aigun, which they did on the 30th August, 1687. In consequence of some information which Golovin received at Yeniseisk regarding Albazin, he sent in advance Lieutenant Bagatiref and some troops. He then continued his journey to Rybenskoi, where he wintered (1686-7). In the ensuing summer the embassy proceeded to Udinsk, and arrived on the 28th September; but they had scarcely set out from this place for Nerchinsk, when an express brought news of the retreat of the Chinese from Albazin. This information induced Golovin to return to Udinsk and continue his journey to Selenginsk, whence he sent Stephen Korovin, one of the attachés, to announce his arrival, and request the Chinese authorities to fix upon a place at which the proposed conference might come off. The monotony of the winter-quarters was somewhat relieved by an attack of a Mongol army, 15,000 strong. Golovin at the time had only two hundred men with him, the remainder having been distributed amongst the villages along the Selinga river. Still he repelled this attack. In consequence of this and other minor defeats, 50,000 Mongol families acknowledged themselves Russian subjects.

Korovin returned from his mission to Peking on the 28th June, 1688. Selenginsk had been chosen as the seat for the conference, and the Chinese plenipotentiaries were at that very time on the way towards it. This embassy had in fact left Peking on the 20th May, accompanied by Thomas Pereyra, a Portuguese, and Gerbillon, a French Jesuit, as interpreters, sixty to seventy mandarins, 1000 horsemen, eight small cannons, and a tremendous crowd of servants. At this period the Mongols were not yet subject to the sway of China, and the wars between the Kalkas and Eluths endangered the onward progress of the embassy. On reference to Peking the embassy was ordered to return to the frontiers of the empire; but before doing so a letter was dispatched to Golovin, then at Udinsk, acquainting him with the reason for the non-appearance of the embassy. The messengers returned on the 30th August, and brought a letter from Golovin, written in Russian and Latin. Golovin therein expressed an earnest desire to come to a final settlement regarding the frontiers, and not allow his time to be wasted in trifles or fruitless discussions. In conformity with the Tzar's wishes, everything should be done to promote the concluding of an honourable peace; and as a meeting during the current year appeared impossible, he would pass the winter near the frontier, in expectation of a more suitable locality being agreed upon. In order to facilitate the making of suitable arrangements, he resolved to send to Peking a gentleman of his suite, who would be treated, he hoped, with all due courtesy.

This envoy, accompanied by sixty-three persons, arrived at Peking on the 13th May, 1689, and made a very favourable impression upon the Jesuits whose convent he visited. He bore a letter addressed to the Minister of the Empire, requesting him to fix a place near the frontier, where the conference might be held. He also desired to know the number of persons who were to accompany the Chinese embassy, so that he might appear with an equal force, and trusted the usages of civilised states would be observed. On the 18th May the envoy received his answer; Nerchinsk was chosen as the place of conference, the embassy would leave Peking on the 3rd June, and their suite was not to exceed the number requisite for their personal safety. Subsequently, however, an express was sent to Udinsk, to announce that some barges also with provisions would ascend the Amur. Golovin was nevertheless not prepared to find the Chinese as numerous as they actually turned out to be.

On the 13th June, 1689, the Chinese ambassadors So-fan-lan-ya and Kiw-Kijew left Peking with 1400 soldiers, numerous servants, and the Jesuit fathers Gerbillon and Pereyra as interpreters. On reaching the Kherlon river (6th July), they sent a messenger in advance to inform Vlasof, the governor of Nerchinsk, of their approach. On the 11th July they arrived opposite Nerchinsk, and the barges which had preceded them in great numbers, ranged themselves along the banks of the Shilka in front of the Chinese camp, hoisting their colours in honour of the plenipotentiaries. In addition to armed junks there were seventy-six barges, which carried sails, but could also be rowed, or towed up the river by boatmen. Three thousand men, of whom 1500 were soldiers, arrived by these barges, and if we add the 1400 soldiers who came by land, the Mandarins, servants, and camp followers, the force of the Chinese can not have been much short of 9000 or 10,000. They had from 3000 to 4000 camels, and at least 15,000 horses. So-fan alone had three hundred camels, five hundred horses, and one hundred personal attendants; Kiw-Kijew three hundred horses, one hundred and thirty camels, and eighty personal attendants. The governor of Nerchinsk naturally felt uneasy at the presence of so large a force. He declared himself quite satisfied with the conduct of the persons who had come by land, but bitterly complained of the people who had ascended the river, and had acted on the road as enemies rather than friends. His fort had been surrounded, some fields had been devastated, and several Russians detained, from whom information was sought regarding the present whereabouts of the Solon Tatars, who had placed themselves under Russian protection. The Chinese Plenipotentiaries replied that the prior arrival of the boats was contrary to the Emperor's orders, and in order to remove any uneasiness, commanded them to retire a few versts. The Chinese patiently waited until the 1st August for Golovin's arrival, but then conveyed a letter to him through the governor of Nerchinsk, in which they expressed their surprise at not having heard from him, and hinted at the possibility of being obliged to cross the river for want of forage (Nerchinsk stands on the left or northern bank of the Shilka). On the same day the governor of Nerchinsk presented the plenipotentiaries with ten oxen, and fifteen sheep, the former in the name of his emperor, the latter in his own. The three Russian officers who took this present, received each a piece of silk in return. On the following day, there arrived from Golovin a messenger, who alleged the bad state of the roads as the occasion of the delay. The nonchalance of this gentleman on embarrassing questions being put to him, surprised even the Chinese and their Jesuit interpreters.

At length, on the 18th, Golovin himself arrived. Two days were spent in preliminary arrangements, and the conferences commenced on the 22nd. A large tent was pitched midway between the fortress and the river, one half appropriated to the Russians, the other to the Chinese. The Russian portion was covered with a handsome Turkey carpet. Golovin, and Vlasof, the governor of Nerchinsk, occupied arm-chairs placed behind a table, which was spread with a Persian silk, embroidered in gold. Upon this table stood a costly clock, and a writing desk. The secretary, Kornitzki, occupied a chair by the side of his principal. The Chinese portion was devoid of all ornament. The chiefs of the embassy, seven in number, sat upon pillows, placed upon a low bench. Behind them stood four Mandarins, and in front the Jesuit fathers. The remainder of the Mandarins and Russian officers were ranged along both sides of the tent. The Chinese had crossed the river with forty Mandarins and seven hundred and sixty soldiers, five hundred of whom remained on the bank of the river, and two hundred and sixty advanced half-way to the tent. In a similar manner, five hundred Russians were placed close to the fort, and forty officers and two hundred and sixty soldiers followed the envoy.

The first conference opened with some questions of etiquette. When these had been settled in a satisfactory manner, Golovin proposed the Amur as the future boundary between the two empires. To this the Chinese objected, on account of the fine sables which the tribes to the north of that river paid as tribute; and, in their turn, proposed to the Russians to surrender Albazin, Nerchinsk and Selenginsk. Golovin of course was not prepared to make so great a concession, and the conference ended in a most unsatisfactory manner. In the second conference, the Chinese offered to permit the Russians to retain Nerchinsk, but simply as a trading post. This proposal was scouted like the first; the Chinese left in high dudgeon, prepared to strike their tents, and refused any longer to confer with people who were unwilling to meet their wishes fairly. At the second conference, a Mongol acted as interpreter. Had the Jesuits been present, this rupture, no doubt, would have been avoided. They now did all in their power to bring about a reconciliation; and, on a visit to Nerchinsk, declared that the Chinese certainly would not feel satisfied unless Albazin were ceded. A Russian officer visited the Chinese camp on the 26th, and

## THE TREATY OF NERCHINSK.

the boundary as finally adopted was pointed out to him on a large map. Golovin however was not yet prepared to make this concession, and on the following day sent in an ultimatum, in which he still claimed Albazin and the surrounding country. On its receipt the Chinese called a grand council. It was resolved to surround Nerchinsk, to incite the neighbouring Tatars to revolt, and send men down the river to take Albazin. The Russians, on their side, prepared for defence; the fortifications of Nerchinsk were strengthened, and the town was barricaded.

Hostilities were not looked forward to with confidence by either party. The Russians would have certainly lost Albazin, the Chinese feared the reception they might meet with at Peking, should a fresh war break out. When therefore a Russian interpreter crossed over to the Chinese camp to ask for renewed negociations, they gladly availed themselves of the opportunity. Father Gerbillon, invested with plenary powers to settle the points in dispute, was despatched to Golovin; and on the 27th of August, succeeded in preliminarily drawing up the terms of the treaty. The Russians, on the following day, requested the insertion of an additional article, guaranteeing liberty of commerce between the two empires; the Chinese however, though recognising such an arrangement as desirable, refused to insert it, as not bearing upon the settlement of the frontiers.

At length, on the 29th August, the ratifications of the treaty were exchanged in a tent pitched for that purpose. The Chinese plenipotentiaries appeared in state; the treaty was signed, sealed, and oaths taken for its maintenance. The philosophic Chinese even declared their willingness to swear upon the crucifix like Christians; but this *auto da fe* was dispensed with. When copies in Manchu, Russian and Latin, had been exchanged, the plenipotentiaries embraced each other; a splendid collation was served, and the company only separated an hour after dusk, and parted in the most friendly manner.

## THE TREATY OF NERCHINSK.

The following is an abstract of the treaty:—

"In order to suppress the insolence of certain scoundrels, who cross the frontier to hunt, plunder, and kill, and who give rise to much trouble and disturbance; to determine clearly and distinctly the boundaries between the empires of China and Russia; and lastly, to re-establish peace and good understanding for the future,

"The following articles are, by mutual consent, agreed upon:—[a]

"1. The boundary between the two empires is to be formed by the river Kerbechi, which is near the Shorna, called Uruon by the Tatars, and enters the Amur; and the long chain of mountains extending from the sources of the Kerbechi to the Eastern Ocean. The rivers, or rivulets, which flow from the southern slope of these mountains and enter the Amur, as well as all territories to the south of these mountains will thus belong to China.

"The territories, rivers, and rivulets, to the north of said mountain chain remain with the empire of Moscovy, excepting the country between the said summit and the river Ud, which shall be neutral until the Plenipotentiaries, after their return home, have received further instructions, when this point may be settled by letter or special envoy.

"The boundary is further to be found by the river Argun, which enters the Amur; the territories south of said river belong to the Emperor of China; those north of it to the empire of Muscovy. The towns, or dwelling-houses, at present situated to the south of the Argun, shall be removed to the northern bank of the river.

[a] As might be expected, the Russian version of this *preamble* differs considerably. It is as follows:—

"The Plenipotentiaries, in order to remove all cause of discontent between the two empires, to conclude a permanent peace, and to settle the frontiers, agree, in their conference at Nerchinsk, to the following articles."

" 2. The fortress built by the Russians at a place called Yaksa (Albazin) shall be demolished, and the subjects of the Tzar residing there shall remove with their property to the Muscovite territory.

"Hunters of either empire shall, under no pretence, cross the frontiers.

" If only one or two persons cross the frontier to hunt, steal, or pilfer, they shall be arrested and given up to the nearest imperial officers, to be punished according to their deserts.

" In case, however, armed parties of ten or fifteen persons cross the frontiers to hunt or plunder, or in case of any person being killed, a report shall be sent in to both emperors; and the parties found guilty shall be punished with death. On no account shall war be declared in consequence of any excess whatever committed by private parties.

" 3. Everything which has occurred hitherto is to be buried in eternal oblivion.

" 4. Neither party shall receive fugitives or deserters from the date of this treaty. Subjects of either empire flying to the other shall be arrested and given up to the nearest authority on the frontier.

" 5. Subjects of Moscovy now in China, or Chinese now in the empire of Moscovy, may remain where they are.

" 6. In consideration of this present treaty of peace, and the reciprocal good understanding of the two empires, persons may pass from one empire to the other, provided they are furnished with passports, and they shall be permitted to carry on commerce, and to sell or purchase at pleasure.

" Copies of the above treaty, properly signed and sealed, shall be exchanged by the Plenipotentiaries. The various articles of the treaty shall be engraved on stones in Tataric, Chinese, Russian, and Latin, to be erected on the frontiers between the two empires, as a permanent testimony to the good understanding subsisting between them."

On the day following the exchange of ratifications, the plenipotentiaries exchanged presents. The first Chinese plenipotentiary received a handsome timepiece, a telescope, a silver basin and jug, gilt inside, and a costly robe of sables. The others were presented with watches, looking-glasses, and ornamental swords. Golovin received a black leather saddle, horse trappings, with gilt stirrups, two red horse tails, two gold cups, eight damask garments, thirty-two pieces of silk, and twelve silk pelangs. Gifts of a similar kind were presented to his companions. The Chinese even talked about erecting a monument in honour of the event.

On the 29th of August the Chinese left Nerchinsk by land and water. The stipulations regarding Albazin were carried out at once. Beiton, with the garrison and their property, returned to Nerchinsk, and the Chinese levelled the fort on descending the river. Years afterwards, the corn could be seen growing on the fields of Albazin; and late travellers have still found traces of the fort, and the Chinese batteries thrown up during the last siege.

In the spring of 1690, Argunskoi Ostrog, which had previously stood on the right bank of the Argun, was removed to its left bank.

Before leaving Nerchinsk, Golovin strengthened its fortifications considerably. He left behind him his cannons; and some of his troops were left there, and at Selenginsk and Udinsk. On his return, he was met by Ivan Skripitsin, with letters from the Tsars, and a number of medals for his men, in recognition of the zeal shewn in the performance of his mission. Arrived at Moscow, he was created a Boyarin and Commissary-General of War.

## IX.

## THE AMUR SINCE THE TREATY OF NERCHINSK TO 1848.

### a.—THE RUSSO-CHINESE FRONTIER.

APPARENTLY the boundary between the empires of Russia and China had been determined with great accuracy by the treaty of Nerchinsk. Such, however, was not the case as regards the actual sovereignty of the tribes inhabiting these frontier regions. The sole object attained by China—and that, of course, was of paramount importance—was to exclude Russia from navigating the river. The Russo-Tunguzians dwelling along the boundary as fixed by treaty are mountaineers, and their existence is inseparable from that of the reindeer, which finds food only in the moss-tracts of the Stanovoi Khrebet, whilst the Manyagers, the principal tribe subject to China, keep horses and confine themselves to the grassy valleys and prairies. Müller, as early as 1742, says that according to an old right of chase the Jakdu (Kœkhkaya) mountains were looked upon as the boundary separating the tribes subject to Russia and China, and that both Russo-Tunguzians from the Ud and Aldan, and Chinese Tunguzians from the Silimji and Dzeya hunted together in these mountains. It thus happened that the Russian government received as tribute furs, which in reality had been procured on Chinese territory as defined by treaty. The Chinese themselves do not appear to have considered the country theirs up to the watershed[a]. At all events, Midden-

[a] These boundary marks consist of heaps of stones, in the form of a pyramid. An inscription, carefully folded up in birch-bark, is left at each revision. At the portage mentioned, the inscription was placed in a hole cut in an old tree. Further details will be found in chap. 13.

dorf and Usultzof on their late exploratory expeditions into these regions, found boundary monuments erected by the Chinese far to the south of the supposed limits, at the confluence of the Gilu and Dzeya, on the Nara, the Silimji, Niman, and Bureya (*see* Map). The most eastern mark stood at the portage between the Ud and Tugur, and the tribes dwelling on these rivers considered the Torom, which falls into the Ud Bay, sea of Okhotsk, as separating their respective hunting-grounds. We do not know whether the Chinese in placing their boundary marks did so with especial reference to the wants of the various tribes inhabiting these regions, or whether we must ascribe their surrendering so large a territory (23,000 square miles) rightfully their own, to ignorance of the country, or the indolence of the officials entrusted with carrying out the article of the treaty referring to the erection of boundary marks.

At another point, the Chinese are, however, accused of an encroachment, due entirely to the imperfect knowledge possessed by the contracting parties regarding the geographical features of the country thus parcelled out—a fertile source of boundary disputes, as is shown by the constantly recurring difficulties with the United States government with respect to the British American frontier. By treaty the boundary on the upper Amur was to commence at the mouth of the "Gorbitza, which is near the Shorna." Unfortunately there are two Gorbitzas and two Shornas. One of these enters the Amur or Shilka about 119° E. of Greenwich; the other, known also as Amazar, some ten miles below the confluence of the Argun with the Shilka. A Shorna river enters the Shilka eight miles above the upper Gorbitza, and a second Shorna, called Ura by the Tunguzians, and Urka by the Russians, enters the Amur fifteen miles below the Lower Gorbitza or Amazar. There is scarcely any doubt the latter was the river alluded to in the treaty, and on the map of China published by the Jesuits it is actually indicated as forming the boundary. Subsequently, however, the Chinese removed their boundary stakes to the Upper Gorbitza, and the event which induced them to do this has been thus communicated by Baer, in "Büsching's Magazine," p. 488. Baer obtained this information during his stay at Irkutsk from a Cossack, who had participated in the transaction.

At the time Pushkin was governor of Nerchinsk (1703 to 1709), a Chinese deserter of Tunguzian origin, by name Shelesin, who in former times had joined the Russians at Albazin, but had been recaptured, escaped for a second time and fled to the upper Gorbitza, where he lived under the protection of the Russians. When the Chinese heard of his presence on Russian territory they claimed his surrender as a deserter; and the governor of Nerchinsk reluctantly sent some Cossacks to take him, and delivered him to the Chinese. Shelesin, however, evaded punishment by denying he ever quitted Chinese territory, inasmuch as the Gorbitza formed the boundary between the two empires. The Chinese were willing to believe him, and in the ensuing year Shelesin guided some officers to the upper Gorbitza, where they erected a boundary monument.

The regulations regarding the crossing of the frontier appear to have been carried out at first with considerable rigour. Witsen (p. 74), for instance, tells us that in 1694 four persons were beheaded at Nerchinsk at the request of the Chinese authorities, because they had been discovered hunting sables in the neighbourhood of Albazin. We can, however, scarcely believe in so severe a sentence being carried out, and think the individuals in question must have deserved their doom by committing an outrage commensurate in some degree with the punishment meted out to them. It is, however, an ascertained fact that many infringers of the boundary law were slain by the natives, who still nourished feelings of revenge against the Cossack freebooters of the Amur.

At the treaty concluded in 1728 by Count Sava Vladislavich Ragusinsky, it was agreed upon that transgressors might under certain circumstances be punished with death. The Chinese Commissioners also proposed a mixed Commission, to settle the boundary near the sea of Okhotsk; but nothing was done in this matter.

Subsequently, China appears to have been unwilling to resent infringements of the boundary, which became of frequent occurrence. The Russian surveyors Shobelzin and Shetilof in 1737-8 extended their labours to Chinese territory at the instance of the Academician Müller. On their first journey in 1737, they came to the sources of the Pendi rivulet, a tributary of the Gilu, where they found an empty winter hut (Zimovie) previously occupied by Russian hunters. Descending the Gilu, they found a second Zimovie also deserted, at the mouth of the Jeltula, and thirty-seven miles above the mouth of the Dzeya they met some inhabitants of Nerchinsk, who had gone there to hunt sables. They descended the Dzeya for twenty-five miles, but were obliged to return from want of provisions. On a second expedition in 1738, they descended the Amur to the mouth of the Bileton, forty miles below Albazin. On the site of Albazin a Cossack and a Russo-Tunguzian family had established themselves. The Cossack had once been taken prisoner by the Chinese; but on stating he had lost his way, was ordered to go back to Nerchinsk. Twenty miles lower down there dwelt another family of Russo-Tunguzians.

In 1805, on the occasion of Count Golovkin's mission to China, it was proposed to send the Academicians Adams and Bogdanovich to explore the frontier, and General Auvrey was to explore the Amur; but neither of these plans was carried out. A Major Stavitsky, however, descended the Amur to Albazin. Subsequently the botanist Turczaninow, author of the Flora Baicalensi-dahurica, investigated the banks of the Amur as far as Albazin. Colonel Ladyshinsky, in 1832, made the same journey with a view to find the boundary-mark said to have been placed by the Chinese at the Lower Gorbitza. He could not, however, discover it; probably because it had been destroyed when they extended their frontier to the Upper Gorbitza.

Of even more interest is the escape of several convicts from the Mines of Nerchinsk across the frontier, to Chinese territory. Middendorf mentions two such cases (iv. p. 155). In 1795 Rusinof and Serkof escaped, but were brought back; and Guri Vasilief spent six years on the Amur, between the years 1816 to 1825. The accounts of this fugitive have been verified by recent exploration. He descended the river to the mouth, and professes to have met many persons able to speak Russian (probably escaped exiles like himself). He describes a burning mountain situated on the right bank of the river, two hundred versts below Aigum. From fissured rocks of a bluish colour, smoke, and dense sulphurous vapours rose here, and at night settled down upon the river. Now and then there were explosions like the discharge of a gun, but without any vibration of the ground.[b] Vasilief, no doubt, is the fugitive referred to by Atkinson in his Travels on the Upper and Lower Amur, p. 416; and who, having been sent by the Russian government to explore the country to the south of the Amur, never returned, and was either killed by the natives, or voluntarily remained among the Chinese; who according to his own statement had on a former journey asked him to become a Chinese subject. Vasilief was evidently a man of education, as is testified by the accounts he gave of the river explored by him.

Middendorf also makes a statement regarding a fugitive, who in 1841 resided at the mouth of the Amur—a statement corroborating the account of the escape of three Polish

[b] This was, probably, some burning coal deposit. Coals have been discovered on the right bank of the Amur, above the Bureya mountains.

exiles published by Atkinson (p. 494). These exiles fled in 1839, and in 1841 visited with their Tunguzian hunting companions the fair or market annually held at the village of Pul on the lower part of the river. They proceeded thence with a Japanese (Aino?) trader to the island of Sakhalin, where one of them died. The others espied an American whaler by whom they were taken to the United States. About ten years after this had happened, one of the Poles came to Paris, and found means of imparting his successful escape to his companions in misery still in Siberia. It was from one of these latter Atkinson obtained the particulars communicated.

We have yet to state the manner in which the Chinese, in accordance with Article 6 of the Treaty, inspected the boundary. Annually in the summer the Chinese officials ascend the Amur on five large barges, preceded by two canoes, upon which are drummers to announce their approach. The barges are each towed up the stream by five men on the bank, who are relieved three times a day; and altogether there are about seventy to eighty persons. The journey as far as Ust Strelka occupies about forty days. Two of the barges remain here on the opposite Chinese bank of the river, where a frontier stone stands; the others continue their voyage up the Shilka as far as Gorbitza. Here they exchange presents with the commander of this Russian station; hire horses, and ride to the boundary pyramid which stands twenty miles above the mouth of that river.

On their return to Ust Strelka they await the detachment coming down the Argun, and in the meantime carry on some bartering trade with the Cossacks. The Argun is inspected by two parties. The first starts from Tsitsikar, and proceeds to the Argun, where this river enters Russian territory, and descends it to the village of Olochi, close to Nerchinskoi Zavod. Here they meet with the second detachment, of about twelve men, from Mergen, and who continue the inspection of the boundary as far as Ust Strelka. There they join the larger party, who have come up the Amur, and the whole then descend the river. In their footsteps follow the Cossacks, to collect tribute from the Oronchon, to carry on the fur trade, and to gather grass for the winter along the banks of the river. The Russian peasants also cross the boundary to hunt squirrels, and are known to have extended their excursions nearly as far as the Kamara.

The frontier pyramid at the confluence of the Gilu and Dzeya is examined every three years, and those on the Bureya annually.

### b.—The Russian Mission at Peking.

After the conclusion of the treaty of Nerchinsk the diplomatic relations of Russia and China were placed upon a more regular footing, and the arrangement of the commerce between the two countries was the cause of many embassies being sent. We do not, however, intend entering upon the details of these various transactions, and the frequent disputes which put a temporary stop to the bartering trade carried on at Kiakhta and Tsurukhaita, but simply offer a few remarks on the colony of Russians at Peking which dates its origin from the wars between the two empires. During these wars the Chinese had taken many prisoners; other Russians deserted, and all were sent to Peking, settled in the north-east corner of that city, and formed into a company attached to the Imperial Body Guard. The Russian settlers, when they first arrived at Peking, built a church dedicated to Saint Nicholas, and a few pictures formerly at Komarsk and Albazin had found their way thither. At the first embassy which Russia sent to Peking subsequent to the treaty of Nerchinsk, that of Eberhard Ysbrand Ides in 1692, it was agreed upon that a priest should be sent to minister to the religious wants of the Cossacks, and a priest actually did arrive in 1698 with the Caravan conducted by Spiridon Langusof. The caravans were lodged at the so called "Russia House" at the expense of the Chinese. At the treaty concluded by Count Sara Vladislavich Ragusinsky in 1727, the Chinese agreed to build a church attached to the Russian House, to which the priest until then ministering at the old church of Saint Nicholas was to be removed. In addition three other priests were to be sent, and four young Russians, and two of more advanced age, acquainted with Latin, were to be allowed to reside at Peking for the purpose of learning Chinese and Manchu, and teaching Russian to some Chinese. China agreed to contribute 1000 silver rubel and 900 cwt. of rice towards the expense of this mission, and Russia the remainder, viz. 16,250 silver rubel, of which sum 1000 rubel were set apart for the instruction of the Albazinians. The church built in accordance with this treaty was consecrated in 1732, and dedicated to the "Purification of Mary." Some pictures brought by the Cossacks from Albazin may yet be seen in it. The term of residence originally fixed for the members of the mission was ten years, but has subsequently been reduced to six. The personnel, since 1857, comprises an Archimandrite, three Hieromonakhs, four students, a physician, and an artist. At the entrance of the Russian House stands an "honorary" guard of Chinese soldiers; no restriction, however, is said to be placed in the free communication of the residents with the native population. The Chinese officials who undergo a course of instruction in the Russian language are promoted; but as yet none of them has gained any proficiency in the language, so as to be able to read and translate correctly. The members of the mission have never engaged in missionary work; their activity is of a scientific and political nature. With respect to the latter, the results can scarcely be appreciated; in many respects they must, however, have been found to answer all the purposes of a regular embassy.

We know, for instance, that Golovin, who in 1805 conducted a mission to Peking, took occasion, though unsuccessfully, to urge upon the Chinese to grant the free navigation of the Amur. The objects of science have, however, undoubtedly been promoted by a number of works which owe their origin solely to the existence of this mission.[c]

The descendants of the ancient Albazinians scarcely exist in name. They still form a separate company of the Imperial Body Guard, but have lost all attachment to the country of their ancestors. Quarters have been assigned to them in the Manchu portion of the town; they speak Chinese, dress like the Manchu, and live entirely in the same manner as the soldiers of that nation, poor, idle, and attached to the superstitions of Shamanism. In 1824 there were still twenty-two who had been baptized, but only three of them attended the Russian service at the Church of the Purification.

Since the treaty of Tientsin, 1858, a Russian ambassador, Ignatief, has resided at Peking, and Russian officers have repeatedly visited that city. The last Mission left Kiakhta on the 8th of August, 1858. On that occasion there was a grand service in the Cathedral, and the street was lined with soldiers. The Mission at present counts fifteen members, including the councillor of State Perovsky, and the Archimandrite Gury. There are besides fifteen Cossacks as servants, and fifty Cossacks are stationed at Kallgan (Syuang-Hoa-fu).

*c.*—THE AMUR AND SAKHALIN UNDER THE DOMINION OF CHINA, 1689 TO 1850.

We will ourselves now cross the forbidden boundaries to enter the regions of the Amur, and see what the Chinese are

[c] For instance, Hyacinthe, Description de Peking, Petersb. 1829; Timkovsky, Reise nach China, Leipzig, 1829; Labours of the Russian Mission at Peking on China, its People, Religion, Institutions, Social Relations, etc. Translated into German by Dr. Abel and F. A. Mecklenburg, 3 vols. Berlin, 1858-9, etc.

doing in the territories restored by the treaty of Nerchinsk. The ancient town of Aigun, on the left bank of the Amur, was the first town occupied by the Chinese in 1683. But in the following year the garrison was removed to the right bank of the river three miles lower down, and the town was made the capital of the newly created government of the Amur (Khei-lun-tsian of the Chinese, Sakhalin-ula of the Manchu). After the peace the seat of government was removed a second time, to the recently (1687) founded town of Mergen, on the river Nonni. A third removal took place in 1700; and from that time Tsitsikar, until then a small village, has remained the seat of government. The government of the Amur, together with that of Girin, which latter included the districts originally owned by the Manchu dynasty, were placed under a governor-general residing at Mukden. The system of administration differs from that of China, and is exclusively of a military nature. Military governors reside at Tsitsikar and Aigun, and in each town there is to be found a yamun or court of justice, with a store-house, granary, prison and school attached to it. The Manchu and some amalgamated tribes of Tunguzians are all of them soldiers; and, besides this, some of the other tribes are incorporated into a kind of militia. The military forces in 1818 numbered two hundred and thirty-eight officers and 10,431 men in the province of the Amur, and three hundred and twenty-three officers and 12,852 men in that of Girin. Small flotillas were also stationed at Girin, Petun, Aigun, and Tsitsikar, with eighteen officers and 1822 sailors. Most of the troops, about 19,000 men, were cavalry with light chain armour, and a considerable number acted as couriers, and others cultivated the soil. The militia organized among the tribes settled along the Sungari and its tributaries numbered about 54,000 men. The revenues are derived from various sources. In 1811 the province of Girin produced £27,784, viz.:—

| | |
|---|---:|
| Land-tax | £16,622 |
| In lieu of rice | 7,319 |
| Capitation-tax | 2,008 |
| Various | 1,835 |
| | £27,784 |

In addition the Nomadic tribes paid a tribute of 2,398 sables or their equivalent, valued at £3,597; and 7,800 quarters of corn; the latter raised, probably, on the government lands.

The Chinese and Manchu population at that time numbered 307,781 individuals; the extent of private lands cultivated was 871,896 acres, and thus each acre pays annually a tax of about sixpence halfpenny. The other taxes are equally trifling. The Nomadic tribes may be estimated at about 12,000; the tribute exacted from them appears to be much more onerous than the taxation is to the rest of the community. In the province of the Amur, 4,497 sables, value £6,746, were paid as tribute, and £557 in taxes. The tribute from the Nomadic tribes was levied by the Mandarins who descended the Amur in their barges, took up their residence in some native village, and having collected the tribute and disposed of their merchandize to the best advantage, returned to their ordinary stations. These Mandarins are charged with abuse of power, and with having made extortionate demands upon the natives, who hailed the Russian, as their liberators. The latter certainly only demanded from one to two rubels annually from each adult male subject to them. On the other hand, the Mandarin is supposed to make a small present of tobacco or silk to every one paying his tribute; and as far as regards the Gilyaks and Negda, this present appears, at least in their estimation, to be of greater value than the tribute demanded. The payment of tribute on the part of these latter tribes has, however, always been voluntary; for the Mandarin did not usually descend the Amur below Pul, and visited Sakhalin island even less frequently. Sakhalin, at least the northern part of it, appears to have become tributary to the Chinese about the beginning of the eighteenth century, shortly after the time when the Jesuits visited the country.[d] Disputes had arisen between the natives and some traders, who had gone there from the Amur. Manchu soldiers were sent to set the matter right. They landed, explored the island, appointed the chiefs of Hoi, Otsis, Gauto and Doga Haratas, i.e. directors, and made them promise to take annually a tribute in sealskins to the village of Deren on the Amur; in return for which they were to receive a piece of silk embroidered with gold, as a mark of the emperor's special favour. The Japanese who had occupied the southern portion of the island carefully avoided coming into contact with the Chinese. The boundary between the two nations may be placed for that time under 49° N. lat.

The jealous policy of exclusion peculiar to the Manchu government of China prevailed also on the Amur. Not only were the Chinese forbidden to emigrate to the thinly-populated Manchuria, but the natives themselves were not allowed to pass the town of Sansin on the Sungari. The privilege of trading on the Amur was restricted to ten merchants, who obtained for that purpose a licence at Peking.

[d] The Emperor Khing-tsu (Khang-hi) resolved in 1707 to avail himself of the services of the Jesuit fathers, then staying at his court, for making a more correct map of his dominions. Their labours extended also to Manchuria and the Amur. On the 8th of May, 1709, the fathers Regis, Jartoux and Fridel left Peking, explored Leaotong, the Sungari Usuri, and the Amur down to the Dondon river. In 1710 they returned to Manchuria, explored its western portions, and ascended the Amur to Ulusu Modon. See Endlicher's Atlas of China, Vienna, 1843; and Du Halde's China.

In reality, however, there were a great many more traders, for the payment of a sufficient bribe to the Mandarins secured the same privileges as an imperial license. A few Chinese, most of them fugitives from justice, found their way across the barrier of stakes, and led a miserable life in the wilds of the Usuri. Others were exiled by government, and settled under military surveillance in the neighbourhood of the towns. At the accession of the Emperor Tao-kwang, in 1820, the restrictions regarding immigration were removed with respect to the regions above the town of Sansin, on the Sungari. The public lands were put up for sale to fill the empty treasury; Chinese immigrated *en masse*; new towns were founded, and the population of others was doubled and trebled. In consequence, the Chinese population preponderates at the present time; and the Manchu language has become almost extinct. Many of these immigrants are Mohammedans, and have mosques in the principal towns. But they also speak Chinese, their teachers alone being obliged to know Arabic, and are not otherwise distinguished from the Chinese surrounding them than by wearing a blue cap. The native tribes gradually yield to the influence of the new comers; and in dress, customs, and even language, assimilate more and more. This of course only refers to the southern portions of the governments of Girin and of the Amur, the regulations forbidding emigration to the Amur itself having been maintained as strictly as ever.

## X.

## THE ROMAN CATHOLIC MISSIONARIES IN MANCHURIA.

THE efforts of the Roman Catholic Missionaries in Manchuria may be said to date from the year 1838, when Leaotong, northern Manchuria, and part of Mongolia, were separated from the diocese of Peking, and created a distinct Vicariat Apostolic. M. E. Verolles, then at the College of Su-chwen in Tibet, was appointed Vicar Apostolic, and arrived at Kai-Cheu in 1841. Soon after, M. de la Brunière proposed the conversion of the Chang-Mao-tse, i.e., long-haired people, on the banks of the Amur, but could not be spared before 1844, when the number of Missionaries was increased. In May 1845 he left Kai-Cheu, with the understanding, of not extending his journey beyond three months. His further progress may be seen from the following letter, dated from the banks of the Usuri, and addressed to the Directors of the Seminary for Foreign Missions.*

" Manchuria, on the river Usuri, April 5th, 1846.

" — — — On the 15th of July, after some retirement wherein I had consulted the will of God, I departed from Pa-kia-tze, a Christian district of Mongolia, accompanied by two neophytes quite unaccustomed to travelling. They were the only guides I could then find. We directed our course eastwards, keeping a little to the north. Seven days' journey sufficed to reach the town of *A-she-ho*, recently founded, and

* Annales de la Propagation de la Foi, vol. xx. 1848.

settled by successive emigrants from China, as had been the case to the deserts of Mongolia. *A-she-ho* is situated forty leagues north of Kirin, and twenty-five west of the Sungari. Its population, estimated at 60,000 souls, increases every day; a Mandarin of the second class governs it. It has within its territory some Christian families, which were visited the preceding winter by our dear brother the Rev. Dr. Venault. I preferred to stop this time with a rich Pagan, a friend of one of our neophytes, hoping that his generous hospitality would afford me the opportunity of announcing to him Jesus Christ. Great was my surprise to find that this man had the faith already in his heart, and sincerely despised the vain superstitions of paganism. And still he remains chained down to that belief; he is insensible to every exhortation, inasmuch as directing a large establishment of carpentry, if he were a Christian, he could no longer make idols for the temples, from which source he derives a considerable profit. In return for my zeal, he eagerly tried to dissuade me from the journey I had undertaken, representing to me the troops of tigers and bears, which filled these deserts; and whilst relating these things he sometimes uttered such vehement cries, that my two guides grew pale with horror. Being already a little accustomed to the figures of Chinese eloquence, I thanked him for his solicitude, assuring him that the flesh of Europeans had such a particular flavour, that the tigers of of Manchuria would not attempt to fasten their teeth in it. The answer was not calculated to reassure my companions; and they did not partake of my confidence when we resumed our route.

"Eight leagues from A-she-ho, the country, hitherto sufficiently peopled, suddenly changes to an immense desert, which ends at the Eastern Sea. Only one road traverses it, conducting to *San-sin* (in the Manchu language Ilamhola), a small village situated on the right bank of the Sungari, twenty-four leagues from its confluence with the Amur. The forests of oaks, elms, and fir-trees, which bound the horizon on all sides, the tall, thick grass, which oftentimes reached above our heads, were convincing proofs of fertility of the soil, as yet untouched by the hand of man. At every ten leagues you find one or two cabins, a kind of lodging-houses, established through the care of the Mandarins for the government couriers, which also as a matter of course lodge other travellers. There you need not ask for a bill of fare. If simplicity be one of the best conditions of a dietary regimen, it cannot be denied but that in this respect the fore-mentioned hostelries deserve to occupy the first rank. You have millet boiled in water, and nothing else. Two or three times the master of the house, in consideration of my noble bearing, brought to me a plate of wild herbs gathered in the neighbourhood. I do not know what these plants were, but I suspect strongly that gentian, an infusion of which is often drunk as a medicinal tea, was a chief component. The choicest dainty in these countries,—which, however, is never served up in the hotels,—is the flower of the yellow lily, which abounds on the mountains and is very palatable to the Chinese.

"Meantime no tigers appeared. But other kinds of animals, no less ferocious in my opinion, awaited us on our journey. I have not words to express to you the multitude of mosquitos, gnats, wasps and gad-flies, which attacked us at every step. Each of us armed with a horse's tail fixed on an iron prong, endeavoured to strike them, and this weak defence only served to render the enemy more vicious in his attacks. As for me, I was completely beaten, without strength either to advance or protect myself from the stinging of these insects; or if, at times, I raised my hand to my face, I crushed ten or twelve with one blow. Two wretched horses, which carried the baggage and occasionally our persons, lay down panting in the midst of the grass, refusing to eat or drink, and could by no means be induced to march. They were all covered with blood. We had been already three days on our journey, and four still remained before we could reach San-sim. We therefore changed our system of travelling, converted night into day, and reached the inn an hour before daybreak. By this procedure we avoided two terrible enemies, the gad-flies and wasps; the mosquitos alone escorted us, in order that we might not be altogether without annoyance.

"Those who know the country best never go out without a mosquito cloth—that is to say, without a thick, double wrapper, covering the head and neck, and having two holes cut for the eyes. As to beasts of burden, to make them travel in the deserts five or six days in succession, under the noon-day's sun, is to expose them to almost certain death. These insects swarm particularly in moist, marshy places, and on the banks of the rivers by which Manchuria is intersected. Beyond San-sim they grow to a monstrous size, particularly the gnats and wasps. As to others, as far as regards the punishment they inflict, it matters not whether they be small or large. The houses are somewhat preserved from them by the cultivated districts which surround them, and by their being fumigated with horse or cow dung; but they are not completely rid of them till the end of September, the time of the severe frosts.

"Another difficulty in these journeys consists in the immense deposits of mud which intervene on the route, and frequently compel a deviation of three or four leagues . . . At last, towards the evening of the 4th of August, San-sim displayed to us its wooden walls and houses. This city presents nothing remarkable but its great street, inlaid with large pieces of wood, six inches thick and joined together with much precision. Its population is reckoned at ten thousand souls. The Manchu mandarin who governs it is of the second class (dark red button), and has under his jurisdiction the banks of the Usuri and the right side of the Amur as far as the sea.

"The city of San-sim, the last post of the mandarins in the North, is to every Chinese or Manchu traveller the extreme limit which the law allows him to reach. To travel beyond is considered and punished as a great infraction of the laws of the state. About ten merchants protected by imperial passports which cost each of them one hundred taels or more annually, have the sole privilege of descending the Sungari, entering the Amur and finally ascending the Usuri, in the forests of which is found the celebrated Ginseng root. Any other traveller is beaten without any form of law, and his baggage, even to his clothes, taken from him. Evasion moreover is difficult on account of the small barges which are continually plying on the river in all directions day and night. The government of San-sim despatch annually three war junks in succession, carrying no guns, and having only a few sabres on board. The first of these goes to Mu-chem, on the right bank of the Amur, in 49° 13′ N. lat. This Muchem (Dondon of the Tunguzians) is neither a town nor a village, nor even a hamlet, but simply a building of deal, which during three months serves as a court-house for the mandarins of the boat. Their business is to receive the skins and furs which the tribe of the Sham-mao-tze (long hair), so called because they never shave the head, furnishes to the emperor, in exchange for a certain number of pieces of cloth. The second barge collects the same imposts from the Yupitatze, or fish skins, from the skins of fish which they make use of for clothing. The third boat has jurisdiction over the Elle-iao-tze (or long red hairs), a wretched and almost extinct tribe, occupying two or three small inlets of the Usuri, and dwelling under tents made of the bark of trees.[b]

"It often happens however that the mandarins and soldiers

[b] The "Long-hairs" of the Chinese are the Manguu or Olcha, the "Fish-skins" the Goldi, and the "Long-red-hairs" the Orochi of the sea coast.—R.

of these boats take more care of their own affairs than of those of the emperor. Not content with the skins of sable, they exact large sums of money before delivering the promised cloth; and in spite of all the natives may urge, they are no less bound down, under pain of being scourged, to this arbitrary impost. Many families on the approach of the boat leave their huts and fly to the mountains. But even this is of little avail; for during their absence everything belonging to them is pillaged, and the cabin itself burnt down.

"For my part, after a few days of rest spent in procuring information and laying in the necessary provisions, I sent back to Leaotong one of my two Christians, whom the experience of the previous journey had disinclined from proceeding further. When we arrived at San-sim it was just the time when the Manchu *Yupitatze* and *Sham-mao* came to exchange the produce of fishing and the chase for cloth, millet, and especially Chinese brandy. I learned from them that about forty leagues below Sansim, also upon the banks of the Sungari, was situated one of their principal villages, named Su-su. They added at the same time, that we Chinese were prohibited entrance, and no one would venture to conduct us thither. This double obstacle was no reason why I should abandon my project. Having then implored the Divine aid, and celebrated for that purpose the holy sacrifice at my hotel, the master of which, a man of the tribe of Xensi, took me for a sorcerer, I directed my way at an early hour of the morning towards the eastern range of mountains. If Providence permitted us to wander on our route, we always did it in such a way, that, meeting with some lonely cabin, we were able either by inquiring or by conjectures more or less correct, to keep without too many deviations the straight road to Su-su. We journeyed full of confidence in the invisible Guide who alone directed our steps, when in the middle of the fourth day, we were met by two horsemen, who bore an air of haughty nobility. It was a military mandarin attended by an inferior officer. He stopped, alighted from his horse, and saluted us very politely. We sat down on the grass and smoked a pipe together. The European countenance, more masculine than the generality of Chinese physiognomies, puzzled him for a moment. He addressed himself to my Christian and desired to know from him the object of our excursion into a country severely interdicted. The latter replied in accordance with instructions given beforehand, that as a simple man and labourer by profession, he had followed me as a domestic, without having any power to take a part in the important affairs which had brought me into these parts. On hearing this answer the mandarin immediately suspected that I was a ministerial agent, charged with examining into the state of the country and the conduct of the officials. This is in reality a common practice of the government, when they have conceived any prejudice against the functionaries of a city or a district. It should also be remarked that the Manchu mandarins are in general illiterate, and very little skilled in business. He therefore turned to me with increased caution, entered into conversation upon the name of my family, the province in which I was born, the products of the south of China, the state of commerce, etc. During all this time there was no inquiry after the object of my mission. He dreaded to compromise himself, and lose my favour. Two hours having thus passed in exchanging compliments, we parted well pleased with each other. He had the kindness to point out to us the best route to Su-su; and the next day, at an early hour, we were reposing in the cabin of a Yupitatze.

" My sudden appearance occasioned great alarm to these poor people; my unusual look; the dress, which in that country denoted somewhat of a high rank; the breviary, and the crucifix, formed the subjects of a thousand conjectures.

Little presents made to the principal persons of the district soon established a familiarity of intercourse, which enabled me to speak openly and with authority of the gospel. My hearers found the religion very fine; but the new doctrine, and the new preacher who announced it, stopped them short at once. One day — it was I believe the fourth of my arrival — I was sitting on the bank of the river conversing with one of the natives, and just beside us were his two sons engaged in fishing. In despair of catching anything they pulled in their long lines and were going away, when I said, assuming a jocose tone,

" ' You do not understand; give me one of your lines.'

"I threw it about ten paces further, not without much laughter from the spectators. Providence willed that a large fish should bite at the very instant; and I drew out my prey, more astonished myself than those who laughed.

" ' This unknown,' said they among themselves, ' has secrets, which other men have not; and nevertheless he is not a bad man.'

"In the evening, at supper, there was much talk about the wonderful capture I had made. They wished to know my secret. Instead of an answer, I contented myself with one single question:

" ' Do you believe in hell?'

" ' Yes,' answered three or four of the best informed; ' we believe in hell, like the bonzes of San-sim.'

" ' Have you any means of escaping it.'

" ' We have never reflected on that point.'

" ' Well then,' I replied, ' I have an infallible secret, by means of which you can become more powerful than all the evil spirits, and go straight to heaven.'

"The first secret gained credence for the second. Thus Divine Providence disposes of all things.

"The next day, three long beards of the village made their appearance in my chamber, armed with a jug of brandy and four glasses.

"'Your secret,' said they, 'is of awful consequence. If our importunity does not hurt your feelings, we would wish to know in what it consists. Let us begin by drinking.'

"Notwithstanding the natural repugnance which I have for Chinese brandy, I thought it necessary to accept the invitation, in order to avoid incurring the aversion of these poor people, who could be made to know or understand nothing but through this channel. I then commenced to develop my 'secret,' by explaining the dogma of original sin, of hell, of the salvation wrought by Jesus Christ, and the application by the sacraments of the merits of the Saviour. It was in the simplest manner, and by familiar comparisons, that I proceeded. But unluckily, my interrogators taking ten or twelve bumpers to my one, became in five or six minutes incapable of understanding anything. However, I gained favour. They lodged me and my Christian in a very spacious house, which had become vacant by the death of the proprietor. One of the most intelligent men of the village was appointed to teach me their Manchu language, which is more pleasing to their ear than Chinese, although they speak the one as well as the other. The Manchu has become a dead language in Manchuria Proper. The natives glory in abandoning the language of their ancestors in favour of that of the new comers—the Chinese. It is not the same with the Yupitatze, whose language is to the Manchu much the same as the Provençal patois is to the French or Italian.

"A week had elapsed when in the middle of the day the sharp sound of the tam-tam was heard on the river. Fear was immediately depicted on every countenance.

"'It is,' said they to me, 'a large boat from San-sim, bearing two Mandarins and twenty soldiers, who at this moment are assembling all the inhabitants of Su-su.'

"In addition to the ordinary apprehension caused by the sudden appearance of the functionaries, the people saw themselves seriously compromised by my presence, which would bring down upon them the wrath of the Mandarin. After a mutual understanding with me, they simply declared me to be an unknown person, who transacted no commercial business, and who, in opposition to their resistance at first, had forced himself upon their hospitality. An officer, followed by seven or eight soldiers, came directly to the house where I was; and, the first usual compliments being passed, demanded of me what business brought me into a country, the entrance of which was strictly forbidden by law.

"'My business,' I answered, 'calls me not only to Su-su; I must go further, and push on even to the Usuri.'

"The officer, without daring to follow up his inquiries, gratefully accepted a cup of tea, and retired inviting me to visit the boat. To anticipate the Mandarin, and pay him the first marks of politeness, was a decisive step; this indication of confidence would remove all suspicion. I went therefore on board attended by my Christian, and was received almost with open arms.

"On the evening of the same day he returned my visit. I offered him some pu-cha, the much-esteemed tea of Se-shwan, the glutinous leaves of which form a roll as hard as wood.

"'My lord,' said he on retiring, 'your presence here causes no inconvenience; I allow you to remain ten or even twenty days, if your business require it.'

"Nevertheless, the crew of the boat exacted from fourteen poor families of Su-su a sum equivalent to two hundred francs. The whole amount of money in possession of the Fish-skins did not amount to more than seventy-two francs. Three days passed in parley. My presence evidently annoyed the collectors. I had become an object of suspicion, and thought it best to return to San-sim, on the 23rd August, where I lodged with a Mahometan.

"My beard and my eyes induced my host first to imagine

that I was one of his co-religionists. His conjectures vanished completely before a plate of pork, which he saw me eat with a great relish. But what was his surprise, when he heard me relate the history of the creation ; the fall of our first parents ; the travels of Abraham ; etc.

"The Mohammedans of San-sim are numerous, and form about one-third of the population; they own a Mosque, which is guarded by a kind of Marabut, called Lao-she-fu. The duty of this man is, every day at sunrise to give the first stroke of the knife to the beast or cow, which is sold in the Turkish shambles. He also opens the school for the young persons, who wish to study the Koran. I received the unexpected visit of a superior officer, a confidant of the chief Mandarin. His mission was not to interrogate me judicially, but by means of certain captious questions and counterfeit politeness to extract my confidence. After a long conversation the officer retired just as wise as he came, but only to return in a short time to the charge. He paid me as many as three visits in the space of six days; so that the Turk, not being able any longer to repress his fears, came to me to humbly ask how much longer I counted on a shelter under his roof. It was therefore necessary to consider anew about my departure.

"I remembered having heard it said by the Fish-skins of Su-su, that towards the east, a little to the south of San-sim, there was a narrow path by which the ginseng dealers annually went to the Usuri. The distance by the long winding caused by the rivers and mountains is reckoned at one hundred and twenty leagues. The Turk, to whom alone I had confided my project, cheerfully assisted my little preparations; and on the 1st day of September 1845 we once more quitted San-sim, without knowing when we might return.

"This time the mule carried along a complete kitchen ; namely a small iron pot, a hatchet, two porringers, a bushel of millet, and some cakes of oaten bread. Whoever makes the journey from San-sim to the Usuri need not look for any other bed than the ground, any other covering than the heavens, nor any other food than what he may have taken the precaution of bringing. The journey, on account of the autumn rains, took us fifteen days. I confess that, in comparison with these, former fatigues appeared as child's play. You must cut and drag trees, light fires, necessary against the cold and the tiger, prepare your victuals in wind and rain, and all this in the midst of a swarm of mosquitoes and gad-flies, who do not suspend their attacks until about ten or twelve o'clock in the evening. Water and wood were in abundance during the first days of the journey; but thirty leagues from the Usuri, the springs became so scarce, that we were compelled to do like the birds of heaven, and eat the millet raw. The forests of this wilderness have scarcely any other trees than an oak, of poor growth in consequence of the rigorous climate.

"At last, towards the evening of the 14th September, the river Usuri came in view; it is as deep but not as broad as the Sungari. We were then forty leagues north of the lake Hinka (Tahu). Our first asylum was a lonely house built by the Chinese merchants, serving as a warehouse for the ginseng trade. Two days had scarcely passed when yielding to the invitation of one of the merchants, I availed myself of his bark to descend the river for a distance of twenty-four leagues, to a miserable cabin, situated ten leagues from the confluence of the Usuri with the Amur.

"This cabin belonged to a Chinese, a native of Shan-tum. With him were ten of his countrymen, from different provinces, whom he employed for six months in the year to traverse the mountains and forests in search of that celebrated root of Zu-leu, about which I will say something further on. The first interview made me imagine myself far from savage districts, and within the pale of Chinese urbanity. But when they learned my quality of Christian priest, then were verified the words of the Teacher, 'The servant is not greater than his Lord' (John xiii. 16). Aversion and disdain were succeeded by wrath, when, profiting by the many questions they addressed me, I openly announced Jesus Christ. In return for the words of salvation and love, they heaped maledictions on me.

"I had been there fifteen days, when a strange accident broke up our meetings. This happened about the middle of October. The trees already bare, and the high grass parched and turned yellow, announced the approach of great cold. At mid-day, there appeared in the horizon above the forests an immense cloud, which completely intercepted the light of the sun. Suddenly, all hurried out of the house, crying 'Fire! fire!' They took hatchets, and destroyed all the vegetation which bordered on the dwellings. The grass was burned and the trees dragged into the river. The cloud kept fast approaching. It opened, and disclosed to us the focus of a raging fire, as rapid in its course as a horse spurred to the gallop. There were concussions in the atmosphere, in violence resembling the shock of a tempest. The flames at hand, as soon as seen, passed a few paces near us, and plunged like an arrow into the forests to the north, leaving us in a sad state of consternation, although we had not suffered any loss. These fires are caused by hunters coming from the banks of the Amur, who find no easier means of compelling the game to quit their retreat.

"A few glasses of brandy having dissipated the late impressions of fear, the conversation turned anew upon religion. The greater part of my hearers agreed that my doctrine was good and true. But the Ten Commandments were universally deemed an insupportable burthen. You will not be astonished at this, when you are made aware what kind of people I had to deal with.

"The entire population of the Usuri and its tributary

rivers does not amount to eight hundred souls. It is divided into two classes, the first of which comprises the Chinese, to the number of two hundred, and the second about five hundred Manchu Fish-skins, subdivided into eighty and some odd families.

"The two hundred Chinese, two upright merchants excepted, are vagrants, felons guilty of murder, highway robbers, whom crime and the fear of punishment have compelled to exile themselves into these deserts, where they are placed beyond the reach of the law. I only judge them from their own account. How many have avowed to me their daring robberies, the number of men whom they had killed or grievously wounded, and the excesses of every kind to which their appearance bore testimony. 'No,' said they, 'misery and poverty alone could never have made us voluntarily undergo such dreadful exile.' And the aspect of the place induced me to believe them without difficulty. Would, at least, that the sufferings of banishment inspired some salutary remorse to these depraved hearts! But they preserve even now, as in their past life, an ardour for crime, to develop which opportunity alone is wanting. Each year is marked by two or three murders. But a very short time ago, even an old man of sixty-eight killed another of seventy-six, on account of some debt which the latter could not discharge on the instant. Four days afterwards I saw the murderer, and he related to me the bloody scene with an air as tranquil, as if he himself had taken no share in it.

"These men, wretched in their entire being, have here no other means of sustaining life than that of giving themselves up, with incredible fatigue, to the search of the ginseng. Picture to yourself one of these miserable carriers, laden with more than twenty-four pounds weight, venturing without any road across immense forests, climbing up or descending the mountains; always left alone to his own thoughts, and exposed to every distemper; not knowing if to-day or tomorrow he may fall a victim to the wild beasts which abound around him, supported by the modicum of millet he brings with him, and a few wild herbs to season it. And all this during five months of the year, from the end of April to the end of September."

[M. de la Brunière here gives a description of the ginseng plant from hearsay. He also encloses some seed with directions how to propagate it. The medicinal virtues of the ginseng, M. de la Brunière can speak of from his own experience; he was cured in a short time of a weakness in the stomach, which had resisted the treatment by Peruvian bark-wine and other infusions].

"I will now give you some details about the Yupitatze, or Fish-skins. This tribe, formerly numerous, at present scarcely counts from seventy to eighty families, who trade from the Lake Hinka as far as the Amur. The Yupitatze inhabit houses differing little from those of the poorer Chinese. In winter the Chase, in summer the Fishing, comprise in two words the history of their arts, sciences, and social state. No government, no laws among them; and how could there be any for scattered members who have not even the appearance of a body? Their whole religion consists in a debasing worship, which in Chinese is called *Tsama* or *Tsamo*. This superstition, equally in favour with the lower class of people in Leao-tong, has for its object the invoking of certain good spirits in opposition to the devil, whom they dread. With the Yupitatze, a tribe fond of the chase, three spirits, that of the stag, that of the fox, and the spirit of the weasel, stand highest in public estimation. If a member of a family fall sick it is ascribed to the agency of the demon. It is then necessary to call upon one of these genii, which is performed by the following ceremony, which I witnessed twice. The great Tsama, or evoker of the Tia-shen (spirit) is invited by the family. At a distance of half a league the sound of the drum announces his approach. Immediately the master of the house issues forth with a drum of the same kind, to receive him. It should be well understood that brandy is always at the reception; and I may as well tell you beforehand, the sun has hardly set before they are all dead drunk.

"When the hour of the Tia-shen has come, the great Tsama clothes himself in his sacred robes. A cap, from which streamers of paper and thin stripes of the bark of trees flutter, covers his head. His tunic of doe-skin or cloth, variegated with different colours, descends to the knees. But the girdle is what seems most necessary for his occupation. It is composed of three plaits, and attached to it are three rows of iron or brass tubes, from seven to eight inches long. Thus accoutred the exorciser sits down, the drum in one hand, a stick in the other. Then in the midst of solemn silence, he intones a lamentation, the music of which is not disagreeable. The drum, which he strikes at regular intervals, accompanies the voice. This lamentation, or invocation of the spirit, has many stanzas, at the end of each of which the face of the *Tsamo* assumes a fearful aspect. Gradually the sounds of the drum become stronger and quicker. The Tsamo contracts his lips, and emitting two or three dull whistling sounds, he stops. Immediately the spectators respond in chorus with a prolonged cry, gradually dying away, the sound of which is that of our open é.

"The invocation ended, the Tsama rises quickly, and with hurried steps and frequent bounds he makes the circuit of the chamber repeatedly, crying out like a man in a transport of frenzy and multiplying his contortions, which cause the tubes of brass to resound with a frightful noise. The spirit is then at hand and shows himself, but only to the exorciser, and not to the spectators. The Tsama I saw called upon the spirit of the stag. It was the commencement of the hunting season. He paused in the middle of his performance and uttered such a cry, or rather howl, that the

Chinese merchants, who at first had laughed at the farce, fled the house and sought shelter for the night elsewhere. An old cook, a native of Peking, assured me he had felt the spirit; but what was his terror when the next day on rising he found an iron pot empty, which he had left full of millet the evening before! It became known some time after, that the spirit, in a generous fit of conviviality, had awarded the dish to the great Tsama and his companions, as a recompense for their labours.

"The natives hunt only during the winter. The snow, which covers the mountains and plains to the depth of six feet, offers no impediment. Two planks cut from the pine-tree, a quarter of an inch thick and at most five inches broad, and six feet long, sloping upwards at both ends, covered underneath with a deer-skin, and bound tightly to the foot by two straps; such are the snow-shoes used by the hunter. Equipped with these, he will skim lightly over the snow follow the track of the stag and deer, and go twenty to twenty-five leagues in the shortest winter's day. Should a mountain lie in the way, he climbs it without difficulty by the aid of his snow-shoes. The hair of the deer-skin, with which they are covered, is put on so as to slope backwards, and sinking in the snow, serves as a means of support.

"The dexterity of the Yupitatze is no less exhibited in fishing. Furnished with a simple iron-pointed javelin, he sits in a skiff made of the bark of a tree, and manages it with the same ease on the water, as the snow-shoes on land. The Chinese call this skiff Kuai-ma, *i.e.*, swift horse. A few strokes of an oar, shaped like our "battoirs de lessive[b]," cause it to glide up the river with extreme rapidity. The Chinese dare not venture in it, for the least motion would upset the venturesome navigator. When the Yupitatze strikes the fish with his dart, the arm alone moves, the body not losing

[b] An oar with a blade at either end.

its equilibrium for an instant. The Usuri and its small tributary rivers abound in fish. That which ranks first is the Iluam-yu, unknown in Europe. I have seen some which weighed more than 1000 lbs., and was assured there were some of 1800 to 2000 pounds. It is said to come from the Hinka Lake. Its flesh, perfectly white and very tender, make me prefer it to all other fresh-water fish. Entirely cartilaginous, with the exception of three small bones in the neck, it has lips formed like those of a shark, the upper protruding much over the lower. Like the shark, it turns itself to seize its prey or bite the hook; and, like it, swims slowly and clumsily. The cartilage and bones are the most esteemed portions of the fish, and sell at San-sim for one and a-half tael of silver the pound. The Mandarins annually lay in a supply for the Emperor's table.

"Towards the end of September, at the approach of winter, another kind of fish called Tamara appears in the Amur and Usuri. It comes from the sea in shoals of several thousands, and weighs from ten to fifteen pounds. Its shape, and especially the flavour of its flesh, give me reason to suppose it a kind of small salmon. God, in His paternal providence, mindful even of those who do not glorify Him, gives it to the poor inhabitants of this country as an excellent preservative against the rigours of winter. I state what I found by experience. Without wine and without flour, supported by very little millet, and a morsel of this dried fish, I have suffered less from a continual cold of 51°, and which during many days reached 65°,[c] than I did in the south of Leaotong, with better food and a temperature of some four degrees below zero. To the Yupitatze the fishing of the Tamara is of the same importance as the gathering in of the harvest is to our rural districts and cities; a deficiency in one or the

[c] Evidently a gross error in M. de la Brunière's thermometer readings. At Nikolaywsk it never exceeds 40°, and at Yakutsk even, such a degree of cold is looked upon as extraordinary.

other will bring a famine along with it. The two fish I spoke of are more frequently eaten raw than cooked. I followed this custom without any very great repugnance, and scarcely believed I might become a savage at so small a cost. You can conceive, gentlemen, that this exclusive regimen of fish, like everything else exclusive, has its inconveniences. The heat which it imparts to the blood, so beneficial in winter, is the cause of severe diseases during spring and summer. Among these maladies I would particularise the small-pox. Its ravages are horrible. The most aged persons dread its attacks as much as infancy and youth. The same individual may suffer from it four or five times in the course of his life.

A GOLDI SLEDGE.

"But though dangerous as a constant article of food, the fish of these rivers are invaluable on account of the imperishable garments made of their skins. In boots made of such fish skins you may wade through rivulets and walk in the snow as on the dry ground, equally protected against the cold and moisture.

"The swan, the stork, the goose, the duck, the teal, appear each year in the month of May in numberless flocks, attracted by the prey which is easily had and in abundance; and the birds are the more daring, as no one disturbs their repose. The natives do not seem to value wild fowl.

"I will conclude with a word on the mode of travelling practised in the winter season. The great and only road during summer or winter is the river or lake. A very light sledge made of thin oaken laths, five or six feet long, a foot and a half high, convex in the lower part, whilst the upper part is level, serves as a general mode of conveyance. Here the dog discharges the same office as the reindeer with the Russians. Every family keeps a pack of fifteen or twenty of these animals. The master eats the flesh of the fish; the dog has for his share the head and the bones. During winter the latter feeds entirely upon the tamara, which produces such heat that he sleeps on the snow during the most severe cold without seeking a more comfortable berth. A team of eight dogs (they are of middle size) draws a man and two hundred pounds of luggage during an entire day with the swiftness of our best coaches. These journeys in winter, and the chase to which the Yupitatze are addicted at this season, bring on here as elsewhere in cold countries where no precautions are taken against it many cases of ophthalmia, which at an advanced age terminates in blindness.

"About the 13th or 15th of May I will buy, if it please God, a small bark in which I may descend the Amur to the sea to visit the Long-hairs. I shall go alone, because no one dare conduct me, and my companion, a poor Christian from Leaotong, returns to his home sick from fear and melancholy. I am well aware how difficult it will be to avoid the barges of the mandarins who descend the river from San-sim; but if it is the will of God that I arrive where I design going, His arm can smooth every obstacle and guide me there in safety, and if it please Him that I return, He knows well how to bring me back. Whatever this future may be, to proceed appears to me in the present circumstances the only duty of a missionary, who in the prayer which the Church enjoins him says often with his lips and in his heart the words of the sacred canticle, 'Shall I give sleep to my eyes or slumber to my eyelids or rest to my temples, until I find out a place for the Lord, a tabernacle for the God of Jacob' (Ps. cxxxi.).

"Have the kindness, gentlemen, to remember me at the holy altar and before the sacred hearts of Jesus and Mary.

"De la Brunière, Missionary Apostolic."

M. de la Brunière did actually descend the Usuri and Amur; but met his death at the hands of predatory Gilyaks. Two messengers were sent to seek him, but they only got as far as San-sim, where the swollen state of the river put a stop to their progress. Further researches were not made, as the situation of the Christian communities in the south of Manchuria did not permit of it. A cathedral had been built at Yang-koan (l'hotel de Soleil) three leagues from the sea, and several oratories and chapels in other parts of the country. A college was founded in the neighbourhood of Kuang-cheng-tzay in the plains of Mongolia; and Christian communities, owing to the activity of M. Venault, existed even at Girin and Asheho—towns of Manchuria. But the progress made by the Missionaries aroused the enemies of the new religion. On the 1st February 1849 when M. Verolles was confessing some Christians, Chinese soldiers and others, to the number of about sixty—in a state of exitement consequent upon an orgie—attempted to enter the oratory to to seize his person and deliver him to the Mandarins. They were prevented by the native Christians, and M. Verolles had time to fly to the mountains. The oratory, however, was watched; messengers ran off to Kai-cheu to denounce the first catechist (a native) for having given shelter to foreigners. In the morning before break of day six neophytes and one catechumen were arrested and taken in chains before the Mandarin. The catechumen and an old man renounced their new religion, but the others remained staunch in spite of tortures. This spread consternation among the neighbouring Christian communities. The men fled before the soldiers sent to arrest them, leaving their women and children behind.

Measures were taken without delay to put a stop to these persecutions. M. Verolles sent his pro-vicar Berneux to Mukden, where the Mandarin at the head of the superior tribunal sold at a high figure the promise to liberate the imprisoned Christians. The Christians were liberated, and their accusers sent to prison. The chief catechist brought an accusation of trespass against the Chinese aggressors. The imperial edict granting protection to the Christian religion was read in open court, and sentence was just being pronounced against the trespassers when the friendly Mandarin himself got into trouble. His successor was hostile to Christianity; he accepted bribes from the Pagans, and decided to refer the case back to the superior tribunal at Kai-cheu where no doubt it would have been lost.

Our catechist, however, presented a petition against such removal; and the government, probably induced to this course by the remonstrances of the French Consul at Shanghai, acceded to his prayer, and at the end of January 1850 the case was settled in his favour. Several Pagans received from twenty to eighty blows, two were deprived of all civil rights, and five soldiers who had robbed the Christians of a sum of thirty-two pounds were expelled the territory, after one month's suffering the infliction of the Cangue. This persecution did anything but promote the number of Christian converts. Many catechumens were shaken in their faith, and Pagans once favourable to Christianity returned to their idols. Nevertheless sixty-six adults and 1200 children were baptized in the course of the year, and in 1850 the number increased to eighty-eight adults and 2081 [d] children. Three new oratories were built.

[d] No doubt many of these children were baptized *in extremis*, by the priest working upon the superstitious fear of their parents.

M. Venault had been active at Asheho, a newly-founded town in northern Manchuria, and resolved to start from there upon an exploratory journey to the Lower Amur. One of the objects of this journey was to clear up the fate of M. de la Brunière still enveloped in mystery. In this he perfectly succeeded, as the following letter will show:—

"MY LORD,

"As soon as the wishes of your Lordships had become known to me I prepared to proceed to the kingdom of Si-san said to exist in the north. I left my residence at Asheho on the 6th day of the first month of 1850 on a sledge drawn by three horses and accompanied by the Christian converts Ho, Cheu and Chao. During the first three days of our journey we met with several hostelries on the road, but after we had passed the river Son-hoa-kiang (Sungari) these became scarcer, and the traveller is obliged to seek hospitality amongst the few colonists dispersed on the western bank of that river—a demand never refused. Numerous military stations are distributed on this western bank of the Sungari, each of which has a Mandarin and a tribunal. The distance from Asheho to Sansin is about fifty leagues, and we passed five days on the road. Sansin is situated at the confluence of the Sungari and the Mutan, on the eastern bank of the former and to the north of the latter. M. de la Brunière had stayed in this town in 1845, and his assassination by the 'Long hair,' still formed the subject of conversation. In order to render my journey as secret as possible I thought it prudent not to stop here. In haste I supplied the deficiency occasioned in our provisions, made during a five days' march, and though night had almost set in proceeded with my sledge across the snow. It was almost midnight when we arrived at a small tavern. The intense cold, or perhaps rather copious libations after supper, rendered our landlord for a long time deaf to our appeals for shelter. At last, however, the door opened and a place was assigned us on the *khang*.* Two took their turn in resting here, whilst the third watched the horses and the sledge on the roadside.

"In order to avoid the Military Station built by the Emperor at the confluence of the Sungari and Amur to prevent all intercourse between Sansin and the Hei-Kin district, we directed our course towards the Usuri (Utze-kiang) and crossed that river where it receives the Imma (Ema), above its confluence with the Moli. Our first station was Wei-tze-keu, ten leagues from Sansin.

"Wei-tze-keu consists of a group of villages situated within a radius of six leagues. Some agriculture is still carried on here and the population is pretty numerous. But going east, hostelries, cultivated lands or roads are no longer met with; only now and then we encounter in the midst of the wilderness the solitary hut of a ginseng dealer. Between Wei-tze-keu and Imma-keu-tze (Ema), a distance of a hundred leagues, there are only a few solitary huts in the mountain-gorges. They are inhabited by old men — a woman is never seen here — whose occupation it is to fell trees which they leave to decay, when a kind of mushroom grows upon them which at Sansin forms the object of a lucrative traffic.

"Scarcely ten leagues beyond Wei-tze-keu the paucity of snow compelled us to abandon our sledge, place the baggage on the back of our animals and travel on foot. We continued crossing the wilderness for twelve days, lodging sometimes in one of the huts just mentioned, but more frequently in the open air. On our arrival at our stopping place in the evening we cut down some wood, cooked our millet, and after supper peaceably fell asleep surrounded by an immense circle of burning embers, which protected us equally against the

---

* The divan, an enclosed bench warmed by the smoke from the fire passing beneath it.

piercing cold and the teeth of the tiger. Thanks to God, we had not yet met during the whole of our journey with a single beast of prey, but scattered bones still covered with pieces of human flesh, and clothing recently torn and besmeared with blood, reminded us of the precautions which it was necessary to take against the dwellers in the forests.

"Imma-keu-tze merely consists of a few houses inhabited by ginseng seekers. These men are homeless adventurers, gallows-birds who live here *en famille* with the proprietor of the house as chief. Gains and expenses are shared alike among all. Such a house is not a tavern, but a homestead of which you may become a member by presenting yourself; a republic where anyone may acquire the rights of citizenship by participating in the labour of all. In such a community I was obliged to stay for two months; it scarcely needed so long a time to make me desire to leave it. But I had neither guides nor a sledge, and, nilly-willy, was compelled to wait until the thawing should enable me to continue my journey in a canoe. During these interminable months we frequently spoke to these ginseng seekers and Chinese or Manchu travellers, who like ourselves sought shelter under the same roof, of God and our holy religion. But we spoke to men who had ears and would not hear, who had eyes and would not see. May the Lord deign to send down upon these vast regions a fire — not to destroy — but to enlighten the stultified understanding of these men, a fire to purify their hearts so profoundly degraded!

"At last the thaw came. I had purchased a small canoe made of the trunk of a tree, about twenty-five feet long and two wide. I engaged a pagan Manchu as pilot, and paid him at the rate of ten taels of silver (£3 12s.) a month. I gave him the helm, my people and myself took to the oars, and on the 19th day of the third month (31st April) we departed for the country of the 'Long-hairs.' Notwithstanding the ten taels which we had paid to our Manchu, he only accompanied us with repugnance and ill grace.

"The many absurd rumours afloat regarding me — I was said to be a Russian in command of a large army, which I was about to rejoin for the purpose of pillaging the country, or a sorcerer having power over life and limb — these rumours made my pilot singularly unwilling and ill-humoured. To these were added the statements of the merchants on our arrival at the Hai-tsing-yü-kiang about the ferocity with which the 'Long-hairs' had murdered M. de la Brunière; their rapacity which would induce them to treat us the same, and rob us of our effects. Fear exasperated our Manchu's naturally irascible temperament, and God knows we had daily to suffer from his violence.

"Apprehensive that he might desert us on the first opportunity, we engaged a second pilot, a Chinaman who had previously visited the Long-hairs and spoke their language. But instead of one tormentor we had now two. Not a day, not an hour, passed without some altercation, and of so satanic a kind that it scarcely is possible to imagine a one thousand tithe of it. Remonstrances would only have still more irritated them, and possibly put a stop to our further journeying, so promotive of the glory of God and the salvation of souls. I therefore held my peace and suffered in silence the insults of these leopards. *He: ecce ego mitto vos sicut agnos in medio luporum.*

"Towards the end of the fourth moon we arrived at Mucheng (Dondon). This is neither a town nor a village but simply an enclosure of palisades in the centre of which stands a wooden house, which serves as a residence to the Mandarin, who comes here annually to collect the tribute in furs from the Tatars and give them in return a few pieces of silk. This official in attending to the interests of his master, neglects not his own. He, as well as the armed satellites, who accompany him to the number of thirty, traffic on their private account. Woe to the natives upon whom he lays his hands, when ascending or descending the river. Having thoroughly exhausted them in pulling the barge with cudgelling at discretion, he compels them furthermore to purchase his merchandize and always at the highest figure.

"As stated above, the emperor has established several military posts on the confluence of the Sungari and Hei-long (Amur), to prevent all communication between Sansin and the tribes to the north. A flotilla of from twelve to fifteen barges is sent down the river under the Mandarin spoken of, and in addition bodies of armed satellites commanded by sub-officers are sent annually to Mu-cheng to prevent the higher functionaries themselves from favouring smugglers. Nevertheless, any one on paying a heavy bribe which the officials divide between them is allowed to pass. But the Son of Heaven may rest assured that these military posts, this flotilla, these armed men, maintained at a large expense, only serve to fill up the coffers of the Mandarins. In order to obviate paying for the right of passage, a great many barges descend to the sea previous to the arrival of the Mandarin at Mu-cheng, and only ascend to Sansin after his return. I did the same. After travelling twenty-four leagues we came to Aki, the first village of the 'Long-hair.' This hamlet, though said to be the largest of the Chang-Mao-tze, is inhabited by only seven or eight families. I observed here with pleasure much more manly features than among the Twan-Moa-tze (Tatars who shave the head), and and almost European physiognomies. I also saw them embrace each other in sign of friendship, which I had seen nowhere in China. When brandy expands their hearts they are particulary prodigal in signs of affection. I made a small present to each family, but they received it without any sign of pleasure. Had it been a bottle of brandy, they would no doubt have better appreciated it.

"Since our departure from Asheho we had generally travelled alone. But from Aki the number of barges following the same route increased much in number, and we were always in company. Great pains were taken to make me give up my intended journey to the sea; all arts of rhetoric were employed to describe the terrible tortures which M. de la Brunière had been subjected to. At last, when they saw I would not yield to the fear of undergoing the same fate, they came to menaces, fearing perhaps that the business which took me to these regions would injure their commerce. Notwithstanding these little friendly disputes, we kept inviting each other to dine on each other's boats. I took advantage of such opportunities to speak eternal truths and to distribute good books.

"In this way we came to Pulo opposite Uktu (Ukhtr), the last village of the 'Long hairs.' There my Manchu, whose fears had kept increasing the further we advanced, declared roundly he had had enough of this voyage, and nothing in the world should induce him to go further. My other companions did not refuse to remain with me, but I could plainly see their hearts began to fail. In my embarrassment, I begged one of the merchants to take me on board his barge and conduct me to the sea; but in vain. Not knowing what to do, I visited Pulo. I there found a man just returned from Sisan (Sakhalin): seven barges had foundered in the bay in a gale of wind, his alone escaping. Great rejoicing consequently took place in the family of this merchant during my stay. I was obliged to share in them, and when the feast terminated availed myself of the good will of my entertainer to interest him in the success of my journey. A nephew of his agreed to conduct me down the river for ten taels. I left part of my merchandize as security, and we were again *en route*, not even excepting my Manchu pilot, who had taken fresh heart. We entered the country of the Ki-li-mi.[f] But scarcely had we advanced five leagues[g]

---

[f] Gilyaks.   [g] Fifty leagues in the original.

when our progress was stopped by a new alarm. We were told that the first village, Hutong, we were about to approach, was the one near which M. de la Brunière had been murdered, and that eight barges were lying in wait for us a little above it to make us share the same lot. The whole of my men refused to go any further. I sought an interpreter who understood the language of the Ki-li-mi, and I sent him forward with three of my companions to ascertain what was going on, and collect precise information regarding the melancholy fate of my former fellow-labourer. They were gone six days. The two men whom I had kept with me augured evil from the delay, and were about to abandon me, when I perceived two Kwai-ma[h] rapidly rowing towards us. They brought back to me my messengers, dripping wet, soaked to the skin. In the joy of the happy termination of their mission, the unlucky fellows had got drunk, quarrelled, and upset themselves in the river. They confirmed the report of M. de la Brunière's death, and in corroboration brought several things which the murderers had taken from his barge. I abstain from giving the numerous versions of the cause of this act of ferocity, and restrict myself to the statement of one of the murderers as most worthy of credit. When my messengers arrived at Hutong, all persons concerned in the murder, one excepted, had fled. This one remained in the village on the assurance of a merchant that I was not come to take vengeance. My people saw and interrogated him. According to his statement, M. de la Brunière was engaged preparing his meal in a small bay, where he had sought shelter against a violent storm, when ten men, of whom the narrator was one, attracted by the prospect of booty to be expected from the strange priest, went towards him armed with bows and pikes. When they arrived at the bay seven of them landed, the others kept on

---

[h] Swift boat, made of birch bark.

their boat. Having hit M. de la Brunière with several arrows, the seven Ki-li-mi went on his boat and struck him with their pikes. The last stroke fractured his skull and proved mortal. During the whole of this tragedy, M. de la Brunière remained seated quietly in his boat, without speaking a word; no complaint escaped his lips. In silence he offered himself a sacrifice before God, in the conversion of the people, whose salvation had constantly occupied his thoughts from his first entrance into Manchuria. It is currently reported among Chinese and Tatars, that after his death the Ki-li-mi wrenched out the teeth of their victim, tore out his eyes, and mutilated the corpse most frightfully. The body was thrown ashore, and after a few days washed away by the river. The natives pretended to have seen the stranger walking the scene of the outrage since, an apparition which caused them much fear.

"This crime consummated, the assassins divided the booty. I have since then seen many children wearing miraculous medals and small crosses. The silver was converted into earrings for the women. The murderer whom my messengers saw appeared to repent of the deed. Of his own will he restored his part of the spoils, consisting in an ornament, a holy stone, a silver cup for mass, the remains of a thermometer, and two compasses. Besides this, my messengers, in concert with three headmen of Kilimi villages, imposed a fine upon him, which he submitted to without much difficulty. It consisted of five pots, two spears, two Mang Pao (dresses embroidered in various colours, such as are worn by the mandarins), a skin dress, a piece of satin and a sabre. The spears will remain in the hands of the interpreters as a memento of the peace concluded between us and the murderers. When these objects had been delivered to my messengers, in presence of the three chiefs, an act of reconciliation was signed, of which one copy remained with the Kilimi, and the other was forwarded to me. It is as follows:—

" ' In the thirtieth year of the Emperor Tao Kwang, Shien-Wen-Ming (M. Venault) and Chen-Tu-Chu (one of the Christians) came to demand satisfaction for a murder committed in the twenty-sixth year upon the person of a missionary called Pao (M. de la Brunière) by men belonging to the villages Arckong, Siöloin, and Hutong, and peace has been restored between both parties. The above villages engage not to incommodate for the future any travellers who may come on barges during the summer, or on sledges during the winter; but promise to treat them as brothers. The relatives and friends of the priest Pao promise on their part not to revenge the assassination of the twenty-sixth year of Tao Kwang. But as the spoken word passes away and is forgotten, these engagements have been put on paper by both parties, in presence of the interpreters, who are charged with seeing them properly carried out.

" ' The witnesses: Chen-Tu Chu and Shang-Shwen.

" ' The interpreters: San In Ho and I Tu Nu of the village of Ngao-lai, Tien-I-Tee Nu and Shy Tee Nu of Kian Pan, Hu Pu and Si Nu of Hutong.'

" But whilst peace was being thus concluded on the one hand, strife broke out on the other. I had promised to distribute among my guides the fine paid by the Kilimi. They did not, however, wait for my decision; each took what suited his fancy, they quarrelled, and from words they came to blows and knife-thrusts. Disheartened by so many disasters my two Neophytes refused to go any further, and I was obliged after all to give up my journey to Sisan. I therefore returned to Pulo, and prepared to proceed home, as soon as the mandarin should have quitted Mucheng with his flotilla.

" I had been there about a month when the news spread that the Chinese were coming to surprise us. We hastily concealed our baggage in a store-house, and with my two Christians I retreated to the neighbouring forest. It was the night of Assumption. Our only provision consisted of some rice-wine, but Providence ordained that we should meet at the skirt of the forest two women, carrying millet and dried fish, part of which they gave us in exchange for our wine. On the following day, towards evening, pressed by hunger, we cautiously ascended a small hill, where I saw on the river, not far from the wood, a solitary canoe with a man in it. He took my belt in exchange for some rice which we cooked in a hollow where the rising smoke would not easily betray us. Our meal was not very copious, and soon finished. Before lying down to sleep, I went aside to pray, when I heard several men advancing towards our retreat, and impatiently calling upon us. I feared the mandarin had received information of our whereabouts, and that he desired a nearer acquaintanceship. I therefore let them shout and beat the bush, concealing myself in the dense shrubs covering the ground. After a time all was silent and I fell asleep. On the following day our first care was to procure food. We walked a long distance without encountering any habitations, but at last came to a village where we heard the good news of the mandarin's return to Sansin.

"Whilst hidden in the woods, my two pilots and the man in whose house I had lodged had been flogged on suspicion of knowing about my evasion, and only got out of the hands of the mandarin on giving up to him their dresses, furs, etc., in short, all they were possessed of. I was obliged to indemnify these unfortunates, not only for their loss, but also for the cudgelling. To increase my misfortune, the Chinese pilot had remained on the spot when I concealed my effects in the stone-house on the day of my flight. My trunk had become an object of affection to his heart, and previous to flying himself, he wanted to have a last peep into it; and on my return, my watch, a silver cup, a compass, and a pair of scissors, were missing.

"Notwithstanding this accumulation of obstacles, I still

thought of Sisan. The refusal of all parties to accompany me obliged me, however, to forego this journey—one of the principal objects of my voyage—and to return to my station at Asheho. I arrived there on the sixth day of the ninth month, nine months after my departure. I only brought back with me skin and bones; more than two hundred and forty taels had been expended on the journey; I had sold my clothes and even lost my breviary.

"Throughout, I was taken for a Russian. Russians frequently make their appearance among the Kilimi and 'Long-hair,' with whom they carry on trade. I have seen with these tribes various objects of European origin, such as pots, hatchets, knives, buttons, playing-cards, and even a silver coin of recent date, which they had obtained in this way. At Pulo I was told that in April 1850 several Russians had come to select the site for building a town. Six days after I had left the Kilimi village of Heng-kong-ta, on my return to Pulo, a boat with seven Russians arrived there. Had the difficulty of ascending the river not detained them, they would have met me at that place. Kilimi, Long-hair and Chinese, all assert, that the Russians are going to build a town and take possession of the country. May not Divine providence have appointed them to open to us the islands north of Japan?

" A few words now on the chances of success which these regions offer to the propagation of the Gospel. Between Asheho and Sansin, few families are met with; there are only soldiers and vagabonds, whose life is passed in gambling, in orgies, in excesses of the most disgraceful debauchery. Sansin, with its environs, is a second Sodom.

" The Yupitatze of the Usuri are big children, affable and hospitable; but unfortunately they have adopted the vices of the Chinese with whom they are constantly in contact. Their superstition on commencing the respective seasons for hunting and fishing, as well as their long and frequent journeyings, present obstacles which the missionary would find it difficult to surmount.

"The Yupitatze of the Amur are gross, more cruel, and addicted to drink.

"The Long-hair and Kilimi surpass all other tribes in ferocity, lust of plunder and thirst for blood, especially when they are drunk, which happens every day. A missionary desirous of converting them would be sure of much suffering: but if the difficulties are great, the power of God is still greater. Courage, therefore, and confidence! The blood of the righteous which the ungrateful earth has drunk, calls for mercy towards it; it renders it fertile and makes it bring forth fruits of salvation.

"I have stated to your lordships the reasons which prevented my going to Sisan. But I will at least give the result of the inquiries I have made respecting it. The Chinese barges which descend the Amur to the sea never visit Sisan, which is separated from the continent by a narrow strait which they dare not cross. The more hardy Yupitatze however go there annually. They depart in the fifth moon, pass the winter on the island hunting or trading, and return in the spring of the following year. Their cargoes consist of millet, spirits and silks, which they exchange for furs. A Long-hair of Heng-kong-ta proposed to take me there in the following year, and a similar offer was made to me by a merchant of Sansin. The shortest route would be to leave the Amur at Cha-She, sixty leagues above Pulo. The country thence to the sea may be traversed in sledges in four days, and another day, with a favourable wind, would suffice to cross the strait.

"From all information Sisan appears to be identical with the island of Karaftu or Tarakai, half of which is subject to Japan, and for this reason the Chinese call it indifferently Sisan or Shepen (Japan)."

After his return, M. Venault remained at Asheho. In

1852 he removed to Girin with the intention of building an oratory. He was, however, denounced by the Pagans, and had to fly for his life. Christians of both sexes were taken to prison in chains, but were subsequently all ransomed on the payment of £120.

In 1856 the Roman Catholics had six chapels and several oratories in southern Manchuria. The number of converts is stated to have been 5000 souls. The chapels are constructed in the Chinese style, but with Gothic windows, doors, and portals. The interior is ornamented as far as their means and other circumstances permit, and it is these outward forms, this appeal to the senses of the people, to which we must mainly ascribe the success of the Romish missionaries.

XI.

RECENT HISTORY OF THE AMUR.

It was not long after the treaty of Nerchinsk, by which Russia had ceded to China her rights to the Amur, when the advantages which might accrue to the development of Siberia generally, and to the settlements on the Pacific in particular, began to be recognised. Müller, the historian, was the first to point out in 1741 how desirable it would be to acquire the right of freely navigating the Amur, and to send down it the provisions for the settlements in Kamchatka. In addition to this, Chirikof, the companion of Bering, advocated in 1746 the establishment of a post at its mouth. The subject was again broached in 1753 by Myetlef, then Governor of Siberia, who handed in a project for provisioning the Pacific settlements by way of the Amur. In 1805 Krusenstern proposed to occupy Aniwa Bay at the southern extremity of Sakhalin, of course as a stepping-stone to further acquisitions on the coast of Manchuria; and in the following year a Russian Lieutenant, Chwostof, actually took possession of the bay in the name of the Emperor by distributing some medals and proclamations among the native chiefs. This proceeding however was disavowed by the government. At about the same time Golovkin went on a mission to Peking, where he was ordered to treat for free navigation of the Amur, or at all events to gain permission annually to send a few ships with provisions down the river. But the Chinese were unwilling to make any concession whatever. To coerce them, Kornilof, the governor of Irkutsk proposed to make a hostile demonstration by constructing an Amur flotilla of gunboats. Again in 1816,

Shemelin of the Russo-American Company spoke very freely on the advantages Russia would derive by again occupying the Amur. He states that 14,000 to 15,000 pack-horses are required every year to carry the necessary provisions for the settlements on the Pacific, at an expense of fifty-eight to seventy-seven shillings per cwt, for every six hundred and sixty miles transport. The price of flour at Kamchatka consequently amounted to thirty-six rubles a cwt.\* Still more recently the opinion appeared to gain ground in Siberia that Russia would again occupy the Amur, and a fur-trader at Udsk, who had on hand a large stock of small brass crosses, effected a rapid sale by working upon the fears of the natives. He told them that a Russian ship would ascend the Amur, and all those not wearing crosses would then be put to death. This happened in 1830, and we can scarcely believe the statement of this merchant to have been entirely a fabrication. Middendorf's journey in 1844 along the supposed frontier, though not of a political character, and undertaken in opposition to the express orders of the Academy, nevertheless served to draw the attention of the home authorities to the regions of the Amur. Another sign of the interest taken in the Amur was evinced by the publication in Russian papers, including several government organs, of numerous accounts of early Russian adventure on the Amur.

When therefore Count Nikolas Muravief became governor of Eastern Siberia in 1847, one of the first acts of his government was to send an officer with four Cossacks down the Amur. Vaganof, the companion of Middendorf, was entrusted with this task. He left Ust Strelka in the spring of 1848, but since then no tidings have arrived from him, and he probably fell by the hand of some natives or was drowned. The Chinese frontier authorities were applied to, and his surrender demanded on the allegation of his being a

\* In 1852 a cow cost eleven pounds, a fowl twenty-five shillings, a pound of flour eightpence-halfpenny, a pound of meat sixpence.

deserter, but they pleaded ignorance. The fate of this pioneer did not however stop the preparations to obtain a footing on the Amur.

Muravief, as a second preliminary step, gave orders to explore the coasts of the sea of Okhotsk and the mouth of the Amur. These preparations, it was also believed, might be

GENERAL COUNT MURAVIEF AMURSKY,
GOVERNOR-GENERAL OF EASTERN SIBERIA.

the means of securing to Russia part of the whale fishery in the sea of Okhotsk, which was being carried on by Americans, English, French, and even Germans, to the entire exclusion of Russians. Captain, now Rear-Admiral

Nevilskoi left Kronstadt in the Baikal in 1848, and several officers of the Russo-American Company were placed under his orders when he arrived out there. Lieut. Gavrilof of the Constantine had in the year previous explored the Liman of the Amur. Capt. Poplonski and Lieut. Savin laid down the coast of the Shantar islands. Lieut. Orlof of the Russo-American Company continued the survey in a boat towards the Amur, and on the day of St. Peter and Paul he discovered the Bay of Fortune (Chastnia), where he founded the post Petrovskoi to serve as a winter station. The position of this post was however very badly chosen; it was scarcely accessible to ships, and was subsequently abandoned as useless.

In 1850 Lieut. Orlof entered the mouth of the Amur.[b] At that time the report was spread generally among the natives, even at some distance from the mouth of the river, that the Russians were coming with a large army to occupy the country. Orlof sent a boat up the river to select a site for a town, and in 1851 Nikolayevsk and Mariinsk were founded by Capt. Nevilskoi to serve as trading posts of the Russo-American Company. Russia had thus got a footing on the Lower Amur. In the following year, 1852, no progress appears to have been made on the Amur itself; but a detachment was sent from Ayan permanently to occupy the island of Urup, one of the Kuriles to which the Japanese preferred a claim, though Urup was not occupied by them, whereas it was occasionally visited by Russian hunters. Lieut. Bashnak discovered Port Imperial (Barracouta Bay) on the coast of Manchuria.

In 1853 Alexandrovsk post in Castries Bay, and Konstantinovsk in Port Imperial were founded. In the autumn Admiral Putiatin, who was then staying in Japan with the Pallas, Olivutzu, Vostok and Menshikof, despatched Captain

[b] In the same year a Russian chapel was built at the confluence of the Bureya and Niman, near one of the Chinese frontier marks discovered by Middendorf.

Rimsky-Korsakof of the Vostok[c] steamer to the Amur, where he wintered. In October Major Busse with one hundred and fifty men occupied Aniwa Bay, where the post of Muravief was established, and a small detachment was sent to Dui, on the west coast of Sakhalin, a place where coals are found.

## 1854-5.

The year 1854 is specially remarkable in the history of the Amur for the first military expedition under the personal conduct of General Muravief descending it from the Transbaikal provinces. Russia had at that time in the Pacific three frigates (the Pallas, Diana and Aurora), and several smaller vessels, and owing to the outbreak of hostilities between Russia and the Western Powers, fears were entertained that the vessels might be left in want of the necessary provisions. The Russian settlements in the Pacific themselves depended at that time upon a foreign supply, and the only feasible plan was to send the provisions from Siberia down the Amur. Muravief easily gained the consent of his own government to that decisive step. That of the Chinese authorities was asked for, but neither the governor at Maimachin (Kiakhta), nor the vice-king at Urga could grant it without reference to Peking. There is no doubt about the answer which would have been returned had the decision of the Peking government been waited for. Moreover, no time was to be lost, and having completed his preparations Muravief started with his expedition, and entered the territory of a neighbouring state, with whom Russia was at peace at that time. We will not pause here to inquire in how far Russia was justified in that step. Supplies were urgently required on the Lower Amur, and "necessity has no law."

Muravief left Shilinsk on the 27th May in the steamer

[c] This steamer was purchased in England, and left Southampton in January 1853 in company with the Pallas frigate, commanded by Admiral Putiatin.

Argun (the machinery of which had been constructed at Petrovsk), fifty barges and numerous rafts. He was escorted by a battalion of infantry of the line and some Cossacks, in all a thousand men, with several guns. In his suite were Permikin, Anosof and Gerstfeldt, entrusted with a scientific mission by the Siberian branch of the Russian Geographical Society, Lieut. Popof of the Topographical Corps who made a sketch survey of the river, Capts. Sverbéef and Bibikof. Most of these gentlemen have published accounts of this journey.[d] On the 7th June the expedition anchored

VIEW OF AIGUN.

off Amba Sakhalin, the first Manchu village, and several officers crossed over and landed, but excepting several old men and three younger ones the inhabitants had fled to the neighbouring town. The young Manchu, however, soon got on a friendly footing, and returned the visit of the Russians

[d] Permikin's Description of the River Amur in Memoirs of the Siberian branch of the Russ. Geog. Soc., vol. ii.; Anosof's Geological Sketch of the River Amur, with map, ibid. vol. i.; Sverbéef's Description of the Governor-General's Voyage down the Amur, ibid. vol. iii.; Permikin's and Anosof's Description of the Amur, in the Viestnik, 1855.

on board their barges where they received a few small presents. On the following day at ten o'clock in the morning, the expedition arrived at Aigun. The steamer anchored close to the town, and the barges and rafts formed a line on the opposite bank. In the "port" were seen thirty-five Chinese junks, each of five or six tons burthen. Several members of the expedition landed and were received by the governor and three other functionaries and invited to enter a tent pitched close to the bank of the river. The whole garrison was drawn up near the tent, in all about 1000 men miserably armed. Most of them carried a pole blackened at the top to represent a lance; a few only had matchlocks, and by far the greater number bows and quivers slung across the back. In rear of the troops stood some guns mounted on clumsy red carriages of very rough workmanship, and protected against sun and rain by a conical birch-bark roof also painted red. A man holding a match, or perhaps only a stick blackened at the top, stood beside each gun. Evidently the Chinese in that quarter had made no progress during the last two centuries. Soldiers as well as other people curiously pressed into the tent whilst the palaver was going on there, and it was necessary to drive them out with sticks. Admittance to the town was refused, the governor alleging he could not grant it without superior orders from Peking, otherwise he would expose himself to the whole severity of the laws prohibiting the entrance of strangers. Muravief not thinking it desirable to provoke any ill feeling, re-embarked and continued his journey down the river. On the 27th June he arrived at Mariinsk, and with part of his retinue he returned by way of Ayan to Irkutsk. Permikin left Mariinsk on the 2nd July in a boat with five rowers, and after seven days arrived at Nikolayevsk. Heavy rains detained him here for two days, when he continued his journey to Petrovsk whence the schooner Vostok took him to Ayan. Muravief hastened from Mariinsk to Port Imperial where he met Admiral Putiatin of the Pallas. Neither the Pallas, nor the Diana, which arrived subsequently, could enter the mouth of the Amur, and proceeded therefore to Cape Lazaref to take in the provisions intended for them.

The commencement of a scientific exploration had been made by the gentleman attached to Muravief's expedition. In the same year however two other gentlemen arrived on the

VIEW OF MARIINSK, 1854.

Amur; we allude to the naturalists Leopold von Schrenck and Charles Maximowicz, the former of whom directed his special attention to the animal world, whilst the latter investigated the botany of the new territories. Leopold von Schrenck had been attached at the instance of the Russian Academy to the frigate Aurora, which left Kronstadt on the 2nd Sept. 1853. She arrived on the 15th April 1854 at Callao, where she found at anchor four French and English frigates awaiting the official news of the declaration of war. Without delay she continued her voyage, crossed the Pacific with a favourable wind, but on arriving near the southern Kuriles contrary winds and the health of the crew compelled her to put in at Petropavlovsk, Kamchatka, 30th June.

Schrenck was here transferred to the Olivutzu, Capt. Nasimof, which was sent by the governor to Castries Bay. On the 6th August he put into Port Imperial, where the garrison at that time consisted of eleven men only, and he arrived on the 11th at Castries Bay. The Olivutzu remained here, but Schrenck was enabled to continue his journey to the Amur on the steamer Vostok which had just come in with coals from Cape Dui. At Cape Lazaref he found at anchor the frigates Diana and Pallas, which owing to the shallow water could not get further. Maximowicz, who was on board the former, joined Schrenck on the Vostok, and after running aground several times both reached Nikolayevsk on the 18th August. Maximowicz had been attached as Botanist to the Diana for the purpose of collecting plants for the Imperial Botanical Gardens at St. Petersburg. The Diana arrived at Castries Bay on the 23rd July 1854, and owing to the outbreak of the war, he was obliged to leave the ship. The time up to his leaving Castries Bay, 6th August, was spent in botanical excursions. Schrenck wintered at Nikolayevsk, but Maximowicz continued his journey on the 19th September to Mariinsk, where he staid during the winter, and in October made an excursion to Castries Bay to explore the marine flora.

The Pallas not proving any longer sea-worthy had her guns taken out at Cape Lazaref, and was then sent to Port Imperial and burnt in the following spring, the small detachment left to guard her returning by land to Mariinsk. The Diana with Admiral Putiatin went to Japan.

At the time of the outbreak of hostilities in 1854, the strength of the Russians on the Amur was very inconsiderable. The post Muravief in Aniwa Bay had been abandoned, the garrison proceeding to the Amur; and the place was again occupied by the Japanese. Konstantinovsk in Port Imperial was guarded by a few men only. Alexandrovsk in Castries Bay had also been evacuated. On the Amur itself Nikolayevsk and Mariinsk alone were occupied; but the garrison of both certainly did not exceed 1000 men. Petrovsk, a block-house, on Fortune Bay, north of the Amur, still existed, but was not capable of offering the least resistance. The military strength of Russia had been concentrated at Petropavlovsk, and reinforcements had been sent there by the Olivutzu from Castries Bay. The naval forces were equally insignificant. The Diana frigate lay at Simoda in Japan; the Pallas, sixty, a hulk in Port Imperial. At Petropavlovsk were the Aurora frigate, forty-four, the store-ship, Dvina, ten, and the transports Baikal, four, and Irtish, six guns. The Okhotsk brig, six, of the Russo-American Company was stationed at Ayan, and at the latter part of the year was drawn ashore at Petrovsk to undergo repairs. Some other vessels of the Company, the Constantine, Turko, Kodiak, Menshikof, were afloat in the sea of Okhotsk, but not being armed no account need be taken of them.

The allies were mustering their forces on the American coast. On the 7th May, the Virago arrived at Callao with official news of the declaration of war, but did not leave before the 17th May, allowing ample time to the frigates Aurora and Diána to reach a place of shelter. The Artemise and Amphitrite, twenty-five, having been sent to California, the allied squadron had the following strength:—

English—President, frigate . 50 guns. Admiral Price.
        Pique       ,,    . 40 ,,
        Virago, steamer . 6 ,,
        Obligado, brig . . 12 ,,
French — Forte, frigate . . 60 ,, Admiral Febvrier
        Eurydice, corvette . 22 ,,   Despointes.

A total of six vessels, with one hundred and ninety guns and about 2000 men, and including but one miserable steamer, of two hundred and twenty horse power. On the 28th August this squadron arrived off Petropavlovsk. The ships were painted black to conceal their strength. In the afternoon Admiral Price reconnoitred the fort on board the Virago. The Russians had made ample preparations for a vigorous defence. The nine batteries of the place mounted fifty-two guns of heavy calibre,[e] and the Aurora and Dvina were moored behind a spit of land in a rather disadvantageous position, their broadsides facing the harbour. The Russian garrison, including ships' crews, was less than eight hundred men. The odds certainly were on the side of the Allies, and considering the weight of their armaments they had a fair chance of success. On the following day the squadron was just moving in to commence the attack, when the suicide of Admiral Price, committed, it would appear, in a temporary fit of despondency, put a sudden stop to further proceedings. The command now devolved upon the French Admiral, a very old and infirm officer.

On the 1st September, the Virago towed in the President, fifty, Forte, sixty, and Pique, forty, but notwithstanding the calm she could scarcely get ahead, and dropped the frigates much further from the Russian batteries than was desirable. A small battery of three guns was however soon silenced, and the guns spiked by a landing party. The circular five-gun battery on Shakof Point was also silenced for that day. The eleven-gun battery on the spit of land behind which were moored the Russian vessels, proved more troublesome, but after a time also ceased her fire. In the evening the Allied ships were hauled out of range of the enemy's guns.

On the following day, the 2nd September, Admiral Price was buried in a sequestered spot of the bay. A stormy war-council was held at night, and it was resolved to take the place by assault, a scheme opposed by the timid French Admiral. Sunday the 3rd September was passed in preparations. On Monday a landing party of seven hundred men—

---

[e] Four Paixhan guns, the others thirty-six and twenty-four pounders.

four hundred and twenty English and two hundred and eighty French—were placed on board the Virago, which again towed in the President and Forte. The frigates took up their positions six hundred yards in front of two batteries of seven and five guns respectively, and having silenced them the landing party was disembarked under the direction of Captain Parker, R.N. It was found impossible to restrain the men, and without any order they scrambled up a hill overgrown with brushwood where they could not distinguish friends from foes. Arrived on the top of the hill, a Russian battery of two guns opened fire upon them and in indescribable confusion they fled towards the sea. Had it not been for the guns of the Virago, which daringly approached to within a few yards of the coast, the loss would have been more considerable. That of the English was one officer and twenty-five men killed, eight officers and seventy-three men wounded. The French had three officers killed and five wounded. The Russians took two prisoners also. On the 5th the fallen were buried in Tarenski Bay, and on the 6th the squadron left. On getting outside two strange sails appeared in sight, and turned out to be the Anadir schooner with provisions for Petropavlovsk, and the Sitka of the Russo-American Company, of seven hundred tons, with military stores from Ayan. Both were taken and the former burned.

The English went to Vancouver, the French to California, whence dispatches were sent to Europe, which arrived there at the end of 1854. Admirals Bruce and Fournichon were appointed to succeed Admirals Price and Febvrier Despointes. The latter officer however died on the 5th March off Callao. Reinforcements were promised, and imperative orders were given to take Petropavlovsk. The Russians at that place were further reinforced by the Olivutzu from Castries Bay, and the Kodiak, which had been staying at Bolsheresh on the west coast of Kamchatka. They strengthened their fortifications still more and repaired the damage done; but on the 17th March orders arrived from St. Petersburg to abandon the place. The guns and ammunition were at once put on board the ships, a passage was cut through the ice, and they left on the 17th April 1855, and safely reached Castries Bay.

## 1855-6.

Considerable activity was displayed by Russia in 1855. Three more expeditions left Shilkinsk in the course of the year, and conveyed down the river altogether three thousand soldiers, five hundred Colonists, with cattle, horses, provisions, agricultural implements, and military stores. Gen. Muravief himself accompanied the first of these expeditions, which started in May. The Chinese were either unwilling or unable to oppose the passage of the Russians, and contented themselves with carefully taking note of the Russian barges floating past. For as yet Russia had not attempted to make any settlement on the upper or middle part of the river, the presence of the allied fleets in the Pacific rendering it necessary to assemble as great a force as possible on the Lower Amur, in case any attempt should be made to land. The Chinese, however, took some notice of the doings of Russia, and in July some Mandarins on four junks came to Nikolayevsk to negociate about the boundaries, but not being of sufficient rank General Muravief refused to treat with them.[f]

Gerstfeldt, in August 1855, remarks upon the progress made on the lower Amur. Mariinsk, which in the preceding year consisted of two log-houses only, now extended for some distance along the bank of the river, and was defended by

[f] According to another authority, these Mandarins came to protest against the occupation of the Amur; their attention, however, was drawn to the guns and military forces assembled, and they left their purpose unattained.

two batteries. A considerable part of the forest had been cleared and a "park" laid out for the enjoyment of the inhabitants.[g] This island of Suchi, where in former times stood Kosogorski, was occupied by a Cossack village, surrounded by "gardens, fields and meadows." The villages of Irkutskoi, Bogorodskoi and Mikhailovsk had been founded in the summer by colonists who came down the river, and who were engaged there ploughing the fields. Their houses had already been built. Progress was however most apparent at Nikolayevsk. The population had been largely increased by the arrival of the garrison of Petropavlovsk, and instead of ten houses there were now one hundred and fitfy. There was a club-house, with "ball-room, dining and reading-room,"[h] a warm bath and two schools, and the town was defended by three batteries mounting sixty guns. In the harbour might be seen the schooner Liman, facetiously called the "Grandfather" of the Russian Navy of the Amur, the first vessel built by Peter the Great having been called "Grandmother." The vessels escaped from Petropavlovsk were lying in the winter-harbour.

Castries Bay had been re-occupied in June, and in addition to four badly built huts, a convenient summer camp for five hundred men, and a winter camp consisting of six large and several small log houses were completed in the course of the year. A small detachment was still stationed at Port Imperial commanded by Lieutenant Kusnezof, but in January 1856 the post was abandoned, and the garrison fell back upon Mariinsk.

The operations of the allied fleets in the Pacific in 1855 were on a much more extended scale than in the year preceding, but the results were equally insignificant. One squadron, commanded by Admiral Bruce, operated in the sea

[g] The neighbouring village of Kidzi was purchased from the Olcha, and settled by a battalion of infantry of the line.

[h] Mr. Gerstfeldt is fond of using high-flown language.

of Okhotsk; and a second, commanded by Admiral Sir James Stirling, in the South. It may be presumption in a civilian to offer any comments on naval operations, but we cannot help thinking that a fleet of seventeen vessels ought to have been sufficient to blockade the northern and southern entrances of the Amur, had it even been found injudicious to attack the Russian stations on the Lower Amur. This attempt, indeed, might have been attended with considerable loss of life, without leading to any commensurate benefit. The naval force of the Russians was utterly insignificant, and, as at Sebastopol, did not dare to show its face. The Diana frigate had been wrecked in Simoda Bay; the Pallas, was lying a hulk in Port Imperial; and of vessels actually in a position to show fight there were but seven, the frigate Aurora, forty-four; the corvette Olivutzu, twenty; the transports Baikal, six; Dvina, ten; and Irtish, six; the small steamer Vostok, four; and the cutter Kodiak. The few vessels of the Russo-American Company were glad to find a refuge in the neutralized[1] territories of North-western America. On the other hand the Allies had at their disposal five steamers and twelve sailing vessels, viz. English: the steamers Hornet, seventeen; Encounter, fourteen; Barracouta, Brisk and Styx, each of six guns; the sailing vessels: President, fifty; Winchester, fifty; Sybille, forty; Pique, forty; Amphitrite, twenty-five; Spartan, twenty-four; Dido, eighteen; and Bittern, twelve: total, three hundred and eight guns. The French had only four sailing vessels, the Alceste of fifty guns; the Sibylle, fifty; the Constantine, thirty; and the Eurydice, twenty-two: their steamers, the Colbert and Jean d'Arc, ran aground and were not available. The grand total is thus seventeen vessels, with four hundred and eighty guns.

A rendezvous was appointed for the vessels belonging to the squadron of Admiral Bruce under fifty degrees north-

[1] The American possessions of Russia had been declared neutral.

latitude and one hundred and sixty degrees east longitude, off the post of Petropavlovsk in Kamchatka. The Encounter and Barracouta arrived there on the 14th of April, and cruized off the port, but owing to dense fogs the Russians, who left the Bay on the 17th, escaped their notice.[j] By the 23rd of May the other vesssels had arrived, and the squadron was composed then of the

> President, sailing frigate, 50 guns.
> Alceste, ,, ,, 50 ,,
> Pique, ,, ,, 40 ,,
> Dido, corvette 18 ,,
> Encounter, screw 14 ,,
> Barracouta, steamer 6 ,,
> Brisk, screw 6 ,,
>
> Total, seven vessels with 184 guns.

and about 2,000 men. All of them, the Alceste excepted, were English. Owing to dense fogs it was necessary to delay entering the port until the 31st, but the town was found deserted, the inhabitants had been removed to the interior and the American colours were flying over one of the stores. The batteries were razed by the Allies and the government buildings burnt down, the latter, however, without the sanction of the Admiral. The Dido was sent to the north to look for a privateer, and on the 3rd of June three boats were sent from the President to capture the Ayan whaler of four hundred tons found in Rakovia harbour. The sails, boats and anchors had been taken from her. She was burnt. Another whaler, the Turko, had safely effected her escape to Kojak, in neutral territory. On the 11th the Amphitrite, twenty-five, and Eurydice,

---

[j] The Heda with Admiral Putiatin entered Petropavlovsk on the 21st of May, and saw four ships cruizing off the port.

twenty-two, arrived with despatches from the south; Admiral Bruce thereupon gave up the pursuit of the Russians in the sea of Okhotsk; but on the 13th he despatched the Barracouta, Pique, and Amphitrite to Ayan, and the Encounter, to reinforce the squadron of Sir James Stirling in Japan. With the remaining five vessels Admiral Bruce returned to the American coast, looked in at Sitka harbour on the 13th July, but finding no preparations made for defence, nor any men-of-war there, he continued his voyage to California. None of his ships took further part in the operations against the Russians.

The three vessels, Barracouta, Pique, and Amphitrite, ordered to Ayan, arrived there on the 7th July. On their approach the Russian flag was lowered, and the town evacuated. A few whalers were at anchor. The batteries had been razed by the Russians. The property of the Russo-American Company, including a small steamer then on the stocks, was destroyed. On the 15th the squadron again left Ayan, and two days after, when off Cape Elizabeth, fell in with Sir James Stirling's squadron.

We now turn to the proceedings of Sir James Stirling in more southern latitudes. The Sybille, forty, Hornet, seventeen, and Bittern, twelve, commanded by Commodore the Hon. C. G. Elliot had left Hong-kong on the 7th April, arrived at Hakodadi on the 29th, and on the 7th May started for the north, on a reconnoitring expedition, to the Channel of Tatary. At Jonquière Bay, where the squadron arrived on the 18th, they met some natives who had seen three vessels pass up the gulf about five or six days previously. These no doubt were some of the Russian ships escaped from Petropavlovsk, and actually, when Commodore Elliot arrived off Castries Bay he could see some vessels under the land. The Bittern was sent to reconnoitre the enemy's position, and when off the harbour signalled a large frigate, three

K

corvettes, a brig, and a steamer.[k] The Hornet in the mean time, had got up steam, and when at five miles' distance from the bay, was ordered to advance, and at two P.M. confirmed the report of the Bittern. The steamer was then recalled, but owing to a strong headwind and the tide, only got alongside the Commodore's frigate at five P.M. After a short consultation the Commodore, with the two other officers commanding, went on board the Hornet, and steamed into the harbour, and when within 2000 yards of the Russian vessels a shell was fired from the thirty-two-pounder at the bow, but fell short. The Russians returned the compliment with equal want of success.

Commodore Elliot did not consider it feasible to attack the Russians in their "strong" position. Had he known how much their ships were encumbered with the women and children and stores brought from Petropavlovsk he would no doubt have done so. His forces were superior (sixty-nine heavy guns) to those of the Russians, who only had a sailing frigate of forty-four, and a corvette of twenty guns, the other vessels being mere transports with a few light guns. No wonder the Russians could not be induced to leave the harbour, to show fight. They were moreover not supported by land-batteries.

The Bittern was sent to the south for reinforcements. The Sybille and Hornet remained near Castries Bay, but the Russians, taking advantage of a dense fog, slipped out, and when the Commodore again looked in at Castries Bay on the 27th the birds had flown. On landing, six rough log-houses, forty by fifteen feet, were found, two of which were habitable,

---

[k] The Russian vessels were the Aurora frigate, forty-four, the Olivutzu corvette, twenty; the transports Baikal, six, Irtish, six, and Dvina, ten, and a cutter, the Kodiak. There was no steamer, as Lieutenant Peshchurof tells me, for the Vostok, the only steamer of the Russians at the Amur, was undergoing repairs at Petrovsk.

the others in an advanced state. In the former were found uniforms, books, and many boxes, containing fur-clothing, and one with Russian documents and letters, and the portrait of a lady. Many barrels of rye-flour, some vegetables and packages with seeds, were made booty of. The Russians had evidently evacuated the place in great haste, for at a short distance from the bay, on the road leading to Kidzi Lake, the ovens in the huts were still hot, and a large quantity of rye-bread, still warm, was found. On the 29th the Commodore turned to the south; reinforcements had looked in at Jonquière Bay, but could not resist the temptation of a fair breeze to return to the south. The Heda with part of the crew of the shipwrecked Diana was met in the strait and chased for some hours during the night, but finally made her escape. On the 7th of June, Commodore Elliot arrived at Cape Grillon where the Winchester fifty, and Spartan twenty-four, were at anchor.

[We will insert here a short notice on the fate of the Diana and its shipwrecked crew. The Diana had left Kronstadt in 1853, and on the 23rd July, 1854, arrived at Castries Bay, whence she proceeded to Osaki in Japan, where Admiral Putiatin concluded a treaty on the 26th January, 1855. This treaty in its main provisions agrees with that concluded by the Americans. Urup is ceded in it to Russia, and with regard to Sakhalin the *status quo* is to be maintained, i.e., the northern part of the island which formerly acknowledged Chinese sovereignty, will remain with Russia, the southern part with Japan. During the earthquake which occurred on the 24th December, 1854, the Diana suffered much injury. With the aid of numerous Japanese boats it was tried to tow the ship to a sheltered bay round Cape Idzu, but a white cloud descended upon the summit of the Fusiyama, a sign of approaching storm, the Japanese left the frigate to her fate, and soon after she sunk. The crew had saved themselves and landed in Heda Bay. Negotiations with a splendid American clipper, the "Young America," to take them to Petropavlovsk failed on account of the desertion of the Yankee crew. A month later, in April, a small American schooner, the Caroline Foote, agreed to take the Russians in three trips to Petropavlovsk. But having conveyed there four or five officers and one hundred and fifty men, a second voyage was thought too venturesome, and the William Penn conveyed this party from Petropavlovsk to Castries Bay. Admiral Putiatin himself had not been idle, and with the assistance of the Japanese built a schooner, the "Heda," with which he, with eight officers, including Lieutenant Peshchurof, and forty men, departed in May for Petropavlovsk, and finding that place abandoned he went to the Amur, which he entered from the south, and continued his journey to Russia by ascending that river.[1]

The remainder of the Russians left Heda Bay in July, but the Bremen brig "Greta," which had agreed to take them to Ayan, was captured when nearly at the port of destination.[m]]

At Cape Grillon, the squadron was joined by the French Sybille, fifty, and Constantine, thirty, which had left Nangasaki on the 31st May. The Colbert, six, steamer, ran on a rock on leaving the bay, and scurvy breaking out on board the Sybille one hundred men had to be landed in Aniwa Bay, and subsequently the ship was sent to the south.[n] We might suppose the squadron would now sail up the Gulf of Tatary, in pursuit of the Russians who were known to have gone there. But no. The unlucky Bittern arrives with some despatches from the home authorities, who could

[1] The Heda was returned to the Japanese in 1856, the Russians otherwise would have been liable for £4,000.

[m] Whilst the Russians were at Heda Bay the commander of the Powhatan, U.S., gave them information about the French whaler Napoleon, cruising off the port, and it was resolved to despatch two boats to capture her. The American, however, feeling qualms of conscience at betraying the Frenchman, gave him information about the intentions of the Russians, and when their boats came to the spot on the following morning, the whaler had disappeared. The same whaler had been met in 1854 by one of Admiral Putiatin's officers, and not made a prize on pleading ignorance of a declaration of war.

[n] The French were very unfortunate with their ships. The Jean d'Arc had run aground in August, 1854, on leaving the Yang-tse-kiang, and it was necessary to send her to Europe for repairs, and out of four fine ships, the Constantine alone remained in a serviceable condition.

not possibly know anything about the state of affairs, and the ships were ordered to the Sea of Okhotsk! On the 10th of July the squadron commanded by Admiral Sir James Stirling left Aniwa Bay for the north. There were the following vessels:—

  Winchester, sailing frigate, 50. Flag-ship.
  Constantine  ,,  50.
  Sybille   ,,  40.
  Spartan   ,,  24.
  Hornet, steam corv. 17.
On the 17th they fell in with the
  Pique, sailing frigate, 40.
  Amphitrite, corvette, 25.
  Barracouta, steamer, 6.

A total of eight vessels with two hundred and fifty-two guns in the Sea of Okhotsk, whilst there was not a single vessel left to guard the Channel of Tatary! On the 22nd the squadron anchored off Baikal Bay. Russian houses could be discerned at the fringe of the forest.° On approaching the northern entrance to the Amur, a Russian brig, the Okhotsk, eight, could be seen in the Liman slowly making her way towards the mouth of the river. The Hornet tried in vain for two days to find a passage, and at last two boats of the Sybille, two of the Barracouta, and one of the Spartan were lowered and towed to within four miles of the brig. They were commanded by Sir Robert Gibson. The Russians had run aground near Cape Golovachef, and when they perceived the enemy they set fire to the brig, and took to their boats. Owing to the strong current it required three hours' hard rowing to come up to the brig, and half a mile before reaching her she blew up, and only a small iron gun, a bell, a few books and papers, and her pendant were saved. One of the boats was left near the burning brig, the others

° This is an error, for no Russian settlement has ever existed there as Lieut. Peshchurof tells me.

went after the Russians, and after twelve hours' exciting chase, the boats being dragged frequently over sand-spits, the cutter of the Sybille overtook one of the Russian boats. The crew of the Spartan, whose boat had stuck fast, ran along the sand and overtook another. The third escaped. At ten p.m. the captors returned with fourteen prisoners, most of them Finlanders. This is *the* great achievement of the naval campaign in the Pacific!

On the 2nd August the squadron put in at Ayan. A search after the guns of the batteries, which were supposed to have been buried, proved unsuccessful, but stores of china and walrus-teeth were dug up. The officers of the squadron were met by Mr. Freiburg, the superintendent of the Russo-American Company, who placed at their disposal his billiard-tables, "from which the English officers carried off balls and cues."[p] The governor had gone inland, but a visit was paid to the Archbishop of Eastern Siberia then staying at Ayan. The Barracouta left on a cruize on the 29th July, and returned on the third of August, having in tow the Bremen brig Greta, which had been captured on the first in 52° north lat. and 145° east long. On board of her were Lieut. Pushkin and two hundred and seventy-six officers and men of the shipwrecked Diana. Lieut. Pushkin and Baron Schelling vainly protested against making shipwrecked mariners prisoners of war. Only a priest, the surgeon and the sick were landed, the others, including Gosh'kevich, interpreter of Count Putiatin and for ten years a member of the Russian mission at Peking, were retained, and distributed on the Barracouta (three officers and one hundred and six men), Sybille (seven officers, one hundred men), and Spartan (two officers and forty men). Lieut. Gibson with a prize crew was placed on board the Greta, and sent to

[p] Habersham, p. 455. Such a statement, coming from an American, requires confirmation. The Russian officers with whom I have spoken know nothing of this pilfering breach of hospitality.

Hong-kong. The Hornet and Constantine went to cruize near the Shantar islands. On the 16th August the Encounter arrived with some bullocks for the French, and the squadron then sailed again to the south. Had they remained a short time longer, and kept near the mouth of the Amur instead of staying at an out-of-the-way place like Ayan they might have made some more captures. Habersham of the U.S. store ship Kennedy met on the 11th September a Russian "gunboat" (the steamer Vostok) at Petrovsk, and further on the Francisco bark "Palmetto," which had been chartered by the Russian consul there, was trying in vain to make her way into the Amur. The boats of the Aurora had fruitlessly endeavoured for six weeks to get the Palmetto into the river, and the Russians offered to pilot the Kennedy through the Liman into the Channel of Tatary, if she would assist in getting the Palmetto off the sandbank upon which she had run. This however was prudently declined, as the Kennedy drew one foot more than the Palmetto.

One other event remains to be recorded, viz. the capture of Urup, one of the Kurile islands where the Russians had made a permanent settlement in 1852. On the 3rd of September the French Sybille, fifty, and the Pique, forty, appeared off the settlement, opened fire, and landed some troops who burnt the store-houses of the Russo-American Company. On the third day they departed, taking with them a cutter laden with furs, and the store-keeper with his clerk a Yakute. A board was put up with an inscription stating that the island had been taken possession of by the allied powers conjointly and would in future be called "Alliance." Inquiries subsequently made in London and Paris with regard to the prisoners proved futile, as it was denied that any had been taken.[q]

The Sibylle and Pique, after this achievement, proceeded to

[q] Annual report of the Russo-American Company, 1856-7. The French moreover are stated to have outraged some native women.

Japan, where at the end of September there was assembled a squadron of eleven vessels with about three hundred and fifty guns. It had been proposed to send the Spartan, Constantine, and some other vessels, up the Channel of Tatary, with orders to penetrate into the Amur, but superior wisdom retained the ships at Japan, and a small squadron only commanded by Commodore Elliot was sent up the Channel. He left Nangasaki on the 2nd October with the Sybille forty, Encounter fourteen and Hornet seventeen. On the 15th the Sybille anchored in Castries Bay, where the American bark Behring was discharging a cargo for the Russians. The boats were sent ashore for water, but when within two hundred yards of land were fired upon, and Lieutenant Chisholm and four men were wounded. The ships opened fire, but without effect, the enemy being hidden in the brushwood and shrubs. On the 16th the boats were once more sent to examine the creeks of the Bay, and on their return were again fired upon, and replied unsuccessfully. It was ascertained from the Captain of the Behring that the Russians had collected a large military force on the Lower Amur. The Hornet was sent to cruize in the north, and on the 23rd had penetrated to 52° 19′ north latitude, thus proving the existence of the channel leading into the Amur. But as she ran aground on a sandbank it was necessary to lighten her of her guns and ballast before she could be got off. The "discovery" of this passage, however valuable it might have been if made in 1854 or earlier in 1855, was now of no avail, the season being too far advanced to take advantage of it. The Sybille, Hornet and Encounter having met on the 29th returned to Japan, and thus ends the naval campaign of 1855.

## 1856-7.

The presence of the Allied squadrons in the Pacific indirectly exercised a baneful influence upon the colonisation of the river Amur, as it had induced the Russians to concentrate the whole of their forces on the lower part of the river. This cause still operated in 1856, for it was June before the news of the conclusion of peace arrived. The operations of the Allied squadrons had been, however, exclusively of a peaceful character. The French Sibylle and Virginie, on the 9th June, called at Castries Bay, where they found an American brig at anchor, and communicated with the Russian officer under a flag of truce. On the 1st of July, when the greater part of the Allied forces were lying in Barracouta Bay (Port Imperial), official confirmation of the conclusion of peace arrived there, and the bay resounded with the ships' artillery in celebration of the event. The Pique, soon after, sailed for Castries Bay to land a few prisoners of war who had remained in the squadron. Thus ends the war in the Pacific, and the Russians were left unfettered to carry on their design of occupying the Amur. Their settlements, up to 1856, were confined to the Lower Amur and Castries Bay. Here they had the towns of Nikolayevsk and Mariinsk, three agricultural colonies between the two, and a settlement at Castries Bay. The colonies on Sakhalin and in Barracouta Bay (Port Imperial) had been evacuated in consequence of the war. In addition to the small flotilla of sea-going vessels enumerated above, and then in safety at Nikolayevsk, they had on the Amur two river steamers, the Shilka and Argun, which had been built on the Shilka, and the Nadeshda, a small steamer of four-horse power and only twenty-eight feet long, brought in 1854 from England. Not a single establishment had yet been founded on the Amur from its origin at Ust Strelka down to Mariinsk, excepting a temporary settlement eighteen miles above Albazin called Kamenskoi, where the steamer Shilka had grounded in 1855 on a voyage down the river. General Muravief was at St. Petersburg to advocate the granting of large means for colonizing the Amur, and during his absence the direction of affairs was left to Major-General Korsakof, the governor of Transbaikal. In the course of the year, six hundred and ninety-seven barges and rafts descended the river, of which one only ran aground and had to be abandoned. These barges conveyed the provisions required by the military forces on the Lower Amur, including 1,500 head of cattle, which were landed every night on the banks of the river. Cossack stations were established near the mouth of the Komar (Komarsk), at the mouth of the Dzeya (Ust Zeisk, now Blagoveshchensk), at the upper entrance of the defile of the Bureya mountains (Khingansk, now Pashkof), and opposite the mouth of the Sungari (Sungarskoi Piket). On the Lower Amur another colony, Novo Mikhailovsk, was established, and at the end of the year consisted of four block-houses. The America, a steamer ordered by the Russian government in America, drawing nine feet, and thus able to enter the Amur, arrived in July. One American merchantman had discharged her cargo in Castries Bay, and in October the clipper Europe arrived off the mouth of the Amur with two small steamers and some machinery on board. It was necessary to lighten her of part of her cargo, before the America could tow her up to Nikolayevsk. The vessel had scarcely cast anchor opposite the town, when the river froze over on the 28th October. Two workshops having been erected on shore, the steamers were conveyed there to be put together during the winter. Arrangements were also made for a more regular postal communication between Nikolayevsk and Mariinsk, which until then had been carried on by dog-sledges. Post stations were built and kept by Cossacks, peasants or discharged sailors. The Russian colonists agreed to supply the necessary horses during the winter months at the rate of twenty-two pounds a pair. During summer, they were to supply the steamers plying on the river with the requisite fuel. This new post-route was inaugurated on the 18th November, when Admiral

Kazakevich, with his staff, travelled from Nikolayevsk to Mariinsk in three troikas to inspect the garrison there. The novel spectacle attracted large crowds of wondering natives.

## 1857-8.

The year 1857 will ever be one of the most memorable in the history of the Amur. Muravief had succeeded at St. Petersburg to secure large means in money and men to carry out the occupation of the river. On the 1st of June a battalion of infantry, six hundred strong, and commanded by Colonel Ushakof, embarked at Shilkinsk for the Amur. Muravief himself started soon after with another body of troops, and altogether one brigade of Cossack infantry and one regiment of cavalry[r] descended the Amur in that year, and formed numerous stations along its left bank. The Amur also served for the first time to convey colonists and provisions to the possessions of the Russo-American Company.

Captain Furruhelm appointed since, in 1859, chief director of the Company, conducted down the river one hundred emigrants and 1,000 tons of provisions. In his company travelled Collins, "Commercial Agent of the United States for the Amur river." Count Putiatin with whom was the orientalist Avvakum, and who was joined at Mariinsk by Captain Chikachef, also availed himself of the newly-opened communication to proceed on a mission to Japan and China. He descended the river in a barge and arrived at Nikolayevsk twenty-five days after his departure from Usk Strelka. On the 13th July he embarked here on board the America, being escorted out of the river by Admiral Kazakevich on the Amur, the shore batteries saluting, and the five American merchantmen hoisting their flags. The passage leading into the Channel of Tatary had been marked out by stakes; Cape Lazaref was reached in twelve hours, and on the 14th,

[r] Two thousand four hundred infantry (four battalions; six hundred cavalry), the total Cossack force at the time in Transbaikal being twelve battalions infantry, and six regiments cavalry.

before sunrise, the America entered Castries Bay. She then crossed over to Cape Dui in Sakhalin, to take in a supply of coal. On his voyage down channel the Admiral entered Olga Bay (Port Sir Michael Seymour), discovered Port Vladimir, and on the 1st August arrived at Port Hamilton, where he obtained the permission of the Koreans to establish a coaling depôt, they consenting to assist in loading and unloading colliers.[s] Continuing his voyage the Admiral came to the Gulf of Pecheli on the 5th August, and after long delays and tedious discussions a Chinese functionary consented on the 16th to receive the letters addressed to Peking, and this only on condition of the answer being sent to Kiakhta. The Admiral however was inexorable, and at last, on the 24th of August succeeded in gaining their acquiescence to send an answer to the Gulf of Pecheli, where it arrived on the 17th of September. It had been Putiatin's endeavour to induce the Chinese to come to some definite arrangement regarding the frontiers on the Amur, but he was not successful. In Allen's Mail (15th December, 1857), we find however a statement from Chinese sources, that Russia had demanded the cession of the provinces of Girin, Helung-kiang (Amur), and another province (Leaotong), promising in return to assist the emperor in putting down the rebellion, by furnishing troops and ammunition. In this statement there is of course a grain of truth; for naturally Russia would be anxious to obtain a legal right to the territories occupied by her on the Amur in defiance of Chinese protests. It was not however likely she would have demanded at once the whole of Manchuria, and with regard to her proffered assistance we may reasonably be allowed to doubt.[t]

The fruitless results of Putiatin's mission were felt on the

[s] As yet the Russians have not availed themselves of this arrangement.

[t] Putiatin on the 24th October concluded a supplemental treaty with the Japanese at Nangasaki.

Amur; for the mandarins, satisfied hitherto with counting the number of barges, men and guns that passed their stations, now again protested against the occupation of the territories by the Russians, and in some instances even molested Russian traders. Muravief hastened to St. Petersburg, where he arrived in November, and explained the state of affairs, expressing a fear of a hostile collision with the Chinese, and asking for reinforcements. General Korsakof, the governor of Trans-Baikal, then at St. Petersburg, supported the views of General Muravief, and the government consented. Admiral Putiatin was ordered to co-operate with the English and French in China, and large bodies of troops were moved towards Amur. The territories of the Amur had previously, by Ukase of 31st October, been separated from the government of Irkutsk, and together with Kamchatka and the whole of the coast of the sea of Okhotsk were created the "Maritime province of Eastern Siberia," with Nikolayevsk as capital. This province, of course, continued to be dependent upon Muravief, as Governor-General of Eastern Siberia. A squadron of seven screw-steamers had been dispatched from Kroustadt in the summer, commanded by Admiral Kuznetzof. They were the Askold frigate, forty-eight, the screw corvettes Plastun Voyevod and Boyarin, of fourteen guns each, and the screw "clippers" (gunboats) Jigit and Strelok, of two guns each. On the Amur itself the two river steamers brought by the Europe were launched, and called "Lena" and "Amur," and both ascended the river with troops returning to Siberia and some merchandise.

Commercial operations were carried on however on the most restricted scale, consisting merely in supplying the troops stationed along the river with provisions. The imports from foreign countries amounted to about £75,000. Of exports there were as yet scarcely any. But more of this in our chapter on commerce.

## 1858.

The operations of the English and French in China were not without their influence upon the state of affairs on the Amur. When, therefore, Muravief arrived in May, he had no occasion to appeal to a decision by arms, but found the Chinese authorities perfectly willing to conclude a treaty of amity. This treaty was concluded at Aigun on the Amur, on the 28th of May. China therein ceded to Russia the left bank of the Amur down to the Usuri, and both banks below the Usuri. The Sungari and Usuri, moreover, were to be open to Russian merchants and travellers, on being provided with proper passports from their government. Veniukof, who in that year ascended the Usuri, was the first to avail himself of this permission, and, though not received in the most cordial manner by the Chinese authorities stationed on that river, no serious obstacles were placed in his way. Just a fortnight after the conclusion of the treaty of Aigun, Putiatin signed the treaty of Tientsin, 13th June 1858, ratified at St. Petersburg on the 10th September, and the ratifications were exchanged at Peking by the Russian envoy General Ignatief and Prince Kung, on the 24th April 1859. Putiatin had been active in China for some time, and to him is to be ascribed the successful conclusion of the treaty of Aigun, the Chinese government considering it best to entrust the arrangement of the boundaries to the local authorities. He had, therefore, every reason to anticipate such a treaty, though not aware at the time of signing the treaty of Tientsin that the other had actually been concluded. The Chinese government during the preliminary negociations, had actually solicited the assistance of the Russians against the English, but were very wisely refused.

The conditions, of the treaty of Tientsin are similar to those contained in the treaties concluded by the other powers. Art. 1 declares that there shall be peace and amity between

the Russian and Chinese governments. Art. 2 recognises the equality of both governments and grants permission to Russia to maintain an embassy at Peking. Art. 3, 4 and 5 refer to commerce. Seven (or more) ports are opened to the Russians; the commerce by land is to be carried on as before; Consuls may reside at the ports. Art. 9 refers to the boundary:—" The undefined part of the frontiers be-
" tween China and Russia will without delay, be surveyed
" by delegates of the two empires, and the arrangement
" concluded between them relative to the frontier line will
" form an additional article to the present treaty. When
" the boundaries are defined, an exact description of them
" will be made, and maps annexed, of the frontier localities,
" which will in future serve for both parties as indisputable
" evidence in all concerns of the frontiers." Art. 10 concedes to Russia the right to renew at will the so-called clerical mission at Peking, and the members may proceed thither by land or sea; Russia, however, will in future bear all expenses connected with it. By Art. 11 arrangements are made for the establishment of a regular postal mail twice a month between Kiakhta and Peking; a heavy mail, for passengers and goods, to be dispatched every three months. The former is allowed fifteen days, the latter one month, to travel the distance. The expenses are to be borne by the two governments conjointly.[u] It will be perceived that Art. 9 of this treaty merely speaks of the " definition " of the frontiers, but tacitly acknowledges the arrangement made at Aigun, of which the Chinese were fully aware, the Emperor himself acknowledging it as binding in an autograph letter addressed to the Commissioner in communication with Count Putiatin. Subsequently, however, the Chinese disavowed the treaty of Aigun on pretence of some informality.

We now return to the Amur. Muravief on the 21st May had laid the foundation of the town of Blagovesh'chensk

[u] The treaty at full length is to be found in the London and China Telegraph, vol. i., p. 417.

(that is "good tidings") at the Cossack station Ust-Zeisk. He then descended the Amur, founded Khabarofka at the mouth of the Usuri, and on the right bank of the Amur, and selected the native village Jai, on the Lower Amur, as the site of a town. This town, called Sofyevsk, is destined to become the chief place of commerce on the Lower Amur, Mariinsk having proved to be unsuitable for that purpose, on account of its being situated on a branch of the river which is not navigable throughout the year. A railway or canal, preliminary surveys for which were made by M. Romanof, is proposed to connect Sofyevsk with Castries Bay, and at both places plots of ground were granted to the Russo-American Company and the merchants of Nikolayevsk. At present a rough road only connects the two places. If a canal were once dug, the dangerous navigation of the Liman would be obviated. It was intended at the same time, to build a dry dock, breakwater, and so forth, at Castries Bay, but up to 1860 none of these improvements had been carried out.

Muravief in the same summer re-ascended the Amur on the steamer Lena, which after running aground several times, and sustaining much damage, took him to Stretyinsk, destined to become the chief port for the Upper Amur. In October we find the indefatigable Governor-General of Eastern Siberia at Kiakhta, making arrangements for the postal service settled by the treaty of Tientsin. At a banquet given by the merchants there, Muravief received the thanks of the community for the services he had rendered to commercial enterprise by opening the territories of the Amur. His government had already rewarded his zeal by creating him Count of the Amur (Amursky) on the 26th August. Admiral Nevelskoi at the same time obtained the grand-cross of the order of St. Anne, and several merchants, citizens and peasants, were honoured with silver medals for the services they had rendered in opening the new country. An Ukase was published on the 31st December, by which the territories of the Amur received a new organization. "Now that Russia has regained possession of this valuable region," thus begins the Ukase, " it becomes the importance due to its future prosperity and social development, to provide for its administration in a well-regulated and durable manner." The newly acquired dominions are then divided into the " Maritime Province of Eastern Siberia," including the districts Nikolayevsk, Sofievsk, Petropavlovsk, Gishigin, Udsk and Petrovsk ; and into the " Amur province," including the territories along the Amur and above the mouth of the Usuri. Admiral Kazakevich remained military governor of the " maritime province," and Major General Busse was appointed military governor of the Amur. The residence of the former remained, for the time, Nikolayevsk ; the latter resides at Blagoveshchensk, the newly founded town at the mouth of the Dzeya. Both governors are subject to the Governor General and his Council of Administration. In the chief places a provincial court, advocate-general and head of the police are established, and a board for the regular troops and Cossacks superintend these branches of the public service. The number of civilian officials for the province of the Amur is fixed at nineteen, with a medical man, and their salaries amount in all to £3,932. The governor receives annually, regular pay £300, table money £300, travelling expenses £225, and £150 for incidental expenses and exercising hospitality towards the Manchu and others ; total £975.

Shortly after the promulgation of this Ukase, the Cossack forces on the Amur received a separate organization. We learn that up to the end of 1858, 20,000 souls of both sexes had been settled along the Amur, most of them being sent from the Transbaikal, others from the interior of Siberia. They are to furnish the following force :—

(a). In the Amur province, with its fine prairies and grazing country, the First and Second Regiment of Amur Cavalry, each nine officers, five hundred and seventy-five non-commissioned officers and men, and fourteen non-combatants. Total of both regiments, 1,196 men.

Two Battalions of Amur Infantry, each of five companies, including one of Rifles, and seven officers, 1,622 non-commissioned officers and men, and sixteen non-combatants. Total of both battalions, 3,290 men.

One of these battalions is reserve.

(*b*). In the Maritime province, two Battalions of Usuri Infantry as above, one of them reserve, 3,290 men.

At the beginning of 1859, the irregular forces amounted thus to 7,776 men. This, however, by no means represents the actual force of Russia on the Amur, for there were at least three Battalions of Line Infantry, each from six hundred to one thousand men strong; and these chiefly occupied the stations between Mariinsk and the Bureya mountains. At Nikolayevsk was stationed the twenty-seventh equipage of the navy, and the naval forces in the Pacific were still further increased by the Griden, fourteen, Rinda, ten, and other vessels despatched from Kronstadt. The screw transports, "Japanese" and "Manchu," ordered in America on account of the Russian government also arrived towards the close of the season.

Commercial enterprise on the Amur was promised a fresh impulse by the foundation of the Amur Company, incorporated by Imperial Charter on the 23rd January 1858, with a capital of £150,000, with power to increase it to £450,000. The object of this company is the development of commerce and industry in the basin of the Amur. It is privileged to open establishments on the Amur and Shilka, to appropriate for its use the coal and wood found in the country, and to trade with the Russians and natives. Government agreed to supply at cost price fifty puds of powder, and one hundred puds of lead from the Imperial stores at Nerchinsk. We must admit that the company lost not a moment in commencing operations. On the 8th of February 1859, the St. Innocentius left Antwerp with two iron screw-steamers[v] of sixty horse-power on board, destined to navigate the Amur; one iron barge, and two iron pack-houses; and soon after, on the 30th March, the Orus, Captain Prütz, left London, also with two steamers, and four iron pack-houses. Both vessels were unfortunately lost, one in Castries Bay, the other in the ice of the Liman. In February, the company proposed to government to lay a telegraphic wire from Moscow to the Amur; this offer was accepted, and the government guaranteed five per cent., and thus ensured the project being carried out. Contracts for laying the wire from Moscow to Kazan were entered into soon after; and Romanof's plan for carrying a wire, by way of the Kuriles and Kamchatka, through Behring's Strait, to North America,—a plan revived subsequently by the American, Collins, thus stands a fair chance of being successful. In a subsequent chapter, we shall see how far the "Company of the Amur" has fulfilled the anticipations entertained at the time of its foundation.

## 1859—60.

Several measures were taken in 1859 to favour colonization on the Amur. The authorities in Siberia are permitted to grant passports for three years to political exiles, in order that they may proceed to the Amur, and, if deserving, this term is extended to perpetuity. The sailors of the Twenty-seventh Equipage, stationed at the Lower Amur may retire after fifteen years' service, when they receive each a plot of freehold ground, £22 10s., and permission to send for their families who are conveyed at government expense. The colonists are maintained two years at the expense of government, after which time they may naturally be supposed to support themselves. The government also renounced its

[v] These steamers were from the famous works of John Cockerell and Co., at Seraing.

monopoly of the mineral treasures of the whole of Siberia; and in future any one, criminals excepted, may search for precious stones, gold, or work mines. Gold was discovered on the upper Dzeya. At the beginning of the year, a body of 10,000 colonists arrived at Irkutsk from Western Siberia and European Russia, on their way to the Amur. Count Muravief-Amursky exhibited his usual activity. By his orders Cossack stations were founded along the banks of the Usuri and its tributary the Sungacha, and a surveying corps was employed under the direction of Colonel Budogorsky to explore the regions of the Usuri with a view to the settlement of the frontier. Muravief himself descended the Amur on a tour of inspection, and in June embarked at Castries Bay, on board the America for China and Japan. At Castries Bay part at least of the projected improvements of the harbour had been commenced, and a lighthouse was in course of construction on Cape Closterkamp. Sailing along the coast of Manchuria, Muravief arrived at the Olga Bay where the Russians were engaged building a naval station, and where he was joined by Colonel Budogorsky, with whom he proceeded to Wei-chai-wey in the Gulf of Pecheli, whence the Colonel departed for Peking for the purpose of coming to some arrangement regarding the frontiers. Muravief then crossed over to Yedo in Japan where twelve Russian men-of-war, including the Askold frigate and five corvettes, all of them steamers, were lying at anchor. On the 1st October, he again arrived at Nikolayevsk, ascended the Amur as far as Khabarofka on the steamer Argun, and then continued the journey up the river on the Lena until the river became covered with ice, when the journey to Irkutsk and St. Petersburg was continued by land.

We had occasion above to remark upon the influence which the operations of the English and French in China exercised on the bearing of the Chinese towards the Russians. When threatened with war, China was willing to make all sorts of concessions; but now, when the Chinese had repelled the advance of the allied ambassadors at the mouth of the Peiho June 1859, she had gained such an opinion of the prowess of her army, that it was not considered necessary any longer to conciliate the Russians on the Amur. They were told again, that China had never ceded the Amur, that they had no right there, and must immediately quit it. The merchants trading on the river were exposed to all sorts of annoyances on the part of the Manchu officials; Maximowicz who, trusting to the provisions of the treaty of Aigun, desired to ascend the Sungari, was compelled to retire before he had reached Sansin, and a war would certainly have ensued had not the allies again done the work of the Russians, and humbled the Chinese government by occupying Peking.

The commerce on the Amur had however made considerable progress, and the Amur Company established new stores in several places. To the five steamers already navigating the river a sixth was added, which had been brought in the preceding year by Mr. Burling from America, and was launched in June 1859, and called the Admiral Kazakevich. The imports at Nikolayevsk and Castries Bay amounted to £152,188. This does not include the value of five steamers brought out for the Amur Company, and the cargo of the Tsarina, 1200 tons, consisting of government stores. The exports as yet were trifling, only amounting to £2,967. Another flotilla had left Kronstadt consisting of the screw corvettes Passadnik and Nayesdnik, and the gunboat Razboynik.

Count Muravief had gone at the end of 1859 to St. Petersburg, as mentioned before, and obtained leave of absence to visit his family then staying at Paris, and to recruit his health, which had suffered from the climate of Siberia. He desired indeed to resign his post as Governor-General of Eastern Siberia, but at the personal request of the emperor, consented to proceed once more to the Amur, where the critical state of affairs made the presence of a man of ability of the greatest consequence. The Chinese persevered in the hostile attitude assumed since the repulse at the Taku forts, and one officer at least, Lieut. Filimonof, was obliged in April to abandon his station on the Sungachan river, a tributary of the Usuri. Elsewhere also the Mandarins resorted to violence, but a letter in the Prussian Gazette, which speaks of "Russian forts blown up, whole villages of peaceful colonists destroyed and plundered, the inhabitants brutally ill-treated, and even in some instances killed, when venturing to offer resistance," is entirely devoid of truth. Certainly the Amur had not fulfilled the anticipations of those who thought to find at once the country there turned into the granary of Siberia, who in imagination saw the navies of the world congregate in Castries Bay to carry away its produce and manufactures. It is quite true also that the Amur was a constant source of expenditure. The colonists did not produce sufficient corn for their own consumption, and the deficiency had to be made up by imports from Siberia. The Cossacks indeed are not the best colonists, a fact of which the government is quite aware. They are not only extremely indolent, but also carry on their agricultural operations in the most primitive manner. To remedy this state of affairs, German colonists had been sent for. Capt. von Bries, proprietor of the steamer Admiral Kazakevich, is going to bring forty German families from California, and they are to be settled at the mouth of the Bureya. One hundred German families, Mennonites from Taurida [*] left

[*] Forty-seven colonies of German Mennonites are situated on the Molocha, in the Steppes of Southern Russia. They were founded between the years 1804 and 1839, and in 1851 had a population of 16,257 souls. The colonists owned in that year 9708 horses, 11,381 head of cattle and 58,595 Spanish sheep. They are noted for the rational manner in which they carry on agriculture. In 1851, they produced 51,700 quarters of wheat, 40,000 qrs. of barley, 19,000 qrs. of rye, 23,000 qrs. of oats, 16,000 qrs. of potatoes, 750 qrs. of cocons 8000 lbs. of silk, and 1500 lbs. of tobacco. They had planted 2,843,289

their homes in 1860. But as they travel with their own waggons and cattle, they could not possibly arrive before 1861. If at the beginning of the year, the aspect of affairs on the Amur was very gloomy, with a Chinese war in prospective, the relative positions of the two governments were reversed by the success of the English and French, of whose victories Russia availed herself to conclude on the 14th November 1860 a most advantageous treaty, much more comprehensive than any treaty ever concluded by China with a foreign power. This treaty was ratified at St. Petersburg on the 1st January 1861 by the emperor. It is signed by Nicolas Ignatief, Russian ambassador at Peking,[x] and Prince Kung, the Chinese Commissioner. The following is an abstract of this treaty :[y]—

Art. 1. "Henceforth the eastern frontier between the two empires shall commence from the juncture of the rivers Shilka and Argun, will follow the course of the River Amur to the junction of the River Usuri with the latter. The land on the left bank (to the north) of the River Amur belongs to the empire of Russia, and the territory on the right bank (to the south) to the junction of the River Usuri to the empire of China. Further on, the frontier line between the two empires ascends the rivers Usuri and Sungacha to where the latter issues from lake Kinka; it then crosses the lake, and takes the direction of the river Belen-ho or Tur; from the mouth of that river it follows the mountain range to the mouth of the River Huptu (a tributary of the Suifun), and from that point the mountains situated between the

---

mulberry trees, 637,269 fruit trees, 1,384,765 timber trees, and 981 vines. The schools were visited by 3288 pupils, or by one out of five of the population. The arrival of such thrifty colonists cannot fail to be advantageous.

[x] Ignatief left St. Petersburg in March 1859.
[y] See Times, 17th January 1861.

river Hun-Chun and the sea, as far as the river Tumen-Kiang. Along this line the territory on the east side belongs to the empire of Russia, and that on the west to the empire of China. The frontier line rests on the river Tumen at twenty *li* above its mouth into the sea.

Art. 2. Defines the frontiers between Russia and China towards the west, and confirms Russia in the possession of the country around lakes Balkash and Issik Kul.

Art. 3. Arranges the appointment of a joint commission for placing the frontier marks. For the inspection of the eastern frontiers the commissioners will meet at the mouth of the Usuri in the month of April, 1861.

Art. 4. On the whole frontier line established by Articles 1 and 2 of the present treaty, trade free of all duty or restrictions is established between the subjects of the two states.

Art. 5. Restores to the merchants of Kiakhta the right of going to Peking, and they may also trade at Urga and Kalgan. At Urga a Russian Consulate may be established. Russian merchants, provided with passports, may travel throughout China, but must not congregate in a greater number than two hundred in the same locality.

Art. 6. Grants to the Russians a site for a factory, with church, etc., at Kashgar. The Chinese government is not however responsible for any pillage of travellers by tribes beyond its control.

Art. 7. At the places thrown open, no restrictions whatever are to be imposed upon commercial transactions, which may be carried on on credit or otherwise as best suits the interests of the parties concerned.

Art. 8. Russia may establish consuls at Kashgar and Urga to watch over the conduct of the merchants, who are to be punished by the laws of the country to which they belong. The Chinese also may send consuls to Russian towns. Commercial disputes are to be settled by arbitrators chosen by the parties concerned. Criminals seeking refuge in either country are to be given up, to be judged by the government to which they are subject.

Art. 9. Annuls the treaties concluded at Nerchinsk 1689, and at Kiakhta 1727.

Art. 10. Refers to the restoration of cattle which may have strayed across the frontiers.

Art. 11. Regulates the transmission of written despatches on a reciprocal amicable footing between the authorities of the respective empires.

Art. 12. Settles the postal arrangements between the two empires. Letters are to leave Peking and Kiakhta once a month; parcels Kiakhta every two months, Peking once in three months. Twenty days are allowed for the transmission of letters, forty days at the utmost for parcels.

Art. 13. Determines that the ordinary correspondence between the two governments is to be sent through post, but that during the residence of a Russian envoy at Peking despatches of special importance may be forwarded by couriers.

Art. 14. Empowers the Governor-General of Eastern Siberia to conclude any additional arrangements with the frontier authorities of a nature to facilitate intercourse.

Art. 15. States that after the exchange of ratifications the treaty will be in full force."

The importance of this treaty can scarcely be over-rated. Russia has now acquired a legal right not only to the country north of the Amur and east of the Usuri, but also to the entire coast of Manchuria down to the frontiers of Korea. The value of this coast with its magnificent bays and harbours is great, quite independently of the Amur, and is fully appreciated by the Russians, who have re-christened Victoria Bay as the Bay of Peter the Great, and one of its ports they call Vladivostok, "Dominion of the East." On the Amur and Usuri however the boundary line does not bear the stamp of permanency. Russia holding one bank only of these rivers, whilst China holds the other, may at any chosen time furnish a government desirous of encroaching upon its neighbour with fertile causes of dispute, and when the time comes when the huge Chinese empire tumbles to pieces, the whole of Manchuria, with Leaotong must become the prey of Russia.

## THE REGIONS OF THE AMUR IN 1861.

Having traced the history of the Amur down to the present time, we will conclude this part of our volume by giving a condensed account of the present condition of Russian power on the Amur.

By Ukase of 31st December 1858, the territories of the Amur are divided into a Province of the Amur, and "Maritime Province of Eastern Siberia."

The area of the former is about 164,000 square miles. The maritime province comprises the following:—

|  | Square Miles. |
|---|---|
| The districts Nikolayevsk and Sofievsk | 179,000 |
| The Northern portion of Sakhalin Island | 18,000 |
| The districts Gishiga (Okhotsk) and Udsk | 78,714 |
| Kamchatka (Petropavlovsk) | 465,208 |
| The Kurile Islands | 3,843 |

The country as yet is very thinly inhabited. In 1851, a census was taken of the population of the Russian empire, and the result, as far as Eastern Siberia is concerned, was as follows:—

|  | Inhabitants. |
|---|---|
| The Government of Irkutsk | 294,514 |
| The Government of Yakutsk (exclusive of Okhotsk) | 199,318 |
| Trans-baikal | 327,908 |
| The District of Okhotsk | 4,712 |
| Kamchatka and Gishiga | 7,331 |
| The Kuriles | 212 |
| Total | 833,995 |

Allowing for the natural increase of the population, and compulsory immigration from European Russia, we obtain about 917,395 inhabitants as the present population of Eastern Siberia, and this would also include the Russian population of the Amur, which has hitherto been drawn almost exclusively from the governments of Trans-baikal and Irkutsk. We are not in a position to state the exact number settled on the Amur at the present time, but believe 40,000 to be near the mark. If we add to these about 24,000 natives, we have a population of 64,000 inhabitants, spread over an area of 361,000 square miles!

MILITARY FORCES. — The Russians have established military posts along the whole course of the Amur, on the Usuri, and at various harbours of the Channel on Tartary, down to Victoria Bay. The forces in the territory in 1859 were as follows :—

| | |
|---|---|
| 5 Battalions of regular Infantry[z] (Nos. 5, 13, 14, 15, 16) | 5,000 men. |
| 2 Regiments of Cossack Cavalry . . . . | 1,196 „ |
| 2 Battalions of Cossack Infantry of the Amur . | 3,290 „ |
| 2     „          „          „          Usuri  . | 3,290 „ |
| 1 Battery of Field Artillery, 12 guns, 60 horses . | 200 „ |
| The 27th *Equipage* of the Navy . . . . | 1,500 „ |
| Total . . . . . | 14,476 men. |

The 13th battalion of Infantry and the battery are stationed at Blagovesh'chensk. The 5th battalion has its head-quarters at Khabarovka, and occupies stations on the Usuri and Kingka Lake. The 14th and 15th battalions occupy forty-eight stations between Pashkof in the Bureya Mountains and Mariinsk, being about forty-two men to a station. The 16th battalion was sent in 1859 to garrison the bays along the sea-coast. Olga Bay for the present is the chief naval station on the coast of Manchuria, but may possibly be eclipsed by Port Vladivostok in Victoria Bay, or the new settlement of Novgorod in Posiet Harbour.

The two cavalry regiments occupy twenty-three stations from Ust Strelka to Pashkof in the Bureya Mountains, being

---

[z] The 5th Battalion stood formerly in Western Siberia

on an average fifty-two men to the station. The four battalions of Cossack Infantry, two of which are reserves, are stationed on the Amur, chiefly about the mouth of the Dzeya, and on the Usuri. There were twenty-four stations along the Usuri and Sungachan at the commencement of 1860, and the settlements now extend probably to Victoria Bay, fresh colonists having arrived.

The villages of colonists between Mariinsk and Nikolayevsk are without garrisons, and at Nikolayevsk, in addition to a detachment of Cossacks who do service as police, is stationed the 27th equipage of the navy.

On Sakhalin, Russians only occupy the village of Dui, near which coals are found, and the post Kusunai. A settlement, Muravief, which they had in Aniva Bay has been evacuated, and all endeavours to induce the Japanese to cede the southern Sakhalin have proved abortive.

The entire military force maintained in 1859 on the Amur exceeded thus scarcely 15,000 men. Since then, however, fresh forces have arrived, but we are not in a position to state their exact numbers. The report of the Minister of War speaks of 18,000 men sent during 1858—60 to the Amur, many for dereliction of duty, and accompanied by about 3,000 women and as many children. On the other hand many of the men annually return to Siberia and Russia on the expiration of their term of service, though great inducements are held out to them to become settlers. Under any circumstances, the available military forces would not exceed 20,000 men; their women and children 8,000; and the number of civilians, including their families 10,000; giving a total of 38,000 to 40,000. The chief centres of population are Blagovesh'chensk with 1306, and Nikolayevsk with 4,000[a] inhabitants in 1860.

With the exception of Nikolayevsk, Mariinsk, and the

[a] In 1858, the population was 2,552. The increase is due chiefly to the arrival, in 1859, of 1,000 convicts. (See p. 199.)

naval forts, the Russian settlements are mere collections of wooden houses, without any artificial defences whatever. Nikolayevsk is the only place possessing formidable means of defence. Fort Constantine has been built upon a sandbank in the middle of the river, and its guns—four 24-pounders, eight 18-pounders, and twelve 100-pound mortars—command both town and roadstead. The harbour battery is called Fort Nikolas, and its armament consists of twelve 36-pounders and two 72-pounder mortars. Four miles below the town, upon the right bank of the river stands the Michael Battery—twenty-one 24-pounders, and two 36-pounders—and eight miles lower down, but on the left bank, at Cape Chnyrrakh, a narrow tongue of land, stood the Alexander Nevsky Battery—fifteen 24-pounders, and two 36-pounder mortars. This battery has lately been removed, and 1,000 convicts in foot irons, who arrived in 1859 from Nerchinsk, are engaged building upon its site a strong stone fort, expected to be completed in 1862.

The battery at Mariinsk was dismantled in 1857, and only a dozen Cossacks guard the port; but several of the ports to the south are defended by batteries. The southernmost settlement is Novgorod, at Possiet Harbour, Gulf of d'Anville.

NAVAL FORCES.—Simultaneously with strengthening her forces on the Amur, Russia reinforced her navy in the Pacific. In 1860, the fleet in the Pacific included nineteen steamers, of 5,150 horse-power, carrying three hundred and eighty guns, and mounted by two hundred and forty-seven officers, and 4,365 sailors and marines, including the 27th Equipage at Nikolayevsk. There were two frigates—the Oleg and Svetlano—five corvettes, viz., Boyarin, Griden, Voyevod, Passadnik, and Kalevala; five screw clippers, viz., Jigit, Oprichnik, Strelok, Nayesdink, and Razboynik; the despatch boat Abriekh; and six smaller steamers. The Griden, Rinda, and Oprichnik returned to Europe in 1860, and the Boyarin, Voyevod and Jigit in 1861. The vessels at the present time in the Pacific, exclusive of the smaller steamers navigating the Amur, are as follows:—

| | | | | |
|---|---|---|---|---|
| 2 Frigates | Oleg | 57 guns | went out in | 1860 |
| | Svetlano* | 48 „ | „ „ | 1860 |
| 2 Screw Corvettes | Passadnik | 14 „ | „ „ | 1859 |
| | Kalevala | 14 „ | „ „ | 1860 |
| 2 Despatch Boats (screws) | Haidemack | 7 „ | „ „ | 1861 |
| | Abriekh | 5 „ | „ „ | 1860 |
| 3 Screw Clippers | Strelok | 3 „ | „ „ | 1857 |
| | Nayesdink | 3 „ | „ „ | 1859 |
| | Razboynik | 3 „ | „ „ | 1859 |
| 1 Gun-boat | Morsh | 2 „ | went out in | 1859 |
| 1 Paddle Steamer | America | 6 „ | from America in | 1856 |
| 1 Steam Schooner | Vostok | 4 „ | went out in | 1853 |
| 2 Strew Transports | Japanese | | from America in | 1858 |
| | Manchu | | „ „ | 1858 |
| 2 Sailing Transports | Baikal | 6 „ | since 1849 or earlier | |
| | Irtisk | 6 „ | previous to | 1854 |
| 1 Cutter | Kamchadal | | „ „ | 1854 |
| 1 Schooner (Sailing) | Liman | | built at Nikolayevsk, | 1857 |

Total, 18 vessels, with 178 guns.

To these may be added the vessels of the Russo-American Company—thirteen in 1858—which are also lightly armed. This force, though large compared with what Russia had in the Pacific previous to the treaty of Paris, need not inspire any apprehension.

The number of river steamers navigating the Amur is twelve, of which nine belong to Government. The imports by sea represent a value of about £53,000, and one-third of this is sent up the Amur. The exports are trifling.

TELEGRAPHS.—The Government authorised, in 1861, the construction of a telegraphic line from Nikolayevsk up the Amur to Khabarovka, thence up the Usuri as far as Novgorod, the southernmost point of the Russian territories on the Sea of Japan. The line from Kazan to Omsk will be opened this year, that from Omsk to Irkutsk in 1862, and the intermediate lines, thence to Kiakhta and Khabarovka, will be undertaken in 1863. The minister of marine will provide the necessary funds.

* Reported to have foundered on the coast of Japan.

# PART II.
# GEOGRAPHICAL, STATISTICAL, AND COMMERCIAL.

# PART II.—GEOGRAPHICAL, STATISTICAL AND COMMERCIAL.

## XII.
### GEOGRAPHICAL DESCRIPTION OF THE RIVER AMUR.

THE Amur, one of the largest rivers of Asia, drains with its tributaries a basin of 766,000 square miles. This basin is bounded on the south by the Shan-alin mountains and a line passing through Korchin and the Gobi desert. Towards the west and north the Yablonoi and Stanovoi ranges separate it from the rivers flowing to the Arctic Ocean and the sea of Okhotsk, and in the east the coast-range from the rivulets entering the Channel of Tatary or Manchuria.

Russian geographers look upon the sources of the Kerlon as the head-waters of the Amur, the Chinese however make it take its rise in the Shan-alin or White Mountains, sacred to the present Manchu dynasty as the cradle of their race. According to the former the Amur is formed by the junction of the Kerlon, called Argun in its lower course, with the Shilka, the Shilka itself being formed by the junction of the Ingoda and Onon. According to the Chinese the Sung Khua Kiang, or Pine-Blossom River, which they consider the head of the Amur, rises from six springs on the north-west slope of the Shan-alin. The Manchu call this river

Sungari, *i. e.* Milk-street River. After a course of three hundred miles the Sungari receives the Nonni from the north, and assumes the name of Kuentong, which with the Chinese it retains until it enters the sea. From the left, this Kuentong receives the Helong Kiang, river of the Black Dragon, called Sakhalin Ula, Black Water, by the Manchu, and Shilka (Silkar) by the Tunguzian Oronchons and Manyargs. This Sakhalin Ula, according the Russian view is in fact the Upper Amur. The Lower Amur, or rather the Amur below the mouth of the Sungari, is called Mango by the Goldi, and Mamu by the natives near its mouth. The Russian "Amur" is believed to be a corruption of the latter.[a]

If we consider that source of a river situated at the greatest distance from its mouth entitled to the honour of being looked upon as the fountain-head of the whole system, then must the Kerlon in the present instance be adopted as such. The development of the Kerlon (and Argun) to its junction with the Shilka is 1000 miles, exclusive of all minor windings, which in the present state of our geographical knowledge of these regions it would be impossible correctly to estimate. The Amur thence to the sea has a development of 1400 miles.[b] On the other hand, from the source of the Sungari to the mouth of the Amur the development of the river is only 1450 miles. It has not yet however been ascertained whether the Sungari or Sakhalin Ula carries the greater quantity of water. Schrenck is in favour of the former, and if we add the fact that the Amur below its junction with the Sungari maintains the north-easterly

[a] According to General d'Auvrey (Stuckenberg, iv. 782) the Amur has derived its name from an usual form of salutation used by the Tunguzians, and meaning "Peace be with you." The Mongols call the Amur Kara-turan, Black River.

[b] Including minor windings, the development of the Amur is estimated at 1890 miles.

direction of the latter to its mouth, we must acknowledge that after all the Chinese may have good cause for maintaining their side of the question.

It is by no means our intention to enter into a detailed description of the head-waters of the Amur. Our purpose will be sufficiently answered by offering a few remarks regarding them.

The Kerlon, Onon and Ingoda, all rise in the Kentei Khan, or Great Khingan, of the Chinese, the culminating point of which on Russian territory, the Chokondo, attains an elevation of 8,259 feet, without however reaching the limit of perennial snow. From this central mass of mountains the Yablonoi Khrebet or Range, branches off towards the north-east; and other branches occupy the country between the Ingoda and the Onon, and the Onon and Argun, forming what are generally known as the Nerchinsk Ore Mountains. In its south-western portion this mountain region is intersected by deep ravines and swampy tracts, and covered with dense, often impenetrable, forests. Further to the north it partakes much of the character of the steppes of central Asia. The country is undulating, and the ridges of the Ore Mountains rise but from two to five hundred feet above the beds of the rivers. There are few trees. Further to the north-east, beyond a line drawn from Stretyinsk on the Shilka to the Nerchinskoi Zavod on the Argun, the country is mountainous and wooded, and tracts favourable for agricultural pursuits occur in the valleys.

The Kerlon river has its source in the Kentei Khan. For five hundred and fifty miles it traverses one of the most inhospitable tracts of the Gobi, it then runs through the Dalai Nor or Lake, and after another four hundred and twenty miles it enters the Shilka at Ust Strelka. In its lower course the river is known as the Argun. As far as Tsurukhaitu the river passes through a steppe, with an area of 8,070 square miles, and an elevation of from 2,000 to 3,000 feet above the sea-level. This steppe is quite unfit for agriculture; there is scarcely any rain, little snow during winter, and early frost in autumn. The soil is a hard clay in which are imbedded pebbles, carneols and onyxes. The numerous salt-lakes frequently dry up.

At Tsurukhaitu the country improves. On northern slopes we find small woods of foliferous trees, and the valleys are decked with a rich covering of flowers. The lower we descend the more promising is the appearance of the country, and between Uryupina and Ust Strelka cereals are cultivated very successfully. Both banks of the river are wooded, the left bank is hilly with wide valleys opening upon the river. The right bank frequently rises in cliffs with exposures of granite. In this lower part of the river the bed is stony and the current rapid.

The *Onon* also rises in the Kentei mountains. In its upper course its banks are wooded, at Chindant it touches the steppe for a short distance, and then suddenly turns to the north, and down to its junction with the Ingoda flows through an undulating wooded country with many fertile tracts fit for cultivation. It is navigable at all seasons.

The *Ingoda* rises north of the Chokondo mountain, and as far as Chita, the capital of the Transbaikal province, flows towards the north-east along the foot of the Yablonoi range. Below Chita it has a breadth of sixty to one hundred yards, is rapid, and encloses many grassy islands. The rocky mountains along its banks are thickly wooded; the rocks often approach the river very closely leaving only a narrow passage through which it forces its way. These rocks are in many parts covered with mosses and a beautiful fern, Pteres pedata, and the rhubarb plant, with its red bulb, appears frequently in warmer sites. The river can be navigated by small boats or rafts below Chita, but this navigation is very dangerous owing to the shallowness of the water and to the rapids. A little above Kruchina a rock called Capitan, in the centre of the river, considerably endangers navigation at low water. The most dangerous of the rapids is that called *Boyets*, "Combatant," below Vorovskaya Pad, where the river forces itself a passage through a narrow defile.

The union of the Ingoda with the Onon forms the Shilka. The river increases in breadth; at Biankina it is four hundred and fifty yards wide. The river thence to the sea is navigable at all seasons in boats drawing two feet of water. The shores are hilly and wooded with large tracts of prairie, bearing rich herbage. The trees are birches and pines with a few larches. Below Shilkinskoi the latter prevail. The country is more mountainous, but wide fertile valleys and plains frequently intervene. The current of the river is

VIEW ON THE SHILKA.

about four knots. Below Gorbitza abrupt cliffs often rise directly from the water, and only small tracts fit for settlement occur at the mouths of some rivulets. A short distance above the embouchure of the Argun, the mountains on the left recede, leaving a narrow level along their base, but on the right they continue as far as the village of

Ust Strelka (Arrow Mouth), situated at the confluence of the two rivers. The thirty Cossacks stationed here engage in fishing, hunting, and bartering with the Oronchons and Manyargs on the Amur. We now embark upon the Amur, about which our communications will be more detailed.

### The Amur from Ust Strelka to Albazin.

Three miles below Ust Strelka the Amur has a width of four hundred and fifty yards with a current of about four miles an hour. The river occupies generally the whole of the valley, and the banks rise in precipitous cliffs, or steep and rocky slopes, leaving but a small space fit for settlement. Numerous tributary rivulets enter the Amur from the left, and also on the right, and when rain falls in the mountains, the waters carried down by them cause the river to rise frequently four yards and more in the course of two or three days—the greatest rise and fall being about eight yards. The most considerable of these rivulets is the Amazar,[c] (twenty-four miles below Ust Strelka) along which the Oronchons proceed to their hunting grounds on the Olekma. At the mouth of these rivulets are generally to be found small plains overgrown with scanty grass and shrubs of birches. At Monastir,[d] the valley of the Amur widens, and meadows extend on either bank to the foot of the mountains. Islands have been formed there. Thirteen miles lower down the Oldoi enters on the left (eighty-four miles); it is equal in size to the Amazar, and in former times its banks were the frequent resort of the Oronchons, who hunted here sables and other fur-bearing animals, whose numbers since then have greatly diminished. Below the Oldoi the Amur makes three abrupt bends, fifteen miles in length, and called Charpel, Dunon and Gonan, after three horses which some Manyarg

[c] At its mouth the Russian settlement Ignashof or Amazarskaya. The distances in miles from Ust Strelka are given in brackets.

[d] In the neighbourhood the settlement Sgibenef.

travellers lost here in the time of Prince Lavkai. There are some small salt lakes in the neighbourhood which communicate with the Amur when the water is high. At the lower end of these bends stands the station of Kutomand or Sverbéef. The river then increases in breadth, the mountains are less high, large fragments of rock have been washed away by the currents and extensive sand-bars stretch into the river, and during low water appear as islands overgrown with rich grasses, but poorer herbage.

The forests are thin, and there is scarcely any underwood. On the mountains larches prevail, with firs in dry situations. In the valleys the white birch predominates, with bird-cherry, aspen and occasionally a few larches. The trees are of very slow growth and hardly ever above a foot in diameter. Grey alders, Alnaster, small fruited apple-trees and willows may be seen at the fringe of the forest.

Spots with pasturage only occur isolated in extensive forests, the grasses are scanty and grow in tufts, and the bare ground may be seen throughout. Bitter, aromatic herbs abound and bear comparison with those of the steppes of Dauria. On the rocky mountain slopes may be seen occasionally some forest trees, the service tree, Alnaster, the grey alder, aspen, poplar and hawthorn, but the prevailing ligneous plants are the Daurian rhododendron and the Geblera. On loose soil Indian wormwood frequently covers a whole mountain-slope with shrubs two or three feet high.

Below Ust Strelka mica slate of unequal cleavage and of a darkish grey colour, with quartz veins, prevails. Lower down as far as Albazin, there is much compact clay-slate, either without any appearance of being stratified, or very irregularly bedded, and of a black colour, produced by oxide of iron.

As we approach Albazin (one hundred and twenty-five miles) the mountains recede, and make room for extensive prairies affording excellent food for cattle and stretching far to the base of the mountains. The features of the country are much more attractive. On the southern slopes oaks and black birch take the place of the larch, and at the foot of the mountains are found elms, ashes, hazelnuts, bird-cherries, willows and wild roses. The grasses are the same as in Dauria. The site of Albazin was well chosen by the Cossacks who founded it. In fact it is the first spot on descending the Amur suitable for a settlement on an extensive scale. Wood and water are found in plenty, and the mountains protect it against the cold northerly winds. The Albazikha or Emuri rivulet opposite Albazin is rich in fish, which are to be caught here with much greater facility than in the rapid Amur. Remains of the ancient ramparts of the town, which had been built upon a plateau about fifty feet above the river, as well as of the circumvallation of the Chinese, may yet be traced, and on the small island at the mouth of the Albazikha rivulet vestiges of a Chinese camp may yet be distinguished. From a plan of these remains in Maack's work Albazin formed a square of two hundred and forty feet; the Chinese camp a parallelogram of six hundred and seventy feet long and about one hundred and forty wide. The Amur has a breadth of five hundred and eighty yards.

## Albazin to the Dzeya.

Below Albazin the Amur expands, the islands increase in number, they form archipelagos and many of them lie in the middle of the river, contributing greatly by their variety to the original and picturesque appearance of the river, but interfering considerably with the navigation. On the right bank the mountains approach again close to the river a short distance below Albazin, and form steep precipices of sandstone; but on the left the plain continues uninterruptedly for a distance of seventy miles to the rock or promontory Malaya Nadeshda, *i.e.* Little Hope (one hundred and ninety-two miles) a bold sandstone cliff projecting into the river in the shape of a semicircular tower.. Above this rock a dangerous bar stretches across the river, having but three feet of water in the summer, and ten in spring. It was here the Russian miniature steamer Nadeshda wintered in 1855-56, whence the name.

The plain thence is at an elevation of from forty to fifty feet above the river, the banks are steep, and partly scooped out or lined with low alluvial deposits, generally overgrown with grass. Upon the elevated plain the hills rise in isolated groups of from one hundred and fifty to three hundred feet in height, and when close to the river form steep precipices. The hills generally have gentle slopes, and are surmounted by masses of syenite frequently presenting perpendicular walls. In their character they bear a great resemblance to the Ore mountains of Dauria. Sandstone formation is more rare. Foliferous trees are more abundant, and at the skirt of the forest may be observed the ash, whilst oaks cover the mountain slopes, and the larch, white birch, with elms and bird-cherry now and then constitute open forests.

The valley of the Burunda rivulet opening into the Amur on the left, thirteen miles below Nadeshda, offers superior inducements to intending colonists, and its advantages were appreciated by the Albazin Cossacks who founded here the village of Andrushkina, remains of which may still be seen. A Cossack station called Burunda (Tolbuzin) has been established in this locality. The soil of the valley is composed of rich black earth, covered with dense grass and herbage. On southern slopes grow small oaks, and black birches with the wild rose, on northern slopes white birches and aspens; whilst the summits of the mountains are occupied by firs and larches. The mountains surrounding this valley consist mostly of carboniferous sandstone and a conglomerate of clay-slate, fragments of quartz and hornblende enclosed in chlorite cement.

The numerous islands lower down are covered with poplar, ash and willow. At the Toro and Angan rivulets beautiful valleys again open upon the Amur. The Russian post of Anganskaya has been established at the mouth of the latter. The rocks on the left bank are granite containing felspar and glands of smoky quartz, without any intermixture of mica. This formation extends to below the Onon, where the felspar is dyed by oxide of iron. The physiognomy of the vegetation remains the same. Among the flowers the rhododendron, white poppy, forget-me-nots, Myosotis, the white-flowered Pæonia, attract the eye.

A few miles below the Onon a steep sandstone cliff of a yellowish grey colour bounds one of the reaches of the Amur for a distance of three miles. This cliff is called Tsagayan (three hundred and two miles). It attains an elevation of two hundred and fifty feet, and at about fifty feet, and one hundred and twenty feet above the level of the river, may be seen two black seams of coal, apparently lignite. The natives look upon this mountain as the abode of evil spirits, and dread it accordingly. The Manyargs who live near assert that smoke rises from the mountain when a human being approaches it, and the Manchu who come to the neighbourhood to fell wood say that the mountain smokes constantly and at times considerably. Neither Permikin, Collins, Maack, nor Maximowize could perceive this smoke when they passed that way. The phenomenon may owe its origin to the self-combustion of some coal seams; or the mountain contains caverns, and the warm air arising from them, on coming in contact with the colder atmosphere, assumes the appearance of smoke. Such at least is the case with several mountains in eastern Siberia. At the foot of the Tsagayan are layers of conglomerate, in which agates, carnelions and chalcedons are to be found.

Beyond the Tsagayan the valleys entering the river are wider, the steep mountains recede gradually, the meadows are richer in grass, and the low islands more numerous. Small groves of poplars, elms, ashes and wild apples, alternate with bushes of red-berried elder, sand-willows, self-heal and wild-briar. Small oaks and black-birch grow on the hills; larches and other conifers become scarcer. The meadows are richer and could afford pasturage to numerous cattle. Hard clay and clay-slate here predominate.

At the promontory Kazakevitch (Ele Khan) (52° 1' north) the mountains again come close to the river. The promontory consists of a reddish mass of deeply furrowed amygdaloid, and rises to the height of three hundred feet. A block projecting from the main mass of the rock assumes the appearance of a colossal human figure which rests upon the foot of the slope, wears a helmet and seemingly gazes down upon the river.

About eight miles further to the south is the rock Korsakof, a similar promontory of a semi-circular shape, and remarkable on account of its having regular steps from the river-side. At its foot the Amur has formed a deposit of sand and shingle, now overgrown with grass.

Thence to the mouth of the Komar (three hundred and eighty-two miles), a distance of forty miles, the left bank of the river shows a continuation of the elevated plain previously mentioned, whilst the right bank is low and undulating. At the mouth of the Komar are several large islands covered with willows, one excepted, which contains pasture land, and upon which stands the Chinese watch station Komar or Humar consisting of two log huts. A little lower down, on the left bank, is the Russian post Komarskoi.

Below the Komar river the banks of the Amur again become mountainous. On the left these mountains begin with the Bibikof promontory, a rugged mass of volcanic rocks, opposite the mouth of the Komar known as Longtor amongst Manyargs, Da-o-she Khada by the Manchu, which on account of its rising directly over the surrounding plain shows to great advantage, although its elevation does not exceed two hundred feet. The mountains do not, however, any longer rest irregularly upon an elevated plain, but form continuous chains as far as the Dzeya, accompanying both banks of the river at a greater or less distance. The prevailing rocks are syenite and porphyry. The course of the Amur itself is here very tortuous, and about fifty-one miles below the Komar it almost describes a complete circle, leaving but a neck of land half a mile in width, upon which the post of Ulusu Modon is built (four hundred and forty-six miles). This post, whilst in possession of the Chinese, consisted of three log huts covered with rush, in front of which stood a small prayer-house dedicated according to the Sinalogue Sychevski to Huan-lo, the god of war. Drift coal of very inferior quality has been found here on a small islet near the right bank. The Russian station in the neighbourhood is called Korsakof.

Below Ulusu Modon the Amur for thirty miles, as far as the Kerlon River, passes between steep mountain slopes, about three hundred feet in height, and crowned with columnar rocks. These slopes are either thinly wooded or altogether barren and formed of débris. Elsewhere precipitous cliffs form the bank of the river, the monotony of which is interrupted only by narrow ravines passing up to the plateau above, or by small basin-shaped valleys where torrents discharge their waters. The forests are nowhere dense, and the Daurian birch prevails, with a few scattered elms. In the ravines are found lime-trees having a trunk one foot in diameter. The mountains consist of felspar coloured by oxide of iron and enclosing concretions of greenish mica and quartz. Further on is found talc slate with a siliceous base, and of a greyish green with a metallic lustre.

Approaching the Dzeya the mountains are frequently interrupted for longer distances and make way for an elevated dry steppe, which is ascended from the river by deep moist ravines washed out by the rains, and containing groups of birches, aspens and poplars, the tops of which reach up to the plain. The soil of the prairie itself is a loose, yellowish and sandy clay, having but a thin covering of vegetable earth. The grass is rather scant, and there is a great variety of flowers and aromatic herbs and shrubs of hazel. In the distance, towards the mountains, the plain grows undulating and bears thickets of black birches and oaks and finally merges in the thinly-wooded mountains. The islands in this part of the river are numerous but far apart, and generally of small extent. Those in the middle of the stream are low and swampy with small pools of stagnant water, and only those closer to the bank are more elevated and bear a dense growth of birch, poplar, aspens with maples and buckthorn.

The upper part of the Amur had been the abode of some nomadic Oronchons and Manyargs only. Here we meet for the first time with isolated huts of Daurians, who come to this part of the river to fell the wood which lower down is scarce. To their labours must be ascribed to a great extent, the fact of the forests being here much cleared. The first Manchu village, Amba Sakhalin, stands about twenty miles above the mouth of the Dzeya, on a rich prairie, on the right bank of the river. It consists of twenty-three houses, built without any attempt at regularity along the bank of the river. The houses are badly constructed of wood, clay and rushes; they have paper windows, and inside may be seen pictures of Buddhist deities, and of the Foist painted on linen cloth by Chinese artists. Attached to each house is a small garden enclosed by palisades or a hedge, where millet, maize, radishes, onions, leeks, garlic, Spanish pepper, cabbages and beans are cultivated. Clusters of elms, birch, maple, poplar and wild apples, have been planted close to the houses. The inhabitants keep plenty of fowls and pigs, and a few horned cattle used for ploughing.

About fifty-three miles higher up, the Russians have the post Narantzum, identical probably with the post Bibikof of the map. At the junction of the Dzeya and Amur (five hundred and forty miles), is situated the town of Blagovesh'chensk, founded in 1858 by General Muravief upon the site of the Cossack station Ust Zeisk. The town is built upon the plateau, and the principal street extends a verst along the river. In April 1860 the population was 1,365 souls. There were twenty-nine buildings belonging to government, four to private individuals, and forty-six wooden huts, covered with earth, and most of them in the ravines extending down to the river. There is a church, and the foundation of a second has been laid. The Amur Company maintain here one of their principal stores. The Chinese from the right bank of the Amur come to Blagovesh'chensk about the fifth day of each month, and for seven days they sell their produce, wheaten and buckwheat flour, barley, oats, walnuts, Usuri apples, fowls, pigs, cows and horses. Occasionally they sell also silk stuffs, peltry, artificial flowers, felt-shoes, matting, etc. Timber has to be brought down the Amur or Dzeya from a distance of sixty miles, for only shrubby oaks and hazel grow in the neighbourhood of the town. The town is the seat of the military and civic authorities of the Amur province. Its site has been well chosen, and in course of time it will no doubt rise into a place of importance. Agricultural operations may be carried on here on the most extensive scale, and with a certainty of success. Coals are found a few versts above the town, and iron is reported to exist in the mountains a short distance up the Dzeya.

## From Blagovesh'chensk to the Bureya Mountains.

At the Dzeya the scenery undergoes a sudden change. Instead of mountains enclosing the valley of the river there stretches before the eye an extensive plain, with no visible limit on the left hand, and bounded on the right by low isolated ranges of hills. The accession of the black and sluggish waters of the Dzeya to the clear and rapid Amur, causes the latter to increase suddenly to a width of two versts. In the vicinity of the Dzeya the prairie is low and liable to be inundated, but a very short distance below it the plain is from twenty to thirty feet above the level of the river. On this plain there are scarcely perceptible elevations between which occur small shallow ponds fringed by rushes. The soil of the prairie is clayey, with a layer of rich black earth, and it is covered with luxuriant grasses attaining often the height of a man. Imperata sacchaliflora, Spodiapogon, and, less frequently, Manchurian panic grass, are those which grow in the greatest abundance and most strike the eye. Shoots of Vicia pallida (vetch) and Pseudorobus intersect the prairie in all directions and, next to the pink gloss of the Imperata, impart to it a striking beauty by their blue, lustrous appearance. Extremely succulent broad-bladed grasses however prevail. Small shrubs of cinnamon rose, two to four feet high, are hidden everywhere by the grass, and with vetches and other climbing plants, render the progress through these prairies excessively difficult. The white flowers of the Polygonum divarica, and the superb Tatar Starwort, with its pinky flowers, are great ornaments of the prairie. Calamagrostis, with Mulgedium, Stellaria radians (stichwort) and Artemisia, are restricted to swampy localities.

Numerous Manchu villages are distributed along both banks of the river, sheltered from the cold northerly winds by groves of poplars and firs, and surrounded by well cultivated fields. Fourteen miles below the Dzeya is situated the town of Sakhalin Ula Hotun or Aigun, the chief place of the Manchu on the Amur, but not otherwise remarkable. The government buildings and several temples are surrounded by a double row of palisades, forming a square, each side of which measures two hundred and thirty yards, and outside this square are several hundred mud houses. The town has a sombre appearance, the houses being for the most part built of wood and plastered with mud. The only variety is produced by the gaily painted temples. The shops in one of the principal streets have open fronts. Here the merchandize is laid out in the most tempting manner, and the merchant, attired in rich silks, gravely smokes his pipe until a purchaser enters. Dragons and other figures cut in paper are fixed to poles surmounting the shops, and paper lanterns hang across the street, giving it a rather original appearance. Heavy two-wheeled carts, drawn by two or three horses each, slowly move through the town. The population is about 15,000. To the north are some long sheds near which the Amur flotilla of the Chinese usually lies at anchor. On an island opposite may be seen traces of ancient batteries erected by the Chinese during their earlier wars with the Russians. Four miles lower down the river, on the opposite bank, is a large village where stood the ancient Aigun, a place described in 1682 by Milovanof, who even then was unable to obtain from the natives any account of its origin. The Chinese subsequently occupied the place, but abandoned it when they built Sakhalin Ula Hotun, the City of the Black River, on the right bank of the Amur.

Below Aigun the country on the left continues perfectly level, and the plain is covered with a rich black soil, in places fourteen inches thick. The banks are formed of a slimy sand. On the right are visible hills of the Little Khingan with their rounded-off contour; an offshoot, the Ilkhuri Alin, advances close to the river. Its slopes are barren, and the foot only of the hill is fringed by a dark line of forests, forming a striking contrast with the brighter hues of the prairie.

About thirty miles below Aigun the river separates into many branches.[f] The right bank is generally scooped out and steep, but on the left are extensive shallows and sandbanks, some barren, others covered with grasses and willows. The villages succeed one another to a distance of about fifty miles. Trees, which in the prairie region had appeared only singly here and there, unless planted by the hand of man, now increase in number, and about the mouth of the Bureya they form small groves. With the forests the villages disappear, and at wide intervals alone may be encountered groups of two or three huts, surrounded by a vegetable garden, and inhabited by Manchu fishermen.

We again enter the country of nomadic tribes, and instead of cultivated fields, tents of wandering Birar Tunguzians meet the eye.

The Bureya river (seven hundred and three miles), passes through a level prairie country enlivened by clumps of oak and maples. At its mouth it has a breadth of half a mile, its current is slow, and its limpid waters may be traced for a long distance after joining the Amur ere they mingle with its dark flood. The character of the country can scarcely be said to change with the Bureya. The right bank gradually rises in height, and the alluvial deposits on the left, are more extensive. Small creeks frequently indent the land, and islands are numerous. The soil in many places is clay or a rich black earth, and offers many advantages to agriculturists, of which even the Daurians, whose chief occupation is the chase, have availed

---

[f] According to the map of the Jesuits, the Amur communicates here with a large lake, situated on the left bank, and near which are three large villages.

themselves. In the prairie there are cavities with pools of stagnant water, surrounded by bulrushes.

The right bank is generally washed away underneath. The hills approach close to the river, and form gradual slopes, steep clayey stratified sections, or precipitous sandstone cliffs. Coal seams have been discovered here in two localities, the seams being three to four inches thick, and upon a trial being made the coal burnt well, with little smoke, and left but few ashes. It resembled cannel coal.

The lower portion of the hills are wooded with small oaks, wide apart. On more elevated spots may be seen a denser forest of young oaks and black birches, with occasionally white birches and Salix caprea. In shady ravines we encounter groves of white birch and aspen, and on the low alluvial fore-shore small poplars and Maackia, and on open situations or on islands, various kinds of willows, bird-cherry trees, small Tatar maples, elms, ashes, and a few cork-trees of small size.

Lespedeza bicolor and hazel-nuts (Corylus heterophylla) form a thick underwood of four feet in height in oak forests. At the skirt of the forest grows the Amurian vine, with its dark blue berries, climbing up the trees to the height of fifteen feet. Acarna and finely slit artemisias are common; but the most characteristic shrub of these forests is the Manchurian Virgin's-bower (Clematis Manchurica), the numerous white blossoms of which contribute not a little to their ornament. Owing to the sandy soil, but little herbage is found where the poplar grows. The willows on the islands or low banks are hung with Metaplexis; or Rubia is enveloped in the dark foliage of the Cornus, contrasting richly with its numerous black berries, and the red grape-berries of the nightshade (Solanum Persicum) bursting forth now and then between.[g]

[g] Between Blagovesh'chensk and the entrance of the Bureya mountains are the following Russian stations, all of them on the left bank:—

THE BUREYA MOUNTAINS.[h]

Ninety miles below the mouth of the Bureya, on the left bank, and at the entrance of the defile formed by the Bureya mountains, is situated the Russian post, Khinganskoi Piket, now called Pashkof (seven hundred and eighty-three miles). On the opposite side rises the bold promontory of Sverbéef, projecting far into the river. The Russian post is situated upon a prairie sloping down to the river, and there are several small creeks above and below it. The mountain nearest to it is a flat-topped cone, consisting of a coarse conglomerate, and separated from the surrounding mountains by narrow valleys with boggy soil. It is remarkable on account of some small fissures on its northern slope, a few feet above the valley, around which ice will form in the middle of summer, and from which issues an icy current of air. A thermometer suspended in one of these fissures fell in the course of an hour to 30° F.

For about twenty miles, as far as the rivulet Oou, at the the mouth of which is situated a small native village, and the Manchu Station of Ulu Biri, and on the left bank the Russian post Radde, extensive meadows may occasionally be seen on either bank, surrounded by terrace-like mountains, groves of oaks, limes and ash trees are found in the valleys; the summits of the mountains are covered with conifers. Below this the river is almost enclosed by walls of stone. From a breadth of two miles, it suddenly decreases to seven hundred yards at most; the depth in many places is seventy

---

Nismenaya, Konstantinof, Tsichevskaya, Poyarkof, Kuprianof, Shobeltsin (Bureya mouth), Inokentievskaya, Kasatkina and Pashkof.

[h] Otherwise called Khingan, or Dousse Alin, from one of the summits. As there are three or four different mountain-chains in China, known as Khingan (*i.e.*, white mountains), Middendorf has proposed to call that under consideration Bureya mountains. Other Russian writers have agreed to this proposed change of name

feet, and the current sweeps along at the rate of three miles, and in particularly narrow places as much as five and a half miles an hour. Within the whole of this extent there are no islands. Small patches of meadow occur, although rarely, at the foot of the precipitous cliffs. Now and then we perceive a small basin-shaped valley, which during high water is converted into a lake. The mountains attain an elevation of about eight hundred feet, and are covered to the summit with dense forests of fine trees – a strange mixture of northern and southern types—conifers however prevailing. On the banks of the few tributary rivulets are found in abundance limes, aspens, self-heal, black currants, and a great variety of climbing plants. At the base of the mountains, we meet the ash, oak, maple, elm, and white birch, and the summits and slopes bear a vegetation of firs. The slopes are bare only where they are formed of loose débris; and occasionally the barren summit of a mountain having the shape of a sugar loaf rises above the vegetation surrounding it. In fact, no accessible spot is void of vegetation. The soil throughout is good; and were it not for the rocks hemming in the river without leaving any space for settlements, this might become one of the most populous sections of the Amur. At present there is but one village of natives to be found here, and a very few huts of Goldi which are inhabited only during summer.

The axis of elevation of the Bureya mountains consists of granites, upon which rest mica schist, clay slate, and similar metamorphic rocks. Porphyry has been discovered in one locality only, at the mouth of the river Oou. Throughout there are indications of precious metals. It is evident that the Amur, before breaking the barrier opposed to it by these mountains, formed a vast lake above them.

About ninety-five miles below Pashkof the mountains recede on the left, and thirteen miles lower down on the right also. At the end of these contracted parts, are two islands. The one on the right is narrow, about a verst long and a few yards high; it is covered with a dense growth of birches and elms, in the shade of which grasses grow to the height of a man. The Amurian vine is plentiful and creeps up the trunks of the trees, and fills the mind of the traveller with anticipations of a flora more abundant than that met with on the prairies on the upper part of the river. The second island is a steep rock of uncertain colouring. The depth of the river is here still seventy feet.[i]

### THE PRAIRIE REGION OF THE LOWER AMUR.

A few hills continue to be seen in the distance, but beyond these the prairie extends so far as the eye reaches. This prairie at first differs but little in the character of its

BELOW THE BUREYA MOUNTAINS.

vegetation from that on the upper part of the river, but lower down grasses are much more predominant, and dotted over it are isolated oaks, limes or elms, with occasionally a wild apple tree, hawthorn, birch or bird-cherry tree. The banks of the river in many places are swampy. It increases in breadth, and its branches enclose numerous islands covered with willows and trees. These islands do not however inter-

[i] The following are the Russian posts situated within the Bureya mountains:— Radde, Pompeyevskaya, Polikarpovskaya, Ekaterin-Nikolskaya, and Pisina.

fere with navigation, as they are ranged along both banks of the river, and leave an open channel between them. The country from the Bureya Mountains to the Sungari is perhaps the most desolate along the whole course of the Amur. The nomadic Birars scarcely ever frequent this part of the river, and it is only occasionally resorted to by Goldi fishermen from the Sungari.[k]

At the mouth of the Sungari (nine hundred and ninety-two miles below Ust Strelka), the Amur is divided into several branches. The Sungari enters on the right, and its dirty waters may be traced for many versts flowing side by side with the clear floods of the Amur, until both mingle and roll on turbidly to its mouth.

Beyond the Sungari the level prairie continues along the left bank of the Amur, and only at the Russian post opposite the mouth of Sungari a range of hills approaches for a short distance and forms bold precipices. On the right bank however a range of hills accompanies the river for a distance of twenty miles and at the villages of Dyrki, Etu, and Kinneli approaches it in bold cliffs of clay slate, granite, and mica schist. These hills are covered with an open forest of foliferous trees. Oaks and black birches prevail, but elms, limes, maples and Maackia are numerous. Aspens grow only on northern slopes. The ground shaded by these trees is covered with a dense growth of Lespedeza bicolor, between which a luxuriant herbage shoots up to the height of five feet. In July the numerous red flowers of the Lespedeza, with the blue blossoms of vetches, large white umbels of the Biotia, and drooping catkins of the Sanguisorba, form a covering of surpassing beauty and of the most charming variety.

The Amur, which below the mouth of the Sungari had become one stream two miles in breadth, divides towards

[k] Russian Stations on the left bank of the Amur from the Bureya Mountains to the lower mouth of the Sungari :— Nagiba (Nagibovskaya), Dobro, Kvasinino, Deshnef, Mikhael Semenof, Voskresenskaya and Stepanof.

CLIFFS OF DYRKI

the lower end of this range of hills into several branches. The islands enclosed by these branches are covered with a dense growth of willows, forming impenetrable thickets, or even with forests of the same trees of large dimensions. On their shores are heaped up the bleached trunks of fallen trees or driftwood often to the height of several feet. On the more elevated ones only a few isolated trees, small-fruited apple trees, bird-cherry trees, maples or poplars, are met with. Some of the islands terminate in a spit of mud or sand, under water during the greater part of the year, and upon which spring up under the influence of the warm sun of summer a great variety of small plants, the seeds of many of which are carried lower than the Sungari and washed ashore.

GOLDI IN A BOAT.

The number of islands is most bewildering above and below the mouth of the rivulet Horolag (Khorok) which enters the Amur on the right, and is resorted to during summer by numerous Manchu for the sake of fishing. At that time the floats of the nets often retard the progress of boats, and conical birch-bark huts, and variously-shaped fishing-boats may be seen in large numbers on every island. Generally speaking, there are however but few permanent habitations along this part of the river. The few villages of the Goldi are situated on the right bank, and built upon prominent points of the land.

Clay slate cliffs again approach the river on the right below the village of Nyungya, where the Amur forms two branches, the main stream continuing an easterly course, whilst the other turns towards the south-east, and fifteen miles lower down receives the Usuri.[1] Maack discovered the remains of ancient fortifications on the summit of Cape Kyrma, above the village Nyungya, which he considers identical with Khabarof's Achanskoi (see p. 19).

## From the Usuri to the Bokki Mountains.

As we approach the mouth of the Usuri (1,179 miles), the craggy summits of the Khœkhtsi Mountains situated on the right bank of that river appear on the horizon. A narrow plain extends along the foot of the mountains. Leaving the willows which grow along the bank of the river, a narrow path conducts us to the huts of the village of Turme, situated at the mouth of the Usuri and imbedded in a thicket of Artemisia vulgaris, where the Urtica dioica and Cannabis grow to the height of a man, and which is rendered almost impenetrable by a great variety of climbing plants. A few steps beyond the village we enter a forest, which in density and the size and beauty of the trees is rivalled only by the forests of the Bureya Mountains. Within a small compass may be found here all the trees peculiar to the Amur: limes, elms of enormous size, ashes, walnuts and maples, the buckthorn, which attains the thickness of a leg, Salix caprea, Maackias, cork trees and others. The rays of the mid-day sun scarcely penetrate the close foliage, and the moisture of the soil is increased by a thick underwood, up which climb the Vine, Maximoviczia, Dioscorea and the

[1] Russian Stations between the Sungari and Usuri left bank of the Amur:—Golovin, Vosnesenskaya, Petrovskaya (Pembrovskaya ?), Lugof and Spaskaye.

gigantic Rubia. In the early part of the year, when the yellow blossoms of the Lonicera chrysantha fill the air with their fragrance, when the syringas bloom and the Hylomecon bedecks large tracts with a bright golden hue, when corydales, violets and pasqueflowers stand in flower, these forests may bear comparison in variety and richness of colouring with the open woods of the prairie country. Later in the year, the scarcity of flowers is compensated by the richness of the herbage, and after a shower of rain delicious perfumes are wafted towards us from the tops of the walnut and cork trees.

As we ascend the slope of the mountains we occasionally encounter a Siberian pine, pitch pine, Ayan spruce, or a solitary larch. The dark foliage of the hazel-shrubs contrasts pleasantly with the grey alder. There is less underwood, and still higher up conifers prevail, and the maple, common lime and ash, are the only foliferous trees met with. The cedar and Ayan fir predominate. On northern slopes, towards the Amur, the forests descend to the bank of the river. Larches grow in the moist ravines, and large tracts are covered with aspens, birches and alder, the ribbed birch appearing but rarely at the fringe of the forest.

Open spaces in the forest are rare, and when they do occur they are moss-swamps, often surrounded by foliferous trees. The meadows, with the short, tender grass, so frequently met with in the forests of northern Europe are not found here. It is at all events only at a great distance from the river. But on some tracts along the bank of the river, where the annual inundations do not permit the growth of trees, we encounter meadows, covered for miles with Calamagrostis purpurea having blades five or six feet high.

Before its junction with the main branch of the Amur, the southern branch forms a wide bay on the right, with many islands, and on its rocky coasts are situated the Goldi villages of Siza and Buri, the latter now the Russian station of Khabarofka,[m] which stands on a picturesque eminence, has a church, with paintings executed by some Russian officers stationed there, and is head-quarters of the fifth battalion of the Line. The left bank below this junction remains a level prairie for a distance of one hundred miles. The flowers of the prairie of the Upper Amur get however more and more scarce as we proceed down the river, and wide tracts are covered almost exclusively with Calamagrostis grass. In the neighbourhood of the river the prairie is swampy and exposed to annual inundations. On the right bank the hills in several instances advance close to the river, and form a series of cliffs composed of layers of glandy, cinnamon-coloured jasper, talc-slate, firm glandy clay, and a flintstone mass two inches thick. Large pieces of clayey sandstone have fallen down, and are deposited at the foot of these cliffs in masses which assume the appearance of ruins of ancient buildings.

The river is studded with islands, some of very great extent, covered with willows, or on tracts liable to inundation with Calamagrostis meadows. Looking from the southern side of the river they often hide the northern bank altogether, and on the summits of the Vanda a branch of the Bureya mountains is visible in the distance. The last of these cliffs is at the village of Uksumi,[n] and between those of Amcho and Khula.[n] The shore below the latter village is level and wooded with a foliferous forest. The villages of the Goldi, who prove useful to the traveller by piloting him through the intricacies of the river, are numerous here. On the right the Sole,[o] or, as it is called after villages situated near its mouth, Dondon or Naikhe[n] enters the Amur. The

[m] In addition to the Khabarofka, the following stations are situated about the mouth of the Usuri :—Korzakof and Kazakevich.

[n] Occupied by the Russians.

[o] Sole, the "Upper," with reference to the Khungar, which is also called Khyddi, *i. e.* the "Lower" (river).

Sole rises in the coast range, has a rapid course, and is frequented only by a few nomadic Orochi.

Below the Dondon the Amur flows for a short distance in one bed, having a breadth of six miles. But below the villages of Emmero and Jare the islands recommence, and the river has a development not hitherto attained. The branches of the river spread themselves over a vast plain, bounded on the south by the rocky heights of Emmero and the Geong Mountains, and on the north by the Ojal ridge and Bokki mountains. The Amur forms here three principal branches, each about a mile and a half wide, and the distance from one bank of the river to the other exceeds fifteen miles, or, including the lakes of Sargu and Boland (Ojal) which communicate with the river, thirty-six miles.

At the island and Cape of Kirile (Cyril) the branches of the river re-unite. The view from here is imposing: before us are a series of precipitous cliffs one hundred feet in height crowned with forest, above which rise the barren summits of the Bokki, on the left the steep slope of the Ojal ridge, and between both the magnificent stream eight miles wide with islands, and mountain-ranges far off on the horizon. In the Ojal or Chotzial Mountains veins of arsenic have been discovered, at first believed to be silver. The natives call these mountains Mungu-hongko, that is, silver mountains, and hold the spot in great dread for fear of the spirits who guard the treasures supposed to be hidden there.

### From the Bokki Mountains to Mariinsk.

The right bank of the river is generally high; on the left mountain-ridges approach at short intervals and form precipitous slopes; here the river is frequently seen expanding into small lakes, extending a few versts inland. The Amur in this part receives numerous tributaries, among which the Khungar on the right and the Gorin (1,520 miles) on the left are the most important. The mountains are composed of a fossiliferous grey sandstone and a conglomerate consisting of ferruginous clay, quartz debris and hornblende. The mountains are wooded with oak and birch. There are still many islands covered with willows. The valleys, though narrow, afford good pasturage, and many points suitable for settlements may be found along the river.

A few miles below the Gorin the islands disappear and the river flows along in one bed, having a breadth of less than a mile. At first the banks are hilly. The hills are covered with forests of conifers, forming an agreeable contrast to the lighter hues of the poplars, ashes and birches growing in the valleys. On either side may be seen the craggy summits of mountain-ranges at greater or less distance from the river, covered in places with snow as late as June. Towards the left, Collins (p. 280) saw two peaks, from which smoke

VIEW OF DERE.

was apparently issuing, and which he took for active volcanoes. Other travellers have not mentioned this phenomenon; it is not however beyond the range of probability. Below Dere the banks of the river form rocky declivities. Porphyry, composed of unequal grains of felspar and hornblende abounds; its colour is greenish. Large quantities of chlorite-slate are also found, and a mixture of it with quartz.

The mountains first recede on the left bank, and a short distance lower down, at Jai, also on the right. On the site of this latter village was founded in 1858 the town of Sofyevsk, which will doubtless become the chief commercial place on the Lower Amur, and is connected with Castries Bay by a road thirty-three miles long, to be converted, if the want of it arise, into a railway.[p] Plots of ground have been granted here to the Russo-American Company and several private merchants. Foreign shipping is admitted on the same terms as at Nikolayevsk, and wharfs and dry-docks are going to be built.[q]

At Sofyevsk (1,640 miles) the Amur again separates into branches, and from an easterly direction suddenly turns towards the north. The eastern branch of the river passes along the foot of offshoots from the coast-range, depressions of which have been invaded by its waters and converted into lakes, those of Kidzi, Kada and Yome being the most considerable. The western branch, which from Sofyevsk flows directly north, is deemed the most considerable, and passes through a wide plain until it joins the eastern branch shortly before the combined streams force a passage through the Amgun Mountains which intersect the river at right angles, one hundred miles north of Sofyevsk. Standing on Cape Jai, above Sofyevsk, this plain may be seen stretching far to the north. Conical peaks rear their barren heads above the heights surrounding it, and in the midst are discernible isolated heights forming, as it were, islands surrounded by

[p] Between the Usuri and Gorin there are seventeen Russian stations, mostly on the right bank of the river. They are called after the native villages near which they are established. Between the Gorin and Sofyevsk we have the following stations:— Gorinskaya, Churinof, Shelekhof, Litvintzof, Yerebtsof, Shakhmati, Feodorovskaya, and Elizevskaya.

[q] Viestnik, 1859. Erman's Archiv. 19, p. 13.

swamps and scrubs. This wide expanse is intersected by numerous branches of the river, which in autumn partly dry up, and lakes, of which the Udal (Chogal) is the largest.

The distance from the head of the Kidzi lake to Castries Bay is only eight and a half miles. Mr. Romanof endeavours to explain the fact of the Amur flowing to the north instead of seeking an apparently more natural outlet into Castries Bay, in the following manner. The waters of the Amur were dammed up in their descent by the opposing coast-range on the east, and the Amgun Mountains on the north, and spread over the extensive plain mentioned above, thus forming a vast inland lake. In its endeavours to reach the sea, it filled up several transverse depressions in the coast-range where now we perceive the lakes Kidzi, Kada and Yome, and would no doubt have succeeded finally in reaching Castries Bay had not the Amgun Mountains previously yielded to the pressure of its waters, and allowed them to find a vent towards the north.

### Sofyevsk to Castries Bay.

Lake Kidzi occupies an area of ninety-three square miles. Its greatest length is twenty-five miles, its breadth twelve miles. The lake consists of two portions, the upper one being the smallest, and they are connected by a channel eight hundred and eighty yards wide. There are two islets in the lake. The first is Boshniak, not far from the Russian station of Mariinsk. It is a rock about fifty feet in diameter, and about thirty five feet high. Its summit and the western slope, from which it may be ascended, are covered with a dense growth of birch, aspen, and other foliferous trees, and its numerous crevices are full of the holes of foxes, with which the island is said still to abound. The Gilyaks look upon it as sacred, and assemble on it from time to time to carry on their Shaman practices. The other islet, Pustoi, is a barren rock covered during high water.

Of the numerous rivulets which enter the lake the Ai or Yai is the largest. It flows through a wide, swampy valley, with mountains on either side, which below the juncture with the Khoil is three to six miles broad. A strip of forest fringes the bank of the river, and beyond it the swamps extend to the foot of the mountains. A few miles above the deltoic mouth of the Ai the forest subsides into shrub, and near the lake we have a plain covered with high grass. The Ai has a very tortuous course, and the current occasionally is five or six miles an hour. Bars and snags occur; the depth over the former does not exceed a foot, but elsewhere it is four to eight feet. The water is transparent. If we follow the course of the Ai, and then of its tributary the Khoil, and cross the watershed between the latter and the Tumji, six hundred feet above the sea, we reach Port Imperial.

Of other affluents of the Kidzi Lake the Taba alone deserves to be noticed. It is the Tabamatsi of Mamia Rinso, and the inhabitants of Sakhalin were in the habit of dragging their boats overland from Musibo, a spot on the sea-coast, to this river and then continuing their journey down the stream and across Kidzi lake to the Amur and the nearest station of Manchu traders.

Kidzi Lake is separated from Castries Bay by the coast-range—Sikhote Alin of the Chinese, Beregovoi Khrebet of the Russians—and where the road from Sofyevsk, or that from the Fedorovsk station on the upper Kidzi Lake, crosses it, its elevation is inconsiderable. Nor are the summits of the range and its branches, which spread themselves north and south of the lake to the banks of the Amur, of any great elevation. They are generally of a rounded shape, surmounted occasionally by a rocky peak, and the flanks cut up by deep ravines through which mountain torrents make their way. All these mountains are covered with dense forests of conifers which are intermixed on the western slope with larches, aspens, birches and even elms. As we descend towards Castries Bay the trees are of a more stunted growth. Above this vegetation some barren summits rear their heads. The absence of trees is however less a consequence of elevation than of the character of the soil, and their being exposed to the full force of the winds, which prevents trees from attaining any height. In some instances, as on the brow of Kloster Kamp, the trees look as if they had been regularly trimmed.

The mountains on the left bank of the Ai do not form a chain, but appear as several groups divided by swampy valleys. Their culminating points, and those of the whole vicinity, are the Cross Peaks (Krestovoi Goletz), a group of five barren peaks, in the shape of a cross and resembling a church with five steeples. Their altitude does not exceed 2,000 to 2,500 feet, yet they are visible at a distance of sixty miles.

### Mariinsk to Nikolayevsk.

Mariinsk (1,660 miles), one of the earliest settlements of the Russians on the Amur, is situated on that branch of the river which communicates with Kidzi Lake. A road leads hence along the north shore of the lake to Castries Bay. It was at first intended to make Mariinsk the chief settlement on the river, but owing to the insufficient depth of water—the branch upon which it is situated not being in fact navigable during part of the year—the government establishments were removed to the newly-founded city of Sofyevsk, more favoured in that respect. One verst below Mariinsk lies Kidzi, which has been purchased by the government and colonised by a battalion of infantry. Two versts further we come to the Cossack station of Suchi. On an island opposite the latter may be seen traces of entrenchments, supposed to be the remains of Stepanof's Kosogorski, from their being situated on an "inclined slope" (Kosoya gora).

As we descend the eastern arm of the Amur we pass in succession the Russian colonies of Irkutskoi, Bogorodsk, Mikhailof and New Mikhailof, in the neighbourhood of all of which the forest has been cleared, and rye, barley, oats and

# THE LOWER AMUR.

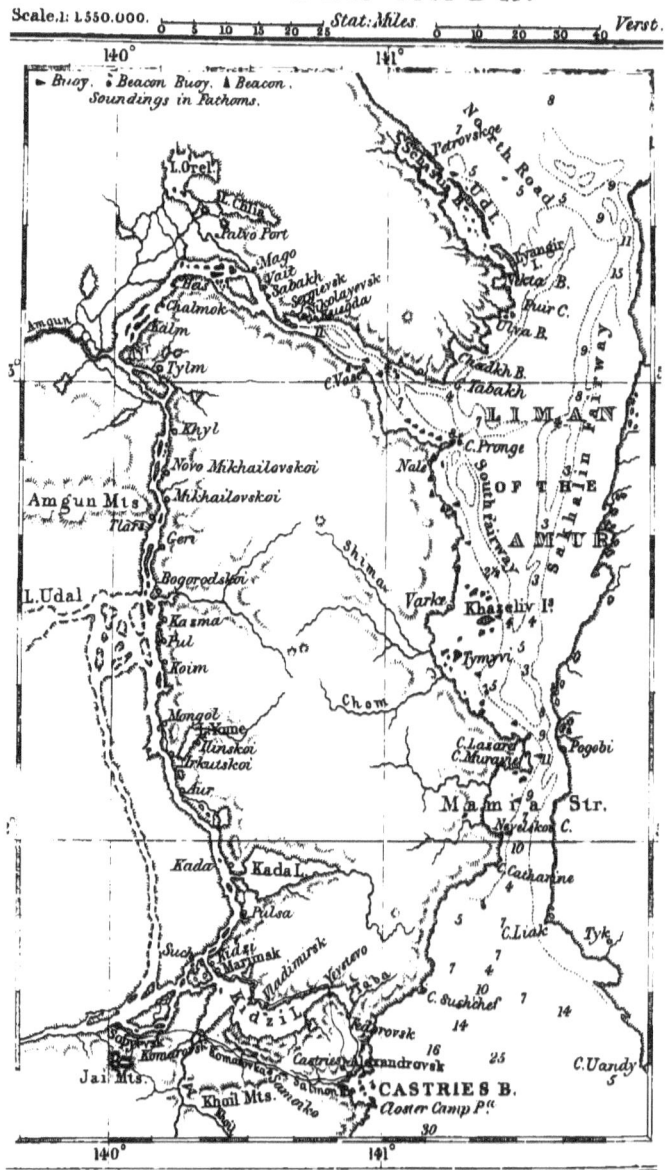

all kinds of vegetables are cultivated successfully, whilst extensive pasturage is found on the islands on the river, and on the plateau in the rear of the settlements. The colonists also profit by supplying firewood to passing steamers in summer, and horses for the post during winter. Accustomed to the rigours of a Siberian climate they are evidently satisfied with their lot, though the country would not by any means appear fertile and desirable in our estimation. But these agricultural settlements were the first established on the Amur, and the government was restricted in its choice of locality from the necessity of securing the settlers against any sudden attack of the Chinese, a defence effectually accomplished by the batteries of Mariinsk; and from solicitude to raise provisions in the immediate vicinity of the troops stationed on the Lower Amur.

On the right bank the range of mountains intervening between the river and coast, often forms precipices of three hundred feet towards the former. The rocks consist of clay-slate of unequal stratification, and a metallic lustre, with indications of iron ores. Near Pul the clay-slate alternates with layers of greyish-green quarzite. The whole mass has evidently been subjected to the action of fire. At Tyr compact limestone is met with. The mountainous country is covered with forests of conifers; birches and a few stunted oaks and poplars thrive only on the lower ground. Herbage is found on the islands, and on some level elevated tracts in the vicinity of the river.

The left bank is undulating, swampy and wooded, and the Amur communicates here with a large lake, the Udal or Chogal. The river Amgun which enters here, passes in its lower course through similar undulating country, and still further down branches of the Amur communicate on the left with the lakes of Orel and Chlia.

Half a mile below the village of Tyr, and not far from the mouth of the Amgun, a bold cliff rises to the height of one hundred feet, and upon its summit have been discovered some monuments and the remains of an ancient temple. The first of these monuments stands two paces from the precipice and is about five feet high. Its base is granite, and the upper portion a grey fine-grained marble. From two inscriptions upon this monument we learn, that in former times a temple or monastery stood here. The

Archimandrite Avvakum who deciphered the inscriptions, believes them to have been made by some illiterate Mongol Lama, not thoroughly acquainted with Chinese grammar, who wrote " Tzi-yun-nin-zy," instead of " Yun-nin-zy-tzi," *i.e.* " Inscription on the Monastery of Eternal Repose." On the back of the monument a similar inscription occurs in Mongolian.

On the left-hand side stand the Sanscrit words " Om-mani-badme-khum," and beneath in Chinese, " Dai Yuan shouch'hi-li-gun-bu," *i.e.* "The great Yuan spread the hands of force everywhere." In a second line, on the same side, the words of Om-mani-badme-khum are written in Chinese and Nigurian. The inscription on the right side contain the same in Chinese, Tibetan and Nigurian.

The sentence " Om-mani-badme-khum " is composed according to Klaproth of four Hindu words. *Om* is an interrogation corresponding to our " oh !" *Mani* signifies "jewel" or " precious stone," *Badma* is the lotus which plays so important a part in the mythology and religion of India, and *Khum* is a mystical interjection in Sanscrit, having no particular meaning. The sentence might thus be rendered,

"Oh! precious lotus! Amen." According to the Lamas, the doctrine contained in these words is immense, and embodies a prayer which believers cannot repeat too often.[r]

A second monument stands four paces from the first, and almost upon the brink of the precipice. It consists of an octagon pedestal upon which rests part of a porphyry column.

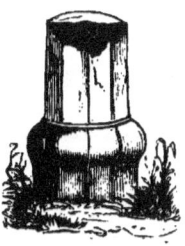

According to native tradition, the upper portion of the column was precipitated into the river by the Russians on their first arrival on the Amur. A third monument of granite similar to the first, stands five paces further; this also bears an inscription. And lastly, about three hundred and fifty yards from the third of these monuments, stands upon a narrow promontory an octagon column, larger than the others. On the plateau, a short distance behind the monuments, are to be seen the remains of ancient walls, nine to ten feet high. Several square stones with a groove an inch deep cut across them lie about, and are probably even now used occasionally by the Gilyaks for sacrifices. The natives look upon this spot with veneration; the Shamans carry on here their religious rites, and Collins found the stones ornamented with wood-shavings fashioned into flowers. The Russians knew of the existence of these monuments in the seventeenth century. We read in Witsen (p. 67), " It is said that some

---

[r] For more details we refer to Huc and Gabet's Travels through China and Tibet.

thirty or forty years ago, Russian warriors found a bell weighing six hundred and sixty pounds, at a place which seemed to have been dug round, and near which stood

several stones bearing Chinese inscriptions. The natives living there said, that long ago a Chinese emperor had come to the Amur by sea, and erected the monuments and left the bell in commemoration, whence it was concluded that China and Japan might be reached this way." A manuscript of 1678 in the library of the Siberian Department mentions the same facts.

The view from these monuments is exceedingly beautiful. Towards the south, dark forests extend as a waving sea, above which rises now and then the barren crest of a mountain ridge. Towards the north is the mouth of the Amgun with deltoic islands covered with forests, and the eye may trace towards the west, the wide valley through which that river takes its course, its banks formed by *tundras*, bounded by impenetrable forests of conifers.

The banks of the Amur north of the Amgun are abrupt, the islands low and to a great extent exposed to inundations. Porphyries enclosing small fragments of felspar and hornblende, with an admixture of lamellæ of mica prevail to a great extent, until they give way in the neighbourhood of Nikolayevsk to a reddish metamorphic clay-slate with metallic lustre. Fir trees prevail here, and birches and some few other foliferous trees occur only in more favoured localities.

NIKOLAYEVSK.

Nikolayevsk, until lately the most important Russian station on the Amur, is situated upon a wooded plateau, on the left bank of the river. The landing-place is available only for small craft, and larger vessels have to lie in the middle of the river, which has a width here of a mile and a half. When we ascend the stairs leading from the landing-place to the plateau upon which the town is built, we have on the right the government machine establishment, superintended by Mr. Barr, who brought over the two first steamers from America, and in 1858 received a gold medal "for zeal." A saw-mill is attached to this establishment. In its rear, a number of log-houses are scattered about, forming the "Slobodka" or suburb of Nikolayevsk. These are inhabited by sailors and workmen; the stumps of trees still remaining between them render walking by night rather unsafe. Returning to the top of the stairs we have Nikolayevsk on the left. The main street runs parallel with the edge of the plateau, from which some "gardens" or rather waste lands separate it. The first house at the corner is a tavern. It was formerly the officers' club; which has been suppressed owing to frequent disputes and personal encounters among its members. Gerstfeldt speaks of a library of 4,000 volumes, a ball-room and large dining-room in the club-house. He also speaks of the principal European newspapers kept there, and not disfigured by the censor's black ink. All this is however very much exaggerated. Capt. Prütz tells me that this famous club can scarcely compare to a low German beer-house. Of newspapers he saw but very few and these were months old. The next building on the left is the Pay-office, the third building the Police-station. Between these two latter is an open space in the centre of which stands the church, very neatly built of wood, the trunks in the lower part being left in their rough state and the roof painted green. This church is ornamented with one large steeple and four small ones. Behind the church, and facing the "square" stands the "chancellerie," a large wooden building, a hundred by fifty feet, surmounted by a mast-head from which the ships in the harbour may be signalled. Of other buildings, most of them in the three side streets, we may mention the hospital, the apothecary's shop, the store-house of the Amur Company, a school for pilots' and soldiers' sons, a bath, the town residence of the governor, a second tavern, and a watchmaker's shop. The houses are of wood with strong doors and windows, and their interior arrangement leaves nothing to be desired. The governor has a country residence about two miles west of the town, on a prominent cliff, whence there is a most extensive view. Attached to it is a kitchen-garden, and in the neighbourhood some Russian peasants have been established, who supply the town with eggs, poultry and butter. The population of Nikolayevsk in 1858 was 2,552, including three hundred and sixty-nine females, and 1,518 soldiers and sailors. There were forty-nine dwelling houses belonging to Government, and two hundred belonging to private individuals; twenty-seven uninhabited houses belonged to government, and there were besides one government and eleven private stores, of which seven belonged to foreign merchants.

The approaches to the town are guarded by four batteries commanding the upper and lower part of the river. The winter station for the shipping is at the village of Vait, fifteen miles above the town. The ships are protected against the floating ice by piles rammed into the river. On the shore have been built a house for the superintendent of the station, barracks for a hundred men, and a bath.

The vicinity of Nikolayevsk is not suited for agricultural pursuits, and the Russian peasants have therefore been settled at the villages extending for about seventy miles below Mariinsk, and mentioned before. Oats, barley and rye, but vegetables especially have been cultivated there with success. Near Nikolayevsk, and in the coast region generally white birches and aspens, the only foliferous trees, are found nowhere but in the most favoured spots. Large forests of conifers, with extensive swampy tracts, cover the country. Ayan spruce prevails, and with the pitch pine and the Daurian larch constitutes the forests. The underwood is formed of Pyrus sambucifolia and Aucuparia, wild rosemary, Siberian dwarf pine. Along the coast wide tracts are covered with Elymus mollis, and at the edge Lathyrus maritimus and Rosa rugosa have become naturalised.

## THE LIMAN OF THE AMUR.

The Amur at Nikolayevsk has a breadth of one mile and a quarter, the current is three to four knots.

Twenty-two miles lower, between the Capes Tebakh and Pronge the river enters the Liman or Gulf of the Amur. The distance between these two capes is seven miles and a half. The depth of the river opposite to Nikolayevsk is eleven fathoms at low water, but further down it is in some places but three fathoms. The banks are generally high and wooded. The rocks consist chiefly of a brownish red lava, enclosing small empty cells with white sides. Sandstones mixed with amphibolite and a fine-grained clay-slate of ash grey colour, occur now and then.

The Liman of the Amur is a wide expanse of water extending sixty-five miles from north to south, and having a breadth of twenty-five miles opposite the mouth of the Amur. The continental coast is steep, with some prominent headlands. The rocks consist of porphyry and lava, or of a reddish limestone, which at Cape Panza was ascertained to contain petrifactions of craw-fish. On an island not far from this cape, was found a hard clay-slate enclosing a great quantity of neo-crystallised sulphureous pyrites. Agates have been found in the alluvium along the coast.

The Liman at the ebb leaves many banks exposed. Its water, as might naturally be expected, is brackish, and the effects of the tide are scarcely perceptible. Its navigation is extremely intricate, and only to be accomplished with the aid of a good pilot, but even then vessels drawing above thirteen feet of water cannot enter the Amur. The main navigable channel called South Fairway* extends from the mouth of the Amur, at Cape Pronge, to the south, and enters the Channel of Tatary between the Capes Lazaref and

---

* On the British Admiralty Chart; in the original Russian "Vaarwater" or waterway.

Pogobi, three miles and a half apart, with a depth of water of from five to twelve fathoms. The current on entering the gulf is five knots an hour. Vessels drawing no more than three feet may proceed from the Gulf of Tatary to the Sea of Okhotsk, if they follow the "Sakhalin Fairway" along the coast of Sakhalin. Vessels desirous to enter the river from the Sea of Okhotsk must sail along this "Fairway" near to the southern extremity of the Liman, and then go along the South Channel. The North Channel which from Cape Tebakh runs beside the mainland has a depth of two and a quarter fathoms, but is closed in the north by a sand-bar, passable only for boats. Buoys have lately been laid down in the South Channel, and a steamer of suitable draft may sail now from Nikolayevsk to Cape Lazaref in twelve hours—a passage which in former times often occupied several weeks. Vessels proceeding to the Amur take up a pilot at Castries Bay.[t]

[t] See Appendix, Observations on the Navigation of the Gulf of the Amur, etc. By Captain Prütz.

## XIII.

### THE COUNTRY NORTH OF THE AMUR.

THE country to the north of the Amur, as far as we bring it within the range of our observations, is bounded by the Stanovoi Khrebet forming the watershed between the rivers flowing to the Arctic ocean and those tributary to the Amur. This country may be naturally subdivided into two portions — the one is mountainous and roved over by nomadic Reindeer Tunguzians and Yakutes, the other a continuation of the prairies noticed previously during our descent of the Amur. The mountainous tract consists of extensive tablelands, wooded, and to a great extent occupied by large mossy swamps. Upon the former repose mountain-ridges capped by conical, barren peaks. The elevation of the table-lands is estimated at from 1,000 to 2,000 feet; that of the passes leading from one river basin to the other may be 2,000 to 3,000 feet, whilst the culminating mountain-peaks do not probably exceed five or six thousand feet. Middendorf has proposed to subdivide the Stanovoi Khrebet[u] into the Olekma, Dzeya, Bureya and Aldan mountains, named thus after the rivers the tributaries of which rise on their slopes.

The prairies along the Amur from the Dzeya to the

[u] "Stanovoi Khrebet" signifies " Framework Mountains," and this name was given by the early Cossacks to these mountains, which they encountered at every point on going to the Amur, in the same way as they named the " Ural," that is "belt" or "girdle." Geographers frequently confound the Yablonoi with the Stanovoi, the former however extend from the Chokondo along the watershed separating the tributaries of the Baikal from those of the Shilka and Amur.

western foot of the Bureya mountains, continue for a great distance along the Dzeya and Bureya rivers and their tributaries. Along the former they extend, with a short interruption about the mouth of the Gilu, to the Byranta; and on the Bureya to the mouth of the Niman. The prairies of the Lower Amur are of less extent, and are bounded by the Bureya mountains and their offshoots.

The principal rivers which enter on the left bank of the Amur are the Dzeya, the Bureya, the Gorin and the Amgun. These rivers in their upper courses are narrowed in by steep and rocky banks, but even near to their sources they are of considerable breadth, and yet have a swift current. The mountains, after a while recede, the rivers are divided into numerous branches enclosing wooded islands, and communicate with shallow lakes forming back waters. Where they enter the level prairie region the current is slow.

Our knowledge of this region mainly rests upon the exploratory journeys of Usultzof and Middendorf. In addition, a number of astronomical points have been determined and published by the Astronomer Schwarz,[v] but that gentleman has not yet published an account of his journeyings. The following account of Middendorf's journey is derived from the "Sibirische Reise," vol. iv. p. 181—194, but we have incorporated some remarks of that traveller dispersed in other parts of the book.

## MIDDENDORF'S JOURNEY FROM THE SEA OF OKHOTSK TO UST STRELKA, 1844—5.

"On the 22nd September 1844, I began my return journey by ascending the Tugur river. The Tugur is formed by the confluence of the rivulets Asyni and Konuni at a place called Burukan. The valley through which it

[v] See Viestnik, 1855; Zeitsch. f. Erdk, 1856. I.

flows varies in breadth from thirteen to twenty miles. The Tugur is divided into numerous branches, and frequently its shallow waters rush over extensive gravel-banks, and though the breadth of the main channel is from eighty to one hundred and sixty-eight yards, it has sufficient depth for small canoes only.

"At the elbow which the Tugur describes at Ukakyt, about eight miles below Burukan, it is separated from the Nemilen, a tributary of the Amgun, by a narrow neck of land, four to five miles wide. The Nigidals who dwell on the Amgun avail themselves of this favourable feature in crossing over to the Tugur, which is on Russian territory (in 1843). At Burukan, where we stayed from the 2nd to 8th October, we found permanently settled three families of Nigidals who at that time were still looked upon as Chinese subjects. They had still continued in constant communication with the other members of their tribe. We also found here a Yurt of Russo-Tunguzians, and three small block houses belonging to Yakute fur-traders, who come to this place annually in December to barter with the Tunguzians, who at that season assemble in great numbers.

"We left the Tugur on the 8th October, and crossed the low watershed which separates that river from the basin of the Amur, in a direction of south-west by south. The distance to the Nemilen is here eighteen miles, and where we came upon that river it flows through a wide-wooded valley towards the north-east by east. The current is strong and the course tortuous. The river encloses many densely-wooded islands, but its depth does not exceed six feet. Ascending it for six miles, we came to a place called Khamykan, where in autumn the Tunguzians congregate in large numbers to carry on the fishing of the Keta salmon, which ascends from the sea and arrives here about that time. On dispersing, many Tunguzians go hence to the Dzeya mountains to hunt.

"On leaving Khamykan we sought, as far as the hilly ground would permit us, to keep towards the south-west in the direction of the Bureya sources, which we were told lay beyond the main mountain-range which now and then appeared in the distance. We crossed over from the Nemilen to the valley of the Kerbi, one of its tributaries, the sources of which are near to those of the Silimji and Bureya. The further we proceeded along the valley of the Kerbi, the more difficult we found it to advance; the trunks of fallen trees proved greater obstacles even than steep mountain slopes and rocky precipices. Near the mouth of the Jaer it was difficult to force a passage even with the aid of the hatchet. At other seasons our progress would probably have been still further impeded by the occurrence of swampy places. At all events, we crossed a large tract, evidently of moor-land, in close proximity to the Pass which leads to the Bureya. Having traversed this, we entered a narrow defile leading to the summit of the pass, where our animals had to jump from rock to rock. On the other side we descended to one of the sources of the Bureya through a valley about one hundred yards wide, and bounded by steep wooded slopes, offshoots from the barren heights higher up. (19th October.)

"We followed the course of the southern head-river of the Bureya[w] upon which we had come, and which little more than sixteen miles in a straight line from the Pass has a breadth of sixty yards, forms wooded islands, and flows along a valley on an average two hundred yards wide. Sometimes precipitous rocks circumscribe the bed of the river; sometimes the river alternately washes the steep slopes abutting upon it on either bank. The declivities are wooded, but in many instances the bare rocks appear. The slopes on the right bank of the Bureya have an angle of thirty-five

---

[w] On the Bureya Middendorf discovered excellent coal, containing 71·475 carbonate, 4·153 water, 8·638 ashes.

degrees, are intersected by deep ravines, and the mountains rise above the region of forests. On the left bank the mountains are at a greater distance, their contours are more rounded, but they frequently abut upon the river in cliffs of little elevation. At the place where the two head-rivers of the Bureya unite, the breadth is one hundred and twenty yards, and the river is divided into numerous branches; the width of the valley, however, does not increase in the same proportion.

"Below Taz Khandyvyt the easy slopes of the mountains frequently enabled us to cross them, and thus to avoid a circuitous course along the river; but as far as the mouth of the Lyukdikan the valley is bounded by high mountains, which only at the Umaltin recede and give way to gentle declivities, which to all appearance form the termination of an undulating plateau. A Chinese frontier mark is said to exist near the mouth of the Umaltin. Below this rivulet, the valley of the Bureya has a breadth of one and a half miles, and the river flows without further obstacles, to the west by south. It still encloses numerous wooded islands frequently above a mile long. Below the Jepko, the river repeatedly communicates with small lakes, forming backwaters. The depth, as far as I was able to ascertain, did not exceed two to four feet. It is however to be observed that the shallower places alone were accessible to me, the deeper places having been covered with ice for some time.

"The Tunguzians avail themselves of a short cut in going from the Bureya to the upper Niman; but as we were unacquainted with its direction, we had to follow the course of the Bureya almost to its confluence with that river, and saved but a few miles by crossing a low swampy tract at the fork of the two rivers. Only in the north and north-east of this level could hills be seen. We came upon the Nimakan, a tributary of the Niman, a few miles above its mouth. It is a rather large mountain stream, eighty yards wide, and enters the Niman between two inconsiderable heights, forming low cliffs. The Niman at the confluence has a breadth of one hundred and sixty yards, and was, of course, covered with ice. I had been told that a Chinese boundary mark stood here, but owing to the deep snow did not succeed in finding it.

"With the Niman we had attained our southernmost point. We now turned towards the north north-west, almost at right angles to our previous route, to go to Inkan on the Silimji. Inkan is a spot far-famed among the nomadic tribes of these mountains, and I expected to meet there a relay of reindeer in accordance with arrangements made during the summer,— as the small herd I had with me would naturally be tired out, and I could not afford to stay to recruit their strength.

"At the fork of the Niman and Bureya the mountainous region gives way to extensive, swampy prairies, which can be traversed only with horses. The natives consider the Niman the chief arm of the Bureya, and that river, down to its mouth into the Amur, is consequently known to them as Niman or Nyuman. The Russians give precedence to the Bureya; but it would be difficult to say which of the two assumptions is the most tenable. The Niman, as far as we ascended it, was bounded by hills inclining steeply towards the river, and approaching often to within one hundred yards, so that, even during winter when the water is low, the river occupies nearly the whole breadth of the valley. The latter is occasionally bounded by low cliffs. These hills are however of no great elevation, have rounded contours, and alternate with low wooded banks. The further we proceeded up the valley, the more it seemed as if cut in an undulating plateau. A few miles below the mouth of the Kerbeli the valley was wider than lower down, but even then its breadth did not exceed 3,000 yards.

"We now ascended for some time the tortuous course of the Kerbeli, sixty yards wide, turned to the north, and advanced along the Kochulyn. This tributary of the Kerbeli flows through a valley of little depth, two and a half miles wide, and bounded by gentle slopes of a swampy nature. The view is almost unlimited, and only on the left could be seen a prominent barren peak. The journey from here to the Silimji offered no difficulty whatever. We advanced across a low and level ridge, and the numerous rivers and watersheds could be crossed without being obliged anxiously to follow the course of the chief rivers.

"At the Kerbeli we met the first human beings since leaving the Tugur. At its mouth stands the hut of a Yakut, who for six years has resided here during the winter, and who has for neighbours four Russo-Tunguzian families.

"The next human habitation is at Inkan, where a Yakut trader owns a small log-house. We reached this hut on the 15th November, having a few miles previously crossed the Silimji, which forms here numerous branches inclosing wooded islands. Lower down, the river has steep rocky banks of middling elevation.

"At Inkan, the nomades of the mountains meet occasionally, and are supplied with the necessaries of life by Yakut traders, who come either direct from Yakutsk or by way of Udsk. The fame of Inkan as a place of trade is spread far and near among the Tunguzians, and even Daurians. We stayed here a week in expectation of the relay of reindeer, which arrived with surprising punctuality.[x]

"On leaving Inkan, we turned to the south-west by south. After ten miles we came upon the Silimji, and followed its course for two and a quarter miles. We then left that river and proceeded towards the Dzeya, in a direction west north west. In this tract also we did not meet with any steep mountain

[x] Here an old Tunguzian was pointed out to Middendorf, who prided himself upon having shot, towards the latter end of the last century, five Russian deserters.

crests, but only gentle ridges of little elevation; and were thus enabled to discard the direction of the valleys and rivers, the more considerable of which even we could cross without any difficulty. Traversing one after another, watersheds and watercourses, we did not again descend into a valley approaching in depth that of the Bureya. In close proximity even to the Silimji, and not far from the Iarakhan heights, we found the Usōurdur rivulet flowing through a shallow valley a mile wide, and the valley of its counterpart, the Usur, was still wider. Nevertheless we were here close to the division between the waters of the Sea of Okhotsk and those of the Amur, for the sources of the Shivili, which flows to the Ud, were but forty to forty-seven miles distant. The only rivers deserving notice, which we crossed on our route to the Dzeya, were the Nara and its tributary the Dukda, and although the former of these is looked upon as the main river, I found its bed which was bounded by low but occasionally steep and sometimes rocky banks, not to exceed one hundred and twenty yards, whilst that of the Dukda had a breadth of two hundred. The Nara may possibly make up by depth what it lacks in breadth. Its undivided straight course at once struck me, whilst the Dukda separates into branches, and at the spot where we crossed it enclosed a wooded island. All other rivers we passed over near their sources, where their breadth did not exceed twenty to thirty yards. The banks throughout were densely wooded.[y]

"We were enabled to continue our direction to the foot of the Kyœkh-Kaya mountains where they approach the mouth of the Gilui. We were however compelled by this mountain range to make a detour towards the south, and reached the Dzeya ten miles below the mouth of the Gilui (15th of December).

[y] According to the statement of the Tunguzians a Chinese frontier mark stands at the mouth of the Mevan into the Nara; and another at the mouth of the Killer into the Silimji.

"The valley of the Dzeya (Zeya) of the Russians (Je-üraekh of the Yakutes and Ji-onikan of the Tunguz) below the mouth of the Gilui has a width of little more than a mile, and is bounded by high mountains with steep declivities, and cut up by deep ravines. The river has a breadth of about two hundred yards and alternately washes the foot of the mountains on its right or left bank, the banks being thus either rocky precipices or gentle inclines, well wooded. We ascended the Dzeya to the Gilui, and I carefully inspected the frontier mark which stands here. It is upon a terrace of a steep slope, and consists of a pyramid about the height of a man and containing eight cubic feet. Close to it a square tablet was suspended on a tree by horsehair, and the inscription upon it, which I copied accurately, showed that the mark had last been inspected two years and a half previously. The Tunguzian who served me as guide, told me that a Mandarin, whose barge was towed by six or seven men, inspected the mark once in three years. I met here a Russo-Tunguzian who saluted me in the Chinese fashion by folding his hands and bending his knees. Our Tunguzians had been constantly warned by the Chinese official, that they had no business there, but on learning that they were poor and had no reindeer, and could not therefore get away, he took no further notice of them.

"The width of the Gilui is about half that of the Dzeya. For several days we journeyed along its banks. It was narrowed in by high precipitous slopes, often barren; and we were compelled slavishly to follow its many bends. Only towards the Kokhan the declivities become more gentle, and at length, a few miles below the mouth of the Dabukyt we were able to leave the valley of the river, and, turning towards the west, came upon the Dabukyt about the middle of its course.[2] We then turned towards the south, and for a

[2] The Tunguzians told me that the great-grandfather of the old woman who lit my fire had seen the first Russians, six or seven of whom he slew in their sleep, on the upper Byranta.

few days travelled in a direction forming an acute angle with the course of the Gilui as far as we had followed it. On the upper Aimkan we found ourselves still confined to a narrow valley. The mountains are however low. At the Erakingra, a tributary of the Aimkan, we again encountered a feature which we had lost sight of for months. Notwithstanding the many mountains which surrounded us, frequently of great height, and of a rocky nature, our route since we had entered the basin of the Ur, daily led across more or less extensive tracts of grassy swamp with small lakes, and easy ridges and declivities. The Tendi, which had been described to us as rich in islands, flowed, where we crossed it, along a shallow valley, and each of its two branches had a width of fifty yards. The main branch of the Ur had a width of ninety yards. The course of this river is very tortuous, and it is divided into branches. At one time it is bounded by steep and rocky banks, in the midst of an undulating country; at others by low and swampy tracts, with small lakes.

"Ascending the tributary valleys of the Ur, especially that of the Kerak, they gradually grow more open and shallow. From the sources of the Kerak, we traversed a slightly inclined open plain, forming a connecting link between the mountains stretching north and south. Having crossed this plain, the basin of the Dzeya, in which we had been travelling for two months and a half, lay behind us, and we entered the immediate basin of the Amur. Where we crossed the Oldoi it has a breadth of eighty yards. On approaching the Urichi I was surprised to see in this wilderness a staggering Tunguzian, whom my sudden and unexpected appearance did not at all disconcert in his then clouded state of understanding. On the contrary, he stuttered, 'Oh! here's the Cossack Captain.' Whence did brandy penetrate into this wilderness? The few nomades whom I had met assured me that fire-water was not to be procured at all, adding, however, cautiously, that even if so, it was only at an unattainable price. The riddle was soon solved, for a few miles further dense columns of smoke rose in the forest, and we came upon a party of frontier Cossacks, who had come to this place with their commanding officer to collect tribute in furs, which the nomades (Oronchon) of this country annually pay to Russia. Tribute was thus being levied on what was undoubtedly Chinese territory. The panic which my unlooked-for apparition produced, was so great, that we had much ado to prevent the party making off in all directions, and we sadly wanted their horses. When I found on nearer acquaintance-ship that these Cossacks were excellent men, open-hearted even to bluntness, and not crafty borderers, I could clearly perceive how much our government had frightened them about the frontier. The configuration of the country naturally leads the Ust Strelka Cossacks to seek the Chinese territory for the purpose of carrying on their profitable fur-trade. The very existence of their horses and cattle depends upon the hay which they collect along the Amur. Many peasants also annually cross the frontier to hunt squirrels along both banks of the Amur.

" We were enabled to exchange our reindeer for horses, and on the 12th January 1845, reached the Amur, and continued on its ice the journey to Ust Strelka, where we arrived on the 14th.

" After a repose of two days we rode across the mountains to Gorbitza, whence levelled roads took us to Nerchinsk."

USOLTZOF'S JOURNEY TO THE SOURCE OF THE GILUI AND
TO THE DZEYA; SUMMER 1856.[*]

THE starting-point of this expedition was Ust Strelka. The provisions were sent from Nerchinsk on rafts down the river,

[*] Viestnik of Russian Geographical Society, 1858, Part iv.; Zeitsch. f. Erdk. 1858. v.; Erman's Archiv. 1858, vol. xvii.

together with instruments, horses, etc., and arrived on the 10th June. Three days afterwards the chief of the Ninagan Oronchons, Grigori Nikolayef, who had been engaged by Lieutenant Orlof to accompany this expedition as guide, arrived. He knew the country well as far as the Khrebet Atychan; Usoltzof hoped to meet with some natives for the journey beyond. On the 14th of June, Usoltzof left Ust Strelka. His suite consisted of the guide, a soldier who had accompanied him on his first journey, two Cossacks, a sub-officer and a hired attendant for the horses. This man acted also as interpreter. There were sixteen pack- and seven saddle-horses. The Amur was descended for eight miles, to the mouth of the Mongalei; the journey thence was continued on horseback. Incessant rains much delayed the progress of the expedition, and it required a month's journey to reach the fork of the Oldoi river, a distance of one hundred and fifteen miles, which under ordinary circumstances might be made in nine days, especially as a track regularly used by the fur-traders leads to it. Usoltzof expected to find Lieutenant Orlof here, but came too late. In the hope of being able to make some reliable astronomical observations he stayed for three days, until the 22nd July, but was prevented from carrying out his intention by foggy and rainy nights. He therefore continued his journey up the eastern branch of the Oldoi. "The features of the country change sensibly; the luxuriant pasture-lands of the Amur disappear altogether. A dense growth of dwarfish larches prevails. Intermixed with these appear groups of birches, red firs and shrubs, and now and then in dry situations some common pines. The soil is moor-land overgrown with moss, but at times the loose subsoil or coarse boulders lie bare. In a word, the country becomes a rough, barren wilderness. The Oronchon are attracted to this district solely by the great abundance of squirrels, but do not stay longer than is absolutely necessary. On approaching the sources of the Oldoi the elevation of the country becomes considerable, the mountain crests are higher and steeper, and in many places barren, lofty glacier-peaks come in view. Forage for the horses was only to be found in the deep tributary valleys of the Oldoi, and but casually in narrow strips along the banks of the Oldoi itself. The length of our day's journey did not therefore depend entirely upon our inclinations; we had to stay where forage could be found.

"On the 2nd August we reached the source of the Oldoi, and having crossed a high mountain range, descended to the source of the Tanda. The valley of the Tanda is swampy; no herbage was to be found. It is bounded on each side by a chain of mountains, rendered almost impassible by ravines, dense forests and high shrubs. At times the thickets were so impervious as to require the use of a hatchet to make a path. Numerous small rivulets had to be crossed, especially near the Gilui. Their proximity might be divined a mile before actually seeing them: as soon as the descent from the mountains began, swampy places, overgrown at first with moss, appeared; closer to the river the moss is replaced by a rugged moor, the hollows of which are filled with water. These pools feed the rivulet which at last makes its appearance, taking its course between steep moor-hills, its banks overgrown with shrubs, and its breadth not exceeding fourteen feet. It would be waste of time to seek for a suitable place to ford it: the character of the country is everywhere the same: up hill and down hill, and again a rivulet. The forest is unbroken by a single meadow; even where fire has passed through it, there is but a scanty growth of short grass on the burnt soil. Large tracts of land, not only along the mountain slopes, but also on the water-sheds are covered with red and yellow mosses. The valley of the Gilui, formed by steep mountain-slopes, consists of a wide-spread carpet of moss, upon which appeared but sparingly some few groves of dwarf-like larches. The natives call such ground 'Uval.'

In consequence of the roughness of the ground we lost seven horses. It was found difficult to devise means to facilitate the crossing of the rivers; the horses stuck fast in the swamps, and the baggage got soaked. Our biscuits grew mouldy, and there were few glimpses of fine weather to dry them. On arriving at the Atychan we had only seven pud of biscuits left, half of which was putrid, and some brick tea.

" However desirable it might appear to me to ascend the Khrebet Atychan and determine its altitude, the swollen rivulets separating us from it, rendered it impracticable to approach its base either on horseback or on foot. Its direction is north-west and south-east, and two peaks one at each extremity bound it distinctly; the distance intervening between them is about three and one-third miles, occupied by several other peaks of various elevation, separated from each other by narrow, deep ravines. They are of pyramidal shape; the slope, which at the foot is interrupted now and then by small terraces, on ascending gets steeper and steeper, until the summits present precipitous masses of granitic rock. In the ravines and on the terraces are found a few trees and shrubs, but the more elevated portions are perfectly barren."

On the 30th August our traveller left the Atychan, and from the eastern source of the Gilui which he reached on the 20th September, ascended the Kuduli rivulet to the watershed, consisting here of an abrupt range of hills, grown over with moss, whence numerous rivulets flowing in all directions take their rise. He soon after fell in with a party of Oronchons. " Our guide had observed the trail of rein-deer whence we crossed a swampy rivulet, and inferred after a careful examination that Oronchons had been in the neighbourhood about three days before. This was good news. I hoped to obtain a guide from them, and, moreover, we had already decided to kill a horse that evening, as our biscuit was unfit for food, and we had only a few pounds of butter and flour left. We followed the footprints and came to the Yurts in the evening. Our arrival surprised the Oronchons not a little. They did not belong to the same tribe as our guide, but nomadised generally in the province of Yakutsk, and merely came across the mountains to barter with the Oronchons dwelling near the Gilui. I purchased from them two small reindeer, but could not induce them to accompany us to the Dzeya. Their Yurts were situated at the source of the Jaltula (a tributary of the Gilui) but they persuaded us not to follow that river, as the Lower Gilui was full of waterfalls and its steep banks rendered travelling with horses very difficult."

Usultzof therefore continued his journey towards the south-east, and on the 14th September came upon the Ilikan.

"We supped here, for the last time, upon reindeer flesh. Early in the morning, I mustered the horses; they were so thin and weak as scarcely to justify a hope of their being able to reach the Dzeya. My travelling companions had become very low-spirited, and, moreover, considered the eating of horse-flesh a carnal sin. My assurances, however, that we should meet with Manyargs on the Dzeya, a distance of thirty-three miles only, and that on their return the priest, would by prayer and fasting purge them of their sins, satisfied them for a time.

"Our road led along the Ilikan. The valley of this rivulet winds its serpentine course along the precipitous mountain-chains which enclose it, and almost entirely consists of Tundras of red moss. Now and then the river passes through a defile. The mountains are not high, and at a first glance the country would appear to form an extensive plateau. Only towards the south-west, and at a great distance, could we see the barren snow-capped mountains near the Gilui."

"On approaching the mouth of the Ilikan, we left it and continued our journey towards the south-west, bearing towards the glacier Tukorinda, which is not far from the mouth of the Gilui. As we went on, the proximity of the Dzeya was perceived in the distance of all mountain-ranges and a gradual inclination of the country towards the south. A large expanse of country consisted of meadow-land, with small lakes, and willow and birch copses scattered about. We came upon the Dzeya quite unawares on the 14th September.

"We had indeed seen it a mile below, but took it then for a long lake stretching out, as we had already passed several on our way, a mistake the better understood by the similar appearance of the country on the other bank of the river. We lost no time in building a raft. Fortunately we had come upon the Dzeya at a place where pines suitable for this purpose were to be found.

"We had yet twelve horses left; and I did not abandon the hope of being able to extend our exploratory journey to the Silimji, especially as the horses might recover their strength whilst we were employed building the raft. The reverse however was the case; from day to day they became more emaciated, and the continuous rains, and even snow, together with the bad forage, rendered them quite incapable of continuing the journey.

"For greater security we built two rafts, which together formed a 'Prahm.' On the 3rd October we loaded the rafts and left in the afternoon. The Dzeya has here a breadth of seven hundred yards, and its current is five miles the hour. For a distance of twenty-one miles, following the windings of the river, meadows entered on both banks as far as the eye could reach. The mountains then gradually approached, first on the right bank then on the left, and the river flowed through a narrow defile. The current was stronger, and sunken rocks lay in the middle of the river, their proximity being indicated by the foaming of the water splashing over them. These rocks increased in number, and in many places made their appearance above the water, which splashed against them and covered the river with spray.

"Our raft was carried along with surprising rapidity, and we dared scarcely lift our eyes from off the river in our anxiety to prevent the raft being knocked to pieces. Swiftly we shot past the narrow defile through which the Gilui takes its course on joining the Dzeya. I had scarcely time to observe the pile of rocks forming the Chinese frontier-mark, placed on a steep high mountain at the fork formed by the two rivers. We continued fourteen and a half miles further through a similar country, but beyond, the mountains receded and formed an open valley, covered with high luxuriant grasses. The river increased considerably in breadth, and the current was so feeble that it sometimes appeared as if the raft remained long in the same place.

"On the following day, 6th October, we met for the first time with Tunguzian Manyargs at the mouth of the Mokcha rivulet. Their birch-bark Yurt stood close to the river, and we saw the inhabitants from afar. On our approach, they took to flight, and it was only after we had staid for an hour in their Yurt, continually shouting, that they ventured to come nearer. However great was my joy at this meeting, my plans regarding further explorations derived no advantage from it. The Manyarg had horses, but could not be induced upon any terms to take us to the Silimji, assuring us, that should his doing so come to the ears of his chief, himself and family might lose their lives. He did not however refuse to accompany us some distance down the Dzeya, and we left after a stay of two hours.

"The Manyarg accompanied us as far as the Umlekau river (10th October), where we found other Manyargs who received us hospitably. They were less timid than those we had met at first, probably because our Manyarg on approaching their Yurts, announced our arrival by several blasts upon a wooden horn. These Manyargs also refused to take us by land to the Silimji but agreed to accompany us down the river to its mouth. We were thus kept, as it were, under surveillance, for every day we came upon some families, who nomadise along the river, where they lie in wait for wild goats. This is their only occupation during that part of the year. Below the Umlekan the navigation became more difficult. The wind was high, and the ice which had began to form on the 7th became thicker. It only disappeared during calms, and as these happened generally during the night, it was only then that we made any progress, whilst during the day we had to combat not merely the wind but ice-blocks too. The moon-light enabled us to distinguish the features of the country. In this manner we continued our journey to the 13th October in company of the Manyargs. The latter, during the night, went to some lakes in the vicinity to hunt deer, and favoured by a clear sky, I took advantage of this opportunity to make some astronomical observations. The site of observation was situated two and a half miles from a small, rocky islet, which separates the river into two branches, the left of which is considered dangerous by the Manyargs and Manchu who ascend the river to this place.

" On the day following we continued our journey under the same difficulties, and on the 15th October arrived at the mouth of the Silimji. This large branch on entering the Dzeya forms an extensive delta consisting of low islands, overgrown with sand-willows, which completely conceal the the mouth. Had not the Manyargs drawn our attention to this, we should have passed without noticing it. Including islands, the Dzeya has here a breadth of three and a half miles; the current is very slow. I was surrounded here by a large party of Manyargs, for this is the Meeting-place of the whole tribe, whence they go to the upper Silimji to hunt squirrels and sable. I took advantage of their hospitable reception to question them about the Silimji and the country bordering upon it, but there were many discrepancies in their statements. The gist of the imformation I obtained is as follows. The Silimji is equal in size to the Dzeya; the current is slow in its lower course but more rapid higher up. The river has not so many windings as the Dzeya or Amur. Among the tributaries the Manyargs mentioned one in particular, about two and a half days' ride from the mouth. As far as this (the Nara of Middendorf), and for a short distance beyond, extensive meadows are found, upon which the Manyargs pasture their horses in the spring and summer. There are some mountain ranges, but they are not very elevated. Towards its source, and also in its middle course, some glaciers are met with. The Manyargs do not often ascend the river to its source, but generally stay at its lower and middle part. We may conclude from this that forage is to be found here. The mountains, forests and swamps higher up, probably afford no pasturage.

" Below the mouth of the Silimji the character of the banks of the Dzeya changes rapidly. Hitherto the river had either passed through small, generally open plains, was enclosed by rocks, or accompanied by mountains on one or the other banks, the summits thinly wooded with pine, red fir, larch and birch. A short distance above the Silimji the mountains recede, and a wide plain extends on both sides, without either rocks or trees. As far as the eye reaches the plain is covered with high, luxuriant grass, intermixed with wild roses; in low parts swamps with small lakes have been formed. Such is the appearance of the country for seventy-one miles. A mountain-chain then gradually approaches on the right, and forms a rocky bank. These are the mountains referred to in Milovanof's report as the 'White Mountains.' They consist of marl upon which rests clay-slate.

" These mountains keep close to the river for six miles, they then recede somewhat leaving a narrow valley, after which they approach for a second time, recede again, and finally form a third promontory, which for one and one-third miles extends along the river. Opposite to the extremity of the second of these promontories are several islands which hide the mouth of the Tomi river. Further on the mountains recede, but still follow the course of the river, and bound a rich meadow-land. About forty miles below the Tomi, the summits along the right bank, and sometimes also the slopes, are wooded, but lower down the forest gradually disappears. The distance of the mountain from the river varies, and both mountain and plain yield good pasturage. The plain extending along the left bank of the river is interrupted only by a few hills; steep mountains are seen beyond. The soil is of loam, at some places covered with black mould fourteen inches thick. These fertile plains offer facilities for founding colonies, and introducing agriculture and cattle-rearing. The breadth of the Dzeya at the mouth of the Tomi is perhaps even more considerable than at the Silimji. The current, especially near the 'White Mountains,' is very slow, and sometimes we could scarcely tell which way the raft was floating.

"On the 18th October we had come abreast the mouth of the Tomi. During the night we lost our last horse. Our Cossacks, who from their youth had been brought up with horses, attributed their death to eating grass which had been submerged for some time. On the following day we continued our journey on one raft, but still made little progress against the ice. The 20th October was our last day on the river. A violent wind arose in the morning, which at night increased to a storm. With difficulty we gained the left bank. During the whole night the storm continued to rage with unabated violence; flakes of ice became more numerous. In the morning we found our raft enclosed by the ice, large pieces of which floated down the whole breadth of the river, which in some places was quite choked up. I remained on shore the whole of that day, in the vain hope that on the cessation of the wind we might be enabled to continue our voyage. Such however was not the case, nor had we any means of crossing over to the right bank. We had yet half a horse left, which might last three persons a week, and we therefore resolved to separate. We hid our baggage in a ravine. Three of my people remained here, and I started with the three others to seek a Manchu village. I ordered those left behind to wait for me during ten days, and in case I should not be able to send any assistance, they were to obliterate the traces of our encampment and to follow me. On the third day we came to the first Manchu village, forty miles from our camp on the Dzeya. Two Manchu conducted us to the house of meeting, where soon afterwards the whole village assembled.

" My first care was to induce the Manchu to fetch the three men I had left behind, and I offered to remunerate them for horses and provisions. They discussed deep into the night as to what was to be done to us. On the following day they brought us thirty pounds of millet, and resolved to escort us onward to Sakhalin-ula-Khotun (Aigun), where we were to be placed at the disposal of the authorities. On the 27th October, they brought us to the village situated opposite the town; the whole of this journey had been made by night, and they always, under some pretence or other, managed to spend the day at a village. My entreaties for us to be sent to the Cossacks who wintered at Ust Zeisk were not noticed, and in the evening of the 28th, when the ice on the Amur was scarcely firm, they took us across the river, and brought us to the government building. In half an hour we were led to our examination. On entering the court of justice we found three officials and several writers there. One of the former, Guzaïda or adjunct of the Amban, commenced the examination by asking our names, and the reason of our traversing territories which they considered their own. They next questioned us about my occupation and travels, etc., putting the same questions repeatedly with the view of confusing me. I did my best to answer concisely, avoiding long explanations, adding, that had I not met with ill-luck I should never have troubled them, but that, situated as I was, I relied upon their friendly feeling towards the Russians. The examination concluded, I was presented to the Amban, who shewed himself very friendly, and without entering into further details ordered us to be taken to Ust Zeisk, and provisions to be sent to the three men I had left at the river. Half an hour afterwards we were conducted out of the town, and on the following day (29th October) I found myself among our Cossacks. The officer in command of the station immediately despatched fifteen Cossacks to convey relief to the men left on the Dzeya, but as the ice was not yet quite firm, they could not get to the left bank of the river.

" On the 1st November the Manchu unexpectedly brought my baggage, instruments and the three men."

Usultzof took advantage of a post which was just then being despatched to Nerchinsk, and without further obstacle travelled up the Amur. On the 16th November he left Ust Zeisk, and on the 20th December he arrived at Ust Strelka.

## XIV.

### THE COUNTRY SOUTH OF THE AMUR.

#### THE COAST OF MANCHURIA.

LEAVING the Amur Liman and following the cliffy coast of Manchuria southward, the first Bay we come to is that of *Castries* (51° 28' north, 140° 49' east), discovered by La Peyrouse on the 28th July 1787, and named by him after the Marquis de Castries, the Minister of Marine of France. As extreme limits of the bay, we may designate the bold Cape d'Assas and Klosterkamp peninsula, a rocky mountain mass separated from the land by a narrow isthmus but eighteen yards across. Upon the summit of this latter a lighthouse has been built, and a guard is stationed there during the summer, which signals vessels approaching the bay. About half-way between these two extreme points is situated the Vostok sandbank, having but two feet of water during ebb. Within this sandbank a chain of four islands, extending from Cape Kornikof to the isthmus of Klosterkamp, separates the open sea from the inner bay. These are Basalt, Observatory, Oyster and South islands. Ships may enter on either side of Oyster Island, where there is a depth (at low water) of five to six fathoms; or to the north of Observatory Island, where the depth is three fathoms. They will find safe anchorage behind the latter island, where they are sheltered against easterly winds, but are exposed in autumn to violent west-winds which sweep down the ravines leading to the bay.

Castries Bay is surrounded by mountains the loftiest of

which is Mount Arbod, having an elevation of 1500 feet. It serves as a land-mark to ships approaching Castries Bay. The mountains form bold cliffs towards the bay, consisting of trachytes and basalts, and about fifty feet in height. Towards the land, the water gradually shoals, and at ebb portions of the bay lie dry. Such is the case with the whole of Salmon Bay, and the upper part of North Bay; in Arbod Bay, to the south, the depth of water is only five feet. Of the numerous rivulets those entering the parts just named are the most important; but Salmon River, the largest of all, is navigable for three miles only, and that in the tiniest of Gilyak canoes. The valley at its mouth is but one-third of a mile in width. Another rivulet near the former bay, the Nelly, is remarkable for its swift current, its pure water, and the fact of its never freezing. At its mouth has been erected the Alexandrovsk post, defended by several batteries. About a mile and a half inland, is the military colony of Castries, consisting of about sixty log-houses, a church and hospital, inhabited by about one hundred and fifty soldiers and their families. They cultivate a few vegetables, and barley, "it is believed," might be grown with advantage. In addition to their ordinary rations these men are served with oyster and fish soup, oysters and fish abounding in the bay. A harbour-master resides at the post, and attached to him is an interpreter speaking English, German and French, Pilots are stationed here to take ships to the Amur (Nikolayevsk). In 1858 it was proposed to carry out improvements on a large scale, to build a magnificent breakwater, dry docks and store-houses. The trifling commerce, however, did not warrant so large an expenditure, and a lighthouse only has been built on Klostercamp. Nor has the railroad been built which was to connect Castries Bay to Sofyevsk on the Amur, but communication between these places is kept up, as formerly, by a road (see p. 192).

Castries Bay remains covered with ice from the middle of

December to that of May, that is for five months. South-easterly winds blow almost uninterruptedly from April to September, and during that time dense fogs frequently continue for days, and ships cruize off Klosterkamp without being able to enter the bay, though they hear the guns fired at intervals at the post. Westerly winds prevail during October, and that season is the best of the year.

The coast south of Castries Bay continues abrupt, the mountains being partially wooded. After a sail of one hundred miles, we reach *Destitution Bay* (49° 46′ north) to the north of a prominent head-land, where there is a safe anchorage. It has a shelving beach upon which there are a few scattered Orochi huts. On landing and crossing a broad bank we come to the margin of a large lake, surrounded by forests and animated by numerous water-fowl; a wide river enters it.

Resuming our journey southwards, we pass Cape Lesseps (49° 33′ north), a bluff headland of columnar basalt capped by yellow sandstone. We have still cliffs along the coast, broken abruptly now and then where a small rivulet enters the sea. In the distance are seen the summits of the coast range covered with snow even in May and June.

We next reach Port Imperial, Haji or Barracouta Bay (49° 2′ north, 140° 19′ east), a Fjord almost entirely surrounded by cliffs. The Haji river enters it, and at the mouth forms some alluvial islands. The bay is environed by dense forests of pines, Scotch firs, larches, yews and alders. The Russians founded a small settlement here in 1853; it was abandoned in consequence of the war, but has recently been re-occupied. This settlement, called Konstantinovsk, consists of a few log-houses, supplied with water from a well, and defended by two batteries mounting eighteen guns. It was intended at one time to make this post the chief naval port on the coast of Manchuria, a project which has been given up in favour of Olga Bay, further south.

We still proceed south along a rocky coast, interrupted at times by wide valleys extending far inland. The hills are wooded, and the summits of the coast-range appear in the distance. Three hundred and twenty miles south of Castries Bay is situated *Suffren Bay* (47° 20′ north, 138° 58′ east) discovered by La Pérouse, an exposed anchorage offering but slight shelter. The water gradually shoals to the shingle beach, and a river thirty to forty yards wide enters the Bay. Oysters and some beautiful corals have been found here. South of Suffren Bay the character of the coast continues the same, but the cliffs are rather lower. The hill-sides are wooded with firs and birches; but the summits are barren. It is not before we reach *Ternay Bay* (45° 13′ north) that the vegetation assumes a more southern appearance. The coast of this Bay is divided into five almost equal portions, and fresh and limpid rivulets fall into the five creeks which form it. These creeks are separated by hills covered with verdure to their summits. Along the banks of the rivulets grow willows, birches, maples, apples, medlar-trees and hazelnuts; higher up oaks, and on the summits pines. The Bay is evidently frequented by the Orochi.

Hence, as we proceed south, the number of bays, some of them very superior, increases, and within a distance of three hundred miles there occur upwards of eight. The traces of Chinese settlements become apparent, and cattle may be seen grazing along the shore. *Bullock Bay* (45° 2′ N. 136° 44′ E.), extends between two headlands, and has a sandy beach. A river enters here, and some hills separate the beach from a lake. Tronson found some forty head of cattle grazing near the shore. Ascending the river for a few miles he came to a Chinese village, the inhabitants of which cultivated dry rice, potatoes and onions. They offered tobacco leaves and some skins for sale, but were very reluctant to part with their cattle. South of Bullock Bay the country is very picturesque and diversified. The coast-line is less bold than further north, and exhibits headlands and banks of yellow clay and sand. Broad park-lands and gentle hillocks, with birch and oak scattered over them extend along the coast. Beyond these, appear wooded hills and winding valleys, and far off may be seen the high-peaked mountains of the coast-range. Eighteen miles beyond Bullock Bay

*Sybille Bay*[b] (44° 44′ N. 136° 22′ E.) opens between two isolated pinnacled heights, consisting of rocks of crystalline structure, vitrified on the surface. There is a river here, and on the slopes of its valley grow oaks and hazel. The hills consist of clay and sand. Two miles to the north of Sybille Bay is *Pique Bay* (44° 46′ N. 136° 27′ E.), into which a river, with a sand-bar, empties itself. A short distance up this river stands a house, built like those in the north of China, and inhabited by Chinese, who cultivate potatoes, turnips, onions, beans and garlic. A village is said to be at a distance of eight miles, and a town at forty miles. Hence southward, as far as the boundaries of Korea, scattered houses and small villages of Chinese are found at a short distance from the sea. "The name of this region," Kimai Kim[c] tells us, "is Ta-cho-su. It is a kind of freed land which was the former resort, and is the resort at the present time, of a crowd of Chinese and Korean vagabonds; some impelled by the spirit of independence, others escaped from the punishment due to their misdeeds or from the pursuit of their creditors. Accustomed to robbery and crime, they have no principles to guide them. They have latterly however, it is said, chosen a chief to check their own disorders, and established some regular form of government. By a general agreement, they have decided that they would

[b] La Pérouse saw a bay under 44° 45′ N. lat.

[c] Kimai-Kim, a Korean convert to Christianity, visited in 1844 the frontier town of Hun-chun on business connected with the Roman Catholic missions. Annals of the Propagation of the Faith, 1846.

bury alive every man guilty of murder; the chief himself is bound by this law. As they have no women they carry them off wheresoever they find them."

Eighteen miles further south, we come to *Shelter Bay* (44° 28′ N. 136° 2′ E.), which is protected against the north-easterly winds by a prominent bluff. It opens between two prominent headlands, and its shore is level and tolerably wooded. A river two hundred yards wide flows into the bay, and is closed by a shallow bar, within which there are nine feet of water. Its banks are marshy and covered with reeds and sedges. Dwarf oaks, birches and elms are thinly scattered on the hill-slopes. Tronson ascended the river for two miles, when it got shallow, and was overhung with willows, birch and alder. Some cattle were grazing, but there were no habitations in sight.

The coast to the south of Shelter Bay continues hilly, and there are several rivulets flowing through valleys affording excellent pasturage. *Port St. Vladimir* (43° 84′ N. 135° 27′ E.) opens between the rocky promontories of Baliuska and Vatovsky, 1,870 yards apart, with a depth of water of ten fathoms at the entrance. The port is one of the finest on the coast of Manchuria. It consists of three inlets of which the southern is the most capacious, and offers great advantages for refitting and arming vessels. A basin of fresh water, separated from the bay by a narrow strip of land, could, at a trifling cost, be converted into a first-rate dock. The surrounding mountains shelter the bay against all winds. Putiatin met here two Chinese and several Manchu; the former occupied in fishing, and the latter tending the horses and cattle of their masters, who reside further north. Both asserted their independence of the Chinese government.

Scarcely twenty miles south-west of *Port Vladimir* we arrive at another bay, which offers equal if not superior advantages as a naval station. This port, *Port Sir Michael*

*Seymour* (43° 46' N. 135° 19' E.), the *Olga Bay* of the Russians, opens towards the south-east, and is protected by high mountains against north-east and south-west winds. Abrupt rocks of granite rise on both sides of the entrance, and the mountains surrounding the bay itself consist of rough-grained granite and red porphyry of coarse crystalline structure. Gilbert or Avvakum river empties itself into the bay. Having crossed a bar of three feet of water, the depth of the river varies between fourteen and twenty feet for a distance of about five miles; it then divides into numerous creeks. The lower part of the valley is marshy and turfy. High mountains form it, but excepting some abrupt and precipitous crags, there is not a spot void of vegetation. The Chinese who are settled along the river cultivate barley, wheat, hemp, potatoes and kitchen plants. A narrow strait separates the body of the bay from the Careening Harbour, called "Calm Landing-place" (Tikhaya Pristanye) by the Russians; it has a depth of from three and a half to seven fathoms, and at its narrow entrance of four fathoms, and is well protected against winds and waves. A rivulet empties itself into this harbour, flowing through a fertile valley, from the direction of Vladimir Bay. The slopes of the mountains are wooded, and excellent timber for ship-building may be procured at some distance from the ·beach. A pass leads through the mountains north of Olga Bay to the Upper Usuri. The Russians have chosen this bay for their chief naval station on the coast of Manchuria; and it is no doubt the one best adapted, though in common with all other bays along this coast it has the disadvantage of difficulty of communication with the the interior of the country, still in a less degree than any of the others, Castries Bay excepted. But the latter Bay is closed by ice during six months of the year, whilst Olga Bay is almost entirely free.

The country south of Olga Bay continues hilly. It is densely wooded with oaks, and there are occasional firs. The coast is rocky, and in places forms precipitous cliffs. In the distance may be seen a granitic mountain-range. In many creeks are discernible the houses of Chinese settlers, and a few boats and canoes are drawn up on the shore. Passing the small Castle and Islet ports, Nakhimof harbour, and the more extensive Hornet Bay, we arrive at *Victoria Bay*, Gulf of Peter the Great, of the Russians. This bay looks towards the south, and is separated by the Albert Peninsula, and the Eugénie Archipelago, a continuation of it, into two Gulfs, those of Napoleon and Guérin. Albert Peninsula is separated from the Eugénie Archipelago by the Hamelin Strait; and upon the north side of this strait is situated Port May, Vladivostok, that is Dominion of the East, of the Russians. This port is well sheltered against all winds by the hills which surround it. The coast consists of clay-slate, heaved up by rocks of red porphyry, and the entire coast-line exhibits marks of volcanic action. The surrounding country is well wooded with oaks, elms, and walnut, and there are large tracts of fine grazing land abounding in various-coloured flowers. The vine grows luxuriantly, and we are led to suppose that the grapes are really edible, and not, as those of the Amur, merely innocuous. The islands of the Eugénie Archipelago, above twenty in number, vary much in size, the largest being about twenty square miles. They are hilly, covered with verdure, and thinly sprinkled with oaks and hazel. The oaks are of superior quality; pines are scarce, but very thick. Some of the islands afford capacious, and well-sheltered anchorages. The islands are inhabited by some "Tatars," probably Chinese and Koreans. Port Dundas, on the northernmost of these islands opens towards the north-west. The land at the entrance of the port is high and rocky, the rocks consisting of a red conglomerate, boulders of granite, and further up the port, red porphyries. The distance from the entrance of the port to its termination is nearly seven miles. Port Bruce, at the west side of Guérin Gulf, is encircled by a high range of hills of granitic structure. It affords a safe anchorage, but during south-east winds is exposed to a heavy swell. Proceeding south along the coast we arrive at D'Anville Gulf. Through a narrow strait we enter the inner part, consisting of Port Louis, and Napoleon or Posyet harbour. Gold has been found here in small quantities in the sands of the rivulets, and coal abounds. A few miles to the south of D'Anville Gulf, is the mouth of the Tumen River, or Mi-kiang (42° 27′ north latitude), the boundary between Korea and Manchuria. About twenty-five miles above the mouth of the river stands the town of Hun-chun (Hwan-chun-ching), besides Tung-Pu-en-men in the south, the only place of trade between Korea and China.[d] About a hundred Tatar families reside here, and a Mandarin of the second class, with about three hundred soldiers maintains order. The Chinese repair hither from a great distance to carry on trade, and the journey from Ningut is performed with clumsy waggons on two wheels. The general trade is restricted to half a day once every two years, and some Mandarins only enjoy the privilege to trade annually for five days. The Chinese supply the Koreans with dogs, cats, pipes, leather, stag-horn, copper, horses, mules, and asses, and receive in return baskets, kitchen furniture, rice, corn, swine, paper, mats, oxen, furs, and ponies, the latter highly prized for their swiftness. Hun-chun is also famous for its trade in *hai-shay*, a marine weed found in the neighbouring sea.

## The Coast Range.

The coast-range, Sihete-alin of the Chinese, may be considered as an offshoot of the Shan-alin mountains in the south. The crest of the range varies in distance from twenty-

[d] Kimai-Kim, Annals of the Propagation of the Faith, 1846.

five to eighty miles from the coast. Its eastern slope drains into the Channel of Tatary and the Japan Sea, the western into the Usuri and Amur. The rivers entering the sea have but a short course, and are navigable only near the mouth. These mountains attain an elevation of from four to six thousand feet, but where passes cross them they are much lower. They are intersected by deep and generally swampy valleys of numerous rivulets. Many offshoots from the coast-range abut upon the Usuri and Amur. The higher parts of the mountains are densely wooded with conifers, foliferous trees being restricted to the valleys, and lower mountain slopes. The passes are frequented in winter by the natives in their trading journeys, but those in the south alone are of real importance, the others being too long and difficult. The road leading from the town of Hun-chun to Ninguta can now even be used by carriages. Another way leads from the same town to the Hinka Lake, which can only be reached by a path from Guérin Gulf, traversed on horseback. The Upper Usuri is reached from Olga Bay by a pass, rather difficult in its present state, but along which a road will no doubt be carried in a very short time, as the Russians have established themselves in this Bay, and the only communication with the interior leads through this pass. Veniukof crossed the mountains near the sources of the Fudza rivulet, a tributary of the Usuri. Among the passes further north that between the Yai, which flows into the Kidzi Lake, and the Tumji river, which enters the sea some miles north of Port Imperial, is the most important. Its elevation is only six hundred feet.

## THE USURI.

The *Usuri* is, next to the Sungari, the most considerable tributary which the Amur receives from the south. Its sources are in 44° north latitude, and the development of the river, from its origin to the mouth, is four hundred and ninety-seven miles. The Upper Usuri (Sandugu) has a very rapid course, and is hemmed in by mountains on both banks. Below the mouth of the Vongo, the mountains disappear on the left, and near the Sungachan also on the right, and the river then flows through a wide plain, until it again enters the mountains, and having traversed them for about one hundred miles, debouches into the vast prairie, partly swampy, and similar in character to that of the Amur. Among the numerous tributaries of the Usuri, the Dobikhan is remarkable on account of gold being found along its course, but the Sungachan which flows from Khingka (Kenka) Lake is the most considerable. This lake extends between 44° 36′ and 45° north latitude ; it is about sixty miles long and forty wide. The north-east and north-west shores of the lake are level, and swampy tracts extend at the mouth of the rivulets which enter it, and of which the Lefu is the largest. The lake abounds in fish, and the neighbouring mountains are rich in game. About ten villages are dispersed along the shore, and among the inhabitants are five Goldi families, the southernmost representatives of this tribe. A sandy strip of low land separates Khingka Lake from the smaller Dabuka Lake, lying within the same basin. Roads lead hence to Ninguta, Hun-chun, and a town (Furden) on the Suifong, which enters Guérin Gulf. At the commencement of last year the Russians had twenty-four stations along the Usuri.

The Usuri was explored in 1858, by M. Veniukof, previous to its occupation by the Russians, and we introduce here the narrative of that traveller.

### VENIUKOF'S EXPLORATION OF THE USURI.

" The desire to explore the river Usuri to its source was expressed at a time, when, though we had gained a firm footing on the Amur itself, we had not yet gained the consent of the Chinese to advance without let or hindrance into a district which they chose to consider their own. It was to be expected, therefore, that the suspicious Chinese and Manchu officials would throw difficulties in the way of an expedition, and try to prevent its reaching its bourn.[e] Even now some obstacles had to be removed; but the treaty of Aigun greatly facilitated my operations, for in it the right to navigate the whole of the Usuri had been granted to us, and if necessary we could treat the Chinese with firmness.

"In order still more to further my proceedings, a special letter, written in Manchu, was given me by order of the Governor-General of Eastern Siberia. In it was set forth my official position, and the Chinese authorities were requested to afford me all the co-operation and assistance in their power. This letter I was obliged to produce but once, at the mouth of the Nishan. At all other places our approach was well known, for the officer commanding the guard at the mouth of the Usuri, had reported along the whole line our intention of ascending it. According to custom the Manchu took measures to prevent any one from rendering us assistance or accompanying us. Fortunately, owing to the good name Russia enjoys in Eastern Asia and possibly also to our own courteous behaviour, the natives, but particularly the Goldi, received us at all times in the most friendly manner. On my return-journey from the sea-coast, I could convince myself of the fact, that the Goldi were rejoiced that Russians at length had made their appearance on the Usuri; Russians, who govern their subjects of another nationality without oppressing them, and who were long expected to free them from the yoke of the Manchu.

"The expedition entrusted to my guidance was not very numerous. It included an officer in command of twelve

[e] M. Veniukof refers here to the time previous to the treaty of Aigun.

Cossacks, an interpreter able to speak Goldi, and my own personal attendants, sixteen in all. Two topographers then staying in the Maritime Province were to accompany me, but the orders sent them from Irkutsk to join me arrived too late. Consequently all the labour devolved upon me. As I did not want my map to deceive those who subsequently might avail themselves of it, I did not like to trust to an estimate of distances by eyesight, but walked the whole distance to the mouth of the Lifule, along the bank of the river, counting the paces. This of course retarded our progress considerably. The road led through high dense grass and swamps, across large stones, or through thick forest, and so overtired me that generally, after having entered my remarks in the journal, I fell asleep on the spot. One of the chief objects of the mission, viz., the collection of the principal products, and a description of the country further from the river, and of the inhabitants, I could not possibly manage by myself. As I desired to ascertain occasionally the accuracy of the map of the Jesuits published by D'Anville, I once entrusted one of my companions with the task of ascending a tributary river. In order to supply to some extent the want of astronomical instruments, I carefully laid down my route from day to day on a Mercator's projection, and am led to believe from it, that the old statements of the Jesuits are very near the truth, and that D'Anville's map (of Manchuria) may be looked upon as the most correct of all hitherto published.

Early on the 13th June we left the post at the mouth of the Usuri. Rapidly we passed the Khœkhtsi range (Khukhchir-Khurgin) on the right bank of the river. This range, it would appear, is a ramification of a mountain-chain which extends eastward from the mouth of the Usuri, and separates the tributaries of the Amur (Dondon) from those of the Usuri (Ky) and the coast rivers (Fish river). These rivers probably rise where this chain joins the coast-range known as Sikhota-Alin. The mountain-ridges everywhere are steep and covered with forest, where we find elm, walnut, oak, black and white birch, aspen, ash and bird-cherry, and a few cedars. There are neither pines nor firs. Vines and jessamines are found on a few spots, and on the southern fringe of the forest surrounding the Khœkhtsi, apples and even bergamot pears, the vegetation in fact reminding one of the most favoured parts of Central Europe. Beyond the Khœkhtsi Mountains both banks of the Usuri are formed by an uniform grass-plain, with a few groves of oaks, elms, aspens and willows. For a distance of almost fifty miles, following the course of the river, the banks are inundated in July, and are therefore little adapted for settlement. To compensate for this the lakes and swamps abound in game. In the lakes are also found fresh-water turtles, which are eaten by the Goldi of the vicinity. A great many of the eggs of these turtles, which they bury in the sand at the margin of the lakes, are destroyed by birds of prey. The abundance of fish in the shallow places of the Usuri is really wonderful. At times, when we passed unruffled and shallow parts of the river, numerous carp, gamboling on the surface of the water, would sometimes jump into our boats. Fish constitutes the chief article of food among the neighbouring Goldi. They do not however make much clothing from fish-skins, but use coarse cotton-stuffs. The name of Yu-pi-da-tzi, *i.e.* "Fish-skin Strangers," given to them by the Chinése, has therefore but little significance.

"On the second day of our journey it began to rain, and this rain continued for forty-five consecutive days. These rains, which owe their origin to the neighbouring sea, constitute a peculiarity in the climate of the valley of the Usuri. They cause that river and some of its tributaries to have a super-abundance of water. To me this copious fall of rain was very inconvenient; it greatly interfered with our labours, and necessitated the seeking of our night's quarters early, so as to have time to dry our clothes before retiring to rest. The banks of the river are occasionally sandy, but for the most part covered with clay-mud, and walking along them was rather a difficult task. The rains caused the grass along the river, which until now had been soft, to get tough. As these rains occur every summer about the same period, future settlers will have to mow the grass first in May, and afterwards in September. The river forms here numerous branches, enclosing islands. The rivulet Ky enters the Usuri from the right, twenty-two miles above its mouth. Near its mouth stood yet in 1855 the village of Kinda, indicated on the map of Maximowicz; it has since been burned down, and the Goldi removed to the left bank of the Usuri, and call their two poor huts the village of Khungari. During the first two days of our journey we found only three villages, viz., Turme, Jacha (Joada), and Khungari, having in all but eight houses. One or two Chinese families have joined the native Goldi.

"In the evening of the third day we came to the mouth of the Khoro or Kholo, erroneously called Por on former maps. This river rises in high mountains at a distance of two hundred and fifty miles, has a very rapid course, and on entering the plain divides into several branches; it carries along with it large masses of stones, and trunks of trees, in an immense volume of water, and enters the Usuri by five mouths, the two northern of which are particularly rapid. The temperature of this current was (in June) three degrees (Reaumur) less than that of the Usuri. As we approached the Khoro we could see localities on its right bank well adapted for settlements, and partially occupied by Chinese and Goldi. The village of Khoicha, forty miles above the mouth of the Usuri, extends along both banks of the river for four miles, but the whole village only contains nine houses, dispersed in the forest. At the time of our visit, half of the inhabitants were absent. We availed ourselves of this opportunity to visit one of the houses, the doors of which were not locked. The household furniture consisted of a few vessels of wood and clay, some fishing implements, and a large cauldron fixed on the hearth. In a store-house, built on poles to preserve it against the rats, we saw a swan hanging, and found traces of peltry. A small temple which stood apart, attracted my especial attention. On a wall inside was a very bad painting of a deity, probably by some Chinese artist. A small box, into which incense is put from time to time, stood in front of this temple. To me this discovery was very interesting; for at the time of the Jesuits not the least trace of public worship existed among the "Yu-pi-da-tzi." The bonzes found nothing to attract them to a country where neither wheat nor rice was being cultivated. But in spite of this the gods of China have found their way to these regions.

"On the 16th of June, we met at the mouth of the river Sim a young Orochi, from the Khoro, who had also been on the sea, among a family of Goldi. He told us that in a canoe made of the trunk of a tree we could ascend the Khoro to its source, which lay in the midst of high mountains, whence the sea might be reached on foot in four days. From the Goldi we heard that the Khoro in its upper course receives a tributary, the Chernai, whence there is a portage to the Samalga, a considerable river flowing into the sea. Maximowicz ascertained that there was a path from the sources of the Khoro to a rivulet falling into the Amur, and called Pakhsa[f] (called Peksha by Admiral Nevilsky). The Chinese who go from the Usuri to the Amur to buy sables take this road, from which we may calculate upon the region being populated (?).

"On the following day, 17th June, heavy rains in the morning made it necessary to make a halt about noon, in

---

[f] The Pakhsa enters the Amur at the village of Khula, a few miles above the Dondon or Sole.

order to take measures against our provisions being soaked. On this occasion, I for the first time got an insight into the relations between Goldi and Manchu. The Goldi fishermen near whose tent we landed were very much frightened when they saw us. At first they were inclined to run away, but finally thought it best to submit to the decrees of Providence, and to the arbitrary conduct of the Manchu, for such at first they took us to be. They were greatly surprised when in return for a large fish which they brought us, we presented them with two or three yards of *Daba*. A woman, who until now had remained in concealment with her boy, three years old, came forth and celebrated our generosity in a song. A great many children, shy as they usually are, surrounded us without fear. Among these poor people, I observed a man whose face and figure differed considerably from the usual type of the Goldi and the Tunguzians in general. He was muscular and rather corpulent, and his long beard and mustaches gave him the appearance of a Russian peasant in a foreign dress. His eyes were round and large, but the large space between them indicated Mongolian race. Possibly exceptions of this kind may have existed among the Goldi when our Cossacks first came to the Amur. The Goldi (of the Usuri) has however no very clear idea of the history of his tribe. He has heard that there are Russians who have come to settle on the Amur, but is afraid to ascertain for himself for fear of the Manchu. When he pays his ordinary tribute to the Manchu official at Turme,—and this consists of all the sables he may be possessed of,—he returns, and in conjunction with some family related to his own, sets to work to secure the necessary food and clothing for the winter. He goes to the forests to hunt, and returns before the inundation, so as to have time to dry a sufficient supply of fish to last through the winter. On the occasion of our visit a great number of fish already hung around the birch-bark tents, and all were engaged in its preparation.

"On the 18th of June, after the usual fogs, the weather was fine and not very hot; but about three in the afternoon clouds gathered on the horizon, the rain descended in streams, and the lightning flashed. This was the second thunder-storm since our departure from the mouth of the Usuri. The rain soon left off, but the heavens continued clouded, and the violent easterly wind gave little hope for improvement. About noon we claimed the hospitality of a Chinese, who had been informed of our approach by the Goldi whom we met the day before. He received us very frigidly, and to all our questions answered 'No.' Once indeed he relaxed from his silence, and that only to deceive us, by telling us we should reach the sources of the Usuri in ten days. He forbade his servant, a Goldi, to hold communication with us. We told the Chinese that we knew as well as he could tell us what awaited us, and that respectable people treated travellers in a less off-hand manner. On this he grew more polite and offered us salad; we would not however accept of anything. The Goldi labourer ran after us and told us that the same kind of reception awaited us everywhere by order of the Manchu authorities, and that we should do well to rely solely upon people of his own tribe.

"On the same day, the 18th June, we came to the mouth of the Aom, which has a course of one hundred and twenty miles. Along the right bank of the Usuri an uninterrupted mountain-chain was visible, which occasionally came close to the river. I found here several pieces of petrified wood, the fibres of which were so distinct that it resembled rather a piece of wood just broken off a tree than a fossil. The view on the right bank of the Usuri changed from this day. On the horizon, we constantly kept in sight the rugged summits of a mountain-chain. On the left bank the plain continued, but in the distance blue hills made their appearance. Localities suitable for settlement are much more frequent here on the eastern bank of the river. Meadows and small groves alternate with forests of oak, birch, elm and service-trees. Fine lilies, orange-coloured and yellow, were in full bloom, apple-trees and roses the same. Notwithstanding the rain, we advanced on that day twenty-six miles, and encamped during the night in face of the hills near the mouth of the Nor.

"The two following days, 19th and 20th June, we spent in crossing the mouth of the Nor, and succeeded in getting friendly with the Goldi who live there. At first they were suspicious and reticent, but a small glass of brandy soon set loose their tongues, and they kept wagging them incessantly. They told me that a town stood near the sources of the Nor, which they knew only as "Khoton." The Sungari thence may be reached in three days. The population along the Nor consists mostly of Chinese, and foot-paths connect their houses. Notwithstanding the pains I took, the Goldi refused to communicate to me any detail about the town, excepting that it was the seat of the authorities upon whom they depended, that is probably the station of a small flotilla, with a few warehouses. At all events, this town is not large. According to my informants, the ascent of the Nor in a canoe requires about twenty days, and the distance therefore is about three hundred miles. An inconsiderable mountain separates its source from that of the Voken, which flows into the Sungari.

"About noon on the 21st we crossed the Abuera, which has a course of several hundred miles, but can be forded at its mouth. The water was cold and turbid, but this may have been in consequence of the rain. A short distance above the Sibku rivulet we came to the village bearing the same name, the largest of all we had as yet seen, for it consisted of seven houses, two inhabited by Chinese, the others by Goldi. The Goldi here have neat vegetable gardens, and even cultivate barley. Above the Sibku, the mountains on the right bank of the Usuri approach close to the river. They occasionally afford a glimpse into valleys about two miles wide, and eminently fit for settlements. About the mouth of the Bikin these mountains attain their maximum height. At the time of our visit the summits were enveloped in fog, which in the morning sinks into the valley. The river Bikin enters the Usuri one hundred and eighty miles above the mouth of that river, and in an undivided stream flows through a valley about two miles wide. It appears to be navigable and much less rapid than the Khoro. According to the 'Chinese geography' it has a length of five hundred *Li*. A road leads from its source over the mountains in five days to the sea, and terminates in a small bay where there is a village. Along the banks of the Bikin are six villages inhabited by Orochi. Chinese are not met with here.

Above the Bikin the Usuri flows through a valley bounded on both sides by picturesque mountains. Here splendid sites for settlements are met with, for instance at the mouth of the Khankuli rivulet, five miles above the Bikin, at the village of Naize and elsewhere. At the rivulet Tsifaku, which has a very broad mouth, the mountains on the right bank of the Usuri recede towards the east, and that rivulet flows along a very extensive plain mostly well timbered. Between the Bikin and Tsifaku just mentioned, the rivers Duman and Kirkin, each about one hundred miles long, enter the Usuri from the left. They flow through narrow valleys where Ginseng (Shen-shen) is found, which has attracted some Chinese settlers. The houses of these Chinese are connected by paths, which also lead to the western slope of the mountain-chain where the rivers rise which flow to the Sungari.

"On the 27th June we were overtaken by some Goldi, twelve miles above the Tsifaku, who were going in their birch-bark canoes from the mouth of the Usuri to the Imma. They had left Turme three days after us, and were the only people during the whole of our journey who brought us news from the Russians. According to their own statement they were on a visit to some relatives on the Imma, but it almost appeared as if they had instructions from the Chinese official at Turme regarding ourselves. At all events we saw them subsequently in company of the Chinese at the Imma. They asked whether the Governor-General intended himself to explore the Usuri, and whether the Russians were coming in the ensuing year to settle along it. When they were told such would not be the case, they communicated our answer to the Manchu official commanding at the Imma.

"At our night's quarters between the Bikin and Nishan we had plenty of leisure to observe the customs of the Goldi whom we met there. One of them having seen silver in our possession proposed to exchange it for sable; and when I asked what he was going to do with the metal, he told me that his old mother was near her death, and that he wished according to custom to place a silver bracelet round her wrist on her death-bed. Another Goldi had his tail cut off as a sign of mourning for a deceased mother. The Goldi are addicted to polygamy, and in many instances from a feeling of duty. One man of thirty, with a very large family, had three wives, two of whom had become his by the death of his younger brothers. He thought it incumbent upon himself fairly to distribute his favours amongst all, and the eldest of them, as it were the mother of the family, exacted obedience from the two others. Like all other nations amongst whom polygamy is in vogue, the Goldi are very jealous. It was only by special favour that our host permitted me and the interpreter to remain in the tent during his absence. Our people he kept as far away as possible. On our departure he expressed himself in flattering terms about the good conduct of the Russians. The Manchu act differently.

"In the course of a fortnight, from the 13th to 27th June, we had but one day without rain.[g] The river wås evidently rising, and on arriving at the Imma we found that many of the sandbanks were covered with water. Owing to the flood, fishing had been given up in the middle of June, and the Goldi were content with catching a few carp for their own use, and they had no fish for sale. To us this was very disagreeable, for we had now to live almost entirely upon salt provisions. Fortunately we were all of us well, excepting some slight head-aches and derangements of the digestive organs.

"On the 29th we crossed the mouth of the Imma, the largest tributary of the Usuri on the right. The current of the latter was all the time very slow, and it is only above the Imma that it becomes more rapid. The whole extent of the river, from the Imma to its mouth, is however very well adapted for navigation, and would not present any obstacle to steam-boats. Its navigation is much easier than that of the Middle Amur, for there are neither so many branches nor sand-bars. The Imma also is probably navigable to a great extent, if we may judge from the level country near its mouth. It has been hitherto navigated only by the small canoes of the Orochi, Goldi and Chinese. According to the Chinese Geography the Niman or Imma, under which name it is better known to the natives, has a course of three hundred miles, and is formed by the junction of the two streams, the Imma Proper and the Akul. According to the statements of the natives the sea may be reached from the sources of the Imma in five days; the mountains are very high and the journey fatiguing. The Chinese do not therefore often avail themselves of this communication. Their settlements are situated near the mouth of the river, the upper part of which is inhabited by Orochi. The Goldi

[g] This is opposed to Veniukof's previous observation of forty-five consecutive days of rain.

told me these latter had five or six villages, but did not know the number of inhabitants. Probably these villages are not larger than those of the Goldi, and contain two or three houses each. This would be a very small population for so extensive a region. The country on the Usuri, above and below the mouth of the Imma, is perfectly level, except towards the north, where may be seen a rather high mountain-chain stretching east and west, but does not reach the Usuri. According to the natives the sources of the Imma and Akul are separated by lofty mountains, and in the upper course these rivers flow rapidly between high banks. The water in them rises about the same period as that of the Usuri, and on our return we found the waters of both inundating the shores and flooding a sandbank or spit, at their confluence. The water of the Imma was dark, and could be distinguished for three miles flowing side by side with the turbid waters of the Usuri. The Imma certainly deserves the particular attention of any future explorer, and near its mouth must arise one of the chief settlements on the Usuri.

"Opposite the mouth of the Imma, on a prominent point of some hills consisting of red marl, forming cliffs towards the river, is situated the Chinese village of Imma or Niman. This has been made a Manchu post. The lower part of the village where we stayed—not yet being aware of the existence of the upper—consists of a large house inhabited by a great number of Chinese, who cultivate extensive kitchen-gardens and corn-fields in the neighbourhood. Our wealthy landlord keeps a kind of hotel or restaurant, and we found there a great many Chinese and Goldi, either as guests or labourers. The arrangement of the rooms reminds one of the hotels of inferior class at Peking, with which one of my companions was acquainted. Small plantations of ginseng are found here; they might probably be greater were it not for the vicinity of the Manchu authorities. At the Manchu post, half a mile higher up, on the banks of the Usuri, I thought it expedient to produce my papers. I made no stay in the village, but observed many horses and oxen of a very excellent breed. These latter, according to Chinese custom, are used exclusively for agricultural purposes and for carrying heavy weights. The horses are of special advantage in communicating with other posts in Manchuria. A road leads hence to the Muren, whence the chief bridle-path leads to Sansin on the Sungari. This no doubt is the road taken by the Roman-Catholic Missionaries de la Brunière and Venault.

" Low hills consisting of a loose reddish earth occur on the Usuri above the Imma. They are not offshoots from the mountains, but form the edge of a plateau densely wooded, and well adapted for cultivation. This plateau, called Dotzili-oforo in the Chinese Geography occasionally approaches close to the river, and then again recedes a few miles. For about a day's journey beyond the Imma, sites adapted for settlement may be frequently noticed. At twenty-five miles above Imma the Usuri receives the northern branch of the river Muren, the most considerable of its tributaries, and the sources of which are in the mountains east of Ninguta. At its mouth it forms a delta, having an area of two hundred square miles. The deltoic branches radiate about forty miles from the Usuri, and none of them separately has a volume of water equal to that of the Imma. The northern arm has a breadth of only fifty to sixty yards.

" The Usuri between the Muren and Sungachan has a more rapid current, its course is very tortuous, and whilst the direct distance between the upper mouth of the Muren and Sungachan is fifteen miles, it is thirty-six following the windings of the river. But though the Usuri is not very wide here, it carries a large body of water, and flowing in one bed, offers no obstacles to navigation. The formation of small inlets or creeks is peculiar to this part of the river, and into these is drained, after each inundation, the water from the plains. There is scarcely a reach without such an inlet or bay, and the water remains in them during summer. The Goldi reap in these bays their richest harvest of fish. The average breadth of the Usuri is here two hundred and thirty yards, and at times only one hundred and sixty, but the depth of the water-way at low water is seven to nine feet.

"Since leaving Imma, we had been accompanied by four Chinese, with a Manchu soldier at their head. These formed our escort by order of the officer commanding at Imma, and acted as spies upon our doings. They were very polite, but always preceded us and forbade the Goldi to accompany us, as I was at that time looking out for a guide. They succeeded very well in foiling my endeavours, and I only found one man not altogether disinclined to serve us as guide. He was an old man from the village Choborka to whom life had become indifferent. 'The Manchu,' he said, 'interdict us from rendering you assistance, and any one acting contrary to their orders would of course fare badly. But I am so old that I should be quite willing to accompany you or to die, had I not a pain in my left leg. I know you are the heralds of other Russians, who will come to free us from the Manchu yoke, but as long as these wild beasts remain here, it is dangerous to be your friend.' I subsequently ascertained that the fears of this old man were by no means exaggerated. On approaching the tent of a Goldi, dwelling above the Sungachan he trembled for fear, thinking we were Manchu; but when I asked him a few questions and tendered payment for some millet, he told us he had cause to fear the Manchu. His father, his mother and his two brothers, driven to desperation by the Manchu collector of tribute, had strangled themselves. These collectors come once or twice annually, and by aid of the stick extort all the sables these poor people may be possessed of. Not putting trust in any of their assertions, they continue the beating after all the furs have been given up to them, in the hope of getting at concealed treasures. Afterwards, on my return, I heard that five Manchu had ascended the Usuri, and called the Goldi to an account for communicating with us. A sincere old Goldi here said to me, 'Look! five men were able to beat above a hundred, and they wanted us—for our own sakes of course—to go to Khœktsir,' at the Usuri mouth, where the Manchu had a station.

"On the 4th July in the evening we reached the mouth of the Sungachan, a river flowing from Lake Kingka (called Sinkai by the Chinese from the northern provinces, and Kenka by the Goldi). Our progress became slower and slower. The Usuri, though passing through a level country, has here a very strong current. I had expected to find the Usuri beyond the Sungachan, reduced to half its former size, but was very much mistaken. Above the Sungachan the current is stronger, and the windings of the river are even more numerous than before."

[Veniukof gives here some details regarding the Kingka Lake, which we have incorporated into our description of Manchuria].

"At length, on the 7th July we succeeded in persuading a Goldi to be our guide to the Kuburkhan. We might for the present have dispensed with his services, but I thought it advisable to avail myself of this opportunity to gain so far the confidence of the Goldi, that they might not fear at any future time to communicate with us. The absence of our Chinese spies facilitated this, and conducted by our Goldi we reached the Kuburkhan in two days. The stream was excessively rapid.

"The country between the Sungachan and Kuburkhan is in most cases well adapted for settlements. Low hills are scattered over the plain, and in the neighbourhood of the

Kuburkhan high hills approach close to the banks of the Usuri. They are wooded with oak, and would well repay gardening and agriculture. In the forests, vines and walnuts abound. Conifers have not as yet been met with. Up to this point the following may be observed regarding the vegetation along the Usuri. Below the Imma, the oak prevails on the mountains. Where the plains are wooded many aspens, elms, walnuts, black and white birches, ashes, maples, and occasionally lime-trees, are met with. In young forests we find vines, roses, and a great many lilies. In the grassland there is much worm-wood; and the pulse, which grows here, renders it almost impossible to walk through the grass, which is five feet high. Then the field-pink-clover, marsh-ranunculus also thrive here. The meadows upon the whole have much resemblance to those about the Sungari, but the forests differ from those of the Amur. The elms attain here a height of one hundred feet, with a girth of ten. The walnuts and limes are also of extraordinary height, but unfortunately the former but seldom bear fruit, and it may be the whole growing power is absorbed by the trunk and leaves. This is however not a solitary case. Humboldt says 'it is remarkable that some plants, though otherwise of large growth, do not flower in certain localities. Such is the case for instance with the European olive, cultivated since centuries near Quito, on the Equator, at an elevation of 9000 feet; the walnut, the hazelnut, and the olive of the Mauritius.' This may possibly be accounted for by the moist climate and cold nights.

"After two days, about noon on the 10th July, we reached the mouth of a small rivulet remarkable for its dark-brown waters. It is identical, probably, with the Carma of D'Anville's map, but known to the natives as the little Situkhu.

"It enters the Usuri through a deep transverse valley, and at its mouth is a splendid site for a settlement, the best of all that I have seen on the Usuri. The heights, which are at a distance of about three or four miles from the right bank of the Usuri are wooded; foliferous trees prevail, but now and then may be seen a cedar or a pine. The current of the river keeps increasing, and its depth in many places in May and to the middle of June is two or three feet only. At the time however when we navigated the river the depth of the water-way was ten feet. This portion of the Usuri, from Sungachan to the Nintu is very thinly populated. To all appearance this tract forms a boundary of the actual territory of the Manchu, for beyond, towards the east, we find Chinese almost independent of them.

"On the 11th July, we passed a remarkable rock of little elevation, rising on an island in the middle of the river. The river here flows through a forest, and a great many trunks of trees, carried down by the current, have been washed ashore, and often impede navigation. Frequently we were compelled to push on our boats with poles or to land and tow it, for owing to the rapid current, it might, through the least carelessness, have been shattered against some of these trees.

"On the 13th July, we came to the mouth of the great Situkhu, the Kurumé of D'Anville's map. Here a small Chinese village has been built, in a fine open spot, the inhabitants of which engage in agriculture and provide the Ginseng seekers, of whom there are many in the neighbouring mountains, with millet. They refused however to sell any millet to us, though they had plenty, pleading ignorance of the Goldi language. Our guide knew Chinese, and they apparently upbraided him for accompanying us.

"On the 14th July, we crossed the forty-fifth degree of latitude, and reached the mouth of the Dobikhu (Khue-bir), where we found a guide who proved very useful by his goodwill and knowledge of the country. To us this day was trebly fortunate: we had got within a degree of latitude from the goal of our journey, found a competent guide, and escaped the espionage of the Manchu officials, who do not often make their appearance so high up the Usuri. The Goldi agreed to accompany us to the mouth of the Nintu, where he promised to get one of his relatives, an Orochi, to go on with us. This promise he kept. To my surprise I heard that the Chinese dig gold in the mountains on the Upper Dobikhu, which they take for sale to China and Korea without much minding the authorities at the neighbouring town of Hun-chun. My surprise was very reasonable, for the jealousy with which the government at Peking watch over the exploration of precious metals even in China itself is well-known. But in Manchuria mining operations are interdicted altogether, for 'it would be indecorous to disturb the earth upon which were born the celebrated ancestors of the reigning dynasty.' My informant was not able to explain satisfactorily the manner in which the Chinese procure the gold, excepting that they find it in the river itself and not in mines.

"Advancing from the Dobikhu towards the south-east, we came through a country bearing traces of a past civilization and a previous numerous population. I allude to some remains of ancient towns and fortresses, which are found along the Usuri between 44° and 45° north latitude. These ruins probably date from the time of the dynasty of the Gin, or Niuchi. It would be difficult to say against whom these earthen walls, which are situated on the summits of high mountains or in the plain, served as a protection. But they were no doubt regular fortresses communicating with each other. Perhaps they were erected as bulwarks against the Mengu (Moho) of the Amur, the Manguns of our days, with whom the Gin were frequently at war. There is no doubt that these walls surrounded large towns, and the natives of the present day simply call them ancient Manchu towns (Manchu-Ballapti-Khoton).

"On the 17th July we came to the mouth of the Vongo; the Usuri here flows between mountains. We found a Ginseng plantation, and inquired into the cultivation of this plant. The settlement numbers twenty hands, all of them Chinese, and belongs to a rich merchant who lives at Peking. Considering the value of this plant in China, the proprietor of these few acres must draw from them an immense revenue. More than thirty beds, each about thirty-five yards long, and four feet wide, are planted in rows with this expensive root. The berries were not yet ripe, but had begun to get red. The beds are protected against the sun by tents or by sheds of wood. The earth must be a rich black mould and loose. When the plant has attained a height of four or five inches it is supported by a stick. The beds are carefully weeded and watered. The plantation is surrounded by a hedge and carefully guarded. The guard is strictly forbidden to sell any root, and our endeavours to purchase one were in vain.

"He probably feared the other labourers might betray him to the proprietors, but when we left he invited us to pay him a visit on our return, and gave us to understand that then he might possibly gratify our wish. I heard that there were many such plantations in the neighbourhood, and was anxious to know where, and at what prices the root was sold. The Chinese themselves answered evasively or not all, but our guide told us they were taken to Hun-chun and there sold to merchants who either carried them across the sea or inland.[h]

"After a difficult navigation of five days we came to the mouth of the Nintu, where we waited for our promised guide. I prepared to continue our journey on foot, further progress by water being impossible. Our Goldi soon brought his relative, who annually visited the sea-coast, but we had much ado to get him to accompany us. We were obliged to

---

[h] Ginseng is imported by sea into Canton. Veniukof's observations on the sale of the Ginseng will be found further on.

agree to his taking us by a road which he knew, and not in the direction which we wished. Early on the 21st July, we started. We had not been able to procure any horses, for the Chinese would not lend us any, though they offered to sell them for about £10 each. We were compelled therefore to walk, carrying our baggage on our backs. Our burthens were heavy and the roads bad, so that we were forced, as early as the 23rd, to leave one of our exhausted Cossacks with Chinese settlers. The 24th July especially will never be forgotten by us. About noon the Orochi led us to a deep ford at the Fudza river which he told us to wade through, as otherwise we should be compelled to ascend the river to its source. We consented; the water reached up to our breasts; we landed, and we were just going to light a fire when we perceived that three more branches of the river had to be crossed. At last the main branch of the Fudza barred our passage. I ordered a raft to be constructed, but having launched it after three hours, three men preparing to navigate it, it was carried away by the current, and thrown upon a small island, where it was shattered to pieces. Our anxiety was great, until we ascertained that the men had been saved. But unfortunately they had been cast upon the opposite shore, and we had no means of getting to them; a rope thrown towards them was not long enough. We succeeded however in letting them have some biscuit and some means of lighting a fire.

"On the 25th, we retraced our steps through the five fords, the water having considerably risen during the night, and rejoined our people. The difficulty we had in ascending a rocky slope on the right bank of the Fudza may be judged of from the fact, that we did so singly, so that in case one of us slipped, the others might not be precipitated through his fall. Having at length regained our former track, I asked the guide whether he was sure we should not again meet with such perilous passages, and whether it was likely we should come out upon Vladimir Bay, the goal of our journey. He gave a satisfactory answer, and we felt the more inclined to believe him, as the Chinese whom we met on the 24th, had given us similar information. But to our great discomfort such was not the case.

" I will state here how we got from the valley of the Usuri to the Fudza, and why, having lost our way, we did not at once return to the right track. The fact is, the inhabitants only call the river Usuri below its junction with the Fudza. The upper part they call Sandugu. When we engaged the Orochi to take us to the sea, I made it a condition that he was to conduct us along the Usuri, and not along the Nintu. During the first two days he did as we desired, but when I observed on the third day (23rd July) that we were going more and more towards the east, instead of south, I asked him the name of the river towards which he was taking us, and we learned that it was upon the Fudza. At first I felt inclined to return to the Sandugu, but as I found from D'Anville's map that the sources of the Fudza were nearer to Vladimir Bay than those of the Usuri (Sandugu), and as I desired to become somewhat acquainted with the country surrounding that harbour, I resolved to continue our journey, and to return by way of the Usuri. Moreover all the natives agreed that the pass towards which we were going was the most convenient. On the 27th July, we did in reality cross a low, swampy, mountain ridge, which separates the Fudza from the Lifule river, running towards the sea.

" The country from the mouth of the Nintu up to this pass presents a large valley half-a-mile to four miles wide, and is well adapted for agriculture. It is wooded, and elms and oaks abound; but as we approach the pass, there are, at first isolated and after a while more frequently, conifers, cedars, larches, and pines, between birches, elms, aspens, and other foliferous trees. The cedars here are of splendid growth. The ridge itself is covered exclusively with pines, and on its slope we find birches also. The Fudza from its source to its junction with the Sandugu is seventy-five miles long. Many Chinese are settled along its banks, and engage in agriculture. They grow millet, barley, wheat, spelt, and also hemp, potatoes, cucumbers, pumpkins, and vegetables. The produce suffices for their own wants and those of the Ginseng-seekers. The fields are cultivated with that industry which distinguishes the inhabitants of the celestial empire. Many of them keep oxen, horses, and fowls. The horses are not large, but strongly built; the oxen are of a large and excellent breed, and in good condition. Besides being used for ploughing, and the conveyance of heavy loads, these animals are employed in the mills, which are attached to almost every house, and the millstone is set in motion by a horse (as shewn on the annexed illustration). The flour when ground

MANCHU MILL.

is put into bins. Some of the Chinese have small distilleries with copper retorts. All Chinese go into the mountains to hunt, and many have match-locks. Among the hunting trophies are the skins of the panther, of brown and black bears, red foxes, and a few sables; the latter however are of very inferior quality. The larger animals are hunted also during the summer. The Chinese are in the habit of hanging up their hunting spoils in the small idol-temples which stand near almost every house; they do this from a superstitious belief that otherwise their next chase might prove unlucky.

"When I got into the valley of the Lifule, called Tadukhu by the Orochi, I saw with pleasure that it extended to the south-east. We did not therefore get any further out of our route to Port Vladimir. We were certainly further northwards than we originally intended, but our divergence was thoroughly compensated for by the discovery of very fertile tracts not far from the sources of the Lifule, and the distance to Port Vladimir, from any settlements which at a future period may be founded here, will scarcely exceed twenty miles. On the 28th July we came upon the first Chinese house on the Lifule; on the following day they increased in number. I had expected to reach the sea on the 29th, for the Lifule has a length of only fifty-five miles, but owing to its many windings, which we had to wade through with care, we did not reach the sea before the 30th — a happy day for us. A strong north-east wind, blowing in the direction of the coast, dispersed the clouds, and the fog, which until now concealed the summits of the mountains, rose and disappeared. Having ordered my people to rest themselves, I ascended a mountain whence I had a splendid view of the neighbouring country. I was not however able to keep my footing upon the top of this mountain, for the wind there blew with the violence of a hurricane, carrying heavy stones before it. Descending, I tried to cross to the right bank of the Lifule, but owing to the depth of the river did not succeed. On my return I gave orders to erect a cross on a small mound, upon which I placed an inscription stating that I had been here on the 30th July, 1858. In the meantime the Cossacks prepared for our onward journey, and engaged in seal-fishing. The Orochi wandered along the sea-shore and gathered Kai-tzai, a well-known sea-weed, of a brownish colour and about seven feet long. The herds of horses and cows of the settlers of the Lifule pastured in this picturesque valley. The nearest village stands about eight miles from the sea, and we only saw the tents of some herdsmen. The Chinese must either be afraid of the sea, or they do not care about it. Besides what advantages would it offer to people who have no boats to navigate it; along the whole course of the Lifule we saw no more than five or six canoes, and these only served to cross the river. But even were they to engage in ship-building no benefit could possibly accrue. It would scarcely be worth while to carry on commerce with the few scattered nomades, and should they wish to be pirates they would find no opportunity for carrying on their pursuits.[1]

"We intended to continue our journey on the morning of the 30th, but I was attacked by a sudden illness, and we were in consequence obliged to retrace our steps to the Fudza. Immediately on taking some food I was seized with violent pains in the stomach and ringing in the ears, as if I had been poisoned.[j] A few drops of water which I took eased my pains for the moment, but they returned with redoubled violence, and very much frightened my people. I was much relieved by a copious emetic, but my weakness scarcely allowed me to walk, and in making the attempt I had to support myself upon the arm of one of the Cossacks. While I was lying on the grass,

[1] Nevertheless trade is being engaged in along the coast of Manchuria. La Pérouse mentions the Bitchy who come from the south in boats to Castries Bay, and Tronson, more recently, met sea-going boats of the natives in some of the coast rivers.—R.

[j] We had dined that day in the house of a Chinaman who wished me to become acquainted with the way in which he prepared his food. His salt no doubt had been mixed with some substance which made it taste sweet, and appears to disagree with Europeans, though not necessarily poisonous.

two miles from our last night's quarters, some thirty Chinese came up and threatened our Orochi guide, who fortunately was accompanied by our interpreter and an armed Cossack. As they drew nearer we found it was their intention to kill the Orochi because he had shewn us the way, and they frightened him so much that he got black in the face and lost the use of his tongue. The interpreter understood the Chinese who spoke Orochi, and explained to me the state of affairs, telling me that the Chinese desired to see the notes I had been taking. I might have resented such impertinence by a few musket-balls without at all deviating from the peaceable character of my mission; the Chinese, however, retreated some distance, but continued to threaten our Orochi. It required a great deal of persuasion to induce the Orochi to keep in our company, and he refused point-blank to guide us to the Vladimir Bay, declaring that he would run away if we used compulsion, and leave us without means to find our way back. I did not think it advisable to separate my small force to fetch the Cossack whom we had been compelled to leave at the Fudza, nor did I feel sufficiently strong myself to continue the journey. We resolved therefore to return to the Nintu where our boats were. On the 4th August we arrived at the Chinese house where our Cossack had remained. He had by this time quite recovered.

" This terminates my exploration of the river Usuri, and of the road from its source across the mountains between the valleys of the Fudza and Lifule, and to the sea!"

The other observations made by M. Veniukof, we have incorporated into the various chapters of this volume.

## The Sungari.

By far the greater part of Manchuria—we exclude here as elsewhere the province of Leaotong—as at present under the dominion of the Chinese, is drained by the Sungari and its affluents. The sources of the Sungari are situated upon the north-west slope of the Shan-alin or White Mountains, which have a belt of thick forests at the foot, fine pasturage higher up, and then precipitous slopes, with glaciers and perennial snow. On their summit is situated an alpine lake having a circumference of above ten miles. The elevation of these mountains probably exceeds 12,000 feet. They form an impassable barrier between Korea and Manchuria. Further to the south they bound the fertile plain of Leaotong, in which stands Mukden the capital of the province, and which is traversed by the Sira-muren river. Towards the north-east, the Shan-alin subsides into a mountainous country forming the water-shed between the Usuri and Sungari. We have not however to do here with a chain of mountains, but rather with a plateau or table-land, densely wooded in the south, and changing in the north into prairie and grass-land, often of a marshy or swampy nature. The rivers run here in deep valleys, isolated mountain-chains are set upon the plateau, and in its main features this tract may be compared with the regions north of the Amur traversed by Middendorf, with this exception, that whilst the forests of the latter consist exclusively of conifers, we find here oaks and elms north of the 45th degree of latitude, pines and firs being restricted to the more elevated and consequently colder regions to the south of that line.

We now return to the Shan-alin in order to trace the watershed of the Sungari towards the south and east. In the south the arid plateau of the Korchin, a continuation of the Gobi desert, from which it is separated by the ridge of the Khingan mountains, here low and barren, separates the basin of the Sungari from that of the Sira-muren or Leaotong river. The Khingan continues to form the watershed further to the north. The mountains increase in height, and the Yalo pass is estimated by the Missionaries to have an elevation of 6,000 feet, which is however probably much exaggerated. The eastern slope of the Khingan partakes of the character of the Gobi, of which it forms the boundary; it is barren, arid and occasionally wooded with pitch-firs. As we approach the summit of the range we enter dense forests of birch and larch, and on the eastern slope, of larch and oaks, until we arrive at the prairies or steppes extending along both banks of the Nonni and Sungari, down to the Amur. It is a branch of the Khingan which forms the rocky banks of the Amur above the Komar, and another branch which separates the small tributaries of the Amur from those of the Nonni and Sungari, and which finally crosses the Amur as the Bureya mountains, formerly called Little Khingan.

"The Sungari, with its low and fertile banks, slow current, and absence of shallows and rapids which might impede navigation, is the most populated portion of Manchuria.[k] The river is navigable below Girin, the largest town of Manchuria, with a reputed population of 600,000 inhabitants, which Kimai-Kim, the Korean traveller, reduces to 150,000 (in 1844), but which even then would be considerable. 'Like almost all Chinese cities, Girin contains nothing remarkable; it is an irregular collection of cabins, built of brick or of clay, and covered with straw, with only a ground floor. It is inhabited by Manchu and Chinese indiscriminately, but by the latter in far greater numbers. Trade is in a flourishing state, and there is a great stir in the streets. It is an emporium for the trade in furs, cotton cloths, silks, of artificial flowers, with which the women of every class deck their heads, and of timber for building, brought from the imperial forests, which may be perceived

[k] The Manchu and Manyargs who navigate the Sungari, spend eight days from the mouth of the river to Sansin; and the voyage to Tsitsikar or Mergen requires a month. They either tow their boats from the land or push them along with long poles.

at a short distance south of the town.' Most boats used for the navigation of the Sungari and Amur are built here. After a course of nearly two hundred miles below Girin, and in a north-western direction, the Sungari receives its most considerable tributary, the Nonni, and then suddenly sweeps round to the north-east, in which direction it continues for above eight hundred miles to its confluence with the Amur. The banks of the Sungari, below Girin, as well as those of its tributaries, the Nonni below Mergen (or Mangar), the Hurka (Khulkha or Mu-twan) below Ninguta, consist of vast prairies often extending for miles inland, and finally merging into the prairies of the Amur. Spurs of the mountains approach close to the river occasionally only. Such, for instance, is the case at Sansin, which in 1844 was still the lowest town to which Chinese colonisation had extended, and which then had about 10,000 inhabitants. Sixteen years have brought about a great change, and at present a numerous Chinese population extends for about fifty miles below Sansin. We insert here an extract from a letter of Mr. Maximowicz, who in 1859 ascended the Sungari, but was compelled to return before he reached Sansin on account of the hostile reception by the Chinese villagers.[1]

"On the 22nd July, 1859, I left the settlement of Yekaterino-Nikolskoi, arrived on the 25th at the mouth of the Sungari, and having engaged, at the last Russian station, another Cossack as a boatman, made preparations, on the same day, to ascend the river. It was my intention to go up the Sungari to the mouth of the Nonki, but the antagonistic position assumed by the Manchu authorities frustrated my plans. At the very mouth of the Sungari, the Manchu official to whom I shewed my passport, forbade me to continue the journey without assigning any reason, and when appealing to the treaty of Aigun, I continued my journey in spite of him, he

[1] Viestnik, Russian Geographical Society, 1859, part xii.

threatened me with his matchlock. On the road I learned from the Goldi inhabiting the bank of the river, that orders had arrived to detain me, and conduct me a prisoner to Sansin. The Goldi however being rather well inclined towards the Russians, I was enabled to travel a distance of one hundred and seventy miles without further molestation. But here, about thirty-three miles below the town of Sansin, where the Manchu-Chinese population is so great that from the left and inhabited bank of the river eight villages may often be seen at one and the same time, the Chinese peasants made a first attempt to surprise me. But seeing a gun on board my boat they precipitately retired, and I resolved at all events to push on to the foot of the mountains which appeared to slope down to the banks of the river, and only to return in case another attack should be made upon me. On the following day, the 9th August, I perceived to my sorrow that the nearest mountain-slopes were at about two-thirds of a mile from the bank of the river, and that in order to reach them I should have to traverse a large village, the inhabitants of which would have attacked either me or the people whom I should have to leave with the boat. Even now they were following us armed with flails, and had it not been for the revolver I carried in my belt, they certainly would have fallen upon the Cossacks who towed my boat up the river. Under these circumstances an exploration of the country was not to be thought of, and in the next village, Chado, which was very large and situated on both banks of the river, I should certainly have been attacked, for the Chinese evidently only wanted some leader. I therefore returned without having reached Sansin and the mountains surrounding it, which we saw at a distance of about twenty-five miles. On the 12th August, I again passed the Chinese guard at the mouth of the river, and on the following day arrived at the station Mikhailo-Semenovskaya, seventeen miles below it, whence I sent a report of my proceedings to the governor of the Amur province. The country, as far as I traversed it, consists of an extensive, monotonous plain, upon which isolated mountain-chains are seen but rarely and at a great distance. One of these chains sends a spur down to the bank of the river, near the village Cham-khoton, and here, and in a small wood near Susu, I made some interesting discoveries. I found a wild apricot, of excellent flavour, the tree having a diameter of at least one foot; a little known species of the cucumber family, Thladiantha, Aristolochia contorta, etc.

"The rest of the country consisted either of grassy plains, with shrubs of willows, or steppes where Mongolian oaks, Corylus heterophylla, and Ulmus campestris grow. The vegetation upon the whole resembles that of similar regions of the Amur, with this difference, that plants which there occur but rarely, such as Lilium callosum, Melampyrus roseum, and others are found here plentifully, and that some Chinese plants make their appearance in the south. The small woods and groves, which are met with in some few localities, are chiefly Usuri apple-trees, mixed with elms and hawthorns. The number of trees is very small. Conifers and even white birches are not found at all, and the black birch and lime are very scarce. These trees are found only in the mountains, at some distance from the river."

## XV.

### SAKHALIN.

The island of Sakhalin extends from Cape Elizabeth (54° 24′ north latitude) to Cape Crillon (45° 54′ north latitude) a distance of five hundred and eighty-eight miles from north to south. The area may be 32,000 square miles. The native name is Taraika or Choka, and to the Japanese it is known as Karafto or Oku-Yeso, that is northern Yeso.

The island in 52° north latitude approaches to within six miles of the mainland, from which it is separated by the shallow Mamia Strait, supposed from the time of La Pérouse till very lately to have no existence, or to afford at most a passage at high water to native canoes only. The Japanese traveller, Mamia Rinso, whose accounts were published by Siebold in 1835, has however clearly proved the contrary, and late Russian discoveries have established the fact to the satisfaction even of the most sceptical, that this strait really does exist, and that Sakhalin consequently is an island. As such it is represented on the map published by D'Anville, as early as 1753, in which it is described as Sahalien ula hata, that is "rocks at the mouth of the black river (Amur)." We have throughout this work called this island "Sakhalin," as the Russians, in the numerous accounts they publish, give it this name, which has thus become domiciled in geographical terminology. It would nevertheless be more correct to call the island Krafto, Taraika, or Choka, Sakhalin simply meaning "black."

A mountain-chain, with craggy summits, and which is

believed to be covered with snow throughout the year, under 52° north latitude, traverses the island from south to north. The coast is generally rocky and steep, but opposite the mouth of the Amur it consists of sandy downs, and a similar region of downs extends on the east coast, both being divided by the mountain chain previously mentioned. As the island extends through eight degrees of latitude there is of course a great difference of climate; and, whilst the rigours of the winter of the Lower Amur are reproduced with even greater severity, in its northern half, the south enjoys a much more equable climate, and one by far preferable to that of the coast of Manchuria under the same latitude.

Aniva Bay occupies the southern end of Sakhalin; it is forty-miles deep, and its two capes, Crillon and Aniva, are sixty-five miles apart. The bay is surrounded by high mountains; the valleys are covered with luxuriant grasses, five feet high; wild briars, raspberries, geraniums, roses and lilies, exhale their perfume, and birches, willows, and other foliferous trees abound in lower situations, pines being restricted to the higher land. The Japanese have within this bay two settlements, valuable on account of the fish which is caught here in great abundance, it being unnecessary even to use a net, as the fish may be taken out of the sea with pails during low water. Krusenstern found the whales so plentiful, that it required the greatest caution to avoid being upset on going ashore. One of the Japanese settlements is at Tomare Aniva on the east side, the other at the bottom of the bay in Salmon-trout Bay. The former place had been temporarily occupied by the Russians, who called their settlement Muravief. At both places there are magazines for storing dried fish, which is exchanged for rice, salt, cloth, and cutlery, and other articles brought by the Japanese. Unfortunately Aniva Bay offers few advantages in the way of havens. It is exposed to south winds, and the harbours of Tomare Aniva, and Port Busse, a short distance south of it, which are pretty well sheltered, are exceedingly small. A Japanese settlement, Siranusi, is situated near Cape Crillon, east of the bay.

We now round Cape Aniva (46° 2′ N. lat. 143° 31′ E. long.), a barren mass of rocks, and proceed along the east coast of the island, which as far as Mordvinof Bay, a distance of sixty miles, is steep and rocky, with bold mountains, densely wooded, in the back ground. The southern shore of Mordvinof Bay (46° 48′ N. lat. 143° 15′ W. long.) is hilly, and wooded with firs; the northern shore is flat. Wood and water are found in plenty, and there is good anchoring ground on a clayey bottom. North of Mordvinof Bay the coast is again abrupt and rocky; the country appears more attractive than further south; the hills near the coast are covered with beautiful verdure, and the valleys are richly wooded; the mountain chain in the interior rises to a considerable height, and attains its culminating point in Bernizet Peak or Mount Spenberg (47° 33′ N. lat.).

The western and northern shores of the Gulf of Patience are low, with a shelving beach; the depth of water half a mile from the shore is four fathoms. The adjoining land is in some places covered with mud five or six feet deep, in others with a rich black soil, but the trees, most of them of the thorn kind, are stunted in their growth. In May snow still remains in many spots. The river Ty, Neva of Krusenstern or Boronci (of the Oroke?), enters the Bay (49° 15′ N. lat. 143° 33′ E. long.). At its mouth it is about thirty yards wide, and seven feet deep. It communicates with a lake at a short distance from the shore. The eastern coast of the bay is rather mountainous and craggy, and the character continues the same after rounding the low Cape Patience (48° 52′ N. lat. 144° 46′ E. long.) as far as Cape Delisle de la Croyère (51° N. lat. 143° 43′ E. long.), for a distance of one hundred and sixty miles. Where there is the mouth of a rivulet small inlets occur, and here generally also native settlements. The hills near the coast are of moderate height, with stunted trees, and only shrubs are found near the sea-coast. From Cape Delisle to Cape Löwenstern (54° 3′ N. lat. 143° 13′ E. long.), a distance of above two hundred miles, the shore consists of a sandy beach, covered with an impenetrable growth of shrubs, but in some parts there are only a few larches. More inland we find not only abundance of conifers, but also foliferous trees of various kinds. The mountain range is either seen at a great distance or disappears altogether. Along the whole of this coast a current sets to the south at the rate of about a mile an hour. At Cape Löwenstern the country again becomes mountainous, and there is a charming valley to the south of that cape. But after doubling it, the appearance of the country is dreary in the extreme. The coast is formed by barren granitic rocks, rising perpendicularly from the sea, and there is not a vestige of vegetation. Cape Elizabeth (54° 24′ 30″ N. lat. 142° 46′ 30″ E. long.), the extreme northern point of the island, is a pinnacled mass of such rocks, but between it and Cape Maria another bold rocky headland, whence a dangerous reef runs towards the north-east, opens a large bay of considerable depth. The land surrounding this bay is of moderate height, and in places even low. The heights are well wooded with magnificent fir trees, and in the valleys fine grass grows. A large Aino village stands at the bottom of the bay, and a smaller one near Cape Maria. There is good anchoring-ground here, on a sandy bottom; the bay is free from all surf, and the only drawback is its exposure to the winds, which however are seldom dangerous.

We now double Cape Maria and return to Aniva Bay by the western side of the island. The country continues mountainous as far as Cape Horner (54° 4′ N. lat. 142° 28′ 30″ E. long.), but the mountains are wooded even to their summits, and the valleys covered with luxuriant grass. At Cape Horner the mountains terminate, and a low and sandy shore with sand-hills, and occasionally small lakes and swamps, extends thence south to Cape Wanda, in the latitude of Castries bay.[a] The shore thence to the south is hilly rather than mountainous, with a coast of steep earth-banks, from one hundred to one hundred and fifty feet high, and interrupted now and then by rocky capes. There is not a single good harbour along the whole of this coast, the bays de la Jonquière (50° 54′), d'Estaing (48° 59′ N. lat.) de Langle (47° 49′) and Nevelsky (47° 15′), being mere open roadsteads. The vegetation is far more favourable than on the east coast. The valleys are covered with luxuriant grass, and though pines and firs prevail north of 48° N. lat., birches, maples and oaks are found at the same time, especially on proceeding a short distance into the interior. There is another feature which renders the possession of this coast of great importance. Coals have been discovered at Dui, near Jonquière Bay, and at de Langle Bay, and are being explored by the Russians, who have also established themselves at Kusunai.

We add to this short notice of Sakhalin the account of a journey undertaken in 1855-6 by L. von Schrenck, into the interior of the northern part of the island.

### Schrenck's Journey to Sakhalin Island.

"*Nikolayevsk, 15th May,* 1856.

"The war having frustrated my desire to visit Sakhalin Island during the summer, I resolved to take advantage of the winter to acquire an exact knowledge of the character of its vegetation, of its birds and mammals, and lastly of the

---

[a] A large bay, Deception, Obman or Baikal Bay, closed by a bar, opens under 53° N. lat. Its greatest depth is ten feet, and it is surrounded by pretty wooded scenery.

various tribes which inhabit it. I left this place for that purpose on the 11th February accompanied by two Cossacks, a sailor, with three sledges and an ample supply of provisions. Having rapidly passed along the Liman of the Amur, we reached the island on the 13th February. On the following day we were at the village of Ty, the inhabitants of which had shown so little hospitality to me during my first visit. Wind and snow detained us this time also for four days much against my will, and we could not continue our journey before the fifth. We followed the coast in a southerly direction; the swamps found in the vicinity of the Liman are soon replaced by undulating rocks of grey limestone and a reddish clay, which latter in places exhibits a bed of bitumen. As far south as Cape Dui, and especially near Jonquière Bay the coast is studded by small villages of Gilyaks, whose language and custom place them between the Gilyaks of the mainland and those in the interior of the island and its east coast. On the west coast these people extend as far as the village Pilavo, which is however inhabited during summer by several families of Ainos. At the village Arkai, which I reached on the 20th February, I left the coast to penetrate into the interior. Snow-storms had completely hidden every trace of the road and none of the Gilyaks of the village was willing to guide us across the three ranges of hills intervening between the coast and the source of the Tymy. I therefore departed on the following morning without a guide. After much trouble, we crossed the first of three mountain ridges and camped for the night in the snow. It was the last night for which we were provided with food for our dogs. Unfortunately a fresh snowstorm rendered our progress on the following day even more difficult, and we could get on only by continually sounding the depth of the snow. At last, this plan also failed, and we found ourselves in entire ignorance of the direction we were to take. Fortunately we met here two

Gilyak sledges which came from the Tymy river, and following the fresh traces they had left, we continued our journey. We crossed two more ridges of the mountains, and in the evening, during a violent snow-storm reached a Gilyak hut on the Tymy. In reality but one range of hills intervenes between the coast and the Tymy, but the natives, in preference to following the course of the rivulets, take the direct route leading across these heights.

"The Tymy is a rather considerable river which runs towards the north-east, through a wide valley, and before entering the sea of Okhotsk, penetrates through the mountains on the east coast. Its source is separated only by a crest of little elevation from the river Ty, which runs towards the south into the Gulf of Patience. During winter the Gilyaks, Ainos and Oroke congregate on the Ty, the banks of which at other seasons are deserted; on the other hand those of the Tymy are the most populated part of the whole of Sakhalin. From the source to the mouth numerous villages of Gilyaks are met with, whose language differs essentially from that of the Gilyaks on the mainland, and both in language and features they form a particular branch of that interesting people. The Tymy has a remarkably rapid current; it never freezes, even when the cold descends below the freezing point of mercury. It abounds in fish, especially during spring; several kinds of salmon are caught here, but particularly, as in the Amur, the Salmo lagocephalus. The Gilyaks of the Tymy collect immense stores of frozen fish, not only as food for themselves and their dogs during winter, but also as an object of trade with Ainos, Oronchons, the Gilyaks of the coast, the mainland, the Ainan, and the Manguns of the Amur. The Ainos bring to the valley of the Tymy Japanese goods, the Oroke furs, the others copper, seals, Russian and Manchu merchandise.

"The study of nature in this valley, as far as the season would permit, was not a little interesting to me. On the

15th January, the temperature of the water of the river was 33·12 F. The river affords a refuge to numerous kinds of ducks and other birds (Anas Boschas, Fidigula cristata, Cinclus Pallasius); on the rocks which bound its banks it is not rare to meet with a very large eagle (Haliaëtus pelagicus), the symmetrical feathers of which furnish to the inhabitants an article of a very advantageous commerce with the Japanese. Having remained for some time in the upper part of the valley of the Tymy, we continued our journey on the 28th February. The weather was clear but very cold; on the 2nd March at 7 A.M., we had $-62°$ F.; on the following day the temperature rose to $-38°$ F. The lower course of the Tymy was frozen, and we found it best to cross the ice several times to avoid its sinuosities. The excessive cold gives Sakhalin the character of a continental climate rather than that of an island. The forests which cover it confirm this opinion. There are many kinds (species) of trees; especially foliferous ones, among which the oak, ash and maple are frequent. There are many very high cedars among the conifers. In the valley of the Tymy the wooded tracts further from the river exhibit an admixture of different kinds of trees. Near the river the foliferous trees predominate, particularly birch and willows; the slopes and crests of the mountains are on the contrary covered with conifers. On approaching the eastern coast of the island the larch becomes more frequent and takes the place of other species, till on the coast itself no other tree is found, and it is there dwarf-like and gnarled. On the west coast, the mainland of the sea of Okhotsk and the north part of the Liman, the larch is only met with incidentally. This tree therefore is typical of the vegetation of this coast.

"The geographical distribution of animals in Sakhalin accords with that of the trees. This island, in fact, or at all events its northern portion, may be included in the same zone with the mouth of the Amur, and the nearest coast of the Okhotsk sea. We find, besides the rein-deer, the common stag (cervus elaphus), the roe, elk and musk ox, which inhabit the depths of the thickest forest in the interior. There is still in Sakhalin a wandering tribe of Tunguzians who keep rein-deer, while among the Tunguzians of the Amur that animal has disappeared, and with it the traces of a nomadic life.

" Proceeding along the valley of the Tymy, which still maintains the same breadth, the crests of the mountains enclosing it grow more and more elevated and their height is sometimes considerable. The summits are capped with snow, which disappears in the middle of summer only. The natives say that it remains throughout the year on the lofty peaks of the Pshangar mountains, situated to the north-east of the valley, and which are called Vakaz on Japanese Maps. The river intersects this chain of mountains, turns towards the east, and runs rapidly to the Sea of Okhotsk. On the lower course of the Tymy, fewer habitations are met with than in the upper part of the valley, and more than once we had to pass the night in the open air. On the 4th March we reached the east coast of the island, and proceeded along it as far as Nyi Bay, and after a stay of two days, from bad weather, among the inhospitable tribe of the Tro-Gilyaks, we returned. The deficiency of provisions obliged us to accelerate our journey as much as possible. Having visited Jonquière Bay and the coal deposits at Khoinjo, we retraced our steps to the north; and on the 17th March arrived at the village of Chkharbakh at the mouth of the Amur, where we found a sledge with provisions and some articles for barter which had been sent to us. The object of this was to enable me to make another excursion to the north of the Liman, and to the south shores of the Sea of Okhotsk into the district of the now abandoned winter station of Petrovsk; to gather information respecting the coast, and the manner of life of the Gilyaks

T

who dwell there, and who are the most northern representatives of this important people. Unfortunately thick fogs and snow-storms continually accompanied us. . . . . On 24th March, after an absence of six weeks, we were again off Nikolayevsk, having made a journey of nine hundred and forty miles with dogs."

275

XVI.

THE CLIMATE.

THE climate of the regions of the Amur is influenced mainly by two causes, first, its position at the eastern extremity of a large continent; and secondly, its being washed towards the east by the Pacific Ocean. The features of a continental and maritime climate thus become blended. The cold during winter is less severe at places situated on the Lower Amur and in the neighbourhood of the sea, nor is the summer as warm as that of places situated under the same parallel, but further inland. Still this equalising influence of the sea is not so great as it would be, were the sea of Okhotsk and Channel of Manchuria as free from ice as is the Eastern Atlantic in the same latitudes. Whilst the difference between the summer and winter temperature in London is 24°,[a] and 62° at Irkutsk in the centre of Northern Asia; it is 58° at Nikolayevsk at the mouth of the Amur, and 75° at Nerchinsk Zavod, or 17° in favour of Nikolayevsk, and 37° in favour of London, if compared with Nerchinsk and Irkutsk respectively.

The following comparative table will at once demonstrate the characteristic features of continental and maritime climate, as applying to London — Barnaul — Irkutsk and Nikolayevsk — Nerchinsk Zavod :—

[a] Fahrenheit throughout.

| Latitude. | Mean Temperature. | | | | | Difference between Summer and Winter. |
|---|---|---|---|---|---|---|
| | Year. | Winter. | Spring. | Summer. | Autumn. | |
| 51° 31' London | 49·69 | 37·80 | 48·97 | 62·15 | 50·03 | 24·35 |
| 53° 20' Barnaul | 35·11 | 6·60 | 42·93 | 61·83 | 29·10 | 55·23 |
| 52° 17' Irkutsk | 31·10 | −1·27 | 2·14 | 61·54 | 30·65 | 62·0 |
| 51° 19' Nerchinsk Zavod | 24·2 | −14·0 | 28·1 | 60·70 | 24·9 | 74·7 |
| 53° 8' Nikolayevsk | 39·42 | 1·27 | 25·70 | 59·05 | 32·23 | 57·78 |

We perceive, by this table, that whilst the summer temperature of the places enumerated differs by scarcely three degrees, that of winter shows greatly in favour of London and Nikolayevsk, both under maritime influences. The difference in the climate of the above places is equally striking, when we compare them with respect to the usual atmospheric precipitation. At London and Nikolayevsk rain (and snow) are pretty equally distributed throughout the year, with a maximum in autumn, but at Barnaul and Nerchinsk scarcely any rain (or snow) falls during the winter and spring.

| | Precipitation in Inches. | | | | |
|---|---|---|---|---|---|
| | Year. | Winter. | Spring. | Summer. | Autumn. |
| London | 19·26 | 4·02 | 3·79 | 5·63 | 5·82 |
| Barnaul | 12·01 | 0·92 | 1·77 | 6·39 | 2·93 |
| Nerchinsk | 17·54 | 0·75 | 0·60 | 8·77 | 7·42 |
| Nikolayevsk | 131 days | 28 days | 36 days | 28 days | 39 days |

We are not in a position to state the amount of rain and snow which fell at Nikolayevsk, but the number of days suffices for our purposes. During winter at Nerchinsk there is hardly a sledge to be seen on account of the scarcity of the snow, whilst at Nikolayevsk the snow lies several feet deep. The regions of the southern Amur being five degrees further to the south, enjoy of course a milder climate, but even here there is nothing to boast of, for the rivers are frozen five months during the year. The minimum temperature observed at Nerchinsk is — 49°, at Blagovesh'chensk — 49°, the Usuri mouth — 18°, at Mariinsk — 36°, and at Nikolayevsk — 40°. After these preliminary remarks, we will enter a little more into detail with regard to particular portions of the Amur.

1. The Upper Amur, down to the mouth of the Komar, enjoys a climate similar to that of Dauria (Eastern Transbaikal). The Shilka below Nerchinsk is free from ice about the 10th April, strong south-westerly winds prevail, and the first rain falls. About the middle of the month vegetation begins to spring forth in favourable spots; and in May, the air is fragrant with the perfumes of many flowers. The greatest heat lasts from the middle of June to the middle of July, when the thermometer in the shade rises as high as 92°; but in the morning and evening a cool breeze blows down from the ravines in the mountains. More continuous rains, with northerly winds, set in about the latter part of June. About the 15th August the husbandman reaps his corn, and after that hoar frost occurs and the leaves wither. But there are occasionally white frosts even in the midst of summer, and near Albazin snow fell during the night of the 4th June 1857. Thick fogs sometimes cover the country in the mornings in August, when nothing can be distinguished beyond a distance of ten or twelve paces; about ten o'clock they disperse in clouds, and the aspect of nature is more charming from the temporary shroud which before enveloped it. September is dry and clear with but little wind, and though hoar frosts fall in the morning, the temperature during the day rises rather high. The first snow falls at the commencement of October; but it is not till November that the weather becomes really severe, and about the 4th of that month the rivers are again covered with a sheet of ice, which remains for five months.

The severe weather lasts until the end of February, and the temperature falls as low as — 35° and — 50°. The snow forms but a very thin covering, rarely sufficient even for sledge-riding, and throughout the winter cattle seek and find the fodder they require. This small quantity of snow has a very serious disadvantage. The thinly-covered soil freezes and crumbles, and is then carried away by the wind, leaving but stones and pebbles behind.

The following table exhibits the monthly temperature of Nerchinsk Zavod, near the Argun, and 2,230 feet above the level of the sea, and the annual fall of rain and snow at the town of Nerchinsk on the Shilka, 1,845 feet above the sea. The former is the average of fourteen, the latter of five years.

| Months. | Mean Temperature. | Rain and Snow. | |
|---|---|---|---|
| | Degrees F. | Days. | Inches. |
| January | —21·2 | 1·4 | 0·10 |
| February | —11·5 | 1·6 | 0·07 |
| March | 8·2 | 3·4 | 0·23 |
| April | 28·7 | 5·7 | 0·30 |
| May | 47·2 | 8·2 | 1·15 |
| June | 59·5 | 7·2 | 3·02 |
| July | 64·0 | 9·7 | 4·60 |
| August | 58·7 | 8·8 | 4·43 |
| September | 46·5 | 3·5 | 2·26 |
| October | 27·0 | 4·5 | 0·72 |
| November | 1·2 | 3·7 | 0·49 |
| December | 13·8 | 2·0 | 0·16 |
| Winter | —14 | 5·0 | 0·75 |
| Spring | 28·1 | 17·3 | 0·60 |
| Summer | 60·77 | 25·7 | 8·77 |
| Autumn | 24·9 | 11·7 | 7·42 |
| Year | 24·2 | 59·7 | 17·54 |

2. The district below the Dzeya, as far as the Bureya Mountains enjoys no doubt a more favourable climate than Dauria, but only in as far as the summer months are free from hoar-frost, which on the Upper Amur often proves

destructive to the harvest. The winter is quite as long, and the Amur at Blagovesh'chensk is frozen over from the 8th Nov. to the 4th May (1856-7); there is scarcely more snow than in Dauria; and the nomadic Manyargs are enabled to keep their horses throughout the winter pasturing in the open air. The Dzeya freezes nearly a fortnight earlier than the Amur, chiefly on account of its slower current.

In 1859-60 the weather at Blagovesh'chensk was fine until the middle of October. On the 4th November much snow fell, and soon after the river became covered with ice. The weather during December and January was fine though cold, the temperature falling occasionally to $-45°$, and at one time to $-49°$, and never rising above $+9·5$. Violent storms occurred during November and again in February. On the 2nd April was the first thaw. Between the 6th and 9th of May the river became free from ice, and the last snow fell on the 12th without however remaining on the ground. The maximum heat during summer is $99°$. The climate is reputed the reverse of salubrious, owing probably to the low and often swampy plains surrounding the town.

3. The *Bureya* Mountains have a much cooler climate than either the prairies higher up or lower down. In August, thick fogs rest upon the river in the morning, and the nights are cold. In 1857, the cold up to the first of November did not however exceed $-40°$; north-westerly and sometimes westerly winds prevailed and the sky was clear; easterly winds brought clouds. The first snow fell on the 6th October, and there was another fall on the 24th, when the temperature during the night was $23°$. By the 2nd Nov. the snow had disappeared everywhere, and during that day, the wind being east, there even fell some rain.

During the night the wind veered round to the north-west, and in the morning the temperature had sunk to $3°$. On that day the first ice-blocks floated down the Amur, and on the 12th November the river was frozen over. Up to the 13th

December, the cold did not generally exceed 10°, and though it was —11° on the morning of the 16th November, it rose to freezing point (32°) during the day. Snow fell again on the 22nd, and on the three following days, to the depth of one foot. The amount of snow throughout the winter is about four feet and a half, or more. The cold during January equals that of Dauria, and varies between 3° and —47°.

4. We now approach those regions of the Amur which have the most favourable climate. But even here the river is ice-bound during five to six months of the year. At the mouth of the Usuri it freezes about the end of November, and opens in the beginning of May. Snow covers the ground to the depth of one foot to one foot and a half, and in exceptional winters as much as two feet and a half. The minimum temperature during the winter 1857-8 was —18° at the mouth of the Usuri. Spring at the mouth of the Gorin is about nine days in advance before that of Mariinsk, only one degree further north; and simultaneous observations of temperature made during sixteen days, at the end of May and June, show a difference of five degrees in favour of the Gorin, where the mean temperature was 61°, whilst it was only 56° at Mariinsk. The minimum temperature, between the Sungari and Mariinsk, observed by Maack with a minimum thermometer during July varied between 53° and 71°. The winds during spring and the beginning of summer are east and north-east, during autumn west and south-west, the former bringing rain. On again ascending the Amur, Maack's minimum thermometer for the first time sunk below freezing point on the 23rd September. The Usuri also has a favourable climate. As on the Amur, south-east winds, with thunderstorms prevail in June and July, and the quantity of rain causes the river to rise nineteen feet at its mouth. Veniukof assigns to the middle Usuri a mean annual temperature of 48°. The climate of this portion of the Amur is

certainly none of the most enviable, but it is nevertheless favourable to the production of the cereals of northern Europe, and of some of the more hardy fruit-trees. The cultivation of the vine is of course out of the question.

5. We now come to Mariinsk and Nikolayevsk, both more immediately subjected to the influence of the sea of Okhotsk. The river freezes at Mariinsk about the 10th November (6th to 14th), at Nikolayevsk on the 16th (14th to 20th). The first day on which the temperature fell below freezing point was the 14th October, 1855, at Mariinsk, and the 9th October, at Nikolayevsk. During the greater part of winter south-west to north-west winds predominated; the barometer then stands high, the sky is clear, and the cold intense. Towards the middle of January, north-east and south-east winds blow; the temperature then rises, sometimes even above freezing point, heavy fogs occur, and large quantities of snow fall. Violent snow-storms take place when the wind changes. On the ice of the river, even where the wind sweeps it away, the snow at Nikolayevsk lies to the depth of three feet and a half; at Mariinsk, under similar circumstances, it is only two feet, a difference accounted for by the coast-range which shields it against easterly winds; for when we cross it to Castries Bay we find the masses of snow equally deep as at Nikolayevsk. In the forest it lies to a depth of twelve or fourteen feet.

The last date upon which the temperature sunk below freezing point at Nikolayevsk, was in 1855, on the 24th April, and in 1856, on the 13th of April. About the 18th of May (14th—21st) the river is free from ice, but on the 25th, it is still found in sheltered bays, and the snow lies deep in the forests. At Mariinsk, the frost breaks ten or eleven days earlier. Southerly winds blow during spring; in summer, the winds are more variable, westerly winds generally prevailing. East wind brings cold and rain.

The following is a tabular statement of meteorological observations made at Mariinsk and Nikolayevsk.[b]

| | TEMPERATURE. | | | | | | | DAYS WITH RAIN OR SNOW. | | | |
|---|---|---|---|---|---|---|---|---|---|---|---|
| | Mariinsk. | | | Nicolayevsk. | | | | Mariinsk. | | Nikolayevsk | |
| | 1854. | 1855. | 1856. | 1854. | 1855. | 1856. | 1857. | 1858. | 1855. | 1856. | 1855. | 1856 |
| January.... | — | 7·73 | — | — | 7·81 | −2·34 | — | −14·37 | 19 | ? | 21 | 9 |
| Feb.uary .. | — | −0·85 | −1·04 | — | −5.24 | −5·43 | — | −3·68 | 12 | 8 | 14 | 7 |
| March...... | — | 16·07 | 14·50 | — | 8.02 | 14·50 | — | 0·43 | 10 | 7 | 10 | 4 |
| April ...... | — | 35·68 | 31·64 | — | 30·79 | 24·89 | — | 31·39 | 10 | 11 | 15 | 11 |
| May ....... | — | 47·34 | 42·35 | — | 40·52 | 36·86 | — | 43·90 | 13 | 13 | 17 | 16 |
| June ....... | — | 59·47 | 57.85 | — | 56·85 | 55·00 | 53·00 | — | 10 | 11 | 13 | 16 |
| July ...... | — | 62·49 | 59·00? | — | 59·47 | 56·07 | 61·12 | — | 18 | 9? | 15? | 13 |
| August .... | — | 63·77 | — | — | — | 67·44 | 59·22 | — | 12 | ? | ? | 11 |
| September.. | — | — | — | 51·30[3] | — | 54.07[4] | 48·27 | — | ? | ? | ? | 10 |
| October .... | — | 37·17 | — | 39·20 | 31·94 | — | 34·16 | — | 10 | ? | 12 | 5 |
| November .. | 9·01 | 14·16 | — | 10·06 | 10·21 | — | 20·01 | — | 6 | 12? | 8 | 11 |
| December .. | 2·45 | 3·73 | — | −4·90 | −0·37 | — | −6·77 | — | 4 | 9 | 15 | 6 |
| Spring ........ | | 31·25 | | | | 25.70 | | | 32 | | | 36 |
| Summer ...... | | 60·21 | | | | 59·05 | | | 36 | | | 28 |
| Autumn ...... | | 34? | | | | 32·23 | | | 30? | | | 39 |
| Winter ..... | | 41·57 | | | | 1·27 | | | 40? | | | 28 |
| Year ...... | | 31·76 | | | | 39·42 | | | 138 | | | 131 |

[1] 15th to 30th November.  [2] 1st to 19th.  [3] 2nd to 29th.  [4] 15th to 10th.

6. Leaving the banks of the Amur and advancing southward into Manchuria, the climate does not apparently improve. This must be ascribed partly to the greater elevation of the country, partly to the vicinity of the snow-covered Shan-alin. At Ninguta violent storms rage at the commencement of spring; there is hoar frost as early as the end of August, in September snow, and in October the rivers are frozen, and do not re-open before April. At Girin the temperature falls to − 22°. The snow lies about six feet deep. Wheat does not succeed on account of superabundant moisture. The climate, however, will doubtless improve as the colonisation goes on.

[b] The observations for 1854-6 were made by Schrenck and Maximowicz; those for 1857-8 at the Meteorological Observatory of Nikolayevsk. The latter are published in Kupfer's Compte rendu Annuel, etc. Petersburg, 1858.

7. We now proceed to the Channel of Tatary. Here the winds blow with great regularity. During summer, when the weather is clear and the barometer high, a light breeze comes from the south, and a thin mist covers the horizon; but when the force of the wind increases, a dense fog spreads over the surface of the sea, frequently intercepting for several days the view of the sky. When the wind ceases some rain falls, after which the weather for a few days continues clear. In September the southerly winds become stronger, but they are no longer accompanied by fogs; the weather is murky, and finally it rains. The season of fogs and southerly winds ceases in October, when strong northerly winds set in, interrupted at times by westerly winds. The fogs do not generally extend to the shore either of Sakhalin or the mainland. At Castries Bay and Port Imperial the weather is frequently fine, while there is a thick fog sea-ward. Whittingham shows that there is often a lane of water, free from fog, and three to six miles in width along the coast; the latter radiating the heat received from the hot summer sun.

In the Liman, navigation is obstructed by floating ice at the beginning of November, but the Liman is not frozen over before January, and can only then be crossed with safety. The breaking of the ice takes place in May or the beginning of June, and is generally accompanied by rain and thunderstorms. South of the Liman ice forms along the coast about November or December. It clears out of Castries Bay about the middle of May, and out of Port Imperial rather later; in 1856 on the 24th May. The climate of Castries Bay is much more unfavourable than that of Mariinsk, and the cultivation of cereals is out of the question. When the trees burst into foliage at Mariinsk, deep snow still lies in the Bay, and there is no trace of vegetation. Port Imperial, though nearly three degrees further south, is scarcely more genial. Cold easterly winds depress the temperature during summer, or beginning in October, westerly and northerly winds frequently cause the thermometer to fall to — 13° and — 24°. On the 4th of June 1856 snow still covered the mountains, the rivers were partly frozen, and yellow violets, anemones, and a corydalis were the only flowers. The temperature was 46°. On the 19th June the ice had disappeared, birches and oaks were in leaf, and there were many flowers. The mean temperature between the 19th and 26th June was 64°. Going southward along the coast the climate improves, and Vladimir Bay (43° 55′ north latitude) is covered with ice only during two months, from the middle of December to that of February. Olga Bay (43° 46′ N. lat.) remains open throughout the winter, the land-locked careening harbour being frozen over however during four months and a half.

8. In the northern part of Sakhalin the climate is even more rigorous than at Nikolayevsk, and on the 1st March 1856, Schrenck observed a temperature of —61° at the Tymy rivulet, in the interior of the island. Vast quantities of snow fall, and the sea on the east coast (52° north latitude) freezes as far as the eye reaches. In Aniwa Bay the cold climate is much less severe, though still sufficiently great. The coldest day during the winter 1853-4 was the 13th January, when the temperature fell to —13°. The middle of the bay is free from ice during the whole of the winter, and the ice along the coast is frequently broken by the waves. At the end of March all snow had gone, and fresh verdure appeared in the middle of May.

## XVII.

## MINERALS.

WE have already noticed the geological formation of the coasts in our geographical description of the Amur and the adjoining regions. Our knowledge as yet is very imperfect, and mainly rests upon the cursory observations of Permikin, Anosof and Maack. Mr. Schmidt is, however, engaged at present in geological researches, and his labours cannot but throw considerable light upon the geological structure of the country.

The rocks of the Amur regions, as far as explored hitherto, appear to belong almost exclusively to the primary, metamorphic and palaeozoic periods. Basalts in large masses occur above and below the Komar river, and with trachytes, amygdaloid, and lava on the coast of the Channel of Tatary. Igneous rocks—granites, syenites and porphyries—occur on the Upper Amur about the mouth of the Onon, and between the Komar and Dzeya rivers. Lower down they form the framework of the Bureya and of the Khœkhtzir mountains. We meet with them for a considerable distance above Sofyevsk; at the mouth of the Amur and on various points of the coast down to the frontiers of Korea. Metamorphic slates and schists are met with near Albazin, opposite the Tsagayan, near Ulusu Modon, in the Bureya mountains, about the Usuri and Gorin. They have also been discovered in Sybille and Victoria Bays. The Palaeozoic series is represented by sandstones and limestones, which Anosof is inclined to believe belong partly to the Silurian formation.

Carboniferous sandstone abounds on the Upper Amur, from Albazin to the Tsagayan; above the Bureya mountains, and below the Gorin. Sandstone has also been discovered in Sybille Bay; limestone in the Bureya mountains and at the mouth of the Amur.

In their structure, the mountains of the Amur offer much similarity to the Nerchinsk ore-mountains, and there is reason to believe that they are equally rich in mineral treasures. But hitherto mining has been carried on in a very restricted manner. Lignite or brown coal has been discovered in several localities; at the Tsagayan on the Upper Amur; a short distance above the mouth of the Dzeya; below the mouth of the Bureya in two places on the right bank of the Amur, and near the sources of the Bureya. Coals have also been found near Dui on Sakhalin, the only place where they are explored at present, at de Langle Bay, and in Posyet harbour. This coal is of very fair quality, one specimen analysed yielding about seventy-one per cent. of carbon. The only other mineral actually explored is gold. The Chinese wash it on the Dobikhu, a tributary of the Upper Usuri, and it has also been observed on the Upper Dzeya and in Posyet harbour. Silver is reported to exist in the Ojal mountains, though the natives led Mr. Maack to a vein of arsenic, as he believes with a view to deceive him, an analysation of which yielded 67·6 per cent. of arsenic, 31·1 of iron, and 1·3 of sulphur. Mr. Pargachevsky was told that there was silver near the Bijan, a river which enters the Amur fifteen miles above the Sungari. Agates, carneols, onyxes, and other stones are found in shingle-beds, and the Chinese wash pearls in the Bijan and Song. Some small pieces of beautiful coral have been picked up in Suffrein Bay. Of building stones there is abundance, and the limestone furnishes greyish marble.

It remains to be seen how far the throwing open of mining to private enterprise will aid in its development. There is here, at all events, great scope for profitable investments, far preferable to the establishment of artificially-supported manufactories. The raising of raw produce—mining, cattle-rearing, and agriculture—must for many years remain the most profitable source of employment of the colonists. A glance at the prosperous condition of Cape Colony, not to speak of Australia, is sufficient to convince us of this.

# XVIII.

## PLANTS.

THE results of the botanical explorations of the Amur have been given by Carl Joh. Maximowicz in "Primitiæ floræ Amurensis, Versuch einer Flora des Amurlandes," St. Petersburg, 1859. The author has not only furnished us with his own researches, during his travels on the Amur, but has also incorporated into his work the observations made by Turczaninow,[a] L. von Schrenck, Maack,[b] and others (see History of Geographical Discovery). Our chief authority for the remarks offered in the following pages is therefore Maximowicz.

### STATISTICS OF PLANTS.

The total number of species as yet found on the Amur is nine hundred and four. Of these eight hundred and seventy-seven are Phanerogams (viz., six hundred and ninety-five Dicotyledons and one hundred and eighty-two

---

[a] Flora baicalensi-dahurica.—Enumeratio plantarum Chinæ borealis, in Bulletin de la Societé de Moscou, X. 1837, etc.

[b] Bulletin de l'Academie de St. Petersbourg, T. xv., p. 257. Trees and shrubs, described by Ruprecht. See also Appendix in Maack's Travels on the Amur.

Monocotyledons). The following tabular view enables us to compare the flora of the Amur with that of some neighbouring countries:—

|  | Total Species. | PHANEROGAMS. | | | | |
|---|---|---|---|---|---|---|
|  |  | Families. | Total. Genera | Species. | Dicotyledons. Species. | Monocotyledons. Species. |
| Amur . . . . . . . . | 904 | 108 | 416 | 877 | 695 | 182 |
| Ditto below Bureya Mountains . . . . | 770 | 105 | 386 | 736 | 580 | 156 |
| Trans-Baikal . . . . | 1201 | 93 | 421 | 1226 | 963 | 263 |
| The Gobi . . . . . . | — | 74 | 249 | 487 | 422 | 65 |
| Peking . . . . . . . | 788 | 123 | 436 | 771 | 638 | 133 |
| Eastern Siberia . . | 533 | 67 | 241 | 510 | 415 | 95 |

Of the 904 species of plants on the Amur, 152 are annual or biennial plants, 621 perennial, 89 shrubs, and 42 trees. Taking the Lower Amur separately, the figures are 136, 512, 122, and 40 respectively. The number of trees in Trans-Baikal is 19,[c] that of shrubs 122; in the Gobi, shrubs 49, trees 5;[d] in the neighbourhood of Peking, trees 40, shrubs 117; and in Eastern Siberia, trees 10, shrubs 63.

If we compare the flora of the Amur with that of neighbouring countries, we find that out of the 904 species of the Amur, 527 are found also in Trans-Baikal, 293 in Eastern Siberia, 276 in the environs of Peking, and 163 in Mongolia.

Considering the flora of the Amur with respect to species having but a limited distribution, we find 143 species of plants, or 15·8 per cent. of the total flora, restricted to the

[c] Including three not found on the Amur, a species of hawthorn (Rh. polymorpha), the Cembra Pine, and Siberian larch.

[d] The trees of the Gobi are a hawthorn, the bird-cherry, a birch, the Scotch pine, and Siberian larch.

Amur; and they include the following new genera, all of them monotypical:—

Plagiorhegma dubium, Max. (Berbery family).
Hylomecon vernalis, Max. (Poppy-worts).
Phellodendron Amurense, Rupr. (Xantholits).
Maackia Amurensis, Rupr. & Max. (Pea and Bean tribe).
Schizopepon bryoniæfolius, Max. (Cucumber family).
Symphyllocarpus exilis, Max. (Composites).
Pterygocalyx volubilis, Max. (Gentian-worts).
Omphalotrix longipes, Max. (Fig-wort family).
Imperata (Triarrhena) sacchariflora, Max. (Grasses).

The last is a sub-genera.

Fifty-six species are restricted to the Amur and the environs of Peking; 25 to the Amur and Trans-Baikal; 40 to the Amur and Eastern Siberia; 6 to the Lower Amur and Japan; 8 to the Amur, Japan, and Northern China; 29 to the Amur, Trans-Baikal and Siberia; 34 to the Amur, Trans-Baikal, and Northern China; 7 to the Amur, Trans-Baikal, and Mongolia; 6 to the Amur, Eastern Siberia, and Peking; and 10 to the Lower Amur and North America.

The remaining 558 species are plants having a more extended distribution; and about one-third of these are found in Northern Asia, Europe, North America, and partly within the tropics, and one-ninth in Northern Asia and Northeastern Europe. Apparently, the statistical data which we have communicated, would show, that, out of plants having a more limited distribution, there are more species of the Amur found in Eastern Siberia and the neighbourhood of Peking, than in Trans-Baikal. Such a conclusion would however probably be erroneous, for the Lower Amur, where Siberian types preponderate, has been examined much more minutely than the upper part of the river adjoining Trans-Baikal.

The following table includes all families of plants, the number of species of which exceeds 2·5 per cent. of the total Phanerogams found in the respective countries.

| Families. | Amur. | | Lower Amur. | | Ayan. | | Trans-Baikal. | | East Siberia. | | Mongolia. | | Peking. | |
|---|---|---|---|---|---|---|---|---|---|---|---|---|---|---|
| | Species. | per cent. | Species. | per cent. | Species. | per cent. | Species. | per cent. | Species. | per cent. | Species. | per cent. | Species. | per cent. |
| Composites | 101 | 11·7 | 82 | 11·1 | 34 | 9·6 | 135 | 11·0 | 50 | 9·8 | 72 | 14·7 | 73 | 9·2 |
| Crowfoot Family | 64 | 7·2 | 47 | 6·3 | 26 | 7·3 | 70 | 5·7 | 43 | 8·2 | 23 | 4·6 | 36 | 4·6 |
| Grasses | 55 | 6·3 | 44 | 5·9 | 16 | 4·5 | 84 | 6·8 | 25 | 4·9 | 31 | 6·3 | 49 | 6·2 |
| Sedge Family | 44 | 4·9 | 40 | 5·4 | 20 | 5·6 | 71 | 5·7 | 29 | 5·6 | — | — | 17 | 2·1 |
| Rose Family | 43 | 4·9 | 34 | 4·6 | 20 | 5·6 | 53 | 4·3 | 30 | 5·8 | 30 | 6·1 | 30 | 3·8 |
| Cress-wort Family | 31 | 3·5 | 25 | 3·3 | 19 | 5·3 | 69 | 5·6 | 33 | 6·4 | 21 | 4·3 | 23 | 2·9 |
| Chick-weed Family | 29 | 3·2 | 23 | 3·3 | — | — | 45 | 3·6 | 26 | 5·1 | 13 | 2·6 | — | — |
| Pea and Bean Tribe | 27 | 3·0 | 21 | 3·1 | — | 1·7 | 80 | 6·5 | 22 | 5·0 | 58 | 11·7 | 60 | 7·6 |
| Lily Tribe | 26 | 2·9 | 21 | 2·8 | 6 | — | — | — | — | — | 14 | 2·8 | — | — |
| Umbelliferous Family | 25 | 2·9 | 23 | 3·1 | 9 | 2·6 | 50 | 4·0 | 12 | 2·5 | 13 | 2·6 | 30 | 3·8 |
| Labiate Family | 25 | 2·9 | 22 | 2·9 | — | — | 28 | 2·2 | — | — | 14 | 2·8 | 23 | 2·9 |
| Buckwheat Family | 24 | 2·8 | 19 | 2·5 | — | — | 32 | 2·6 | — | — | 17 | 3·4 | — | — |
| Fig-wort Family | — | — | — | — | — | — | 42 | 3·4 | — | — | 34 | 6·9 | — | — |
| Salsolaceæ | — | — | — | — | — | — | — | — | — | — | — | — | — | — |
| Willow Tribe | — | 2·3 | — | — | — | — | 37 | 3·0 | 21 | 4·1 | — | — | — | — |
| Ferns, per cent. of the total flora | — | — | — | 2·7 | — | — | 1·5 | — | — | 1·8 | few | — | — | 1·2 |

## Physiognomy of Vegetation.

Maximowicz distinguishes eight regions of vegetation along the Amur. In giving their chief characteristics we refer for more detailed accounts of particular localities to our geographical description of the river Amur.

1. The first region includes the Amur down to Albazin. In the valleys the forest is composed of white birch, bird-cherry and aspen; on the mountains and in dry places larch and pine prevail; the spruce and pitch-pines are very scarce. The forest is nowhere thick, and there is no underwood. The meadows are of small extent, and resemble the steppes of Dauria, the grass growing in tufts and there being an abundance of bitter aromatic herbs.

2. The second region extends down to the Dzeya. Coniferous woods are scarcer here, and foliferous trees and meadows occur more frequently. The oak, elm, ash, lime and black birch, which are not found at all above Albazin, or only of a dwarfish growth, constitute the forests. The steppes on the plateau on both banks of the river bear a vegetation of tufty grass and herbs, and are covered with shrubs of hazel and cinnamon roses.

3. The region from the Dzeya to the Bureya Mountains forms an immense prairie, with a few groves of trees. Forests occur again below the Bureya River, and on the mountain-slope grow oaks, birches, walnuts and aspens. Maackia amurensis, a tree-like species of the Leguminosæ, and the Cork-tree (Phelodendron amurensis) are first observed here, and at the fringe of the forest may be seen the Amurian vine, which lower down appears more frequently. The Bureya Mountains form the limit of many plants peculiar to the Upper or Lower Amur. The Manchu lime, the maples, excepting the Tatar maple, the Manchu cedar, the ribbed birch, and many other trees are not found

to the west of them, whilst the Scotch pine and other plants do not extend below them.

4. The prairie region of the Lower Amur extends to the Usuri, and is distinguished from the prairie of the Upper Amur by a greater preponderance of grasses and more luxuriant herbage, though the number of species of the latter is less. Scattered over it are trees of large dimensions. The prevailing trees are oaks, elms, limes, maples, with aspens, bird-cherries, birches, cork-trees and hawthorns. Thickets of willows grow along the banks of the river and on the islands.

5. The fifth region extends down to the Gorin. The prairie continues for some distance along the left bank of the river, but on the right bank thick forests of foliferous trees commence at the mouth of the Usuri, where the trees indigenous to the Amur country are found of the largest dimensions. Cedars, larches and other conifers are confined to the mountain summits or northern slopes.

6. The region hence to Sofyevsk forms a connecting link between the foliferous region of the Amur, and that of the coast region. The trees typical of the more southern portion of the Amur are replaced by Erman's birch, the Lonicera and elder-leaved apple; the white birch, aspen and Acer spicatum are more frequent.

7. The seventh region extends from Sofyevsk to Tebakh, where the Amur suddenly turns to the east. Foliferous trees are scarcer here, and are restricted to Prunus glandulifolia, a few ash-trees, two species of maples and the elm. The hazel frequently forms a thick underwood, but coniferous forests predominate.

8. On the Lower Amur, a few birches and aspens are confined to some favourable spots, and the forests, intersected by large tracts of swamp, are composed chiefly of Ayan spruce, pitch-pine and larches.

For further details regarding the distribution of plants on

the Amur, etc., we must refer to Maximowicz's important work; that gentleman in 1859 for a second time visited the Amur, and the plants recently collected by him and others will no doubt form a large supplement to his Primitiæ Floræ Amurensis. We will proceed now to a consideration of the various plants applied to useful purposes, or which may become of importance in a commercial point of view.

## Food-Plants.

An agricultural country, properly so-called, is to be found only on the river Nonni, where the Daurians till the soil from time immemorial, and in southern Manchuria. Breadstuffs are cultivated to satisfy the wants of the inhabitants, and even sufficient for exportation. Here we find four out of the five bread-stuffs of China; Sorghum of various kinds, wheat, millet and barley. Most of the rice is imported from Mukden; but the Chinese, settled near the Gulf of Manchuria, cultivate it in small quantities. Tobacco of a superior quality is grown here, with soy and many other plants. In 1812, the number of acres brought under cultivation in the province of Girin was 905,000 acres, and in that of the Amur 49,500 acres.

This, of course, is but a small portion of a country containing about 193,000,000 of acres.[e] Along the banks of the Amur, agriculture, on a larger scale, is carried on only in the vicinity of the villages immediately above and below the town of Aigun. We meet here with extensive fields sown with millet, barley, oats and sometimes Soja hispida. Numerous herds of cattle graze on the prairies, and in some places, where Imperata sacchariflora abounds, the grass is regularly mown and gathered into small stacks with the seeds of the Imperata outside, so that the wind may carry it away, and it may produce a fresh crop. To each house is

[e] The province of Tsitsikar has an area of 177,000 square miles; and that of Girin, within its present limits, of 135,000 square miles.

attached a garden, where tobacco, maize, beans, cabbages, radishes, pumpkins, cucumbers, melons, capsicum, Chinese mustard, lettuces, carrots, red pepper and some other plants are cultivated in small quantities. We even find some flowers, such as hollyhocks, cockscombs, globe-amaranths, Indian cress and marigold, which the women put into their hair, the red, white and lilac flowers of the hollyhock being especial favourites with the fair sex.

The agricultural produce of Aigun and its vicinity more than suffices for the wants of the inhabitants, and millet and tobacco of very superior quality are annually exported up the river to the Manyargs, and as far as the Russian villages of Trans-Baikal, and down the river to the tribes dwelling there; or they are exchanged on the spot itself for furs.

For a distance of two hundred miles above and below this agricultural district, we occasionally find a solitary hut of a wood-feller or a trader surrounded by a small garden, where millet, tobacco and the like are cultivated; the proprietors of these houses are not, however, natives of the soil, but generally immigrant Chinese or Manchu. The natives on the Lower Amur do not cultivate the ground at all, and it is among the Goldi only that we find now and then a small garden, never exceeding four hundred to eight hundred square yards, where they grow some tobacco, which they smoke before the leaf is ripe, pumpkins, cucumbers and beans. These gardens are very carelessly attended to, and the produce is looked upon rather as a luxury than a necessary article of consumption. No hay is mown for the few horses which the Goldi keep at the mouth of the Usuri, and during winter they must get fodder in the best way they can. The Chinese settled among the Goldi have larger gardens, and, in addition to the plants mentioned above, they grow water melons, potatoes and Chinese onions.

The further we descend the river, the more exclusive is the use of fish, and, during winter, the flesh of some animals.

The Goldi procure brandy, tobacco, beans and wheaten-flour on their annual journeys to Sansin, a town on the Sungari. The natives living on the Lower Amur do not however undertake these journeys so regularly, and are dependent for these luxuries upon the Chinese merchants who every year descend the Amur in their well-filled barges, and stay during the winter at some village—the lowest is Pul—bartering with the natives. Maximowicz found the cargo of such a barge to consist of the following: —Three varieties of millet; wheaten flour, which the merchants generally use themselves; small brown beans (Lablab vulgaris); white beans (Phaseolus vulgaris); large red beans; small white ones, about the size of a pea, with blue marbling; peas; sorghum grits of a reddish variety; barley; bundles of large-leafed tobacco; sesamum oil (?) mostly for their own consumption; a very small quantity of rice, at an exorbitant price; rice brandy; white and coloured cotton stuffs, thread, etc. The supply of these articles is however very small, and in consequence of the high prices demanded the natives cannot often enjoy the luxury of vegetable food.

Previous to the occupation of the country by the Russians, the lowest point on the Amur to which the cultivation of vegetables extended was Tsyanka, not far from the mouth of the Gorin. Here a Chinese merchant owned a small garden in which he raised, among other things, spinach, onions, coriander seeds and red pepper. The Russian colonists who were sent in 1855 from Trans-Baikal, at once set about cultivating the cereals of their native country in the villages between Mariinsk and Nikolayevsk, and with very fair success. Less could scarcely be expected from the virgin soil, the hot summer, regularly distributed and not very continuous rains, and the dry, fine autumn. Vegetables had been introduced simultaneously with the first settlement of the river, and at a horticultural show held in

1857 at Nikolayevsk, contributions were received from fifty-five gardens. Cauliflowers, cabbages, potatoes, carrots and other roots had thriven best; and even in the most unfavourable localities, such as Castries Bay and Nikolayevsk, where the cultivation of cereals could never be expected to be remunerative, very excellent vegetables were produced.

In addition to these cultivated plants, there are several herbs and roots which the native puts in his soup; but few of these would be approved by European palates, or contain much nourishment. Most of them are of very indifferent taste, and are such as we might gather on a walk through any of the lanes of England. Not one of them compensates by aroma, tartness or acidity, the total want of spices. To this class of plants belong the long-rooted garlic, spear-leafed cacalia and the groundsel, the last of which is put into soup, in Sakhalin; the young stems of the water-pepper and goosefoot; Limnanthemum nymphoides; the sprouts of the common mug-wort and Selenga mug-wort, are said to have a very fine flavour; the stems of cow parsnep; the young sprouts of the willow-herb; the fresh leaves of the red-berried alder, as well as several others known only from reputation, and probably belonging also to quite common plants.

Some others are eaten raw or cooked for the sake of the mucilage they contain. The small tasty bulb of the Kamchatka fritillary are dug up in large quantities and strung upon ropes to dry. The bulbs of the Lilium spectabilis are also gathered. Chives and Iceland moss are eaten. Less general, and perhaps only for a make-shift, is the use of the roots of the obovate Pæony; of the thick, white roots of Platycodon and Adenophara; as also some others of unknown origin which Schrenck found among the Gilyaks on Sakhalin. To these may be added the slender-leafed lily, the bulbs of which are dug up in large quantities by the Daurian Cossacks. In southern Manchuria, the blossoms of the yellow lily are said to form one of the dainties of the Chinese, who also value highly some mushrooms which grow on the trunk of a decayed tree.

We now proceed to the fruit-trees. These also play a very subordinate part in the household of the tribes living there. The tree yielding the bird-cherry (Prunus Padus) is generally spared by all. The cherries are dried, bruised, stones and all, and formed into small flat crumbling cakes of a dark violet colour, and a bitter almond-like taste. They are either eaten alone or put into the soup. The Gilyaks gather large quantities of cow-berries, which abound in their territory, and keep them frozen during winter. The Goldi collect the water-caltrops and walnuts, which are thrown into the fire to crack the shells; and also of the Manchu pine and hazel-shrub. These nuts are eaten however more as a pastime by young and old. The Gilyaks may occasionally be seen with small baskets containing fruit of the cinnamon-rose—the Goldi give the preference to the Rosa acicularis — of the hawthorn, crow-berries, and Lonicera Maximowiczii. A great many other kinds of fruit are found; they are generally liked, but only gathered when accidentally met with during a walk through the forest. Little regard is paid to fruit which does not strike the eye by quantity or size, and which, however good its flavour, might entail trouble in gathering it. The natives are not even aware of the existence of the strawberry and dwarf crimson bramble.

Grapes are found along the Amur from forty miles below Aigun to the neighbourhood of Kidzi, and are most abundant below the Bureya Mountains. They are blackish-blue and nearly half an inch in diameter, but not very juicy. Those growing in the neighbourhood of Ninguta are said to be superior, and are exported to Peking. Besides the bird-cherry (Prunus Padus), there are four species of Prunus, viz., Prunus (Cerasus) glandulifolia, with small black cherries, spare of flesh, and tart; the Prunus (Padus) Maackii, with small black plums a quarter of an inch in diameter; and Prunus Maximowiczii with small cherries. A wild apricot has lately been discovered on the Sungari. The service-tree (Sorbus Aucuparia) bears vermilion fruit, ripe about the end of August. The small-fruited apple (Pyrus baccata) is found along the whole course of the Amur and Usuri, and it ripens in September. The Usuri pear-tree bears a small fruit about an inch in diameter, and shape of a bergamot, ligneous and tart, and of a dirty green, but on being kept it gets brown and soft. At Peking this tree is cultivated.

Pyrus (Sorbus) sambucifolia, the elder-leaved apple, is a shrub found on the Lower Amur and the sea-coast only, and bears a large vermilion fruit. The number of edible berries is very great. We find blackberries, cloud-berries, the crimson and stone bramble, red and black currants, gooseberries, raspberries, cranberries, strawberries, whortle and blea-berries, cowberries, berberries, cornelian cherries, and the Maximowiczia Chinensis, a dioecious shrub, with a thin aromatic bark, fragrant pink blossoms, and a tart scarlet berry; it climbs up the trees to the height of from twenty to twenty-five feet, and is found in foliferous woods below the Bureya Mountains. Mulberries are said to exist in Southern Manchuria. Mountain apricots with a large red fruit grow near Ninguta, and are made into marmalade. There is also a kind of small white pear, having an excellent flavour, and with which the emperor's table is supplied.

## Trees.

Undoubtedly one of the greatest riches of the Amur consists in its abundance of fine timber, which is available not only for ship-building, but also supplies some fine woods for cabinet work. We will therefore enumerate all the trees found along the course of the river, stating at the same time their size, and some of the uses to which they are applied by the natives.

*Limes.* Tilia cordata is found along the whole course of the Amur, from the Komar to the neighbourhood of Kidzi, and on Sakhalin. Above the Dzeya, the tree generally grows on the level sandy banks of the river, and has a height of forty feet, with a diameter of two feet. But on the lower part of the Amur it grows in foliferous forests together with maples and oaks, and attains a height of sixty feet, whilst its trunk is three feet and a half in thickness. The Manchu Lime (T. Manchurica) is met within the same limit as the preceding, but its trunk scarcely exceeds three-quarters of a foot in diameter. The wood of the limes is white and soft, and the Goldi twist the bast into ropes.

*Maples.* There are four species of maples, Acer spicatum, A. Mono, A. tegmentosum, and A. Tataricum.

The first of these—A. spicatum—is found along the Amur below the Bureya Mountains, on the sea coast and on Sakhalin, and appears to be rather scarce on the Amur itself. It prefers moist and shady situations along the fringe of foliferous forests and in pine clearings. On the Lower Amur it is a fine tree from twenty to thirty feet high, and with a trunk six inches thick. Its wood is yellow and hard, and is used by the natives in the manufacture of various household utensils.

A. Mono—which takes on the Amur the place of A. truncatum—occupies the same area as the preceding, exclusive of Sakhalin. It is most abundant between the Sungari and Mariinsk, and grows either in open foliferous forests or on rocky mountain slopes. The largest trees observed were about fifty feet high, with a trunk two feet in diameter. Its wood is excellent, of a yellowish colour, and much harder than that of the other maples.

A. tegmentosum—analogous to the Pennsylvanian maple—

is found between the Bureya mountains and Kidzi, but in the upper part of this area it is merely a shrub, and only at the Usuri it assumes larger proportions. On the banks of that river trees have been observed about thirty feet high, with a trunk nine inches thick, but higher up, on the same slope of the valley, it is much larger, and trees fifty feet in height with a trunk two feet and a half in diameter are frequently met with. Its wood is white and rather hard.

The Tatar maple extends along the Amur from the Komar to below Kidzi, and frequently occurs as a shrub about fifteen feet high, on the islands and alluvial banks of the river. Below the Bureya mountains it is occasionally met with as a small tree about twenty feet high in forests, together with oaks and elms.

The *Cork-tree* of the Amur (Phellodendron amurense) is distributed along the Amur from the neighbourhood of Aigun to the village of Onmoi (50° 10′ north latitude). According to native information, it is found also lower down, but in the mountains at some distance from the river. At first the Cork-tree is found on the islands exclusively, but lower down it grows on the mountain-slopes together with other foliferous trees. The largest trees observed on the Middle Amur were about fifty feet high, with a straight trunk, two feet thick, and a fine and dense top. The bark of the older trees consists of two distinct layers, the outer of which is above half an inch thick and of the usual cork colour; the inner is one quarter of an inch thick or more, and lemon-coloured. Pieces of cork were seen, however, among the natives three inches thick. The natives along the Middle Amur use the cork to float their fishing-nets, and the very firm wood of the tree is made into snow-shoes.

The Daurian *Buckthorn* (Rhamnus daurica) occurs in the foliferous region of the Lower Amur and in the woods of the Middle and Upper Amur. The tree is about thirty feet high, and the trunk frequently a foot thick. The wood is very hard, of a reddish yellow colour, and beautifully watered. It would be eminently fit for cabinet work.

The Manchu *Walnut* (Juglans Manchurica) is found between the Bureya mountains and the Komar river, in foliferous and mixed forests. The largest trees are about sixty feet high, with a straight trunk two feet thick, and bare of branches for thirty feet. The wood is very hard. Another kind of walnut (J. stenocarpa, Max.), similar to the former, is restricted to the hilly tracts, and does not occur on the banks of the river.

*Maackia* amurensis, Max., is found from above the Dzeya to Pul on the Lower Amur. It grows as a shrub on low and sandy islands, and as a small tree intermixed with maple, bird-cherry and hawthorn, on mountain-slopes. At the Usuri it attains its maximum development, and is here above thirty-five feet high, with a trunk one foot in diameter. The wood is brown and watered.

Of *Prunes* there are four species, viz., Prunus glandulifolia, P. Maackii, P. Maximowiczii and P. Padus.

*P. glandulifolia* is most frequent on the Lower Amur, and is here about forty feet high and one foot thick. The wood is soft and white.

*P. Maackii* is found in foliferous woods in the Bureya Mountains, and on the Lower Amur. It has a straight trunk about thirty-five feet high and nine inches thick ; on the Lower Amur it is only ten feet high.

*Prunus Maximowiczii* is a small tree found in coniferous woods on the Lower Amur.

*P. Padus*, the bird-cherry, is the most important of all, and abounds along the whole course of the Amur and on Sakhalin, and on the Upper Amur especially, covers large tracts on the islands and banks of the river. At the Usuri mouth, trees fifty feet high, and with a trunk one and a-half to two feet thick are not scarce.

The *Hawthorn* (Cratægus sanguinea) occurs on the whole of the Amur and on Sakhalin, either as a shrub or a small tree, the latter twenty feet high and with a trunk ten inches thick.

The *apple-trees* have been mentioned before. Pyrus baccata, the small-fruited apple, is found throughout the whole course of the Amur and along the Usuri, on islands and in open shrubberies. The Usuri apple-tree is found in foliferous forests along the Lower Amur, the Usuri, and extends to Korea and northern China. Its maximum height is forty feet, and the diameter varies from a foot to five inches, the latter being more frequent.

The *Service-tree* (Pyrus [sorbus] aucuparia) thrives on the whole of the Amur and on Sakhalin. It grows on mountain-slopes and occasionally wooded islands.

*Dimorphantus Manchuricus*, Rupr. et Max., is a small tree in the Bureya Mountains and along the Amur to below the Usuri.

The Manchu *Ash* (Fraxinus Manchurica Rupr.), is found along the Amur from Albazin to Kidzi, the largest trees occur as usual about the mouth of the Usuri. They are here about sixty feet high, with a trunk four feet in diameter. The wood is hard, and of good quality.

The Mongol *Oak* (Quercus Mongolica, Fisch.), is met with first at Albazin, as a shrub; below the Komar it occurs as a stunted-tree, and it is not before we approach the Bureya Mountains, that it assumes larger proportions and on the Middle Amur is one of the most frequent forest-trees, growing together with the bird-cherry and ash-tree on level tracts, and with other foliferous trees on the mountain-slopes. On the Lower Amur it is again of dwarfish growth, but on the sea-coast, south of Port Imperial, the tree is once more highly developed. The largest oaks were about forty feet high with a trunk five feet thick, but unfortunately generally rotten to the core. In one locality only, in the

Bureya Mountains, have good, sound oaks been found. But as a rule, the oak of the Amur is much inferior to that of Europe.

Out of nine species of *Willow* found on the Amur, three attain the dimension of trees. The early willow (Salix præcox) is found on the Lower and Middle Amur, at some distance from the river, and the diameter of its trunk is frequently four feet. The Bay-willow (S. pentandra) is restricted to the Upper Amur. The great round-leaved willow (S. caprea) is found along the whole course of the river, somtimes as a shrub, at others as a tree, with a trunk two feet thick. Its wood is very tough and flexible. The other willows are found along the whole course of the river, and most frequent on its low banks and islands are the almond-leaved willow (S. amygdalina), the common osier-willow (S. viminalis), the auricled-willow (S. stipularis. These grow to the height of fifteen to twenty feet, but are not trees. Restricted to the Lower Amur are the weeping-willow (S. depressa), the myrtle-leaved willow (S. myrtilloides), and the creeping or bog-willow (S. repens).

To the natives, the willows are of importance in many respects. The trunk of the early willow is hollowed out on the Lower Amur and on Sakhalin, and shaped into canoes. The thin branches serve for the frame-work of the summer or winter habitations. The Goldi manufacture ropes from the bast of several sorts, especially the osier, which they use for their fishing nets, and for towing their boats. Chips of willow wood are used to kindle a fire, a piece of burning tinder being put in the midst of it, and the whole is swayed to and fro until the flame bursts forth. In rainy weather the capillary roots of the willow answer the same purpose. These roots form a kind of fungus at the foot of the trunk, as far as the water reaches in periods of inundations, and during rain ; they are found dry in protected situations.

The *Aspen* (Populus tremula) is found along the whole

course of the Amur and on Sakhalin, and the tree attains its largest dimensions near the Usuri, where it is fifty feet high, with a trunk three, and even four, feet in diameter.

*Poplars* (Populus suaveolens) also are found along the whole course of the river, but most frequently for a distance of one hundred and sixty miles below the Usuri, where they attain a height of forty feet, with a trunk of one foot and a half thick.

*Elms.*—The mountain elm (Ulmus montana) chiefly abounds from the Bureya mountains to the village of Borbi, above Mariinsk. On the sea-coast it occurs first to the south of Port Imperial. It is a large tree, forty feet high, with a thick and far-spreading top. Varieties of the small-leaved Elm (U. campestris) occupy a far wider area, and are found from the islands above the Dzeya to nearly the mouth of the Amur. The tree attains a height of fifty feet, and has a sound trunk from one to four feet thick. The wood is of a dark colour and very hard, and may be advantageously used as a substitute for oak.

There are various kinds of *Birch*, amongst which the common or white birch (Betula alba) is the most important. It is met with along the whole course of the river, and on

MANGUN BIRCH BARK BASKET.

Sakhalin. In spring, the natives peel off the bark of the tree in strips two to four yards in length. The coarse outside of the bark, and the ligneous layers on the inside are scraped off. It is then rolled up and softened by hot steam, which renders it very pliable. Several of these strips are sewn together, and supply the natives with a portable waterproof blanket or mat, extremely useful under many circumstances. In winter encampments, when hung across some poles before the fire, it shields the traveller against the cold winds. In summer, it forms the covering of the rudely built huts. It is also used for laying over and wrapping up merchandise. And lastly, small canoes, neat baskets, platters, cups, and pails, are made of the bark. The wood of this birch supplies the material for sledges and various household utensils.

The Daurian birch (B. daurica) differs from the preceding by its darkish brown bark, which peels off in lamellæ, and is consequently not available for the many purposes of the former. It is found along the whole course of the Amur to the vicinity of Mariinsk, and grows on mountain slopes and grassland, in company with the white birch, oaks, and other trees. Its trunk attains a thickness of two to three feet.

Erman's birch (B. Ermani) is found on the Lower Amur in moist localities, and forms a chief feature of the forests of Sakhalin. Its trunk attains a diameter of above one foot.

The ribbed birch (B. costata) found from the Bureya mountains to below the Usuri, and has a trunk seven inches thick. In addition there are two stunted birches, the shrubby birch (B. fruticosa) and Middendorff's birch.

*Alnaster fruticosus*, Led. (Alnobetula fruticosa, Rupr.) flourishes on the Amur to a degree not noticed elsewhere. It generally grows as a shrub having several branches, and is twenty feet high, but has also been found in the Bureya mountains as a small tree with a straight trunk, about three inches thick, and for nine feet free of branches.

The hoar-leaved *Alder* (Alnus incana) is found on the whole of the Amur and on Sakhalin; but in more southern localities only on northern slopes. It grows as a shrub along the bank of the river, and in the level country generally, and on slopes, attains a height of twenty feet, with a trunk half a foot thick.

The *Yew* (Taxus baccata) exists in several spots on the Lower Amur and on Sakhalin as a branchy shrub, three to five feet high. In Port Imperial, however, and elsewhere along the coast, it is a tree; and according to the statements of the natives it has, at some distance from the river, a trunk one foot thick.

The Siberian Fir or *Pitch* (Pikhta of Russian travellers, Abies Sibirica) is one of the most frequent trees met with along the Amur. On its upper course it generally occupies with other conifers the more elevated portions of the mountain slopes; in the Bureya mountains it is found with cedars and larches on the middle of the slope, and still lower down the river it descends to the valleys. Its height is fifty feet, with a trunk two-thirds of a foot thick.

The *Siberian Spruce* (Picea obovata) is found along the whole of the Amur, down to the village of Patt (52° 40′ north latitude). It is most developed in the Bureya mountains, where it grows near the summits in company with Scotch firs. The trunk of the larger trees is about one foot thick, and twenty-five feet from the ground bare of branches. The tree itself is fifty feet high.

The *Ayan Pitch* (Picea ajanensis) is confined to the Lower Amur, the sea coast, and the Upper Usuri. The tree has a straight trunk, sixty to seventy feet high, and of a diameter of two to three feet, and is admirably suited for shipbuilding.

The Daurian *Larch* (Larix daurica) is abundant along the whole course of the river, but especially so in its upper and lower part, where it forms a chief component of the forests. Trees sixty feet high, and with a trunk three or more feet in diameter, are frequent, especially in those valleys and plains on the Lower Amur, protected against storms. It is an equally fine tree on Sakhalin, and well adapted for shipbuilding.

Of the *Siberian* or *Cembra Pine* (Pinus Cembra) a stunted variety only is found on the Amur itself; but the tree is supposed to exist in the neighbourhood of Ninguta, whence its nuts are exported to Peking. On the Amur it is replaced by the *Manchu Pine,* or *Cedar* of Russian travellers (Pinus Manchurica, Rupr.), which extends from the Bureya Mountains to Kidzi, and first appears on the sea-coast south of Port Imperial. It is a fine tree, with a trunk seventy feet high, from which deals three feet wide and fifty-six feet long may be cut.

The *Scotch Fir* (Pinus sylvestris) abounds on the upper part of the Amur, but is not met with below the Bureya Mountains.

The wood of the Conifers is very valuable to the natives, for owing to their very imperfect implements they cannot avail themselves of the harder woods, which in many respects would be preferable. Of the former they build their houses, carve many of their household utensils, and their idols. The Gilyaks and natives of the Lower Amur make their boats of the Pitch fir or Cedar, and on the Upper Amur the Scotch fir answers the same purpose. The bark of the larch supplies materials for the roof and walls of the summer habitations on the Lower Amur.

## Medicinal Plants.

In speaking of the Medicinal Plants of Manchuria, the first place must of course be assigned to the far-famed Ginseng root (Panax ginseng), which the Chinese call Orhota, *i. e.* first of all plants. They consider it the most costly produce of the earth, diamonds and some other precious stones excepted, and ascribe to it the most wonderful healing properties. It is vaunted to be a specific in all kinds of bodily ailments, to cure consumption when half the lungs are gone; to restore to dotards the fire of youth, and to act as a sure antidote against the most powerful poisons. European physicians have proved rather incredulous, and according to Richard (Botanique Medicale), many common European plants have the same properties. On the other hand, Roman Catholic missionaries of former and recent times, acknowledge from their own experience the beneficial effects of the ginseng. Jartoux (Lettres édifiantes, Paris, 1713) declares it to be a first-rate tonic; and de la Brunière cured himself of a complaint in the stomach, which had resisted even an infusion of Peruvian bark.

At all events the fame of this medicine has spread to the Goldi who live on the Amur, and it is known to them as Manchu medicine. If we are to credit the statements of the missionaries, the prices paid for this root are enormous. A single root is worth from £250 to £300 in Manchuria, and in China as much as £2,000 are stated to have been paid for a pound of it. A ginseng-seeker has to search for five, ten, or even fifteen years before he finds a root. These extravagant statements have however been completely upset by Veniukof, who ascended the Usuri, and visited the very localities where the best ginseng is said to be found. At the Imma river he was offered a bundle of from twelve to fifteen roots for £4, and on his return the native interpreter procured twenty for £1 10s. The members of the Russian Mission at Peking were on several occasions presented by the emperor each with half a pound of this invaluable root,—a munificent gift were the price really as stated by the missionaries.

The ginseng is found chiefly in the valleys of the Upper Usuri up to 47° N. lat., and it prefers moist forests and recesses never visited by the rays of the sun. That which grows wild is said to be the best, but little of it goes into the market.

During summer several hundred Chinese come to seek the root, and on an average they find forty plants each. Of these, fifteen are spent in provisions, procured from the Chinese settled on the Upper Usuri, and the remainder are taken to the ginseng plantations, where a root five inches long generally fetches five shillings. The gain of the ginseng-seeker is thus about from £6 to £7, with which he is enabled to live through the winter, even if he does not engage in hunting. It is but exceptionally that his profit is more, that is if he finds roots of about eight inches long and half an inch thick, for the value of the ginseng is calculated in the same manner as that of a diamond. In one of the ginseng plantations Veniukof found 12,000 roots in beds. The manner of cultivating the plant has been noticed previously. When prepared for sale, the leaves are cut off and the root is boiled in water, apparently to remove some injurious quality, and then carefully dried and wrapped up in unsized paper. The Chinese on the Usuri are scarcely ever without a root, and make use of it boiled in case of cold, fever, head-ache or stomach-ache. The Goldi and Orochi do not esteem the root so highly, and if by chance they find one sell it to the Chinese.[d]

We will now mention some other plants applied to medicinal purposes by the natives on the Amur. The Manguns use infusion of yellow Rhododendron against stomach-ache; the Goldi, for the same complaint, marsh wild rosemary (Ledum palustre). The latter take Rock Woodsia (W. ilvensis) for pains in the chest, and the roots of the tokose herb are considered a cure for diarrhœa, produced by feeding on fish. The burnt heads of burdock are laid on ulcers: at Peking they are used in a similar manner. Wounds are

---

[d] For detailed descriptions of the Ginseng, see Nees von Esenbeck's Medicinal Plants, Plate 112; C. A. Meyer in Gauger's Repertory for Pharmacy and Practical Chemistry, i. 517.

covered with agaric. The small buds of a plant called toors by the natives, are resorted to by the Gilyaks in case of sexual diseases; they have scarcely any taste, and are slightly astringent.

The ancient doctrine of the Signatura plantarum is borne out by the application of the root of Solomon's seal (Polygonatum) for pains in the throat; and that of the hand-shaped bulb of an orchid for ulcers. The latter bears a great resemblance to the fragrant gymnadenia and is called by the Gilyaks Macherlaga-tymyk, *i.e.*, child's hand. The Goldi, Gilyaks and other tribes are also in the habit of making a wooden model of the limb suffering, which they carry about with them attached to the arm or leg, as the case may be.

It would appear, however, that only old women put any trust in the use of vegetable medicines. The more enlightened portion of the community resort to the services of a Shaman, by whom a cure, if at all possible, is affected with much greater dispatch and certainty. We shall describe the ceremonies practised on such occasions when speaking of the native inhabitants. But the services of the Shamans even are considered inefficient in case of infectious diseases. The small-pox has committed dreadful ravages amongst the natives since its first introduction by the Chinese. The only chance of safety is sought in dispersing through the forests, where each family lives for some time, without having any intercourse with others.

MISCELLANEOUS PLANTS.

We cannot avoid putting tobacco at the head of plants of a miscellaneous character, for the native generally feels its want much more acutely than that of food plants. In many instances when tobacco cannot be procured, substitutes are

## NETTLES AND HEMP.

used, such as mistletoe, the leaves of hare's ear, Limnanthemum, and on Sakhalin a kind of moss, Polystichum spinulosum—plants which we recommend to the notice of the London tobacconists.

Among the herbs which are of importance in the household of the natives, the common sting-nettle occupies the first rank, and next to it hemp. Both grow in large masses in the vicinity of every native hut. The natives manufacture rope from the nettle. In autumn the stems are cut, soaked in water, and during the winter they are kept drying, tied up in bundles. On the approach of spring they are split with a sharp wedge, then flattened with a piece of wood, and shaken until the fibres separate. These are spun into thread by the women on a spindle (shown in the illustration). They

THE SPINDLE.

are afterwards made into ropes by the men. The thread is wound on as many spindles as the rope is intended to have strands. These spindles are then fixed to a bench, and the ends of the thread pulled through a ring fastened to a beam of the roof, until they nearly reach the ground. They are then fastened to another spindle which is kept suspended and revolving until the rope has acquired the necessary firmness. The portion thus completed is rolled up, another portion of the thread is pulled down, and the operation repeated until the rope is finished. Ropes manufactured in this style are equal in evenness and strength to the better kind of our hemp ropes and cannot be distinguished from them after being in use and consequently bleached in the water, for owing to the dirty hands of the women, the rope leaves the manufacture quite black. Coloured threads, with which garments, etc., are embroidered, are purchased from the Chinese. Dyestuffs are not, however, wanting entirely for colouring furs and fish-skin clothing, boots, tobacco-pouches and so forth. Red dye is prepared from a red earth, said to be found in small pieces on the sea-coast; or from a Chinese product called Yukha. A fine blue is procured by squeezing out the leaves of the Commelynæ, which is even cultivated for this purpose in several villages. A decoction of the bark of the Alnaster fruticosus furnishes a brownish-yellow. For black they use Indian ink. Green is procured from the Satrinia scabiosæfolia.

Sedge-grass (Calamagrostis purpurea) is generally employed for roofing the houses, and in the south for covering the conical summer huts. Reeds are worked into matting, laid upon the benches in the houses. In addition to these, there is another grass which the Chinese consider one of the three treasures of Manchuria, sables and the ginseng being the other two. We refer to the *ula*, which during winter is placed in the boots to keep the feet warm. In northern countries, where severe frosts are of frequent occurrence, it is by no means rare among the peasantry, to wrap up the feet in hay or straw. The grass used for this purpose must be sufficiently strong and elastic to resist being crushed together by the pressure of the foot. Several varieties of the Carices would answer these requirements, and a specimen of "ula" which the Paris Society for Acclimatisation. presented to the Russian Academy, in reality belonged to the species Carex, or at all events to the Cyperaceæ.

Bog-moss is used for calking of boats and houses. The fungus used for tinder is procured chiefly from the trunks of larch trees. The Goldi and Manyargs, in lieu of it make use of the Rhaponticum atriplicifolium, and in case of emergency resort to dry decayed willow wood.

## XIX.

## ANIMALS.

##### MAMMALS.

THE country of the Amur is by no means distinguished for having many mammals peculiar to it; for if we except two species of field-mice (Arvicola Amurensis and A. Maximowiczii) we only met with animals which occur also in other regions of the globe. It is remarkable however that animals indigenous to regions far removed in latitude meet here. The Bengal tiger, for instance, is a constant inhabitant of the country up to 51° of north latitude, and on its predatory excursions to the left bank of the Amur, to 53°, it feeds upon the reindeer, seals and the Delphinapterus. We also find here the Antelope crispa, and the Racoon dog, natives of Japan and China. The stag ranges here to 56°, the wild boar to beyond 52°, and the badger to 53°, their extreme limits in Europe being 63°, 55°, and 54° respectively. On the other hand, animals peculiar to the Arctic regions extend further south in the Amur countries than elsewhere. The polar Pika hare, which in Europe is not found to the south of 50° north latitude, is met with on the Amur under 47°; and the reindeer and glutton, whose extreme limits in Sweden and the Altai are 50° and 60° respectively, are found here to 49°, and on Sakhalin to 46°. The white whale comes from 10° to 15° further to the south than in the Ob or Yenisei. Recent researches on the Amur have further shown that some animals have a much wider longitudinal range than was believed formerly. The common European hedgehog, the eastern limit of which was believed to be the Ural Mountains, inhabits the prairies of the Amur; and at its mouth we find a bat, Vespertilio mystacinus, which was believed not to exist beyond the Ukraine.

Another peculiarity in the Mammals is the prevalence of dark colours. It had been previously noticed with respect to the sables and squirrels of Siberia, that the further we proceed towards the east, the darker is the colouring of their furs. But on the Amur the same holds good with very many other animals, as the badger, wolf, fox and hedgehog. The squirrels and sables of the Amur are nevertheless of a darker colour than those near the sea of Okhotsk or in Sakhalin, and the polar Pika hare increases in darkness as we proceed towards the south and west.

The following is a complete list of all Mammals hitherto discovered on the Amur.

| | | | |
|---|---|---|---|
| GLIRES | Sciurus | Vulgaris | Red or common squirrel. |
| | Pteromys | Volans | Flying squirrel. |
| | Tamias | Striatus | Ground squirrel. |
| | Mus | Decumana | Rat. |
| | Arvicola | Amurensis, rutilus, saxatilis, Maximowiczii | Field mice. |
| | | Amphibius | Water-rat. |
| | Siphneus | Asphalax | Mouse. |
| | Arctomys | Bobac | Bobac. |
| | Spermophilus | Eversmannii | Marmot. |
| | Lepus | Variabilis | Changing or Alpine hare. |
| | Lagomys | Hyperboreus | Polar Pika hare. |
| CHEIROPTERA | Vespertilio | Mystacimus, Daubentonii | Bats. |
| | Vesperugo | Borealis | |
| | Plecotus | Auritus | Horse-shoe bat. |
| DIGITIGRADA | Canis | Lupus, alpinus, vulpes, procyonoides, familiaris | Wolf, red wolf, fox, racoon-dog, dog. |

MAMMALS.                                  317

| | | | |
|---|---|---|---|
| DIGITIGRADA | Felis | Lynx, tigris, irbis, domestica... | Lynx, tiger, panther, cat. |
| | Mustela | Zibellina, Sibirica, erminea, vulgaris. | Sable, polecat, ermine, weasel. |
| | Lutra | Vulgaris | Common otter. |
| | Enhydris | Marina | Sea otter. |
| PLANTIGRADA | Ursus | Arctos | Brown bear. |
| | Gulo | Borealis | Glutton. |
| | Meles | Taxus | Badger. |
| | Erinaceus | Europæus, auritus | Hedgehogs. |
| | Sorex | Vulgaris, pigmaeus | Shrews. |
| RUMINANTIA | Bos | Taurus | Ox. |
| | Ovis | Aries | Sheep. |
| | Antelope | Crispa | Antelope. |
| | Cervus | Capreolus, tarandus, elephas, alces | Roe, reindeer, stag, elk. |
| | Moschus | Moschifera | Musk deer. |
| SOLIPEDES | Equus | Caballus, asinus | Horse, ass. |
| PACHYDERMATA | Sus | Scrofa, domestica | Boar, pig. |
| PHOCACEAE | Phoca | Nummularis, barbata, Ochotensis, equestris | Seal, sea-calf, Okhotsk, and ribbon seal. |
| | Trichechus | Rosmarus | Walrus. |
| | Otaria | Ursina | Ursine seal. |
| CETACEAE | Balaena | Australis | Whale. |
| | Balaenoptera | Longimana | Fin-fish. |
| | Delphinapterus Leucas | | White whale. |

Total, thirty-six genera with sixty-one species.

Of *domesticated animals* there are the dog, the reindeer, the horse, ass and mule, the ox, the sheep and the cat. The *dog* is the most widely distributed. Among the Goldi and other tribes of the Lower Amur and Sakhalin, it is used as a beast of draft; among the Manchu and Chinese to guard the houses, and among all to hunt.[*] Its skin supplies a

[*] The dogs are harnessed to the sledges in pairs, preceded by a dog acting as leader. Neither whips nor reins are used, the occupant of the sledge directing them exclusively by his voice. These animals

material for dress. The *reindeer* appears to have been much more widely distributed formerly than at present, for we now find it as a domesticated animal only among the Orochons of the Upper Amur and the Oroke of Sakhalin. There is even a tradition among the Goldi and Manguns that they also had reindeer in times long gone, but lost them in consequence of an epidemic, and were driven thereby to seek their sustenance in fishing. The very name of the Tunguzians of the sea-coast — we allude to the Orochi, testifies this fact, for Oro or Oron is the Tunguzian name for reindeer, and Oronchon, Orochi, or Oroke, simply mean reindeer-keepers.

The Tunguzians north of the Amur keep reindeer in larger numbers, and with their herds cross the Ud and Tugur. They have occasionally supplied the Russian garrison at Nikolayevsk with reindeer fresh meat, and also find the necessary animals for the postal service to Udsk and Ayan, and likewise train some of the domesticated to hunt the wild ones. The huntsman retains the decoy by a strap, and when the wild deer approach, he is enabled with his bow to commit great havoc before they are aware of the proximity of their enemy. Among the Orochons of the Upper Amur, the reindeer is used as a beast of burthen, and the Oroke of Sakhalin make it draw the sledges during winter.

*Horses* are numerous among the Manyargs, who use them as beasts of burden. They appear to have come originally from the Russian Cossacks of the Shilka and the Argun, and even now the Manyargs frequently procure horses from ·the Russians, and sell them to the Chinese and Manchu. The

---

are very intelligent. M. Maack one morning missed his pots which he had left full of meat the evening before, and, on search being made, they were found empty in the forest, several dogs prowling about them. They had evidently feared being interrupted in their meal ; and to avoid this, carried the pots off, to consume the contents at their ease.

breed is rather small, but robust and strong. Among the Manchu and Chinese, the horse is used, as in Europe, for riding, draft, and for carrying loads. The communication between Tsitsikar, Aigun, and the Sungari is kept up with horses, and the mountains across which the road leads from Aigun, are known to the Birars as "Morre-urra," or horse mountains. Among the Goldi there are but few; those which they kept at the Usuri mouth have recently (in 1855) been destroyed by tigers. *Asses* and *mules* are reserved by the Manchu and Chinese for riding. The *pig* abounds among the Manchu, Chinese, and Daurians, and the Goldi of the Sungari. It is scarcer amongst the Goldi of the Amur, and even more among Olcha, who only now and then procure one from a Manchu trader. The Russians had introduced some pigs in 1854 and 1855, but in 1856 they had either been killed or had gone astray.

*Horned Cattle* are kept only in the neighbourhood of the agricultural settlements on the Amur, the Sungari and Usuri, where they find excellent food in the prairies. They are large and strong, and employed mostly in agriculture. Numerous herds have been recently imported by the Russians, and there will, no doubt, be in time a sufficiency to supply the garrisions with fresh meat throughout the year. *Sheep*, strange to say, are not reared on the Amur; though the natives are well acquainted with sheepskins through the resident Manchu and Chinese merchants, who hold them in high esteem. The Russians in 1856 had not yet introduced the sheep. The nomadic life of many of the Amur tribes is not favourable generally to *cats*, but among the more stationary Goldi, Manguns, and Gilyaks, puss is a great pet. Since the arrival of the Russians, cats are easy to be had, but in former times, when the only supply came through the Manchu, a cat fetched a high price, and even then castrated Toms only came into the market. To these domesticated mammals, we may add the ermine, which the Gilyaks keep in their houses to catch rats.

We now proceed to those animals which the natives hunt, sometimes for the sake of the furs or skins, sometimes for the flesh, and sometimes for all together. At the head of these we place the tiger, which is said to be frequent on the Sungari and Usuri. This beast of prey is naturally much dreaded and regarded with great superstition; but nevertheless the Goldi and Manguns dare face ·it, and when they succeed in killing one, sell the skin to the Manchu. On the Lower Amur the tiger is very rare, and the Gilyaks are even more superstitious with regard to it than their neighbours higher up. No instance is known of their having killed a tiger, and they look upon it as a kind of bogy who appears to individuals who have committed an evil action. The remains of persons killed by a tiger are interred on the spot without any observance of religious ceremonies. They believe, in fact, in a migration of souls in which the tiger and bear play a part, and this belief is typified in some of their idols, which are half beast half man. Occasionally the tiger crosses over to Sakhalin. The panther is met within the same limits as the tiger, but more rarely. Similar superstitions are entertained with regard to it, and even the Goldi do not dare to hunt the creature. The only other animal of the genus *felis* is the Lynx, which is found in the forests of the Amur and Sakhalin; but is very scarce. Its fur is highly valued, and a Gilyak in possession of one does not wear it, but preserves it as a kind of curiosity, which confers on the owner the reputation of great wealth. Sometimes a kind of cap is made of it for the women.

Next to the tiger and panther, the most formidable beast is the bear (Ursus arctos) which is found in a black and light brown variety, the former prevailing. Another variety with a white collar (U. collaris Gadd.) or with spots on neck and breast is also to be met with. The Ursus maritimus has never been seen, but the light variety of the U. Arctos is often confounded with it. The bear inhabits the mountainous districts of the region of the Amur and Manchuria and is never so good-natured as on Kamchatka. Feared as a powerful beast of prey it enters strongly into the religious ideas of the natives, who frequently catch it alive and confine it in a cage. But this we have referred to at length elsewhere.

Of all animals valued for their fur, the Sable is the most esteemed. It is found along the whole of the Amur, and varies in colour between black and light brown. The best black sables are at the headwaters of the Gorin, Amgun, and Dzeya. As we proceed to the east or south, it deteriorates, and on Sakhalin is almost worthless. On the Argun and Upper Amur the animal has become extinct, but the hunters find compensation in the great number of squirrels.[b] The *polecat* abounds in the hilly tracts north of the Lower Amur, and is trapped sometimes in the snares set for sables, to the great annoyance of the hunters. The *weasel* exists in the same locality, but is very rare. The *ermine* again has a wider range and extends to Sakhalin. The common *otter* is not numerous. Its fur is highly prized by the Manchu and Chinese, and next to sables, supplies the most important article of trade on the part of the natives. Schrenck also noticed a sea-otter (Enhydris marina), but it is not hunted by the natives. The *fox* ranks next in importance to the otter, as other furs are either too scarce or of no great value. It occurs in all varieties, black, red, and crossed.

The skin of the *wolf* is thought very highly of. This animal chiefly preys upon reindeer, and in the prairies, upon roes. Sometimes, famished herds of wolves approach the villages of the natives to kill the dogs. The *red-wolf* (Canis Alpinus) is generally left alone from a superstitious apprehension, dictated probably by the fact of this creature

[b] The Marten (Mustela marten) has not been found on the Amur, but sometimes a light-coloured variety of sable is confounded with it.

traversing the forests in herds, often very numerous. The winter skin of the *Racoon-dog* is highly valued by Manchu and natives, and during summer the animal is killed only for the sake of its flesh.[c] The *badger*, of a darker colour generally than in Europe, is most abundant in the prairies, and does not extend to Sakhalin. The *glutton*, in a dark and light variety, appears throughout in the mountainous tracts wherever there are rein-deer.

*Squirrels* are numerous, especially so on the Upper Amur, where, too, they are of superior quality. Annually in September and October, the Cossacks of the Argun and Shilka disperse in small hunting parties, and every huntsman calculates on bringing back several hundred skins. The squirrel during winter varies in colour; some are darkish grey, others brown, and some almost black, these latter being considered the most valuable. By the Russians this difference of colour is ascribed to variety of food. The black squirrels live upon mushrooms, of which they gather stores for the winter; the brown ones feed upon the cones of the cedar and other conifers, and the reddish variety upon hazelnuts. As a rule, squirrels abound most where sables and polecats, who prey upon it, are about. Ground-squirrels are found on the Usuri; *Hares* along the whole course of the Amur. The *Bobac* is esteemed not only for its fur, but also for its fat. Among the ruminating animals an *Antelope* (A. crispa) is the most interesting; it is found only in the mountains near the sea-coast, and is alluded to by travellers as a wild goat. The *Roe* abounds on the Amur as far as the Gorin, and is occasionally met with down to the first Gilyak villages. It is hunted chiefly in Autumn for the sale of its flesh and skin. The *Stag* is equally abundant on the Upper Amur, and is the most valued game of the Orochons, Manyargs and Birars. Its

---

[c] The Polar fox (Canis lagopus) is not found on the Amur.

flesh, fresh or dried, constitutes with them a chief article of food; the skin is manufactured into garments, and the soft antlers are sold to Chinese and Russians, the former considering it a very effectual confortative. This animal is less important to the tribes below the Bureya, who depend more exclusively upon fishing for their sustenance. The *Elk* is the largest and most widely distributed of all; and for that reason the Tunguzians simply call it Buyu or Boyun, that is the "Animal." It is particularly numerous on the Upper Gorin, where most of the Samagers dress in elk-skins. The flesh is eaten. The *musk-deer* is most abundant in the coniferous woods along the Amur and on Sakhalin. The skin is made into clothing, and the flesh eaten, though not very much liked. The thin tubular bones of the legs are made into arrow heads. *Reindeer* are found wild in all mountainous districts north of 50° N. lat. and on Sakhalin. The wild *boar* is most frequent in the prairie region; its flesh is eaten and the skin converted into covers or blankets, used to cover the summer tents or in travelling. Of smaller animals the rats alone deserve to be mentioned specially. It is owing chiefly to the rapacity of the *Mus decumana* that the Tunguzians built their store-house on four poles, to keep the contents beyond its reach; and among the Goldi the Manchu are nicknamed "Singare," *i.e.*, rats, on account of the rapacity with which they exact tribute.

Of aquatic mammals, the *Seals* are the most important. The animal is killed with harpoons, or in the winter, when the Liman is frozen over, its retreat, when venturing upon the ice, is cut off, and it is killed with sticks. The flesh and oil serve for food for man and beast, the skin is used for clothing; and that of the sea-calf, being very stout, is cut into thongs, or boots are made of it. The common seal ascends the Amur as far as the village Yrri, 51° north latitude. The *whale* abounds in the Channel of Manchuria, but is only got by the natives of Sakhalin when washed ashore. They sell the oil to the Japanese, and make use of the whale-bone for their sledges, bows and snow-shoes. The white whale (Delphinapterus Leucas) appears in May in large shoals north of the Liman, and the Gilyaks kill a great many with their harpoons. When the Amur is free of ice it ascends the river to Yrri. The *Fin-fish* is sometimes washed ashore, and the Gilyaks give the flesh to their dogs, and use the bones for the soles or keels of their sledges. Walrus teeth are procured sometimes by the Gilyaks from their northern neighbours or the Russians. They are not however much in demand, as the antlers of the elk and reindeer suffice for their wants.

## Birds.

The birds of the Amur belong for the most part to species which are common also to Siberia and Europe, but in addition to these, we meet with some birds of passage, natives of southern and south-eastern Asia, China, Japan, the Himalaya, the East Indies, Philippine Islands and even Australia and South Africa. Seven-tenths of the birds are found in Europe, two-tenths in Siberia, and one-tenth in the tropical and sub-tropical regions to the south. Among the birds found in Siberia, there are, however, some which may be more properly assigned to America; for instance, the Canada woodcock and the water ouzel (Cinclus Pallasii), and, as might be expected from the close proximity of the two continents at Behring Straits, there are several birds common to the east and west coasts of the Pacific, belonging to the genera Mormon, Uria and Phaleris. With regard to land-birds this affinity is however scarcely perceptible. The ornithological fauna owes some of its more peculiar features to a number of birds of more southern latitude, which do not extend to Europe or Siberia. Acanthylis cauducata, and Zosterops chloronatas, Australian birds, visit the Amur. We find the Pericrocotus cinereus, of a group otherwise represented only within the tropics; the Ardea virescens, a native of tropical and subtropical Africa, Asia and America; the Ardea cinnamomea, of southern Asia. Of Chinese birds, there are the ring-pheasant, the Mandarin-duck, the Cochin-china oriole, the Cuculus sparverioides, (a cuckoo), Caprimulgus Jotaka (night-jar), Emberiza personata (a bunting), Sturnus cineraceus (a starling), Pastor sturninus (starling ouzel), the Turdus daulius and T. chrysolaus (thrushes), Salicaria Aëdon (red wren), Muscicapa cinerea-alba and M. hylocharis (fly-catcher), and probably several others. The laughing dove, which, in Europe, is not found beyond the Balkan and Southern Russia, extends on the Amur to 51° north latitude. The white stork frequents the Amur, though not met with in Siberia. The Alpine accentor which does not extend beyond central Europe, and is wanting in Siberia, frequents the Amur, and even reaches the sea of Okhotsk. The Pica cyana of Spain, China and Japan, also occurs on the Amur. These birds of tropical and sub-tropical regions, are, of course, most abundant at the southern bend of the Amur, about the mouth of the Sungari and Usuri, but, advancing along the valley of the river, some of them reach Dauria and Mariinsk. It would be in vain, however, to look for them on the eastern slope of the coast range, in Castries Bay, or even the more southern Port Imperial.

The number of stationary birds on the Amur is not very large, owing to the excessive cold during winter, and the great fall of snow on the lower part of the river. Schrenck gives the following list of birds as stationary on the Amur below the Gorin, the result of two years' observation by himself and Maack.

The goshawk; short-eared owl, hawk-owl, little owl; five species of wood-peckers; the common and white-winged cross-bill; four species of tits; the nut-hatch; the two jays;

the magpie; the nut-cracker; the carrion crow, Japanese crow and raven; the creeper; the water-ouzel; white grouse; grouse; Canada woodcock, and hazel hen. To these may be added a few birds for localities where there is open water also during winter, most of them probably old individuals, viz., the white-tailed eagle, the wild duck, golden eye, and Phaleris cristatella; and the following which arrive in autumn for a shorter or longer period:—the snowy owl; the bullfinch, pink bullfinch, pine gros-beak and redpole. We have thus named all those species, thirty-nine, which are met with during winter. There are naturally several others which escaped notice. The birds of passage generally arrive at the end of April or during May, and leave in September and October. It is a remarkable fact, that they come generally later to Nikolayevsk on the Lower Amur than to the town of Yakutsk, nine degrees further to the north. The cuckoo, for instance, is heard at Nikolayevsk about the 28th May, at Yakutsk between the 15th and 21st. The geese arrive at the former place on the 2nd May, but at Yakutsk as early as the 26th April. Many other instances are quoted·by Maximowicz. The cause of this late arrival of birds of passage is to be sought for in the climatological and orographical features of the Amur country and adjoining regions. The Lower Amur is remarkable for its large quantities of snow, and at Nikolayevsk it remains on the ground until the beginning of June. The seasons above the Usuri are more favourable; but to the south is the snow-covered Shan-alin, which arrests the progress of the birds. These unfavourable circumstances do not exist on the Upper Amur and in Trans-baikal, where little snow falls, and where there are no high mountains to the south offering obstacles to birds proceeding to Northern Siberia.

The feathered tribe are not of very much importance in the household of the native tribes. The Manchu keep fowls and swan-geese, and the Russians introduced pigeons in 1855. The natives on the Lower Amur sometimes keep eagles, kites, owls, hawks or jays captive. The tail feathers of the two former are used to wing their arrows. They are glad to see chimney-swallows build in their houses. Woodcocks, grouse, all kinds of aquatic birds are caught by the natives and eaten.

In conclusion, we give a tabular view of all birds described in Schrenck's "Reisen," vol. i. part 2. The last column gives the number of species supposed to exist on the Amur, though not yet actually found. Sakhalin has been included.

328

ORDER I. NATATORES (Swimming Birds).

| | Genera. | Species described by Schrenck. | Total Species. | English Name. | Total Species. |
|---|---|---|---|---|---|
| Short winged | Alca | Cirrhatum | — | Razor-bill hawk | 1 |
| | Mormon | Cristatella | 1 | Puffin | 4 |
| | Phaleris | | 1 | | 2 |
| | Uria | Carbo, antique | 2 | | 4 |
| | Colymbus | Arcticus, septentrionalis | 2 | Northern and speckled diver | 4 |
| | Podiceps | Cornutus, subcristatus | 2 | Grebe | 4 |
| | Mergus | Merganser, Serrator, albellus | 3 | Goosander, saw-bill, smew | 3 |
| | Anas | Galericulata, Penelope, Boschas; Crecca, glocitans, falcata; acuta, clypeata, clangula, histrionica, fuligula | 11 | Mandarin duck, widgeon, wild duck; teal; pintail duck, shoveller, golden eye, harlequin duck, tufted duck | 21 |
| Duck tribe | Anser | Cygnoides, grandis, segetum, cinereus | 4 | Swan-goose, great goose, bean and grey goose | 7 |
| | Cygnus | Musicus, Bewickii | 2 | Singing, and Bewick's swan | 2 |
| Steganopodes | Pelecanus | | — | Pelican | 2 |
| | Phalacrocorax | Carbo | 1 | Cormorant | 3 |
| | Sterna | Leucoptera, longipennis | 2 | Tern | 2 |
| Longipennes | Larus | Argentatus, canus, ridibundus | 3 | Herring gull, common & laughing gull | 8 |
| | Lestris | | — | Skua | 2 |
| | Procellaria | Glacialis | 1 | Fulmar | 1 |
| | Phalassidroma | Leachii | 1 | Petrel | 2 |
| | | Total | 36 | Total | 72 |

## Order II. Grallatores (Waders).

| | Genera. | Species described by Schrenck. | Total Species. | English Name. | Total Species. |
|---|---|---|---|---|---|
| Macrodactyli | Fulica | Atra | 1 | Common coot | 1 |
| | Gallinula | | — | Moorhen | 1 |
| | Ortygometra | (To Grex, Rallus or Gallinula) | — | Rail | 2 |
| | Scolopax | Gallinago | 1 | Snipe | 4 |
| | Limosa | Cinerea | 1 | Godwit | 3 |
| | (Totanus | Glottis, glareola, ochropus | 3 | Greenshawk, Pratincole, green sandpiper | 6 |
| Longirostres (Long bills) | Actitis | Hypoleucus | 1 | Common sandpiper | 1 |
| | Recurvirostra | | — | Avocet | 1 |
| | (Tringa | Crassirostris, Canutus, subarquatra, cinclus, Temminckii, minuta, sub-minuta | 7 | Sandpiper, knot, curlew sandpiper, Dunlin sandpiper, Temminck's stint, little stint | 9 |
| | Calidris | | — | Sanderling | 1 |
| | Machetes | | — | Ruff | 1 |
| | Phalaropus | Cinereus | 1 | Phalarope | 2 |
| | Numenius | Australis | 1 | Australian curlew | 2 |
| | Platalea | | — | Spoonbill | 1 |
| Cultrirostres | Ciconia | Nigra, alba | 2 | Black and white stork | 2 |
| | Ardea | Cinerea, virescens, cinnamouea; stellaris | 5 | Herons; bittern | 10 |
| | Grus | Leucogeranus, cinerea | 2 | Cranes | 5 |
| Pressirostres | Haemotopus | Ostralegus | 1 | Oyster-catcher | 2 |
| | Charadrius | Pluvialis, Mongolicus, curonicus | 3 | Golden plover, Mongol plover | 6 |
| | Squatarola | Helvetica | 1 | Grey plover | 1 |
| | Vanellus | Cristatus | 1 | Lapwing or peewit | 1 |
| Bustards | Otis | Tarda | 1 | Great Bustard | 1 |
| | | Total Waders | 32 | Total | 63 |

ORDER III. GALLINAE OR RASORES.

| | Genera. | Species described by Schrenck. | English Name. | Total Species. |
|---|---|---|---|---|
| Pheasants | Phasianus | Torquanus | Pheasant | 1 |
| | Gallus | Gallinaceus | Domestic cock | 1 |
| | Perdix | — | Partridges and quail [d] | 3 |
| Tetraoninae | Tetrao [d] | Urogalloides, Tetrix, Canadensis, Bonasia | Woodcock or grouse, black cock, Canada grouse, hazel-hen | 5 |
| | Lagopus | Albus | White grouse | 1 |
| Columbinae | Columba | Turtur, risoria, livia | Turtle dove, laughing dove, pigeon | 4 |
| | | | Total Gallinae | 15 |

ORDER IV. SCANSORES (Climbing Birds).

| Cuckoos | Cuculus | Canorus, sparverioides | Cuckoo | 2 |
|---|---|---|---|---|
| | Yunx | Torquilla | Wryneck | 1 |
| Sagittilingues | Picus | Canus, martius, leuconotus, major, minor, trydactylus | Grey, black and spotted woodpeckers | 6 |
| | | | Total Climbing Birds | 9 |

ORDER V. AMBULATORES (Walking Birds).

| Coracinae | Coracias | . . . | Roller | 1 |
|---|---|---|---|---|
| Halcyoninae | Alcedo | Ispida, var. Bengalensis | Kingfisher | 1 |
| Upupinae | Upupa | Epops | Hoopoe | 1 |
| Colopteridae | Thaumaleae | . . . | . . . | 1 |

[d] Found by Tronson in Barracouta Bay.    [e] Tetrao Urogallus, the Capercailzie, in Barracouta Bay.

331

ORDER V. AMBULATORES (Walking Birds)—*Continued.*

| | Genera. | Species described by Schrenck. | Total Species. | English Name. | Total Species. |
|---|---|---|---|---|---|
| Corvinae | Corvus | Monedula, corone; Japanensis, corax | 4 | Jackdaw, carrion crow, raven | 5 |
| | Pica | Cyana, caudata | 2 | Magpie | 2 |
| | Nucifrega | Caryocatactes | 1 | Nutcracker | 1 |
| | Garrulus | Infaustus, glandarius | 2 | Jay | 2 |
| | Fregilus | | — | Chough or red-legged crow | 1 |
| Paradiseinae | Oriolus | Cochin-chinensis | 1 | Cochin-china oriole | 2 |
| Sturninae | Pastor | | — | Starling-ouzel | 1 |
| | Sturnus | Cineraceus | 1 | Starling | 1 |
| | Fringilla | Linaria, spinus, montifringilla | 3 | Rose-linnet or redpoll, siskin and bramble finch | 6 |
| | Loxia | Curvirostra, leucoptera | 2 | Common and white-winged cross-bill | 2 |
| | Pyrhula | Sibirica, vulgaris, erythrinae, rosea; Enecleator | 5 | Siberian bullfinch, common bullfinch; Pine gros-beak | 5 |
| Finches | Emberizza | Aureola, rustica, Pithyornis, cioides, rutila, personata, spodocephala, Schoenidus, pusilla | 9 | } Hammers and buntings | 12 |
| | Plectrophanes | Nivalis, Lapponica | 2 | Snow bunting, Lapland lark, bunting | 2 |
| | Passer | Montanus, domesticus | 2 | Tree and house sparrow | 2 |
| | Coccothraustes | Vulgaris | 1 | Gros-beak, finch, or haw-finch | 1 |
| Larks | Alauda | Alpestris, arvensis | 2 | Shore-lark, sky-lark | 4 |
| Parinae | Parus | Caudatus, cyanus, palustris, ater | 5 | Long-tailed tit, blue tit, marsh tit, cole tit | 9 |
| Certhianae | Regulus | Cristatus | 1 | Golden-crested warbler or Wren | 1 |
| | Sitta | Europaea | 1 | Nuthatch | 1 |
| | Certhia | Familiaris | 1 | Creeper | 1 |

332

ORDER V. AMBULATORES (Walking Birds)—*Continued.*

| | Genera. | Species described by Schrenck. | Total Species. | | English Name. | Total Species. |
|---|---|---|---|---|---|---|
| Nectarinae | Zosterops | Chloronatus | 1 | | | |
| Turdinae | Turdus | Daulius, chrysolaus, Naumanni, fuscatus | 4 | | Thrushes | 13 |
| | Cinclus | Pallasii | 1 | | Dipper or water-ouzel | 2 |
| | Moticilla | Alba, sulphurea, flava | 3 | | Wagtails | 4 |
| | Anthus | Arborens, pratensis | 2 | | Tree-pipit, meadow-pipit or titlark | 3 |
| | Accentor | Alpinus | 1 | | Alpine accentor | 1 |
| Motacillinae | Saxicola | Saltatrix, rubicola | 2 | | Stonechat | 5 |
| | Lusciola | Kamchatensis, phoenicura, cyanura | 3 | | Kamchatha nightingale, red start | 7 |
| | Sylvia | | | | Nightingale | 1 |
| | Phylopneuste | Rufa, sibirica, superciliosa | 3 | | Chiffchaff | 5 |
| | Salicaria | Aëdon, Maackii, certhiola, locustella | 4 | | Red wren and warblers | 7 |
| | Muscicapa | Parva, luteola, Sibirica, cinereo-alba, hylocharis | 5 | | Fly-catchers | 7 |
| Muscicapinae | Perierocotus | Cinereus | 1 | | Chatterer | 1 |
| | Bombycilla | | | | Shrike | 5 |
| Laniianae | Lanius | Phoenicurus | 1 | | Chimney-swallow, martin, sand-martin | 5 |
| | Hirundo | Rustica, urbica, riparia | 3 | | Swift | 1 |
| Chelidones | Cypselus | | | | | |
| | Acanthylis | Caudacuta | 1 | | | 2 |
| Nyctichelidones | Caprimulgus | Jotaka | 1 | | Night-jar | 2 |
| | | Total Walking Birds | 83 | | Total | 138 |

333

## Order VI. Raptores (Birds of Prey).

| | Genera. | Species described by Schrenck. | Total Species. | English Name. | Total Species. |
|---|---|---|---|---|---|
| Strigidæ | Strix | Uralensis, otus, brachyotus, nyctea, funerea, passerina, bubo | 7 | Short-eared and long-eared owl, brown owl, snowy owl, hawk-owl, little owl, great-eared owl | 12 |
| | Falco | Gyrfalco, peregrinus; subbuteo, vespertinus, tinnunculus | 5 | Gyrfalcon, peregrine falcon; hobby, red-legged falcon, kestrel | 6 |
| | Circus | Cyanus | 1 | Hen-harrier | 2 |
| | Milvus | Niger, var. melanotis | 1 | Black kite | 1 |
| Accipitrinae | Buteo | | — | Buzzard | 1 |
| | Astur | Palumbarius, nisus | 2 | Gos-hawk, sparrow-hawk | 2 |
| | Aquila | Naevia | 1 | Spotted eagle | 2 |
| | Haliaëtus | Pelagicus, albicella | 2 | Sea-eagle, white-tailed eagle | 2 |
| | Pandion | Haliaëtos | 1 | Osprey or fish-hawk | 1 |
| Vultures | Gypaëtos | | — | Vulture | 1 |
| | | Total Raptores | 20 | Total | 30 |
| | | Grand total | 190 | Grand total | 327 |

## Fish and Reptiles.

Fish yield to the natives one of the chief articles of their food, and, indeed, on the Lower Amur, almost the only one. The skin is made into dresses, and the oil supplies the lamps.

In spring, they ascend the rivers to spawn; and remain until about August, and then descend again towards the sea. It is in autumn that the native procures his chief supply of fish. Having watched, in spring, the channels by which the fish ascend, he lies in wait for their return; for it has observed that they always come back by the same channels. The number of fish is prodigious, and there are many kinds not known in Europe. Sturgeons and salmon of extraordinary size are the most important. We find here the common sturgeon (Accipenser sturio), the kaluga and bieluga of the Russians (A. orientalis and A. huso), the grayling (Salmo thymallus), Salmo lagocephalus, S. Proteus, trout (S. lense), and chad (Silurus). Of smaller fish there are carp, pike, and perch, the eel pout (Encheliopus lota), bream, and many others. Along the coast, cod and plaice are the most valuable, especially the former.

Fresh-water turtles are found at the mouth of the Usuri, and their flesh is much relished by the natives. Among the reptiles there is a poisonous viper. Gerstfeldt enumerates nine genera of reptiles, with fourteen species, viz., Zootoca (lizards), Eremias, Coelopeltis (adders), Vipera, Trigonocephalas, Trionyx, Bufa (toads), Rana (frogs), and Triton.

## Insects, etc.

About one thousand species of insects have been hitherto collected on the Amur, and among them are above three hundred new ones, including of butterflies alone thirty-five. The proportionate number of new species is consequently very much greater than that of plants, mammals, or birds, and with the insects also we find representatives of distinct types. In the prairies of the southern Amur, where various Colias and Vanessæ bask in spring, we meet in July, according to Radde, the splendid Papilio Maackii, and whilst about noon the widely distributed Aglia Tau darts rapidly along, or large species of Limenites hide in the thick foliage of the oak, there buzzes at dusk a large Saturnia. The insect fauna of the Amur has, in fact, affinities with that of Central Europe, Dauria, and in the south, with that of subtropical regions. Among others we find here a gigantic moth of the genus Tropæa, which has been found in Southern China, and a variety in the East Indies and North America.

In the forests of the Bureya mountains and along the Usuri the innumerable gad-flies are a great plague to man and beasts. On a fine summer evening, when there is no wind, they appear in swarms, and after a rain, gnats and

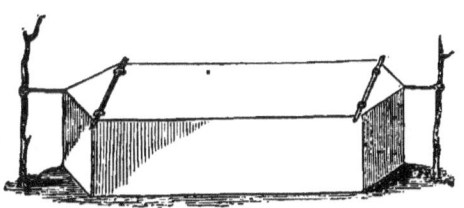

SLEEPING TENT OF THE GOLDI.

flies. No animal is safe against their attacks, however thick its skin, and they often torment it to such a degree, that it is unconscious of the approach of the huntsman, who thus makes it a more easy prey. Before retiring to rest it is absolutely necessary to smoke these insects out of the tents, and then close it hermetically. This is the only sure way of obtaining a night's rest. The Goldi and Orochi have small portable sleeping tents, which are fastened to two poles or trees, as shewn in our engraving. As a protection against the sting of these insects, a veil is worn over the face, while a thin cloth also covers the head and neck. The Chinese, when working in their fields, fasten a small piece of burning tinder to a ring, which they wear round the head, to keep off these plagues.

Pearls (Unio dahurica) are found in some of the rivers, and have been explored hitherto for the benefit of the Chinese Government exclusively.

The following is a summary view of the insects, etc., described by Gerstfeldt in Maack's work on the Amur:—

I. Insects.
  (a). Rhopalocera, in 27 genera, with 72 species.
  (b). Heterocera in 55 genera with 69 species.
II. Myriapoda: the genera Julus, 3; Platydesmus, 1; Craspedosoma, 1; Arthropomalus, 1; Lithrobius, 1. Total, 5 genera, 7 species.
III. Crustaceæ: the genera Cypris, 1; Cymothoa, 1; Glammarus, 8; Astacus, 1. Total, 4 genera, 11 species.
IV. Platodes: the genera Planaria, 3; Clepsine, 1; Nephelis, 1; Aulacostomum, 1. Total, 4 genera, 6 species.
V. Molluscæ.
  (a). Pectinibranchia: the genera Paludina, 3; Bythinia, 3; Hydrobia, 1; Melania, 1; Valvata, 4. Total, 5 genera, 12 species.
  (b). Pulmonata: the genera Limax, 1; Arion, 1; Vitrina, 1; Succinea, 1; Helix, 20; Bulimus, 2; Achatina, 1; Pupa, 3; Auricula, 1; Limnæus, 8;

Physa, 2; Planorbis, 10; Ancylus, 1; Choanomphalus, 1 (a new genera). Total, 14 genera, 53 species.

(*c*). Pneumopoma: the genus Acicula, 1.

(*d*). Pelecypoda: The genera Cyclas, 3; Pisidium, 2; Unio, 5; Anodonta, 3. Total, 4 genera, 13 species.

Total Molluscæ, 24 genera, 79 species.

XX.

NATIVE INHABITANTS.

GOLDI HUT NEAR THE SUNGARI.

THE native population of the Amur, even if we include emigrant Chinese and Manchu, is far from numerous. It may be estimated at 24,000, for the whole of the territory at present in possession of Russia. With two exceptions, the tribes of the Amur belong to the Tunguzian stock. The language of the Gilyaks, on the Lower Amur, differs from the Tunguzian dialects along the river; but the features of these Gilyaks are still Mongol, they have small obliquely set eyes, prominent cheek bones, and scanty beards. With the

Ainos on Sakhalin, the language differs both from the Tunguzian and Gilyak; their features are decidedly not Mongol, and they are distinguished by a great profusion of hair.

In order to enable our readers to judge of the close affinity between the various Tunguzian dialects, and the differences existing between Tunguzian, Gilyak, and Aino, we append a short vocabulary.

|  | TUNGUZIANS. | | | | | Gilyak.[4] | Aino.[5] |
|---|---|---|---|---|---|---|---|
|  | Yeniseisk.[1] | Nerchinsk.[1] | Manyarg.[2] | Manchu.[1] | Orochi.[3] | | |
| One...... | ummukon | onion | omun | emu | omoho | niun | chine |
| Two...... | dzyur | jur | zur | juo | dhu | morsh | tu |
| Three .... | illün | ilan | ilan | ilan | ela | chiorch | che |
| Four .... | diggin | dyggin | digin | duin | dhi | murch | yne |
| Five...... | tungya | tongua | .... | sunja | thungha | torch | ashne |
| Six ...... | niungun | niungun | nugun | ninggun | nungo | ngak | yhampe |
| River .... | birrya | bira | ... | birá | bila or widhi | .... | .... |
| Sea ...... | lamu | lamu | .... | namu | namu | atui (rur) | choiza |
| Water.... | mu | mu | mu | muke | mu | .... | wakka |
| Sun ...... | shiggun | shivun | .... | shûn | su | ... | tsuhu |
| Reindeer . | oron | sokje | ... | oron | .... | .... | .... |
| Thunder.. | addi | akdi | .... | akjan | .... | .... | kanna-ka-mui |
| Dog ...... | ninakin | nenaki | .... | indakhun | euuk | kan | tamui or sheta |

[1] Klaproth, Asia Polyglotta.  [2] Maack, Travels on the Amur.  [3] Tronson (Barracouta Bay).
[4] Furet, Letters sur l'Archipel. Japonais (Jonequière Bay).
[5] La Pérouse, Pfizmaier's Vocabularium der Aino Sprache, Vienna, 1851, and other works by the same author.

The Tunguzian tribes either are nomads, keeping herds of reindeer or horses, or they subsist chiefly upon the produce of their fisheries. The reindeer Tunguzians are called Oronchon or Oroke, a word signifying reindeer-keepers, and are met with on the Upper Amur, and on Sakhalin. Among the other tribes, a tradition prevails of their having owned reindeer at some remote period; and there is one tribe along the sea-coast still called Orochi, or Orochon. The Manyargs and the kindred Birars, and Solons, on the Nonni, who occupy the vast prairies above the Bureya mountains, keep large herds of horses. The Goldi, Olcha (Manguns), Gilyaks, Orochis of the sea-coast, and Ainos, are fishermen, but are hunters also; and the Goldi, especially those settled on the Sungari, cultivate the ground to some extent. It is, however, only the Manchu and Chinese, and the Daurians living amongst them on the Middle Amur, who till the ground to a larger extent, the Daurians doing so even at the time the Russians first appeared on the Amur. At that period their settlements extended into Dauria,[a] whilst at the present day they are but rarely found above the Dzeya.

The Chinese classify the natives of the Amur according to their way of dressing the hair. The Goldi, and others who have assumed the habit of shaving the head are called Twan-moa-tze, that is, "people who shave the head"; the tribes who use fish-skins, as one of the chief materials for making their garments, are called Yu-pi-ta-tze; the Olcha and others on the Lower Amur are called Shang-moa-tze, *i.e.*, long-haired people, and the Orochi, Elle-iao-tze, red-haired people. There are, besides, Chinese, who have fled to the wilds of the Usuri, and are called Kwang-kung-tze, that is, people without family. In the Chinese geography, we find the following tribes enumerated as being tributary. The Nair, Geikere and Hushihar, on the rivers Hulha and Sungari (they are registered as soldiers); the He-tzin-hara, on both banks of the Sungari and Amur; the Edengara, below the former on the Usuri; the Mulin, a tribe on the Usuri; and the Kilerkhaji, on the Upper Gorin. All these seem to be tribes of Goldi. The Feiaka (Viyake) and Lerkoye are identical probably with the Olcha; the Tsiagara, on the sources of the Niman are the Orochi of the sea-coast; the Tsiler (Kiyakla) are the Gilyaks. Another tribe, the Kwiara, live on the frontiers of Korea, on the north bank of the Tumen river, and these are probably also Orochi. On the Upper Amur, the Chinese enumerate the Dakhor (Dagor or Daurians), the Oronchons, the Solons and the Builar (Birars).

[a] That portion of Transbaikal, east of the Yablonoi Khrebet.

Reverting specially to the native tribes now subject to Russia, with a view to estimate their numbers, we obtain the following results:—The Oronchons of the Upper Amur numbered, in 1856, two hundred and six individuals of both sexes, roving over an area of 28,000 square miles, which would give one hundred and seventy square miles to each individual. Next come the Manyargs. Their numbers, including the Birars and the Solons, on the right bank of the Amur, are about 20,000, of whom one-sixth at most are under Russian sway. The agricultural population about Aigun, estimated at from 40,000 to 50,000, is also confined chiefly to the right bank of the river, those on its left bank hardly amounting to 2,000. The Goldi occupy one hundred and fourteen so-called villages on the Amur, with three hundred and twenty houses, and 2,560 inhabitants. The Manguns, forty villages, with one hundred and ten houses, and 1,100 inhabitants. The Kile on the Upper Gorin, and Negidalze on the Amgun, do not probably exceed 1000 souls. The population along the Usuri is estimated by Veniukof at 1,400, of whom about four hundred are on the left bank of the river. The vast tract extending between the Usuri and the sea-coast, from Castries Bay in the north to the frontier of Korea, is very thinly populated, and it is only in the south, where there are several Chinese settlements, that the population is comparatively numerous. Veniukof reckons the population between the Usuri and the coast, north of Port Imperial, at 1,600; and we believe that 2,500 might be the approximate population of the entire coast-region under consideration. The Gilyaks on the Amur occupy thirty-nine "villages," having one hundred and forty houses, and 1,680 inmates. The population of Southern Sakhalin, up to about 49° of north latitude, was calculated by Mamia Rinso at 2,850, in four hundred and thirty-eight huts, which would allow 2·1 square miles to each inhabitant. If we assume a similar population for the northern (Russian) part of the island, we obtain 8,550, which is, however, in all likelihood beyond the actual number.

Combining these results, we may infer the following as the native population of the Russian territories on the Amur:—

|  | Square Miles. | Natives. |
|---|---|---|
| Province of the Amur | 164,000 | 5,200 |
| Usuri, Sofyevsk, & Nikolayevsk | 179,000 | 9,800 |
| Northern (Russian) Sakhalin | 18,000 | 8,500 |
| Total | 361,000 | 23,500 |

Or, arranging this population according to tribes, we obtain:—

| | |
|---|---|
| Oronchons of the Upper Amur | 260 |
| Manyargs and Birars | 3,000 |
| Daurians, etc. | 2,000 |
| Goldi on the Amur and Usuri | 3,560 |
| Olcha (Manguns) on the Amur | 1,100 |
| Negidals and Kile (Samagers) | 1,000 |
| Orochis of the sea-coast | 1,000 |
| Orokes on Sakhalin | 1,000 |
| Gilyaks on the Lower Amur and on Sakhalin | 8,180 ? |
| Ainos on Northern Sakhalin | 1,000[b] |
| Chinese on the Usuri, etc. | 1,400 |
| Total | 23,500[c] |

[b] On Southern (Japanese) Sakhalin about 2,850 additional.

[c] No account has been taken in this estimate of the nomadic Tunguzians who annually cross the Yablonoi mountains, from the Government of Yakutsk, to pasture their reindeer.

THE TUNGUZIANS OF THE UPPER AMUR.[d]—ORONCHONS AND MANYARGS.

The banks of the Upper Amur, down to the mouth of the Dzeya, are in the occupation of the Tunguzian tribes of the Oronchons and Manyargs (Monagirs, Manègres), the principal difference between whom is, that the chief domestic animal of the former is the reindeer (Oronchon = reindeer-

ORONCHON.

keeper), and of the latter the horse. The horses are small, but strong and of great endurance. Before going on a long journey the Manyarg keeps his horse for a day without food, and on his return also the poor beast is made to undergo five or six days' abstinence. This is done with a view of keeping the horse in working condition. Among the Manyargs

[d] Orlof. Viestnik, 1857; Zeitschrift für Erdk. 1858, iv.; Gerstfeldt, Viestnik, 1857; Erman's Archiv., vol. xvii., R. Maack, etc.

the influence of the Chinese with whom they live in close proximity is very apparent, not only in their dress but in their general demeanour. The oppressions of the Mandarins have broken their spirits, and they are much more submissive than the Oronchons. They are compelled to tow the boats, and are rewarded for their labour by harsh treatment and heavy blows. They pay the usual tribute in skins, and are, besides, liable to military conscription, and are sent to the Sungari to serve their term. Now that the Russians are in possession of the left bank of the river, the Manyargs living there are of course no longer exposed to these severities.

The Oronchons originally lived in the province of Yakutsk, whence they voluntarily emigrated to the banks of the Amur in 1825, and occupied there part of the territory of the Manyargs, whom they compelled to withdraw further down the river.[d] There are two tribes of Oronchons. One of them, the Ninagai, occupies the left bank of the Amur, between the rivers Oldoi and Amazar, and the country up to and beyond the crest of the Stanovoi mountains. In 1856 it mustered sixty-eight males and sixty-six females, and twenty-seven of the former paid annually five shillings and fivepence of tribute each, or in lieu thereof twelve squirrel-skins, to the officer commanding the post of Gorbitza. The other tribe, the Shologon, occupy the right bank of the Amur, down to the Albazikha rivulet. They number seventy-two individuals of both sexes, including forty males, of whom seventeen had to pay to the commandant of Ust Strelka a tribute of six shillings and four pence each. They owned eighty-two reindeer.

The Manyargs, as stated above, occupy the Amur below

---

[d] The chief of this small tribe has still in his possession a hunting-knife with a silver handle, upon which are engraved the initials of Catherine II., and which was presented to one of his ancestors.

the Oronchon, but in spring and summer they ascend it for the sake of fishing, to the Ignashina and Sester, leaving their horses below the Albazikha. They also dwell in the valley of the Dzeya, and generally speaking, the whole of the Prairie region down to the Bureya mountains, where their horses find forage; whilst the Oronchons, on account of their rein-deer, are confined to the mountainous districts. The Birars residing along the Bureya river are a sub-tribe of the Manyargs, and the Solons, north of Mergen, are probably related.[e]

The Manyargs and Oronchons are rather small and of

Woman.    Girl.    Man.
MANYARGS.

spare build. Their arms and legs are thin, a feature most striking in their half-naked children, whose belllies moreover are very protruding. The face is flat, but the nose in many instances, large and pointed. The cheeks are broad, the mouth is large, and the lips are thin; the eyes very small and sleepy-looking, and generally of black or reddish-brown. The hair is black and smooth, the beard short and

[e] The Manyargs are not known to Chinese geographers by that name, but they mention the Solon and Builar (Birar).

the eye-brows very thin. The Manchu features frequently found among the Manyargs are traced by Maack to the officials who annually collect the tribute, and to whom their women are freely yielded up.

The ordinary dress of the men consists of a kind of frock called "gulama," made of fur or leather, and reaching down to the knees. Under this they sometimes wear a gown (samsä) purchased from the Chinese, or at all events made of Chinese cotton-stuffs, after Chinese patterns. Shirts are not worn at all, unless one has been procured in barter from a Cossack. They wear short and wide leather-drawers girthed round the waist. The frock is confined by a belt of leather or horsehair, attached to which they carry a great many things of daily use, such as a knife, a tobacco-pouch, flint and steel, a pipe, an iron tobacco-stoker, ear-picks, a small pair of tweezers for pulling out the beard, a purse, and so forth. Most of these things are of Chinese workmanship, and are ornamented with glass beads and Chinese copper coins. The boots reach up to the middle of the calf, and the remainder of the leg is inclosed in a hose made of leather or cotton-stuff, and reaching from the ankles to the middle of the thigh. Instead of boots the feet are often wrapped up in reindeer leather, the hair inside, and the outside embroidered.

The hair is cut short on the forehead and temples, and plaited behind into a tail hanging down the back, and ornamented with ribbons and leather straps. Some of the Oronchons, who have been for a longer period tributary to Russia patronise tails no more. Old men alone allow the beard and moustaches to grow, but the whiskers are always carefully tweezed out. The head-dress is a structure of several semicircular caps of fur and leather, with a silk tassel. Chinese felt hats are also in vogue. Most of the men wear a ring on the thumb of the right hand, made of bone, wood or some such material, which was originally of assistance in bending the bow. The gradual introduction of fire-arms has superseded its original application, but it still forms a formidable means of attack in the pugilistic encounters between the natives.

The dress of the women does not materially differ from that of the men. The frock and gown are however longer, and trimmed with stripes of coloured cloth. In a girdle or belt they generally carry everything requisite for smoking,—for women and children even are equally addicted to this habit. There is besides attached to this belt a sort of housewife, with needles and thread, proofs of their domestic virtues.

The hair is parted down the middle, the plaits are wound round the head, and fastened behind above the forehead with ribbons. The head-dress is either a piece of cloth, or a structure resembling that of the man, but many-coloured and decorated with ribbons hanging down the back. During summer they sometimes wear a kind of a conical hat made of cotton, and resembling an extinguisher when looked at from behind. Unmarried girls may be recognized by their head-band embroidered with beads, and adorned with buttons, copper coins and small pieces of tin. The women wear brass bracelets, rings of silver and copper, ear-rings with glass beads, and necklaces made of small pieces of cypress wood and Chinese copper coins slung on a string.

These Tunguzians lead a wandering life. During spring and the beginning of summer they generally reside on the banks of the river, engaged in fishing, but in the autumn and winter they retire to the interior of the country to pursue the chase. In these migrations the reindeer or horse carries the scanty property of its owner. The only other domestic animal is the dog. We need not be surprised, considering this mode of life, if their habitations do not

---

[f] Among the tribes on the sea-coast, these rings protect the thumb when cutting fish open.

bear the stamp of permanency. They are in fact conical yurts or tents, easily built and more easily removed. Some twenty poles are stuck into the ground to form a circle of from ten to fourteen feet in diameter, and they are tied together about ten feet above the centre of the circle. This frame is covered with birch-bark, and above that with skins of the reindeer and moose. An opening is left in front to serve as the door, and a hole in the top for a chimney. During winter the door is closed by furs or skins. In case of a temporary removal, the bark and the skins are taken away, but the poles are left standing.

A hole in the centre of the tent serves as a fire-place, and above it the most important household utensils, a shallow iron pot with two handles, is suspended from a tripod formed of three wooden staves. The floor is covered with felt carpets, manufactured from the hair of the reindeer or moose. Low wooden benches on the sides serve as beds, and are covered with furs. The seat of honour is opposite the entrance. It is reserved for guests, and must never be occupied by the women. On entering, the guest sits down there; the host offers him a pipe, which is then passed round the circle until it is smoked out, when gruel with small pieces of meat in it, is served up in birch-bark cups.

In front of the yurts are scaffoldings for drying fish and meat, and at a greater distance are store-houses, placed upon poles, beyond the reach of animals, where all those things are kept which are not taken upon the migrations. These store-houses are religiously respected, and are never known to have been plundered.

The fisheries during spring and summer prove very productive. They catch sturgeons, taimen, bielugus and kelugas of a very large size, the caviar of which often weighs thirty-six pounds and more. The fish caught they either reserve for their own use, or sell it to the Cossacks, from whom they get from thirty-six to fifty-four pounds of rye-flour for thirty-six pounds of fish, or from one hundred and twenty-six to one hundred and forty-four pounds of rye-flour for a pound of caviar. In catching fish, they make use either of harpoons or of a snare (*samolof* in Russian). The management of the former requires a great deal of skill, and is employed only for large fish. During calm weather, one man will mount upon a prominent rock on the bank of the river whence he can espy the fish as it passes. On perceiving one he calls to his companion below, who is in readiness in a small birch-bark canoe, and provided with a harpoon fixed to a long pole, with a long line attached.

MANYARG HARPOON.

The latter then pursues the fish, and having harpooned it he lets go the line, and by skilful manœuvring contrives to drag the fish ashore, where it is killed.

Snares or samalofs are laid in the following manner. To a rope of from two hundred and eighty to five hundred and sixty feet in length, cords of thirty inches, with iron hooks (*c*) attached, are tied at intervals of thirty inches.

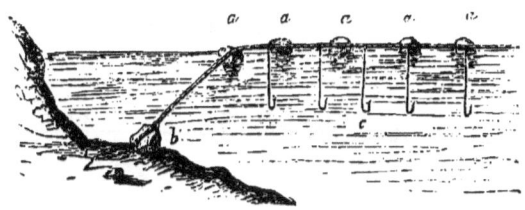

FISHING APPARATUS.

Floats made of birch-bark (*a*) are fastened to the rope, and to its ends heavy weights are attached (*b*). It is then stretched across the river. The fish passing are caught on the unbaited hooks; and all the fisherman has to do is to collect his booty from time to time from his small birch-bark canoe (*omuroch*). Small fish alone can be caught in this manner; a large one pulls the whole apparatus after it, and it is rather difficult, often impossible, to recover it.

Wild animals are numerous, especially on the right bank of the river. During summer many are killed for the sake of the flesh; above all, elks near the small lakes at some distance from the Amur. During winter the Oronchons disperse in small hunting parties in the forests, returning from time to time to carry their booty to the yurts. They hunt squirrels, martens, sables, roedeer, reindeer, elks, foxes and sometimes bears. Squirrels in particular are found in great numbers, and those from this neighbourhood are highly esteemed in the markets of Siberia, and on the spot itself fetch fivepence halfpenny a piece. A good sportsman may bag a thousand in a season, and five hundred is considered an average yield. Sables are very scarce, and not more than fifteen or twenty altogether are procured here annually by traders. Bears, otters, gluttons, lynxes and wild boars are scarcely ever met with. Wolves are plentiful, but only few of them are killed, for during summer they leave no track, and in winter they easily get away. The Oronchons are very good marksmen, and Orlof, who staid among them for a long time, did not see a single squirrel

MANCHU MATCHLOCK.

through whose head their small bullet had not passed. Bows and arrows have been almost entirely superseded by fire-arms, but spears are occasionally used. The Manyargs also set snares consisting of a crossbow fastened to a trunk of a tree. The arrow is smeared with putrified fat in order to accelerate the death of the animal hit. The poison spreads with great rapidity from the wound through the body, and the carcase exhales a most nauseous odour, which is also the case even if the animal is killed before succumbing to the strength of the poison. Nevertheless the Manyargs eat the flesh without disgust, and without its entailing any evil consequences.

Women hold a very inferior position. Girls marry before the age of puberty. Not only is the whole of the domestic labour assigned to the women, but they have to build and take down the yurts, load and unload the reindeer, prepare the hides, manufacture cloth, birch-bark matting, etc.

The Oronchons are nominally Christians, but they resort to the practices of Shamanism almost every night. On one occasion the Shaman astonished his auditors by waking a woman from a lethargic sleep, and in doing so he shook the poor woman most unmercifully, constantly calling out, *amnidu, aya aya-kokendu,* her soul has gone far very far away. Idols made of wood and fur may be seen in the yurts, and the teeth and claws of animals are worn as talismans. Diseased parts of the body are cured by wearing a carved resemblance of them; a lame person may thus be seen carrying about small legs of wood; an individual suffering in the chest, a little heart; and so forth. The dead are buried in the neighbourhood of the yurts, and a small house or wooden roof, ornamented frequently with carvings, representing the heads of horses or the like is placed over the grave.

Orlof, in a paper on the nomadic Tunguzians of Bauntovsk and the Angára, east of Lake Baikal, and north-west of the Oronchons, gives an interesting account of the manner in which these tribes are engaged in the course of a year. These tribes are the Kindigir, one hundred and seventy-six males and one hundred and forty-seven females; and the Chilchagir, four hundred and forty-nine males and four hundred and seventy-seven females. The Tunguzians divide our year into two parts, a summer and winter-year, of six moons each. The summer year begins with the first new moon after the spring equinox, and to make up the deficiency between the lunar and solar year, a seventh moon called oktynkiro, *i.e.*, the time is up, is added after the six winter months.[g] The names of the moons are as follows:—

*a*. Summer Year:
   1. Turan corresponds to our March.
   2. Sonka or Shonkon  ,,  April.
   3. Dukun  ,,  May.
   4. Ilyaga or Roga  ,,  June.
   5. Ilkun  ,,  July.
   6. Irun  ,,  August.

*b*. Winter Year:
   1. Yrkin corresponds to our September.
   2. Urgun  ,,  October.
   3. Ugdarpyr  ,,  November.
   4. Miro  ,,  December.
   5. Otki  ,,  January.
   6. Giraun  ,,  February.
   7. Oktynkiro  " Time is up."

We will now proceed to describe the occupation of the Tunguzians during each moon of the year. In the first moon of summer (March), the snow which had choked up the ravines and defiles has become settled, and its crust is sufficiently hard to enable the Tunguzian to venture upon it

[g] Viestnik, xxi.; Zeitsch. f. Erdk. 1858, v.

in his snow-shoes, whilst cloven-footed animals sink down. The Tunguzian avails himself of this circumstance and pursues the game with or without dogs, and shoots it when he finds it. In some instances he is even able to approach the game with his hunting-spear, or the dogs overtake and kill it, and surrender their prey to the huntsman. Elks, roe- and musk-deer, wild reindeer and goats constitute the chief objects of the chase in that month, and the Tunguzians fix their tents in the neighbourhood of valleys, defiles or ravines where the snow lies deepest.

In April the ice on the rivers begins to move, and when the banks are inundated in consequence of the melting of the snow, the Tunguzian hastens to the small rivulets or to the sources of the larger ones; and in swampy localities or places overgrown with sedge, he casts his fishing-nets and catches great numbers of taimen, perch, pike and eel-pouts. The fish not required for immediate consumption is dried in the sun, and put into the store-houses, to be made use of in the following month, which is considered one of the worst of the year.

May is a very dreary month. Preparations for attracting game to certain spots have been made in the preceding autumn, by burning down some of the high grass in the valleys, where the young grass sprouts forth earlier than elsewhere; and the game at night comes to pasture. The Tunguzians, concealed by the high grass, lie in ambush in expectation of getting a favourable shot. This manner of hunting is not always successful, for the Tunguzians from under their cover cannot always obtain a sight of the animals, and these are remarkably shy. Moreover a shot in the dark does not always tell. A huntsman who, during that month, kills three goats, or a reindeer and a goat, is considered very lucky. The Tunguzians dwell at this period in the vicinity of large valleys, but do not altogether leave the rivers, nor give up fishing.

The fourth summer month—*Ilyaga*, June—supplies them with soft-roe antlers, filled with blood, and having a thick woolly covering of a grayish colour. These antlers are sold to the Chinese, who use them as a remedy for irregular menstruation. The roe is of a very hardy nature, and prefers the rocky heights and mountains, where it is pursued by the natives. The Tunguzian keeps the skin and flesh, and sells the antlers to merchants who visit him towards the end of that month bringing tea, tobacco, salt, powder and lead, grain, butter and so forth, and he is often able to procure in this way provisions to last himself and family for half a year. No wonder June is considered one of the best months of the year.

In July—*Ilkun*—the Tunguzians descend from the mountains to the rivers and lakes, and spend the first part of the month in fishing. At rapid places of the rivers they cast their nets, and catch grayling and pike. On the lakes they use small horsehair-nets, which they throw out from a birch-bark canoe, containing two or three persons. The fishery here is very productive; they catch large sturgeons, taimens, trout (Salmo lenoc), perch and pike. The fish are cut lengthways into strips, and exposed on a horsehair-net to the sun; or they are smoked under the hole in the roof which serves for their chimney. Fish prepared in this way, called in Tunguzian *baptsiany*, are very palatable, and much liked by Russian travellers. Towards the end of this month, when the night is favourable, the Tunguzians provide themselves with torches, and visit in their canoes the retired bays of the lake, where they harpoon the fish found near the shore; when the rivers rise in consequence of heavy rains, they hasten to the rapids, and kill the large sturgeon, taimens, and pike cast ashore and left by the waters. In the course of this month they also spear the elk near the lakes. This animal is very fond of a water-plant—Lycopodium solago—and at night or at the break of day resorts to shallow lakes covered with it. He wades into the water, and whilst engaged tearing out the plant with his teeth, the Tunguzian draws near in a canoe, and kills the beast with a spear. Sometimes the Tunguzians hide in the vicinity of the lake and way-lay the elk. This kind of sport is not however frequently crowned with success, for the elk is not only very shy and scents human beings at a great distance, but approaches the lakes only during dark nights, or when dense fogs lie upon them.

In the sixth month—August, *Iren*—the natives catch birds. It is well known that wild-fowl, swans, geese, divers, scoters, ducks, gulls, etc., migrate in summer to Siberia, where they seek retired places, to breed undisturbed. Such localities are generally found in the vicinity of lakes or creeks. The Tunguzians are sure of a good capture at the beginning of August, for at that time the young birds are not yet fledged, and the mothers are moulting their feathers. On their small birch-bark canoes, the men visit at night the retired creeks and bays of the rivers and lakes, and spear the birds in great numbers. Their flesh, excepting that of the swans, is eaten, and the feathers and down are exchanged for tobacco, ear and finger rings, bracelets, beads and the like. About the middle of the month, the Tunguzians leave the lakes and go up the mountains and glaciers, to trace the burrows of the Bobak, which they unearth, or smoke out. The skins of these little animals are used to ornament the holiday dress, or they are sold. The fat—and in autumn these little creatures are nothing scarcely but fat—is esteemed a delicacy. It never freezes and is kept in a small leather bag expressly made for that purpose.

This is their mode of life during the six months of the summer. In the beginning of September they leave the mountains and again descend to the rivers, where they prepare for their winter-pursuits. At this season the larches turn yellow, and the leaves fall off the trees. This is the rutting period, and from the opening of the month may be heard at day-break the call of the roe-buck, and the response of the doe, who has gone to the valley with her fawns to seek forage. The Tunguzian avails himself of this, and by cleverly imitating the call of the doe on a wooden horn, entices the buck near enough to shoot him.[h] The elk is also now hunted, but as it does not call, it is necessary to follow its track, which is not very difficult after the first snow has

MANYARG HORN.

fallen. Generally speaking the Tunguzians have more meat at the end of September than at any other time of the year. But if fortune should not smile upon them in their hunting expeditions, they live upon service-berries and bilberries, which they mix with reindeer milk. Other berries, such as cloud-berries, whortle-berries and currants, are considered unwholesome. They also gather the nuts of the Manchu-cedar, and the dwarflike Cembra-pine. These are generally eaten with the shell on, and on extra occasions are mixed up with kukuru, that is dried meat cut small. The latter part of September and beginning of October is again employed in fishing, for the fish then ascend the rivers to spawn. The catch at that time is very large if not interrupted by a premature frost. Having procured a sufficiency of provisions against the winter, the Tunguzians about the middle of October remove to the forests and enter upon the chase of fur-bearing animals, of all game the most profitable. They stop here until the close of November. Their first care is to

[h] The Manyargs employ the same stratagem for hunting stags.

set various kinds of snares, which are inspected from day to day. They hunt and trap sables, foxes, bears, wolves, otters, martens, lynxes, gluttons, squirrels and polecats.

At the beginning of the fourth winter month, December, the Tunguzians take their furs to the localities fixed upon for paying the Yassak, or tribute in furs, and where they also carry on barter with merchants who come for that purpose. Each male between the years of fifteen and fifty pays annually two silver rubles, or the equivalent in furs. No other taxes are levied upon them. In some instances, the Tunguzians evade the payment of this impost; but as, in such cases, the other members of the tribe have to make good the deficiency, they are all of them interested in discovering the defaulter. Sometimes a Tunguzian remains away from the "fair," as this annual gathering is called, because he is greatly in arrear to the merchants, and is afraid of being compelled to surrender the whole of his furs, without receiving means to sustain life. In that case, he generally visits another fair, where he sells his furs and pays the Yassak due.

The merchants always manage to keep the Tunguzian in debt, and the price of commodities is most exorbitant. His purchases made—they consist for the greater part in grain— the Tunguzian returns to the forests, and during January and February continues to hunt fur-animals.

In conclusion, we will say a few words about the Solon, a nomadic tribe, allied to, if not identical with, the Manyargs, and who occupy the country north of Mergen. They claim to be descendants of the ancient Sushi, by whom was founded the dynasty of the Gin. The word *Solon* signifies "Shooters." They are indeed expert huntsmen, and even their women mount on horseback and pursue the game. Besides horses, they have dogs for hunting, sheep, oxen, and camels.[f]

[f] Du Halde, China, iv.; Lange in Pallas Beiträge, ii.

## Manchu, Daurians and Chinese.

The most populous part of the Amur is that immediately below the Dzeya, where for a distance of forty to fifty miles, some twenty-five or thirty villages are scattered along its banks, above and below the town of Sakhalin-ula-hotun or

MANCHU.

Aigun. These villages number ten to fifty or even one hundred houses each, and are built either on the high banks of the river, where plantations of trees protect them against cold northerly winds, or on sandy islands or peninsulas, among the willows. Between these villages their clumsy carts may be seen going. These have two wheels fixed to the axle-tree, and they all turn together. They are drawn by oxen, and move but slowly along the wretched roads. Labourers are engaged in the gardens and fields surrounding the villages, and herds of cattle and horses graze on the

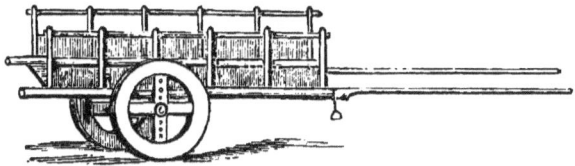

MANCHU CART.

intervening pasture-lands. The river is enlivened by junks and fishing-boats, the former carrying sails and streamers. They are towed up the river by men on the banks. Leaving this populous district, the mud-houses again become scarce, and in their place we find yurts covered with birch or larch-bark, sedge or twigs. But whilst the inhabitants of these yurts resemble the Oronchons and Manyargs in dress, they are in feature more akin to the Daurians.

This population consists of Daurians and Manchu, who can scarcely be distinguished from each other in appearance. They are taller and stronger than the Orochons; the countenance is oval and more intellectual, and the cheeks are less broad. The nose is rather prominent; and the eyebrows straight. The skin is tawny-coloured, the hair brown. The lower classes do not shave the head, and their hair resembles an ill-constructed hay-stack, around which they twist their pig-tail to keep it in place. The higher classes shave the head in front and over the temples, and cultivate a tail which hangs down behind. Some of the women are well-favoured, generally round-faced, fleshy and of a very ruddy complexion. Collins noticed several old people and young children afflicted with sore eyes, and among the women several cases of goitre.

The dress is very much like that of the Chinese. The men wear a long blue coat of cotton, loose linen trousers fastened at the knee or made into leggings, and Chinese shoes or boots made of skin. They wear also a kind of vest or Kaftan of skin or fish-skin, and a belt to which is attached a case containing a knife, Chinese chop-sticks, tinder, a small copper pipe and tobacco. Both sexes are passionately fond of smoking, and, as in China, constantly carry a fan about with them. The women dress in a blue cotton gown with short loose sleeves, above which they wear a cape or mantle of silk reaching down to the waist. The hair is brushed up and fastened on the top of the head in a bunch, which is secured by a comb ornamented with beads, hair needles, and decked with gay ribbons and real or artificial flowers. The ear-rings, finger-rings and bracelets exhibit much taste. The women are in the habit of carrying their youngest children about with them, tied on their back. The girls on being released from their swaddling clothes, are dressed like their mothers, but the boys up to six or seven years of age, only wear a pair of loose pantaloons. The use of fur or leather in their clothing is restricted almost to the inhabitants of the yurts.

The houses generally stand in a square yard, having a fence of stakes or wickerwork. The frame-work of the house is made of wood, and the walls are plastered with mud-clay, for wood is here rather a dear commodity, and men go to the Upper Amur to fell the wood necessary for the consumption of the inhabitants of the prairie, and float it down in rafts. The roof is covered with sedge or grass. The interior is not generally divided into compartments, but when it is, all culinary operations are carried on in the entrance-room, and we meet here also with the children, sucking-pigs, calves, chickens and dogs of the proprietor. There is a large window of paper soaked in oil on each side of the door. During summer the paper windows are replaced by matting which rolls up like our blinds. The fire-place is generally to the left as you enter, close to the wall. A large iron pan is set up into this fire-place, and the smoke passes through wooden pipes leading from it and carried underneath the low benches which encompass the apartment, and continued to a sort of high wooden chimney, stuck up in the yard. Great economy is thus practised as regards the smoke. The wooden benches, which are about eighteen inches high, and five or six feet wide, serve as places of repose by night or day. Cupboards are let into the wall for articles of clothing and utensils, such as wooden and clay vessels, baskets, boxes, iron kettles. A clay-pot with charcoal is placed in front of, or on one of the benches, to light the pipes, which are in constant requisition. When a guest enters, one of the women at once fills and lights a pipe, and having taken a few puffs herself, and wiped the mouth-piece with her hand or apron, she presents it to him. On the walls we perceive pictures of Buddhist deities, or of Foism, painted on linen. Outside many of the houses there is a shrine containing idols, in front of which stand small basins with incense. We noticed in addition opposite the door of many houses, and standing within the yard, a square wooden screen several feet high. On that side of the screen facing the door there is a pole attached with an arrangement for raising it when required. The upper part of this pole is ornamented with the skulls of beasts of prey, small flags, horse-hair or the like, and during prayer it is set up whilst the worshippers are lying prostrate on the ground downward. Maack noticed a rude calendar in the house of the Manchu official residing at the mouth of the Sungari. It consisted of a bent bow, to the cord of which thirty wooden bells were attached, and one of which was pushed every day to the other side.

There are several temples at Aigun, and at a few of the military stations. Maack describes a temple of Confu-tze which he found standing in the midst of a grove of oak-trees, near the river Gaijin. It is a square house, the walls of which are made of thin poles set up side by side, and the interstices filled up with clay, and smoothened. The sloping roof is thatched with straw. As you enter you find yourself in a kind of ante-room, separated from the inner compartment by a pink curtain running along the width of the temple, and suspended from slender pillars. Upon this curtain are three inscriptions, in Chinese, viz., " Erected in the tenth month of the fourth year of San-tin, of the Dai-tsin dynasty;" "Three suns govern spring and autumn;" and " Built by the pious and humble Yan-khai-tsin." Drawing aside the curtain, we see before us a table against the wall, upon which stands a picture painted on deal and representing some deity with a deformed face, the head surrounded by a variegated nimbus. He sits cross-legged on a bench, and on each side of him are three human beings with a similar nimbus.

At the lower corners of the picture two animals are crouching, one resembling a lynx, the other a tiger. At the foot of the deity two men without nimbus are wrestling. Dried stems and leaves of Artemisia, some Chinese coins, and a Russian farthing (half kopeck) lie on the table in front of the picture. There is also a semi-globular vessel of cast-iron, with three holes on each side, which is struck by the worshipper, after he has made his obeisance, to attract the notice of the god.

It has been remarked before that the Tunguzians about Aigun till the soil, and breed cattle; but they carry on fishing and the chase with the same zest as their neighbours. The Manchu and Chinese[a] are more addicted to the former,

---

[a] Called Nikans by the Tunguzians.

the Daurians to the latter. Their boats are made of the trunk of a hollowed-out tree, cut into two pieces, fastened with wooden pegs, and secured from leaking with pitch. They also make flat-bottomed boats of planks. Occasionally

MANCHU BARGE.

may be seen the large junks of the Chinese or Manchu, most of them built on the Sungari, with a small tub-like house at the stern, and a mast with a knob, a bird, or trident at the top. They have nets, hooks, and fishing forks, or harpoons. A peculiar kind of fishing apparatus was observed near Aigun. We give an illustration of it. The net is lowered by means of a rope, and the apparatus can be pushed into the water and pulled back as required.

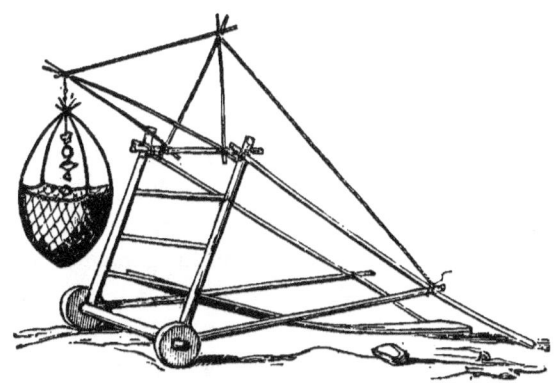

FISHING APPARATUS.

During winter, when the river is covered with ice, the Daurians practise a mode of fishing known to the Cossacks as chekacheni or "malleting." Where the ice is transparent, the fish may be seen almost immoveable near the surface of the water beneath it. A few strokes on the ice with a mallet stun the fish, and a hole is then made, and they are taken out with the hand or a small net.

The Daurians dwelling on the Upper Sungari, in the neighbourhood of Tsitsikar, have been visited by E. Ysbrand Ides.

"They occupy Naun-kotun (now Tsitsikar) and the six villages south of it, and are called Daori or Daurians.

"They carry on agriculture very successfully, and cultivate vegetables and much tobacco. Their religion is very impious and diabolical, for according to their own admission they are Shamanists, and serve and worship the devil.

"At midnight, the neighbours frequently meet, both men and women. One of them prostrates himself upon the ground, and those surrounding him set up a hideous howl. Others beat a kind of drum, and after a short pause, the shouting recommences, and this continues for an hour or two. After some time, the person lying upon the ground, and who appears to be mad with enthusiasm. raises himself, and tells the others where he has been, and what he heard and saw. Sometimes one or the other of the company desires to learn something about the future, and the information is of course afforded him. Not a night passed whilst I staid in the place without these devil-worshippers yelling in this way.

"The dead are kept in the house for three days; they are then half-buried in a funereal hut in the garden or field. It is daily visited by the nearest relatives, who bring all sorts of meat and drink. The food is put to the mouth of the deceased with a spoon, and the drink is placed in small cups outside the hut. A few weeks pass in this manner, and then the decomposed corpse is buried deeper.

"These Daori live in houses made of loam, or earth,

thatched with reeds or thin bamboos. The walls are whitewashed inside. On a pillar, about six feet high, are suspended the entrails of an animal, with a small bow, arrows, spears, and other arms arrayed around it. Before this they bend now and then in adoration. The houses are not divided into compartments; nearly half the room is encompassed by a bench, about a yard high and two wide, which is covered with reed matting. The fire-place is outside the house, near the door, and the smoke from it passes through a pipe conducted beneath the benches through the house. This arrangement replaces but imperfectly our stove; and imparts but little warmth to the room, though the persons lying upon the divan are pretty comfortable.

"Two iron kettles always form part of the household utensils, one of them contains water for the tea, and the food is cooked in the other. The houses have large square windows, pasted with paper. They are hinged at the top, and opened for ventilation by raising the bottom part with a stick.

"These people are well made, especially the women, and dress like the Manchu in China. The secretaries of the Mandarins who are sent to this part, are privileged by a letter from the Khan to select any women or young girls whom they may fancy whenever love prompts them. I have myself frequently been present when the best-looking females were taken away in a cart, as if they were going to the slaughterhouse. Some of the men whose wives had been taken in this manner, still persist in considering it a a special favour to have such fine gentlemen as brothers-in-law. Others, though discontented, are compelled to conceal their chagrin from fear of punishment and disgrace."

The *Targachins*, mentioned by Ysbrand Ides and Brandt, are probably also Daurians. They are Shamanists. During summer they dress in Chinese cotton stuffs or prepared hides, but in winter they wear sheep-skins. They live in huts made of reeds or bamboos; but unlike the Orochons and Manyargs of the Amur, they subsist chiefly upon agriculture, and cultivate barley, oats, etc., and sell the surplus at Tsitsikar. They keep horses, camels, oxen and sheep, the latter having fat tails. They frequently ride on oxen, and are expert in the use of the bow.

## THE TUNGUZIANS OF THE LOWER AMUR. — GOLDI, MANGUNS, OROCHIS.

THESE tribes exhibit so great a similarity in outward appearance, customs and manner of life, as to induce us not to describe them under separate headings, which would necessitate our repeating the same kind of information in almost

GOLDI.

every instance. We shall merely state where one of the tribes mentioned possesses some peculiarity distinguishing it from its neighbours.

The Tunguzian tribes are the Goldi and Manguns, along the Amur, Sungari and Usuri; and the Orochis along the sea-coast from Castries Bay to about 44° N. lat.

The Goldi inhabit both banks of the Sungari below the town of Sansin, the Usuri below the Dobikhu and the Amur to the village of Niurguya below the Gorin. Maack calls the Goldi living along the Amur down to Nyungya "Kileng"; and those about the mouth of the Usuri, "Hodseng." Below the Goldi the banks of the Amur are occupied by the Manguns or Olchas as far as the village of Kadema, below the Russian settlement of Irkutskoi. The Orochis, lastly, occupy the sea-coast and the country bounded by the Amur and Usuri, having for neighbours the Gilyaks, Manguns and Goldis, and coming into contact on the Upper Usuri with Chinese settlers.

These Tunguzians have the usual Mongol features, prominent check bones, and small oblique eyes. The nose is not in all cases flat. The eyebrows are more defined and arched. The mouth large, the lips thick and of a dull red colour. The complexion is fair and ruddy. The colour of

OROCHIS.

the hair and eyes are black, but occasionally grey eyes are seen. The size of the head is large compared to that of the body. According to M. Rollin, the average stature of the men whom he met in Castries Bay was five feet one inch, the circumference of the head 22·38 inches, and the diameters 9·59 and 5·69 inches. The bodies are lank, but the muscles well developed, and the men by no means deficient in strength.

The fashion of shaving the head has only in few instances been adopted from the Manchu. Ordinarily the hair is tied up in a bunch and allowed to hang down the nape of the neck, or it is plaited. The beard and moustaches make but a poor show, and many natives are not provided with hirsute appendages at all, or tweeze them out for very shame. The women wear their hair parted in the middle with two plaits hanging down the back, like Russian peasant girls, or twisted round their heads. Both sexes are in the habit of tattooing the face, a custom not observed amongst the Daurians, though met with occasionally amongst the Oronchons. The tattooing is restricted however to four spots placed on the forehead in the shape of a cross. In their dress much has been adopted from the Manchu, and though few can afford to purchase cotton stuffs, not to mention silks, the fish, dog and deer-skins are fashioned according to Chinese patterns. The materials most in request for summer dresses are fish-skins, which are procured from two kinds of salmon. They strip the skin off with surprising dexterity, and by beating it with a mallet cause the scales to fall off, and render it very supple. Clothes thus made are impervious to rain. The men wear a kind of blouse made of this skin, fastened in front, and confined round the waist by a leather belt, to which are suspended a number of articles of daily use. These articles are worked with much neatness, and consist of a large knife in a fur sheath (1); an iron instrument for cleaning the tobacco-pipe, the constant companion of men and women, for both sexes and even children are inveterate smokers (2) ; a curved knife for cutting fish (3) ; a tinder pouch (4) ; a steel for striking a light (5); a bone for smoothing their fish-skins and loosening knots (6); a bag of fish-skin for tinder (7); a small bag with a whetstone (8); and a needle-case (9). In addition

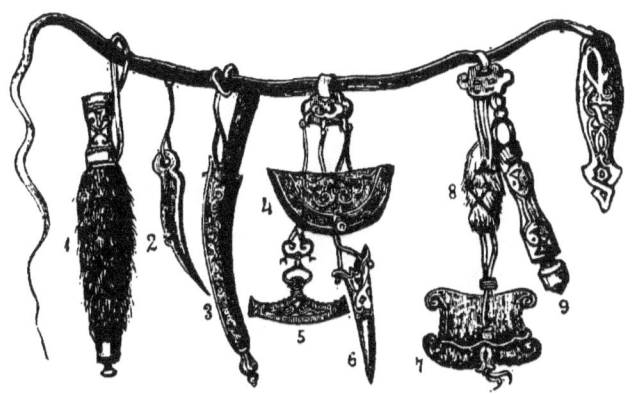

MANGUN BELT.

to the blouse, the men wear a short loose pair of trowsers, and shoes made of deer or seal-skin. During summer however, and when they are in their houses, they generally go bare-footed. They have leggings of birch-bark or cotton stuff up to the knee, tied round with strips of raw hide. Their hats are made of various materials, felt, birch-bark, straw, and in winter fur, and are of various shapes. One of the Goldi in the wood-cut wears a conical hat of birch-bark, of a Chinese pattern, and beautifully carved. The other wears a peculiar head-dress, consisting of two ear-lappets attached to a head-band. The Orochi wears a straw-hat with a very wide brim. In winter the fish-skin dress is replaced by dresses made of dog and reindeer-skin and fur, the hair turned outside, and the fine Mangun gentleman, with his jovial face, dandified moustaches and beard à la Henri Quatre, conveys a good idea of the comfort which such a dress affords.

MANGUN.

As might be expected, the dress of the women here as elsewhere is of a more elaborate character. The loose gown of blue or white cotton stuff or fishskin is trimmed along the hem with coloured pieces of cloth or silk ribbons, small shells and Chinese coins. The skirt and body are embroidered in red, blue, black or yellow, in various designs

GOLDI IDOL.

exhibiting much taste. They also wear aprons similarly ornamented to which are attached sometimes a small idol or two as charms. Their shoes and leggings are similar to those of the man. There is no lack of jewellery. Sometimes two or more pairs of ear-rings made of brass, silver or copper wires, with a glass-bead or Chinese coins as pendants are

EAR-RING

worn in the ears. The Goldi and Orochi occasionally wear a small nose-ring. Copper bracelets and necklaces of glass-beads are also worn.

The habitations are regulated by the season and occupation. Fishing is by far the most important of their employments, for it not only supplies them with the chief article of food for themselves and dogs, but also with a material for their dress and lamp-oil for the winter months. They occasionally hunt in the summer, but only such animals as are valuable for their skins or flesh, and reserve the hunting of fur-bearing animals for the winter months. They are not thus nomades in the ordinary acceptation of that term, but nevertheless lead a very roving life, being frequently absent from home for months. During these temporary absences they occupy temporary dwellings, which they build where the fishing of the season promises to be most productive. The materials employed in the building of these summer-huts are birch-bark, sedge, the flexible boughs of the willow or very thin poles. The shape of the huts is either that of a bee-hive, or they are conical or square, the latter are called Da'urs. In front of these huts there are generally various fishing utensils, baskets, hatchets, small tables to cut the

SUMMER HUT AT THE USURI MOUTH.

fish-skins on, and so forth. The interior is lighted by means of fish-oil kept burning outside the door, as there is no chimney.

We find here again the small birch-bark canoe of the Manyargs, which carries one man. He propels it with a paddle, having a blade at each end, and which he dips alternately into the water on either side. They also have larger boats made of three principal planks, mostly of cedar-

BIRCH-BARK CANOE.

wood, and fastened by means of wooden-pegs, and caulked with willow-bast. These boats are about fifteen feet long and sometimes carry sails. The bottom plank curves above the water and extends beyond the bow. There are wooden-pins on the gunwales, and the oars fit into them by holes, and the prow is often ornamented with a bird's head. Boats of this construction easily pass the many shallows of the river.

These oars are nicely carved and painted black and red. One man takes his place at the stern, and the boat is rowed European fashion. The boatmen chaunt in a monotonous strain keeping time to the stroke of their oars. They are indeed expert rowers, and intimately acquainted with the intricate navigation of the river upon which they spend a great part of their life. As pilots they have been of great assistance to the Russians. In going against the stream the boat is often towed by dogs. Another kind of boat is hollowed out from the trunk of a tree, and is about ten feet long. The bow has the same construction as in the larger boats.

The fishing-tackle consists of harpoons, hooks and various kinds of nets. The harpoon is about five feet long and is

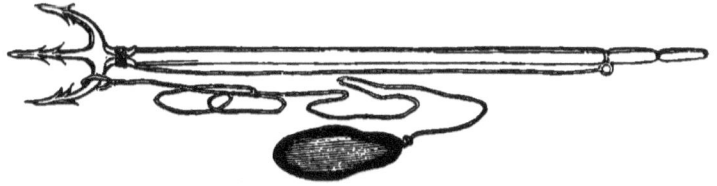

HARPOON.

provided with three iron prongs with teeth. To prevent the prongs being detached by the exertions the fish naturally makes to get rid of the unwelcome visitant, they are secured by a rope to a ring at the end of the handle of the harpoon. There is also an ingenious arrangement to indicate the position of the fish when once the harpoon has been thrown, for the fisherman does not retain it by a line. This consists of an inflated fish-bladder fastened to one of the prongs by a line thirty-five feet long. This bladder floats of course. When the fish has become exhausted, it is pulled out with a hook, and killed with a mallet. Ordinary fish-hooks fastened to a long switch, are also used: They are concealed by the tail of a squirrel, and vary in size according to the kind of fish it is intended to secure. The native smith displays great skill and dexterity in the manufacture of these fish-hooks. He sits on the ground with an anvil on his right hand. This

ANVIL.

anvil is square; on one side it has two projections, on the opposite a long incision, and on the top a circular hole. There is a basin with charcoal between his feet and he blows it with a pair of bellows, the nose of which passes through

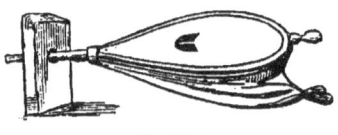

BELLOWS.

the hole of a stone, and which he works with his right foot. Having heated the iron in the charcoal, the smith shapes the hooks in the small cavity on the top of the anvil. He does not however confine himself to making hooks, and as far as the scarcity of iron admits of it, he manufactures other articles, and the annexed illustration of a spear-head may pass as a fair specimen of native industry.

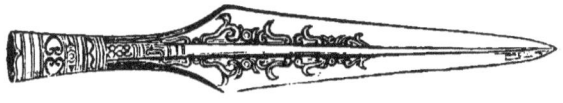

SPEAR-HEAD.

The nets of hemp or nettles, are made chiefly during the winter, when the whole family engages in this kind of work, sitting round a lamp fed with fish-oil. A small net of hemp, with floats of corkwood and a heavy weight of clay in the centre is used for catching small fish. On narrow rivers they employ a net above fifty feet long and seven feet wide, and without weights. This net is stretched across the river, and one of the men drives the fish towards it by making a great noise. Another kind is used for catching sturgeons and salmon in the Amur itself. This net is a sort of sack, with a circumference at the top of five feet, and a depth of two feet and a half. The meshes are two or three inches wide. One half of the top is provided with leaden weights, and the other with corks. At each end, where the corks and leads meet, is fastened a heavy stone and a rope. Two persons at least are required to drag this net. They sit each in his own boat, holding an end of one of the ropes, and drag the net between them. The leaded part of the net goes to the bottom, and the corks float, leaving thus an opening for the fish to get in, and the booty is cleverly pulled ashore.

Another plan, and one most in vogue among the Goldi during autumn, when the fish descend to the sea, is this. For a distance of sixty feet from the bank of the river, a series of tressels, connected by crossbeams, are firmly fixed in the bottom. The space between them is filled up by a wicker-work of willows, leaving but a small opening for the fish to pass through. At this opening the Goldi lies in wait with his ordinary fishing net, and the number of fish he is thus enabled to take, with little trouble, is enormous.

The fish, after being skinned and dried for a few days in the smoke of the cabin fires, is hung up in the sun, and in time acquires the hardness of wood. To prevent birds preying upon the fish hung up, they are covered with a net, or guarded by a eagle, chained to the scaffolding.

We will now leave these temporary cabins or lodges of the

Tunguzians, and pay a visit to one of their villages, inhabited during winter, and at other periods of the year also, when not absent on a fishing expedition, or trading journey. The houses are built upon the plan of those of the Daurians

INTERIOR OF A MANGUN HOUSE.

which we have described before. They are commodious, about thirty-five to forty feet square, and afford accommodation to a grandfather and the whole of his descendants, often to the number of thirty or forty of both sexes. The walls of the house are formed of poles, the interstices being plastered with a mixture of clay and straw. The roof is of birch-bark, with some poles and heavy stones placed upon it to prevent its being carried away by the wind. There are two or more windows, with wooden lattices, pasted over with paper during winter. In summer the window is closed by mats which roll up like blinds. Against one of the walls is the fire-place, with a large deep pan let into it, and a pot suspended over it from a rafter. Wooden pipes lead from this fire-place below the divan, and finally pass out of the house, as previously described. The floor is covered with clay, stamped down, and there is a hole in it, with charcoal burning summer and winter, for lighting the pipes, and warming the brandy (rakki), of which they are very fond. In the houses of the Manguns there is a table in the centre specially reserved for feeding the dogs, which they keep in much greater number than the Goldi.

The household utensils are hung upon the rafters of the roof, and clothes and other articles are kept in cupboards. Part of one wall is reserved for religious purposes. Some pieces of coloured cloth, horsehair, fishes, bear-skulls, etc., are strung up here, as offerings to the idols. The Goldi have also pictures of Chinese workmanship, but very badly executed, and for which they pay two or three sables each. In front of their houses they have idol-poles, facing the river. Maack describes some standing in front of a native hut at Silvi, below the mouth of the Sungari. The top of the centre pole is fashioned

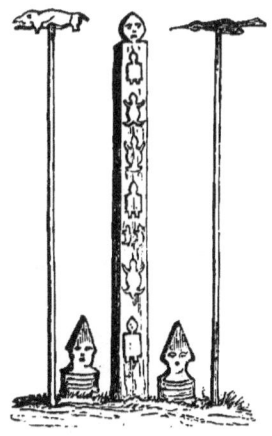

GOLDI IDOL POLES.

into a head—the eyes and mouth being indicated by incisions. On the flat surface of the pole towards the house, are represented, beginning from the top, a human being, two animals, without tails, resembling frogs; another human being; two quadrupeds; an animal with a short tail, and a third human being. On the side facing the river, the same objects are represented, excepting that two serpents take the place of the quadrupeds, and that the two animals without tails are provided with them here, and the other one is deprived of it. At each side of this pole stands a block of wood in the shape of a human head, and outside these are two staves, one surmounted by a bird, the other by a quadruped. These idols are very rudely carved, and with nothing like the taste exhibited in the funereal huts and household utensils. As we descend the Amur we lose sight of these idols in front of the houses. Manchu influences are less perceptible, and in the houses of the Orochis we miss the ingenious arrangement for warming the hut, and carrying off the smoke. Their houses are built of wood and covered with birch-bark, but the fire-place, with its large cauldron, is in the centre, and the smoke escapes through door, roof, or window, as best it may. Ophthalmia is in consequence a frequent complaint. The huts which Tronson saw in Barracouta Bay (Port Imperial) appear to have served as a temporary residence during the fishing season only. From a ridge pole about six feet high, ribs of fir-wood reached to the ground and were covered with birch-bark. The door was a mere hole at the end of the hut, covered with skins. Within, the family squatted round a wood fire. The young branches of the fir spread on the ground served as beds, and the skins of foxes, dogs, bears, and stags, for covering. During winter, the Orochis occupy large subterranean dwellings similar to those of Kamchatka.

Close to the dwelling-house is a scaffolding for drying fish and nets. To this are often chained tame eagles; they are supplied with fish, and are supposed to prevent other birds from preying on it. The tail feathers of this bird they use for winging their arrows, or they are taken to Sakhalin, and

purchased by the Japanese, who highly value them as an ornament. To secure an eagle (Haliaëtos albicella), the natives watch the eyrie and wait until the young birds are just able to fly. The tree is then felled, and the young eagles carried away.

The storehouses are of wood, and stand upon poles five feet from the ground, to preserve the contents against wild animals. They are not locked, nor are their dwelling-houses, for honesty is one of the virtues most strictly observed among the savages, and theft is unheard of.

There is another thing in each native village which deserves to be mentioned specially. We allude to the bear-cages. They are built of strong planks, and on one side they have an opening for the trough, above which is attached a peculiar kind of head-dress which the Shaman wears at funeral ceremonies, and a tassel of the bark of the lime-tree fixed to a small stick, which also appears to embody some religious idea. The bear (Ursus arctos) being feared as a fierce antagonist is respected accordingly, and plays a part in the religious notions of these tribes. They speak of him as " Mafa," *i.e.*, Chief, Elder, or, to distinguish him from the tiger, who is also "mafa," Sakhale mafa, *i.e.*, Black chief.

MANGUN SPEAR.

In hunting the bear the natives exhibit a great deal of intrepidity. In order not to excite his posthumous revenge, they never attempt to surprise him, but have a fair stand-up fight. When it is not desired to secure a bear alive, the Tunguze uses a spear, which he holds firmly planted in the ground, with the point directed towards the bear, upon which the beast throws himself. It is much more exciting sport to catch a living beast. A party of ten men or more, enter the forest provided with straps, a muzzle, and a collar with a chain attached to it. Having discovered the whereabouts of the beast, a battue is instituted. The individual near whom the bear debouches jumps upon his back in the twinkling of an eye, and seizes hold of his ears. Another man then rapidly throws a running knot round the neck of the beast, and almost suffocates him. He is then muzzled, and the collar is fastened round his neck, and the chain passed between the hind legs. He is led in triumph to the village, and put into his cage. These bear-hunts do not always pass without accident, and one frequently encounters an individual frightfully mutilated, a living witness of the dangers encountered with this redoubtable denizen of the forest. Once in his wooden cage, the bear is fattened on fish. On high festivals, when it is desired to lead him forth, some of the planks of the roof are taken out, and the beast is teased until it stands upon its hind legs, when a sling is thrown round its body, and the roof uncovered sufficiently for him to get out. Having succeeded in dragging him forth, one of the men jumps upon his back, again getting hold of the ears, whilst the others tie his paws, and place an iron chain in his mouth. He is then bound between two fixed poles, an involuntary witness of the frolicking going on before him. On very grand occasions, he takes a more direct share in the festival, by being killed with superstitious ceremonies, scrupulously observed on all such occasions. The skull, jawbones, and ears are then suspended on a tree, as an antidote against evil spirits; but the flesh is eaten and much relished, for they believe that all who partake of it acquire a zest for the chase, and become courageous. Sometimes Bruin escapes this fate by scraping a large hole beneath his cage, and escaping to the forests.

The bear has thus become, so to say, domesticated. Of other animals, besides the bear and the eagle, we find in the houses of the Goldi and Manguns the horned owl (Strix

Bubo), of value for catching the numerous rats; the jay (Garrulus glandarius), the hawk (Astur palumbarius) or kite (Milvus niger), kept for no particular object, or merely for the sake of their feathers, which are used to wing arrows. The natives are also very fond of seeing swallows build in their houses, and to induce them to do so fasten small boards under the roof inside, to which the swallows have free access through the windows, doors or smoke-holes.

Among the Goldi of the Sungari the pig is of some importance, but owing to its being fed exclusively upon fish it has a very disagreeable flavour, not at all palatable to Europeans. We also find a few cats, which are great favourites, but the clever Manchu introduce only castrated males in order not to spoil their trade. There are a few horses. But of all the domestic animals the dog is the most useful. He not only accompanies his master in the chase, drags the boats during summer and the sledge during winter, but his skin supplies a material for dress. We are not aware whether dog-flesh is considered a culinary article; at all events it would prove a very tough bit of meat. The dogs used in hunting do not generally draw the sledge.

Agriculture is unknown among the tribes now under consideration, and the Goldi of the Sungari alone cultivate small plots of ground, which produce vegetables and tobacco.

In hunting they employ bows and spears, and in winter

GOLDI SPEAR.

pursue the beasts on snow-shoes. A snare is laid for sables; those on the Lower Amur however are of little value, but other beasts are frequently caught in it, much to the disappointment of the huntsman. It consists of a cross-bow, strongly bent, and fixed in the cleft of some tree, the arrow being retained merely by a horse-hair. A string with a bait is placed in the track frequented by the sables, and the arrow is discharged at the slightest touch. To be struck by the arrow is not however certain death, and to impede as much as possible the flight of the animal after being hit, the arrow-head on striking becomes detached from the shaft, but being still connected with it by a string, the shaft gets entangled in the low brushwood and prevents the animal from extricating itself.

SNARE.

The most redoubtable foe encountered by the natives is the tiger, and they are consequently very superstitious with regard to him, and are reluctant even to speak about him for fear of evil consequences. Images of the tiger are carved in wood and placed at the foot of large trees in the forest, or worn as charms, which are supposed to protect the bearer against his attacks. Still the Goldi occasionally kill a tiger, and appear very proud of the achievement; when this happens they fasten the animal to a wall of their houses, and the whole family passes in review before him, doing homage by bending low, and sarcastically addressing him as "My Lord." The skin soon finds its way into the hands of the Manchu, and is worn by high officials. The panther (Felis Irbis) is more feared than the tiger, and even the Goldi dare not attack him.

As regards the religion of these tribes, they certainly have some notion of a Supreme Being, but as this Being is ever benevolent they do not deem it worth while to address to him any particular worship. Their worship is addressed to good and evil spirits, who must be appeased or propitiated by the intercession of the Shaman. Images of these genii carved in wood may be seen in abundance everywhere. They sometimes represent human figures bedizened with bits of coloured cloth or with furs,

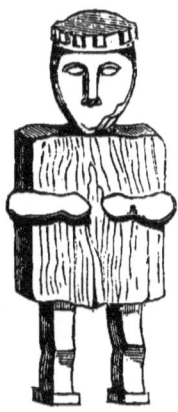

MANGUN IDOL.

and about a foot and a half high. Others resembling animals, such as the bear, tiger, frog or serpent, are worn as talismans. A third kind of idols, also carved in wood, are intended as companions to the native on his journeys. They are the gods Tanya and Panya, and when addressed in prayer are placed upon a pillow, which at night serves to support the head of the supplicant. There are also idols on the summits of mountains, before which stand small boxes containing millet or sand, and iron pots. The supplicant having elicited sweet sounds from the pot by striking it with

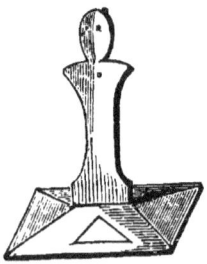

THE GOD PANYA.

a stick, throws a small piece of wood or straw into the box as an offering to the god. They use moreover a kind of libation, for when the Japanese traveller Rinso passed the so-called Tatar monument at Tyr, the natives, looking up towards them, threw some millet into the river.

It is the special business of the Shaman to invoke the assistance of the good spirits and to propitiate the evil, for sickness and all other mishaps are ascribed to the working of malignant spirits. Thus when a person falls sick, both doctor and patient deck themselves with wooden shavings, and the Shaman, beating his drum, chaunting his monotonous strain, and burning bog-moss as incense, calls upon the particular spirit to leave his patient. Or instead of making a direct appeal, he addresses himself to its idol, bearing a branch of the sacred Ayan pine in his hand. There is a distinct spirit for every disease. A bandage round the head with images of serpents, toads and other animals stuck on, is worn for headache; a dog cut out of grass-leaves against sexual diseases, and so forth. The custom of wearing an image of the diseased part as a kind of amulet has been mentioned before, and the manner of invoking the aid of the spirits at the commencement of the fishing or hunting season has been graphically described by M. de la Brunière (p. 93).

It is seen thus that the Shamans wield a great power; but their responsibility is equally great, for whilst ordinary people pass after death without fail to heaven, the Shaman is liable to go to hell should he during his lifetime abuse the power he possesses over evil spirits to the detriment of his fellow creatures. This hell is of course a loathsome place, where the soul of the departed is tormented by gnawing insects. But neither is the heaven particularly inviting, for the departed lead a life there, the very counterpart of that they lead on earth. We may suppose however that fish and

SHAMAN TOMB.

game are more abundant, and that the influence of evil spirits ceases within its sacred precincts.

Much respect is shown to the dead. The corpse is placed in a rude coffin made of the trunk of a tree or of some planks, and a very neat house erected over it, in the building of which the artistic taste of the Goldi and Manguns allows itself free scope. The funeral huts, of the Shamans especially, exhibit native workmanship of a very superior order. Near these tombs are hung up nets, bows and spears which the deceased is supposed to require, and offerings of food are made to the soul of the departed. They also make an idol of wood, the face of which they besmear with oil, and believe that it is entered by the soul of the deceased, before passing to the subterranean heaven, when the idol is broken. Those of the Orochi are of a more humble kind, and contain several coffins placed side by side. Poor people are simply laid in a coffin and lodged in the forked branches of some tree, out of the reach of wild animals.

The character of these tribes is pourtrayed as being rather timid and good-natured, and strictly honest. They reverence old age and are kind to their children. The latter, while infants, are kept among the Manguns and Orochi in an

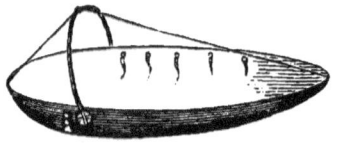

CRADLE.

oblong box; whilst the Goldi strap them down in a basin-shaped cradle, ornamented with small coins, and suspended by means of an iron hoop to a rafter in the house. The Orochi women suckle their children until they are three or four years of age.

The females assist their lords in many ways, but are by no means oppressed. The heavier work is undertaken by the men, and though the women row boats, and evidently delight in doing so, this is not degrading, compared with what we may see any day at Boulogne, where old women toil up hill with a heavily-laden truck, whilst the husband stands by, smoking *imperial* and drinking his litre on the fruits of her labour. There is no regular form of government unless we may so name that which is exercised by the Manchu, whose only care is to extort as many sables as they can. Children up to a certain age are under the tutelage of their parents. The father chooses his son's bride, while that son is still in his infancy, and the intended bride with the consent of her parents comes to live with her future parents-in-law, and both are brought up as brother and sister. When the boy is eighteen and the girl fifteen, marriage is generally consummated, but there are some wise old men who see in these early marriages the decay of their tribe, and make their children wait until they are twenty or more. Polygamy is not generally practised, for if anything the number of women is inferior to that of the men. It is nevertheless usual that a man should inherit his deceased brother's wife as well as his personal estate.

Wrestling is one of the favourite amusements of the men. They lay hold of their belts, and in this way seek to throw their opponents. A literature of course is not to be sought for among a people who have no written language, and but few of whom know how to read or write Chinese. Nor do any traditions of past times appear to exist amongst them. They improvise songs, which are however devoid of any artistic arrangement. One of the guides of Veniukof on nearing his home, sang of the rapid river, which he should not much longer navigate; of his being soon at home where a pretty wife expected him, whilst his mother was fretting at his absence. He introduced into this strain—which according to circumstances was joyful or plaintive—the Russians, the country traversed, the difficulties surmounted—but all this pell-mell, and without any inherent connection. Still Veniukof appears too severe when he denies to the Goldi and Orochi all feelings of poetry.

In one respect we cannot withhold our admiration from

the Tunguzians. The manner in which they adorn their tombs, dresses and household utensils cannot be sufficiently praised. They make use of the colours at their disposal with much taste. Blue is the favourite, and they also use red, black, green and brown. For cutting out their fish-skin

MANGUN KNIFE FOR CUTTING OUT FISH-SKIN ORNAMENTS.

patterns, or carving in wood they have a short knife. We cannot resist the temptation of giving a few specimens of

native designs. The first is a small bag for tinder, which would be no discredit to Bond-street.

The second is a box made of birch-bark, and the third a design cut in fish-skin.

## THE GILYAKS.

The Gilyaks inhabit the banks of the Lower Amur, below Pul, and the northern portion of Sakhalin, their limits on the island being on the west coast the village of Pilyavo, 50° 10′ N. lat.; and on the east coast about 50° 30′ N. lat.

GILYAKS.

There are several tribes of these Gilyaks, those of the mainland, the Smerenkur of the west coast of Sakhalin, and the Tro of the east coast, but the distinction between them is trifling. Nor do they differ much in outward appearance from their Tunguzian neighbours. The features are still Mongol, the nose is rather flat, the eyes are small, the lips are voluptuous, the eyebrows bushy, and the beard is stronger than with the Tunguzians. They do not shave the head, but wear the hair tied up into a thick tail or in tresses. The Russians describe their women as frights, but tastes are not always the same, and Rimso, the Japanese, says they are very comely, and doubly attractive on account of their daily ablutions. Their dress does not vary much from that of the Tunguzians. They wear large boots of seal-skin, or sometimes cotton, and a blouse of Chinese pattern. The use of fish-skins is much more restricted.

Their habitations are wooden houses, the interior often partitioned off into two apartments, the first of which serves as a kind of ante-room, whilst the second is that generally inhabited. The fire is in the centre of this second room, and the smoke escapes through a hole in the roof. Father Furet[a] describes a dwelling-house in Jonquière Bay, constructed on the same principle as the store-houses of the Tunguzians. This house was built upon stakes, about four feet above the ground. It was about thirty feet long and fifteen wide, and there was a small platform in front, access to which was gained by the trunk of a tree, which had rough steps cut into it. On this verandah, arrows, bows and spears, with light sledges were disposed in pleasing variety. The walls and floors were made of the trunks of trees, the interstices filled up with birch-bark or leaves, and the roof was covered with birch-bark. There were two rooms. The dogs have admittance to the rooms, but are generally tied up underneath the building, or to a rail near the houses. They are neither vicious nor cowardly, and their masters show great reluctance to part with them. In addition to dogs, the Gilyaks keep sometimes an ermine (Mustela erminea) to kill rats. Wealthy individuals keep a tom-cat. They also have bear-cages near their villages, and when they kill the beast, they split the skull and suspend it in their houses. Fish, prepared with herbs, roots and

[a] Lettres sur l'Archipel Japonais et la Tartarie Oriental. Par le P. Furet. Paris, 1860.

train-oil, constitutes their principal food. Sometimes they procure a little millet or rice from the Manchu or Japanese in exchange for furs. At meal-time much attention is shewn to the position of each individual, and the person highest in rank occupies the centre seat. The character given to these Gilyaks is far from favourable. Schrenck says, that the Gilyaks of the mainland are avaricious and covetous in their commercial transactions, but that among those of Sakhalin this propensity seeks satisfaction in theft and robbery. The Gilyaks of the northern portion of the island are particularly notorious in this respect, and never fail to exhibit such friendly sentiments towards ship-wrecked whalers. It will be remembered that the missionary, De la Brunière, met his death at the hand of Gilyaks, who were induced to commit this outrage by the little merchandise he had with him. Murder is of frequent occurrence among the Gilyaks, and it is often the result of trifling causes, a feeling of jealousy or an offensive allusion. Blood demands blood, and the family of a murdered man is bound to avenge his death upon the murderer or one of his relatives. There are instances where this blood-feud has been carried on for generations.

If we may credit the statement of Rinso, polyandry prevails among the Smerenkur Gilyaks, and the women are treated with the greatest indulgence. Only those however skilled in the use of the needle can expect to get married. The children, as among the Goldi, are strapped down on a kind of board serving as a cradle, and hung up in that position to a rafter of the roof.

The Gilyaks, like the Tunguzians, put their faith in wooden idols, representing good or evil spirits, and whom they worship with the assistance of the Shamans. They are even more superstitious than the Tunguzians. A Gilyak would not for instance permit any fire to be taken from his hut, not even in a pipe, nor would he allow any to be imported for were he to do so, he would have ill-luck in the fishing or the hunt, or lose one of his relatives by death. The tiger is much more feared than among the Goldi, and its appearance portends evil. If the remains of a man are found who has been killed by a tiger, they are buried on the spot without any further ceremony. The burial rites ordinarily are of a rather ·imposing character. The body is first burnt on a funeral-pyre, and a small wooden house is erected over the carefully-gathered ashes. The favourite dog of the deceased, having been fattened previously, is killed on the grave, and the soul of the deceased, which until then took up its abode in the dog, is thus released and descends into—heaven. Small sacrifices of fish, tobacco or similar objects are from time to time taken to the tomb, the shed above which is cleared away after a lapse of two years.

In each dwelling-house, there is small shrine with an idol, and the heads of seals and fishes are sacrificed on the shore to the sea-god.

## THE AINO.

THE Aino occupy the southern portion of Sakhalin, part of Yeso and some of the Kuriles. Our remarks have of course especial reference to the Aino of Sakhalin. Aino, in their language, signifies "Man." In the historical records of the Japanese, they are referred to as Eastern savages, and about 660 B.C. they still occupied the northern provinces of Nippon. It was not until the close of the ninth century that the Aino of Nippon became really subject to the Japanese. In course of time they disappeared on Nippon as a separate people, they were either exterminated, emigrated to Yeso or became amalgamated with the Japanese. In the fourteenth century the Japanese extended their dominion to Yeso, and at the commencement of this present century they crossed over to Sakhalin, by them called • Oke or Northern Yeso where they formed several settlements.

In language and appearance the Aino differ totally from their neighbours the Gilyak and Oroki, and the Tunguzian tribes of the Amur. Their average stature is five feet four inches, none of them being above five feet nine inches. They are squat and strong-built, and have the muscles of their body well-defined. The head[a] is large, and the face broader and more rounded than with Europeans. Their countenance is animated and agreeable, though destitute of that regularity and grace which in Europe are deemed essential to beauty. They have large cheeks, a short nose, rounded at the tip, with very broad nostrils. Their eyes are of moderate size and lively, for the most part black, though occasionally blue may be seen. The eyebrows are bushy; the mouth of the common size and the voice strong. The lips are rather thick and of a dull red; several have the upper lip tattoed or tinged blue. Their teeth are white and regular, the chin rounded and a little retreating. The ears are small and ornamented with glass-beads or silver ear-rings. The nails are allowed to grow long. The skin is of a tawny colour. It is however the quantity of hair which distinguishes these savages most strikingly from their neighbours, and the Eastern Asiatics generally. They wear moustaches and long beards reaching down to the middle of the breast. The arms, chest, neck and back are very hairy; individuals, however, quite as hairy may be found in Europe. Krusenstern examined a child of eight years of age in Mordvinof Bay (east coast, 47° north latitude), the body of which was entirely covered with hair, whilst its parents were not hairy. The women are much smaller than the men; they

---

[a] Circumference of the head 23·80 inches; its longest diameter 10·30 inches; its shortest diameter 6·83. Rollin in la Pérouse's Travels vol. ii. p. 298.

are not very prepossessing. Whittingham says they are ugly. They wear the hair long and flowing, tattoo their upper lip and sometimes the hands. But though Whittingham is rather hard upon the fair sex, he does ample justice to the men. "One of them was a magnificent savage: tall, lithe, straight and strong, with hair, beard and moustaches never desecrated by the touch of scissors; with a high, broad brow, dark eyes, straight nose and oval face, he was a far nobler creature than the Red Indian whom I always fancied was the pride of wild men."[b]

The Aino of Aniva Bay show their subjection to the Japanese by shaving the crown of the head, and wearing a Japanese dress.

The Aino are acquainted with the use of the weaver's loom, and manufacture cloth from the bark of the willow-tree. They also employ the spindle to make thread from the hair of animals, willow-bast or the great nettle. They generally wear a loose robe of such material or of nankeen, buttoned in front and bound by a girdle round the waist. During winter they dress in dog-skins or seal-skins. Their boots are made of seal-skins, in Chinese style. They are very fond of ornamenting their clothing with small bits of coloured cloth which they obtain from the Amur. The natives whom Krusenstern found at Mordvinof Bay wore a cotton shirt underneath their seal-skin robe, which in every instance was scrupulously clean. Most of the men wore no head-dress at all; some wear straw hats, a band of bear-skin round the head or a seal-skin hat.

Their houses are rough log-huts, the interstices filled up with birch-bark and dry leaves; the roof is covered with birch-bark or thatched with straw. The door, at the gable, is very low. The fire-place is in the centre of the apartment and the smoke escapes through the roof. Benches

[b] Whittingham.

eight or ten inches high run round the wall. Sometimes the house is divided into two rooms. During winter they dwell in subterranean habitations. The store-houses are similar to those of the Tunguzians. They also have cages with bears near their habitations, and the captive is well fed with fish.

AINO ELDER.

La Pérouse found in d'Estaing Bay fifteen to twenty stakes standing, each surmounted with the head of a bear, in a more or less advanced state of decomposition. The festival *Omsia* takes place in autumn, and the bear plays an important part. A neat hut covered with branches of trees is erected outside the village and in it the head of a newly-killed bear is fastened to the wall, surrounded by a trophy composed of arms. The Aino squat down on mats in front of this hut, and pass the time in eating, drinking, singing and dancing. The principal dish at this festival is soup with bear's-meat, with which they drink sake or rice-brandy.[c]

The Aino do not cultivate the ground, but are satisfied with collecting some plants—the roots of the yellow lily and

[c] Siebold, Nippon, xvii.

angelica — which they dry in the sun. Their chief supply of food is drawn from fishing. They throw away the head, tail and backbone of the fish, and dry and smoke the remainder. On the thumb they wear a thick ring of ivory, horn or lead, to protect themselves when skinning the fish. In the preparation of food little salt is used, but the more train-oil, which they pretend keeps off the stomach-ache. Their arms consist of bows and arrows, javelins and pikes. They make use of poisoned arrows when hunting the bear, but sometimes the poison does not take instantaneous effect, and the enraged beast falls upon the hunter, who has to defend himself with his spear. The produce of the chase is trifling, and dried fish and oil supply the chief articles of export. They carry on commerce with the Japanese and with the Manchu on the Amur. Their boats are made of a hollowed-out oak-tree, or of planks fastened with wooden pegs. They never venture far from the land. At night they pull the boat ashore, and erect a temporary hut of birch-bark, which they carry along with them for that purpose. Rinso informs us that when the "Santans" — the country on the Lower Amur is called Santan by the Japanese — arrive in their small boats they place the merchandise they wish to sell on the shore and retire. The Aino then approach, inspect it and replace it by the furs they desire to exchange. Sometimes the Aino wish to eschew payment altogether, but if the accounts are not adjusted in the following year, the Santans carry off a brother, sister or child of the delinquent as security. According to the same authority, trade in human beings is carried on along the west coast of Sakhalin, and the people of Yeso come here to sell slaves to the "Santans," that is the Manchu. Poor or valueless persons, such as widows or widowers, old maids and bachelors, orphans or idiots, are disposed of in this way for three to seven pieces of gold-stuff a head. If this is true, the character given to the Aino by European travellers—that they are solemn and striking in their bearing, distinguished by goodness of heart, and strangers to avarice and rapacity—requires to be considerably modified. This statement is corroborated in so far as slavery is an institution in Manchuria, where many slaves are found in the retinue of the military nobles.

We know but little of the religious notions of the Aino, except that they appear to resemble in this respect the

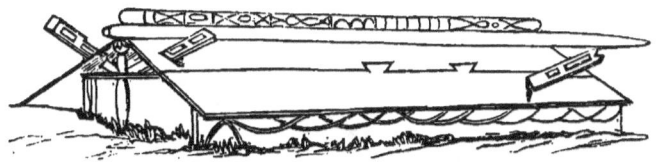

AINO TOMB.

Gilyaks and Tunguzians. After death the entrails are taken out through the anus, and this last service is performed by some relative or friend, who had already undertaken this obligation during the life-time of the deceased. The body is then exposed in the open air for thirty days and dried, when it is put into a tomb, above which a small wooden house is erected. Poor people merely cut down a tree near the place

PLACE OF BURIAL.

of burial, to within a short distance from the ground, carve designs round the stump, and set up the symbols of the Aino protective deity, Inao,—a short pole with a tassel suspended from the end of it. (See p. 379).

THE OROKE, OR OROTSKOS ON SAKHALIN.[d]

OROTSKOS WITH REINDEER.

THE Orotskos are few in number, and occupy the interior of Sakhalin and its eastern coast. Their language differs from that of the Aino, and according to Schrenck, they are Tunguzians. They do not shave the head, but allow the hair to fall over the shoulders, or tie it up in a tail which hangs down behind. Their women plait or curl the hair, and according to Mamia Rinso, the Japanese traveller, are very good-looking. They moreover possess the art of making themselves agreeable to the male sex, wash the face and body, and comb the hair. They wear large ear-rings. The

[d] Mamia Rinso, in Siebold's "Nippon."

men wear smaller ones. Their dress is made of fish or sealskin; the trowsers of deer-skin. The gowns of the women are ornamented with brass baubles, and they wear linen aprons, the material being procured in trading journeys to the Amur. The Orotskos have no permanent habitations, but dwell in yurts like the Orochons of the Upper Amur. Their store-houses are also similar, and are left standing when the owner removes. The only domestic animal of this tribe is the reindeer, and a man owning twelve of them is considered well off. The reindeer carry burthens or draw the sledge. During summer, they are pastured in the plains, and in thé winter taken to the mountains, where their food consists of lichens and mosses. They are afraid of dogs, and will not enter a village where these are kept. The character of the Orotskos is described as rough and unbridled.

A murderer is obliged to surrender the whole of his property to the relatives of his victim. The dead are placed in coffins, and exposed in the open air, in the same manner as with the Orochis of Castries Bay.

The food of the Orotskos consists of fish, meat, roots, and herbs. They use bows, arrows, and spears. Their boats are of the same build as those of the Ainos, but larger and stronger.

## XXI.

## COMMERCIAL RESOURCES, AND GERMS FOR THEIR DEVELOPMENT.

In considering the commercial resources of the Amur country itself, we need say but little, all of the products having been enumerated in previous chapters. We have seen that there is an inexhaustible stock of timber and firewood. Varieties of excellent hard wood are supplied by the maple, walnut, buckthorn, ash, elm, a good substitute for the oak, which on the Amur is often rotten to the core, and generally inferior to the oaks of Europe; the cork tree not only supplies cork, but also a superior hard wood; the Maackia is well suited for cabinet work. Trees with soft wood are the poplar, aspen, larch, pitch, spruce, cedar, and Scotch fir; the conifers, besides furnishing excellent timber, yielding also turpentine, pitch, tar, and rosin. There are various kinds of apple and plum (cherry) trees, and some of our European fruit trees, which do not succeed in Siberia, might no doubt be cultivated on the Amur. Such is not however the case as regards the vine; for though grapes half an inch in diameter are found on the southern Amur, the berries are tart and not juicy. Humboldt says (Kosmos i. p. 350), "In order to produce a drinkable wine, the mean annual temperature must not only exceed 49° F., but a mild winter of 32° 90′ F. must be succeeded by a summer temperature of at least 64°." These climatological conditions do not exist on the Amur, for though the summer temperature on the southern parts of that river exceeds 64°, the winters are extremely severe, and moreover frosts in spring and autumn are unfavourable to the cultivation of the vine. This does not however refer to Victoria Bay, where the wild vine has also been found to grow luxuriantly, and where the climatological conditions are much more favourable.

With regard to the produce of the forests we must observe, that the export of timber is strictly prohibited, though any one is permitted to cut trees for building purposes or for fuel, and many square miles of forest are burnt down annually through the carelessness or thoughtless avarice of huntsmen. In Canada the exports of timber and ashes amount to 48 per cent. of the total exports of the country!

Among the cereals which may be and are cultivated on the Amur, rye, no doubt, will occupy the most important place. Barley, oats, and wheat, are also cultivated successfully. In addition we find various kinds of millet (sorghum). Maize would certainly thrive well if introduced. The cultivation of cereals promises however to become remunerative only between the Dzeya and Mariinsk. At Nikolayevsk and Castries Bay even barley does not succeed, and on the Upper Amur, including Dauria, the yield is rendered precarious by early frosts in autumn. Of other food-plants, we may mention buck-wheat, potatoes, and most of our European vegetables.

The extreme moisture of many localities, as for instance along the Usuri, caused by a superabundance of forest land, will no doubt injuriously affect agriculture for some time to come. We are however justified in believing that with the partial destruction of the forests, the climate will become drier. Dauria, for example, which in by-gone times had a moist climate, now suffers occasionally from drought, and this is the case, to a much greater extent, in the now desolate regions west of the Quathlamba mountains in South Africa.

Tobacco, hemp, flax, and linseed will become of value.

The natives also use a kind of nettle for manufacturing their ropes.

Passing next to the animal creation, we find a great abundance of fish, and numerous fur-animals. The former, in fact, furnish most of the natives with their principal article of food, but with an increased settlement of the country this resource may be exhausted. Such is the case even to a greater degree with the fur and other wild animals, which future generations will exterminate. West of the Yablonoi mountains the scarcity of game is even now the cause of great distress, and as a proof we select the following extract from a lecture by Mr. Radde, delivered before the Russian Academy of Sciences, in March, 1860.

" There, in the dense forest, where the sable loves nightly to follow his prey, and the huntsman pursues his daily toil, we see a human being, stagger panting towards the valley, where a flickering flame indicates the resting-place of all he most cherishes. It is late. Five days have elapsed, and he has captured no game, which, formerly so abundant, has quitted these regions; the small store of flour has been consumed; and weeks ago the last tame reindeer was killed. The muscles of his enfeebled body are powerless, and the star-light shines upon a visage full of cares. The savage has a father's heart too, which sinks within him as he pictures grinning death hovering round that fire.

" Anxiously the looks of the expectant ones meet those of the comer; no other demonstration; no word is exchanged. The infant at the breast sucks a piece of leather, and silently the mother turns her back towards the fire, to sleep, perchance the sleep of eternity."

But independently of game and fish, the Amur is valuable as a cattle-breeding country. There are thousands of square miles of excellent pasture-land, where millions of sheep, cattle and horses might find an easy sustenance. With proper management, the severe winter and snow would prove no obstacle; the real obstacle must be sought for in the character of the Russian population at present settled there. German colonists from the steppes of Southern Russia, well acquainted with the breeding of cattle, have however been sent for, and are expected in this or the next year.

Nor are the mineral riches of the Amur to be despised; and since the whole of Siberia has been thrown open to private enterprise, we may reasonably expect to see them explored at some period not very far distant. Coals have been discovered at several places on the Amur itself, on the Bureya, and on Sakhalin island. Gold is found in several localities; iron is reported to exist, whilst there is every probability of there being other minerals in the country.

Among minor articles of export, large quantities of the ginseng-root which is cultivated on Russian territory by Chinese settlers on the Upper Usuri will form no inconsiderable portion. The ginseng (Panax ginseng) is superior, at all events, to the so-called ginseng (Panax sessiflorum) of the United States, the exports of which in 1858 amounted to 366,053 pounds, valued at 193,736 dollars.

These then are the various articles of raw produce, available as exports. A manufacturing industry does not as yet exist, but might be advantageously established for some branches. A great abundance of cattle would favour the manufacture of leather, and that of sheep the manufacture of coarse cloths. Cotton stuffs, for the present at least, are not to be thought of. We are not however very sanguine as regards manufactures. Siberia has hitherto been obliged to rest satisfied with the miserable and expensive manufactures of the country, but would cease to do so if once the Amur were thrown open to foreign commerce with unrestricted competition. The settlers would then find it more advantageous to supply raw produce in return for manufactures and colonial goods.

Now as regards imports. Merchants desirous to trade

with the natives ought to supply themselves with cotton stuffs, cloth, *daba* (a coarse woollen stuff), common Russian tobacco (which, owing to its narcotic qualities, is preferred to the Manchurian and even American), powder and lead, knives, millet, rice, brandy, small nicknacks of gilt or silvered copper, common glass and amber beads, and blue and black plush. Red, black and blue are the favourite colours. Spirits however meet with the surest sale among natives and Russians alike.

The wants of the Russian garrison and colonists are far more comprehensive. Colonial goods, sugar, coffee and spices; tea, spirits, wines and beer; rice and for some time at least, wheat and other cereals; arms, cutlery, cigars and superior kinds of tobacco; manufactured goods of all kinds, agricultural implements, dress-stuffs, glass-ware, etc., would meet with a ready sale. For though many articles are produced in Siberia, they cannot compete in price or quality with European goods. Nor have the manufacturers of European Russia any chance as long as free-trade obtains on the Amur.

We will next look at the countries with which the Amur provinces have entered into commercial intercourse. Of these the province of Transbaikal is the most important. It not only sent the first colonists to the Amur, but at a great sacrifice supplied them with the necessaries of life, and still does so, the imports by sea far from supplying the wants of settlers and garrisons. The government of Transbaikal had in 1851 a population of 327,908 souls, on an area of 213,547 square miles. We will here confine our remarks to that part of Transbaikal east of the Yablonoi range, and at the head-waters of the Amur. Here, as elsewhere in Siberia, the population is a mixture of involuntary immigrants, belonging to the various tribes of European Russia, with the aborigines. The result has not been favourable, and indolence, and the vices which follow in its wake, distinguish the population. Need we therefore be surprised that in spite of the well-meant exertions of government, agriculture and every other branch of industry are still in their infancy? The chief riches of Transbaikal consist in its mines.[a] Silver, gold, lead, tin, copper, iron, coal, mercury and black-lead are found, but the three former alone appear to be explored to any extent, and yield annually 145 cwt. of silver, 54 cwt. of lead, and from 25 cwt. to 70 cwt. of gold. The mines have been hitherto worked by government exclusively, and with forced labour, but have been thrown open to private enterprize since 1859. There is a great deficiency of iron implements. Radde saw four looking-glasses of the value of £28 each in one room of a rich Cossack. But if you were to ask for a nail in this establishment, your host, though he owns one thousand horses and five hundred bullocks, and is said to have hoarded up £1,500, would not be able to supply your want. And when he sends his people into the forest to fell wood, he has to borrow hatchets from his neighbours.

Cattle-rearing might become of equal importance with mining. In 1849, there were in the whole province 300,000 horses, 300,000 head of horned cattle, 500,000 sheep, and 5,000 camels, besides pigs. Radde found on the steppes of Southern Dauria,—steppes having an area of 5,200,000 acres —70,000 sheep, 24,000 horses, 20,000 head of horned cattle. In Southern Russia, the relative proportion of the animals is very different; 2·7 acres are reckoned to a sheep, and one horse or head of horned cattle is reckoned to from 150 to 250 sheep. The number of sheep might thus be easily increased twenty-five fold. Moreover the population here is not at all acquainted with the treatment of cattle, and if you suggest any improvement, they merely

[a] Transbaikal, by N. S. Sh'chukin, in the Journal of the Ministry of the Interior, 1853.

shrug their shoulders, and tell you they do not understand these things, they do not suit them, their fathers before them did as they do, and so forth. The wool is allowed to remain on the sheep until it is ready to fall off, and then it is plucked off with the hand. Butter cleanly prepared is scarcely ever found among the Cossacks. A good round sum might nevertheless be realised by making butter and cheese. At Irkutsk a pound of bad salt butter costs sevenpence, and a pound of fresh butter one shilling. An exiled Pole, residing at Petrovskoi Zavod, made some cheese in 1856, and sold it at one shilling and sixpence a pound.[b]

Many localities are suitable for agriculture; but Dauria can never expect to become an exporting country on a large scale, for the harvest, on account of the early frosts and dry summers, is often precarious. On favourable soil, six or seven-fold is considered a good harvest, but exceptionally, after three or four bad years, it is sixty-fold. In their agricultural operations the inhabitants are as far behind as in their cattle-rearing. No manure is used, though plenty may be had; the field is allowed to lie fallow for a year, and there is no regular rotation of crops. Ploughs are unknown, and the Siberian sokha alone is used. Vegetables, even potatoes, are cultivated only in the gardens. The quantity of hemp raised is very small. The present colonists of the Amur, having most of them been transferred from Transbaikal, are imbued of course with this ignorance and these prejudices. The manufacturing industry is extremely restricted. Leather is made on the Argun; but this manufacture will naturally be removed to the Southern Amur, where oak-bark for tanning is abundant. There is a glass manufactory at Shilkinsk, producing glass and bottles of a very inferior description, which cannot expect to find a market

---

[b] These are wholesale prices, and about fifty per cent. must be added as salesmen's profits.

beyond the country and Mongolia. At Chita a large manufactory for making candles, soap and rope, has been established, but on account of the difficulty of procuring the raw material, its activity is much less than the proprietor could wish. At the same town a number of establishments for curing and smoking beef and pork have been opened, but their meat can scarcely be called edible. A Hamburg merchant, in conjunction with a St. Petersburg firm, has therefore resolved to send some person acquainted with this business. The salt which can be procured in the steppes, and may become of importance as an article of trade, is at present taken from some lakes, where it crystalizes spontaneously after a hot summer. Vast tracts are covered with worm-wood and other true salt-plants, and potash might thus be procured easily, and in abundance.

It now remains for us to see in how far Transbaikal and Eastern Siberia generally would profit by the Amur being opened to navigation. The conveyance of a ton of merchandise from London to Nikolayevsk amounts to £4 or £5, or about five shillings the cwt. Thence to Chita on the Ingoda, the head of navigation on the Amur, is a distance of 2,260 miles,[c] but owing to the want of steamers of suitable draft, Stretyinsk, 250 miles below Chita, is the highest point to which steamers usually ascend. In 1860 the charge for conveying a cwt. to Stretyinsk was as much as twenty-one shillings; but during 1861, in consequence of the addition of several steamers, the charge has been reduced to 12s. 6d. The conveyance from Stretyinsk to Irkutsk, the commercial centre of Eastern Siberia, a distance of 730

[c] Up to the Dzeya, the Amur may be navigated by vessels drawing four feet; thence to Shilkinsk vessels drawing two feet may proceed throughout the year, and during high-water (spring) they may get as far as Chita. A boat journey down the river occupies fifty days, and up the river one hundred days. A steamer may descend in twenty days, and ascend in thirty.

miles, is about 8s. 6d. a cwt. The total expense for carrying one cwt. of goods from Europe to Irkutsk amounts thus to 26 shillings.[d] If we compare this amount with the expense of conveying a cwt. of goods from Nishegorod to Irkutsk, we find a gain in favour of the Amur route of sixteen shillings, and it would result from this that European produce may compete on equal terms with the produce of European Russia at a point situated 1,100 miles to the west of Irkutsk.

This expense certainly is heavy, and adds considerably to the price of goods, even without taking into view the large profits Siberian merchants are accustomed to make. The proportionate expense varies greatly with the character of the merchandise. The imports of our Australian colonies, for instance, have a value of 25 shillings a cwt.; their conveyance to Irkutsk would add above 100 per cent. to this. In the case of dress-stuffs the addition is however but 3 per cent.; with cigars 5 per cent.; hardware and tobacco 18 per cent.; coffee 43 per cent.; sugar 60 per cent., and so forth —a percentage in most instances far below the duties charged in the tariffs of European and American States. Loaf-sugar at Irkutsk cost formerly about 2s. 6d. a pound; it might now be sold for 10d. at a good profit. Coffee cost 3s. 2d. a pound; imported by way of the Amur, it might be sold for 1s. 8d. We are however far from affirming that these reductions have actually taken place, or in other words that the Siberian community have availed themselves of the advantages of the Amur route: up to 1859 they had not. Western Europe might thus reasonably expect to compete with the manufacturers of Russia in the very heart of

[d] An enterprising American, Mr. Collins, has proposed to build a railway from Chita to Kiakhta, but such a scheme, though feasible, cannot be expected to be remunerative for many years to come. Much less could a railway through Siberia to Europe compete with the small charges at present in force for land-transport.

Siberia, if not excluded by high protective duties. The Russian manufactures are not only inferior, but on account of the high prices of raw material, more expensive also. Cotton for instance costs at Moscow £3 12s. to £4 7s. the cwt.; in London, only £3. Indigo, Moscow, £45; London, £22, and so forth. There are however manufactories in Siberia several of which procure their raw material on the spot. In 1849 there were :—

| Manufactories in | Tobolsk. | Tomsk. | Yeniseisk. | Irkutsk.[c] | Total. |
|---|---|---|---|---|---|
| Leather | 77 | 20 | 11 | 19 | 127 |
| Soap | 21 | 17 | 3 | 15 | 56 |
| Tallow and Candles | 19 | 4 | 1 | 10 | 34 |
| Wax | — | — | 1 | — | 1 |
| Glass | 9 | 1 | 1 | 2 | 13 |
| China | — | 1 | — | 2 | 3 |
| Hardware | 3 | — | 1 | — | 4 |
| Oil | 1 | — | — | — | 1 |
| Rope | — | 1 | — | — | 1 |
| Paper | 2 | — | — | — | 2 |
| Cloth | — | — | — | 1 | 1 |
| Chemical Products | 2 | — | — | — | 2 |
| Total | 134 | 44 | 18 | 49 | 245 |
| Workmen | 718 | 186 | 183 | 366 | 1453 |

The government iron works at Petrovsk, on the western slope of the Yablonoi Mountains, have not been included in this return. About 360 cwt. of bar-iron are produced here annually; there is an iron foundry, and the machinery for three of the steamers now navigating the Amur was made here. The quality of the iron however is not good, and the price is so high, that large quantities are brought from the Ural, 2,000 miles distant. Coal abounds in the neighbourhood, but is little used.

More dangerous rivals might be found in the government of Perm, employing 48,436 persons in five hundred and twenty-seven manufactories (two hundred and twenty-six in

[c] Including Transbaikal.

leather, one hundred and seventy-seven hardware, etc.). On the Amur itself their competition need not however be feared.[f]

With China and Mongolia a considerable commerce is carried on by Russia by way of Kiakhta. According to official statements the value of export was as follows:—

|      | Exports in Manufacture and Raw Produce. | Exports in Bullion and Specie | Customs Receipts. |
|------|-----------------------------------------|-------------------------------|-------------------|
| 1852 | £1,190,800                              | none                          | £732,530          |
| 1854 | 881,020                                 | none                          | 429,360           |
| 1857 | 903,740                                 | none                          | 834,080           |
| 1858 | 858,554                                 | £227,840                      | 800,430           |

The trade was, up to 1858, entirely a bartering trade. Of the Russian manufactured goods above forty-one per cent. are woollen-cloths, twenty-five per cent. cotton-stuffs, four to twenty per cent. peltry, ten per cent. leather and skins, two per cent. cereals, and seventeen per cent. silver and gold ornaments. The export of specie has been permitted since 1858, and before that time the Russian merchants, in order to evade the law, were in the habit of having silver and gold cast into rough candlesticks and the like, to barter away as manufactured goods. The Chinese imports consist of tea exclusively, and it had formerly to pay a duty of nearly 75 per cent.! With such oppressive imposts we need not wonder that a large contraband trade was carried on; and to arrive at the true appreciation of the Kiakhta trade, we may double the above statements.[g] The customs receipts are paid on the tea being cleared from the custom-house, and are not

[f] We have not taken into account here the import duties which Russia may levy upon foreign merchandise. For the present, the trade of the Amur is free.

[g] The duties on tea have been considerably reduced by a decree of 30th March, 1861. At Kiakhta a pound pays 1s. 1d., 5½d., or 1¼d., according to quality. In European Russia the duties are 2s. and 1s. 3d. for southern ports, and 1s. 10d. and 11d. for northern ports.

therefore in proportion to the actual annual trade. The question now arises in how far will this Kiakhta trade be influenced by the acquisition of the Amur? We believe very little, if at all. The cost of conveying a cwt. of merchandise from the Chinese frontier across the Mongolian Steppes to Kiakhta, varies from nine to twenty shillings, according to the greater or lesser abundance of fodder.[h] The conveyance of a cwt. up the Amur alone to Stretyinsk, costs twelve shillings and sixpence, to which must be added the cost of conveyance from some Chinese port. Stretyinsk and Kiakhta occupy about the same position with respect to Irkutsk, the centre of Siberian commerce, and are nearly equal in point of expense. A third route from China to Siberia is available for trade, we mean that to the head waters of Sungari, and thence down to the Amur; but as a simple glance at a map will show, it offers even fewer advantages than that by sea, there being several hundred miles of land-transport.[i]

China being now thrown open to foreign commerce, the Amur country, when more developed, will no doubt take its share. It can export copper, lead and zinc, which in China are extensively used, but procurable only in the southwestern part of the empire; woollen cloths, the consumption of which is on the increase; glass-ware, a manufacture not in a very advanced state in China; leather, which owing to the scarcity of cattle there, every inch of ground almost

[h] In 1860 the charges made were 17s. for ordinary merchandise, 21s. for furs, 25s. for silver bullion.

[i] Russia also carries on a considerable trade on the western frontier of China, by way of Kulja and Chuguchak. In 1841 the imports from China, the Kirgiz Steppe and Turan amounted to £898,000 including 1315 lbs. of tea. In 1852 the imports were valued at £552,000 including 666,000 lbs. of tea, valued at £71,000. In 1854 the imports had increased to £780,000 including 1,668,096 lbs. of tea; in 1856 they were £1,016,692.

being applied to agricultural purposes, is in much request; and furs. China, in return, will send tea, sugar, porcelain, indigo and silk.

Commercial intercourse has also been opened with Japan, which exports cotton, rice, tea, camphor, silks, porcelain, lacquered ware; and would take in return hemp, woollen stuffs, linen, lead and zinc procurable from Siberia and the country on the Amur. The other countries with which the Amur has already carried on some commerce, are the United States, England and Germany. The imports thence consist of brandy, wine, tobacco, colonial and manufactured goods. The exports as yet are very trifling.

## COMMUNICATIONS.

The river is the great highway during summer and winter. Up to the Dzeya, the Amur may be navigated by vessels drawing four feet; thence to Shilkinsk, vessels drawing two feet may proceed throughout the year, and during high water (spring) they may get as far as Chita, though the current is strong. A boat journey down the river occupies about fifty days, and one up the river one hundred days. A steamer descends in twenty days, and ascends in thirty. This calculation is of course exclusive of all delays on the road. The Dzeya, Sungari, Usuri, and Bureya, are also navigable for a considerable distance.

The following are the steamers at present navigating the Amur:—

| | | |
|---|---|---|
| Shilka, | 20 H.P. | ⎧ Wooden steamers, built on the Shilka in 1854, the machinery having been brought from Petrovsk. In 1860, they were undergoing repairs. |
| Argun, | 20 „ | |
| Amur, | 60 „ | ⎧ Iron steamers, built in America; brought to the Amur in 1856, and launched in 1857. |
| Lena, | 35 „ | |

| | | |
|---|---|---|
| Mechanik, | 15 H.P. | Built at Nikolayevsk, the machinery having been brought from Petrovsk. Run aground on the Usuri, 1860. Ascended to Kingka Lake in 1861. |
| Dzeya, | 70 „ | Iron steamers built by Geoffroy at Hamburg, sent to the Amur in the St. Francisco, and launched in 1860. |
| Onon, | 40 „ | |
| Chita, | 30 „ | |
| Ingoda, | 30 „ | |
| Kazakwich, | „ | Wooden steamer, having a wheel in the stern, brought from America in 1859. Property of Captain Vries. |
| —— | 60 „ | Iron steamer, brought from America in 1860. Property of Bordtman and Co. |

All, except the two last, are government property. The screw-steamer Nadeshda, eight horse-power, brought from England in 1854, foundered in 1860, and has not been recovered. The Muravief-Amursky, sixty horse-power, built by Cockerell, at Seraing, for the Amur Company, and taken out in 1859, struck upon a rock below Ust Strelka, and is irretrievably lost. The Company are engaged however in putting together a steamer with the iron saved from the shipwrecked Orus. Mr. Lühdorf has a steamer building at Liverpool, and another lying ready at Hamburg. The number of steamers actually navigating the Amur is thus eleven, to which three will be added this year or next. The chief carrying trade is however effected by means of barges of twenty-five tons, large boats and rafts. They are constructed on the Upper Amur, and if not required for a return-journey are sold for fire-wood.

We have already stated the cost of conveyance in force for taking goods up the river. Coming down, the charges are naturally more moderate; and, supposing it to be the same as on the Lena, they would amount to seven shillings from Shilkinsk to Nikolayevsk. Arrangements for passenger traffic have also been made, and in 1859 the fares, including board, were as follows:—From Nikolayevsk to Kidzi,

£3 15s.; to Khabarovka, £11 5s.; to Blagovesh'chensk, £18 15s.; to Ust Strelka, £26 5s.; and to Shilkinsk, £30. Half these fares are charged descending the river.

With respect to land-transport much remains to be done. There is a good post road from Nerchinsk to the Selenga, the only one crossing the Yablonoi range practicable at all seasons, though difficult in spring owing to the melting of the snow. On leaving Chita, 1,880 feet above the level of the sea, this road ascends the steep gradient of the Yablonoi mountains, and after twenty miles reaches their summit, according to Maack 4,010 feet above the sea. It then descends to the Shaksha Lake, 3,270 feet, and after crossing the low but swampy water-parting between the Khilok and Uda, continues down the valley of the latter to Verkhne Udinsk, 1,560 feet above the sea-level, and nearly three hundred miles from the culminating point of the road. During summer, goods may be sent from this latter place by water to Irkutsk; in winter, the sledge takes the course of the Selenga River, and crosses the ice of Lake Baikal; but at other seasons a very circuitous and different road leading round the south-western extremity of Lake Baikal must be taken. A courier travelling by the direct road, may proceed from Chita to Irkutsk, a distance of five hundred and twenty miles in sixty-five hours, including delays on the road. Mr. Collins, an enterprising American, has proposed to build a railway from Chita to Irkutsk, but such a scheme, though feasible, can scarcely be expected to be remunerative for many years to come. Much less could a railway through Siberia to European Russia compete with the small charges at present in force for land transport.

From the head-waters of the Amur we descend at once to Mariinsk and the Kidzi Lake, the latter separated from Castries Bay by a low range of hills, five miles across. Several tracks have been cut here through the forest, practicable for carriages, one leading to the head of the Kidzi

Lake, and the other direct to Sofyevsk; and there have been proposals to connect the latter place with Castries Bay by means of a railway. But though the distance between the two places scarcely exceeds forty miles, nothing has been done to carry out the scheme. Castries Bay is in most respects far superior to Nikolayevsk as a port of entry; but for some reason or other the authorities have neglected to proceed with the requisite works. There is no warehousing accommodation, and the merchandise, when landed, lies on the beach, exposed to all kinds of weather. Mr. Esche obtained permission to construct a warehouse; but the site pointed out to him by the authorities was too far from the beach to be of any service. Nor can vessels safely winter here.

We are told that roads connecting the various stations are in course of construction; but we are not able to inform our readers how far the work has progressed. A carriage road from the Upper Usuri to Victoria Bay is said to be completed.

## The Government.

The Russian government is evidently anxious to promote commerce on the Amur and in Eastern Siberia generally. A lighthouse has been built upon Cape Klosterkamp, Castries Bay; an accurate chart of the Gulf of the Amur has been published, and the channel leading to Nikolayevsk marked with buoys and beacons, thus rendering navigation comparatively safe, and enabling a captain to navigate his vessel even without the services of a pilot. In fact, it is almost better to do so. Those usually stationed at Castries Bay are Russian soldiers or "sailors" totally unacquainted with the management of a vessel. Under any circumstances merchants are strongly recommended to send a pilot from Nikolayevsk to meet expected vessels. Government requires no payment of harbour dues, wharfage, or any other imposts of the kind. An Ukase published in May, 1861, declares Nikolayevsk a free port for the duration of twenty years, and merchandise may be sent up the Amur and imported into the whole of Eastern Siberia without paying any customs' duties. Foreigners are admitted to trade on payment of the usual corporation tax, and enjoy all privileges of Russian subjects.

These well-meant arrangements could not but fail to exercise a most beneficial influence upon commerce, if their spirit were acted upon by the local authorities. That such liberal regulations exist at all, is due entirely to the enlarged mind of Count Muravief Amursky; and we fear that now, when the resignation of that nobleman as Governor-General of Eastern Siberia has been accepted by the emperor,[k] they may be rendered nugatory by local arrangements of officials totally incapable of developing the resources of a newly-opened country like that of the Amur. One of the chief complaints is the refusal of the government to admit Consuls, who might act as mediators between the authorities and foreign merchants. At the same time, the perpetual interference of the police in affairs with which they have no concern, and the absence of any fixed laws by which to regulate one's conduct, are a constant source of anxiety. In spite of the free-trade, no vessel must be loaded or unloaded without the presence of two policemen, and in several instances two Cossacks have been placed as a guard before a store—and this for a period of several weeks—with the right of searching all persons entering or leaving. The Governor, Admiral Kazakevich, is evidently not the right man in the right place. He is avowedly hostile to foreigners, and his

---

[k] The resignation of Count Muravief, on account of ill health, was accepted on the 3rd March, 1861; and as a reward for the services he had rendered, the emperor appointed him a member of the Council of State, and invested him with the Grand Cross of the order of St. Vladimir.

amiable private character does not compensate for his ignorance of commercial affairs, an ignorance which places him at the mercy of unscrupulous functionaries. The uncalled-for manner in which he interfered in 1859 in the winding-up of the affairs of the ship-wrecked "Orus" and "Innocentius," gave just offence to the captains and insurance companies concerned, and is perhaps one of the reasons why the latter now demand a premium of six per cent. upon vessels sailing to the Amur. Foreigners have been arrested upon a mere verbal order of the director of the police, and in two instances were threatened with the knout. Legal redress is difficult to obtain, if the complainant be in any way obnoxious to the powers that be, or the defendant enjoy their friendship. A criminal information was laid in consequence of theft and incendiarism on board the wreck of the "Innocentius" lying in Castries Bay; but one of the defendants being a personal friend of the governor's, the affair was hushed up.

The best way to make our readers acquainted with the manner in which commercial affairs are regulated is to lay before them an order issued by the Governor, on the 28th June 1859. It refers to the sale of spirits, which up to that time had been unrestricted. The merchants received one day's notice of its proposed publication; one vessel with a large consignment of brandy had already arrived, and several others were expected. The orders, literally translated, were as follows:—

"With a view of preventing the evil consequent upon an unlimited sale of spirits and liquors to soldiers, sailors and exiles in the service of government, His Excellency, the Military Governor, considers it incumbent upon himself to issue the following regulations.

"1. The Police are ordered to seal up all spirits, such as rum, whisky, gin, cognac, brandy, cordials, etc., brought to this place. As the sealing up of each separate case or cask would require too much time, each merchant is bound to provide a separate room or compartment in which he intends to keep his stores of spirits. This room is sealed up by the police in the presence of the proprietor or his agent, and of a deputy elected by the commercial community. These persons have to make a return of all spirits, their quality and quantity in gallons and bottles, to which they affix their signatures, and which is then delivered to His Excellency the Governor.

" 2. The merchant is allowed a quantity of spirits for his own consumption and for sale to officers, officials, and other persons authorised (!) to become purchasers. If a merchant desire a further supply he has to send a written request to the chancellerie, he will then receive the authorisation required, signed and sealed by His Excellency the Governor. The store is then unsealed by the police, in presence of the deputies, and after each delivery, the magazine is again sealed up.

" 3. Permission to sell spirits is granted only on producing an order from the chancellerie, the staff or commander of the Naval *Equipaye*. This order must be kept by the merchant, and must be sent to the chancellerie at the same time as a request for a further quantity of drinks, and a memorandum stating the quantity already sold and consumed.

" 4. In case of infringement of the above regulations, the spirits belonging to the offender are confiscated for the benefit of the town, and he will have to pay a fine to be hereafter determined.

" 5. The above regulations are not to interfere with the unlimited sale of wines, porter and ales, which may be sold without special permission.

" Merchants trading in spirits and their clerks are required to affix their signatures to these regulations, in testimony of their having read and understood them.

"Nikolayevsk, 16-28 June, 1859.
  "For translation, ALEX. PHILIPPAEUS,
       "Government translator."

The desire of the Governor to prevent drunkenness, one of the chief vices of the Russians, is no doubt laudable; but the bungling manner in which he attempts to do it would be unworthy even the King of the Cannibal Islands trying to set up a civilised government. The merchants were more than ever exposed to the arbitrary oppression of the police, whose favours they had to purchase, as is the case throughout the Russian empire. The only person who really profited by it, and was indeed most instrumental in getting this order issued, was Mr. Philippaeus, government translator, shareholder and manager of an hotel and billiard-room. In one instance, the privilege of selling spirits was altogether withdrawn from a merchant on the unsupported statement of a soldier, that one of his clerks had sold a mixture of cherry-cordial and rum, which was against some regulation. Mr. Bodiscol, one of the satelites of the governor, marched into the store, and after a good deal of vile language threatened to have the clerk flogged. On the merchant's sending in a protest to the Governor-General, the prohibition was withdrawn.

Unfortunately the grievances complained of by the mercantile community are not likely to be redressed for the present; for Admiral Kazakevich, who lately visited St. Petersburg, was confirmed in his post, appointed Aide-de-Camp, which confers the right of reporting to the emperor direct, and has returned to the Amur laden with orders for his subordinates.

### PRESENT COMMERCE ON THE AMUR.

The commerce of the Amur is yet in its infancy; a foreign export trade scarcely exists, and the few European and American ships which enter at Castries Bay or Nikolayevsk, merely supply the wants of the Russian garrisons along the river, a trade by no means profitable, these garrisons having to be maintained at the expense of the government. Even before the occupation of the country by Russia, some trifling bartering trade was carried on there by Chinese and natives. Chinese traders not only descended the Amur itself down to the Gilyak village Pul, but also ascended some of its tributaries, and in winter they supplied the Samagers and other tribes north of the Amur with the merchandise they required. At Pul they met natives of Sakhalin through whom the products of Japan came to the Amur. This trade was of no great importance : the natives exchanged furs and skins for the few necessaries and luxuries they required, powder and shot, spirits and tobacco. Since the arrival of the Russians the trade has assumed somewhat larger proportions, though far yet from satisfying the expectations of oversanguine persons.

Transbaikal which had furnished the men, had also to furnish them provisions. This trade was and still is in the hands of Siberian merchants[m] and contractors. The foreign import trade however is in the hands chiefly of the Amur Company, the Russo-American Company and the foreign merchants established at Nikolayevsk.[m] The grievances of

---

[m] Five foreign firms were permanently established at Nikolayevsk in 1860, viz., Fr. Aug. Lühdorf; Bordtman and Co. of Boston, represented by Mr. H. G. O. Chase; H. Pearce of Boston, represented by Mr. H. H. Freeman; O. Esche of St. Francisco; Cohen and Newman of St. Francisco. Several others occasionally carry on trade, viz., Mr. Burling and Mr. Friesius of St. Francisco, Mr. Pitman of Boston, and Mr. Melchars of Honolulu.

these latter shared in of course by the resident Russian merchants we have mentioned above. We will now give a short statement of the operations of the Amur Company.

The Amur Company was established in 1858, with a capital of £450,000. They are privileged to open commercial establishments on the Shilka and Amur, to appropriate for their own consumption the coal and wood they may find, and to carry on trade with Russians and natives. They are also supplied with fifty pud of powder and a hundred pud (3,600 lbs.) of lead at cost price from Nerchinsk. The company undoubtedly had a fair chance of success, but mismanagement, and the dishonesty of many of its officials have brought it to the verge of ruin. The company has opened stores in the chief stations on the Amur, and might carry on a most profitable trade there, if its officials thought it worth while to study the wants of the colonists. These latter, however profit but little from its operations, as may be seen by the following extract from a letter addressed by Dr. Holtermann, the government physician at Blagovsh'chensk, to Professor —— at Dorpat, and dated 14th July, 1860 :—

" You will no doubt be anxious to learn where we all obtain our daily supplies of food, and I will therefore say a few words on this subject. The Amur Trading Company was started with a paid up capital of £450,000, for the express purpose of furnishing our new settlements with all the necessaries and many of the luxuries of life. This was so generally understood that all private enterprise was stopped, no merchants being bold enough to think of entering into competition with such a powerful company, since, having to get their goods sent by the expensive land conveyance all the way from St. Petersburg, they could not dream of underselling the prices asked by the company. And what is the real state of the case? Why, that after all we find it cheaper and more profitable to have our orders executed at St. Petersburg, and sent out here by the post, which, though the expense is very heavy, being not less than ninepence the pound, comes still much cheaper than if we bought them on the spot from the company, so exorbitant are the prices they ask. This may appear to you incredible, exaggerated, and incomprehensible, but I am nevertheless stating nothing but the plain naked truth. The company have fulfilled only a part of their engagement, and their factories are over-loaded with goods of all descriptions; but the quality they sell is very indifferent, and by their being in virtual possession of a monopoly, they consider themselves at liberty to screw as much profit out of us as they can, and they are certainly not bashful in their extortionate demands. No wonder the shares of the company command such a high premium at St. Petersburg, though it is highly probable that the shareholders, if acquainted with the manner in which their high dividends are derived, would many of them prefer a smaller return for their money, with the conviction of having gained it by fair trading, instead of taking advantage of the wants of the settlers, and forcing them to become purchasers of very inferior goods at the startling and hitherto unheard-of prices."

Another letter dated Nerchinsk, 14th October, 1860, and published in the "Nord," says, that notwithstanding the Amur is navigated by steamers, American sugar has not penetrated into Dauria. "The Amur Company boast of their success and the merchandize which they carry to the Amur, but when spring comes, and any article is asked for, it is not to be had. The company dispose of a large capital, but do not appear to know as yet the wants of the inhabitants."

Dr. Holtermann is however mistaken, if he supposes the shares of the company are at a premium: they are almost worthless. The original value of the shares was 250 rubles, in 1859 they stood at 175, and last year they were offered at 85. The manner in which the company manages its affairs may be judged of from the following statement of their operations in 1859. In that year the company sent three vessels from Europe to the Amur, the " S. Theodosius," the " S. Innocentius," and the " Orus." The " S. Theodosius," 312 tons, had on board an iron steamer, an iron barge, an iron house, and a miscellaneous cargo valued at £7,500, and arrived at Nikolayevsk in safety. The " Innocentius " arrived at Castries Bay in October. She had on board two iron steamers from the works of Cockerell at Seraing, one iron barge, two iron houses, and a cargo valued at £7,500. The Company had neglected to send some person to Castries Bay to receive this vessel; and the captain, unacquainted with the Bay, and apparently not provided with a chart or sailing directions, anchored in an exposed position. A few days afterwards a violent gale blew from the north-east, and the vessel was thrown upon the rocky coast. The loss of this vessel must be ascribed solely to the improvidence of the officials entrusted with the affairs of the company; but a still more glaring instance of incapacity brought about the loss of a second vessel. The " Orus," Captain Prütz, having on board two iron steamers and four barges, and a cargo valued at £20,250, arrived a few days after the " Innocentius" in Castries Bay, and waited there for orders twenty-three days in vain, though the season was far advanced. At last Captain Prütz proceeded to Nikolayevsk in person. Mr. Bellegobovoi, at that time chief manager of the company, shrunk from the responsibility of ordering the " Orus " on to Nikolayevsk, but after a consultation with Admiral Kazakevich the vessel was ordered to proceed to Liman, where the government steamer " America " was to meet and lighter her. This was done in spite of the advice of competent persons to send the vessel to winter at Hakodade. Captain Prütz reluctantly obeyed. Blocks of ice were floating in the Liman, and on nearing the Khazeliv islands the ship sprung a leak. At that critical moment the "America" hove in sight, and pulled the "Orus" on a sand-bank. Part of the cargo was transferred to the "America" and "Japanese" to be taken to Japan, and the remainder, including the hulk, sold for the trifling sum of 8,000 rubles. The merchandise alone was resold subsequently by the purchasers for 50,000 rubles, and in 1860 the Company repurchased the iron taken from the wreck for 30,000 rubles, and are now engaged in putting a steamer together with it!

The steamer brought by the "S. Theodosius" was launched in 1860, and baptized "Muravief-Amursky," but on her first ascent of the river, she struck on a rock and sunk. The Company is said to have lost £60,000 in the first year, £45,000 in the second year, and even a larger sum last year. Its operations now are of a very limited kind, and no orders for steamers or merchandise were given in Europe last year. The bankruptcy of its Director, Carl Brandt, has occasioned still further losses, and the Company, in all probability, will soon have to be wound up.

The *Russo-American Company* also maintains a few stores on the Amur, and the furs intended for Kiakhta are now sent up that river. The Company however enjoy no special privileges, its monopolies being restricted to the American territories and the Kurile islands. In 1862 these also will cease, and they are not likely to be renewed.

The number of foreign merchants established at Nikolayevsk in 1859 was seven, of whom six were American, and one German. There were also two Russian merchants of the second guild and two of the third (in 1860 three of the second, and four of the third guild).

The imports brought to the Amur by sea have of late attained considerable dimensions; we must not however infer from this the increasing wealth of the country, for the goods imported were mainly required for supplying the military colonists; and there are scarcely any exports. In

1857, seven merchantmen entered the Amur (three from St. Francisco, two from Hong-Kong, and two from Boston), the united cargoes of which were valued at £75,000. Besides these, a screw steamer from Hamburg, and the brig "Sitka" arrived for the Russo-American Company. The market had apparently become glutted, and in the following year, 1858, four vessels only arrived, with cargoes valued at £26,197. A rapid increase took place in 1859, and we will here enter somewhat into detail. The following table gives the details of the vessels entered, I., at Nikolayevsk; II., at Castries Bay.

| I. | Tons. | Nationality. | Port of Departure. | Value of Cargo. |
|---|---|---|---|---|
| Constantine | 282 | Russia. | Petropavlovsk | £11,937 |
| Melita | 198 | U.S. | Hong Kong | 15,697 |
| Lewis Perry | 130 | ,, | S. Francisco | 1,821 |
| Bering | 376 | ,, | Boston | 2,220 |
| Emma | 130 | New Granada. | S. Francisco | 10,763 |
| Hero | 108 | Hawai. | Honolulu | 6,699 |
| Theodor & Julia | 300 | Holstein. | Altona | 39,437 |
| S. Theodosius | 312 | Russia. | Antwerp | 7,500 |
| Total | 1836 | | | 96,075 |
| II. | | | | |
| Melita | 275 | U.S. | Boston | 10,500 |
| Tsarina | 1200 | Russia. | Kronstadt | — |
| S. Innocentius | 450 | ,, | Antwerp | 7,500 |
| Orus | 503 | ,, | London | 20,250 |
| Caroline E. Foote | 150 | U.S. | S. Francisco | 17,863 |
| Total | 2578 | | | 56,113 |

The cargoes of the S. Theodosius, S. Innocentius and Orus, for the Amur Company, are estimated at European prices, and the value of the five iron river steamers, six iron barges, and three iron houses, on board these vessels, is not included. Information supplied to us by Mr. Lühdorf, enables us to furnish some details. When a vessel arrives, the captain or consignee is bound to supply government with an invoice stating the prices at which it is intended to sell the goods at Nikolayevsk. The merchants, to avoid subsequent disputes, state higher prices than they actually expect to realize, and the estimates given in the above return are consequently too high. We have already mentioned the loss of the Orus and S. Innocentius, but must observe here that part of the cargo of the Orus was transferred to the America and Japanese, and taken to Japan, and the portion actually entered at Nikolayevsk did not exceed £7,500. A deduction ought also to be made from the cargo of the Innocentius, which suffered shipwreck in Castries Bay. Besides the Orus and Innocentius, one vessel was shipwrecked, and two others sustained trifling damages. The American bark, Melita, 275 tons, ran on a sandbank near Sakhalin island, on her way from Castries Bay to the Amur. The captain prematurely ordered an anchor to be thrown out, the waves lifted the vessel upon it, and she sprung a leak. Otherwise she might have been got off at high water. The Theodor and Julia arrived at Nikolayevsk on the 8th October in tow of a steamer of the Russo-American Company. The consignees detained the ship until the 27th October, and before she could leave the river she was frozen in, and remained in the ice. The damage caused by the ice having been repaired, the vessel left on the 12th July, 1860, for Shanghai, with a cargo of ice for the Russo-American Company. The Caroline E. Foote froze in at Castries Bay, but sustained only trifling damages. The Emma, on leaving Nikolayevsk had the misfortune to lose her captain and four sailors by the capsizing of the only boat on board. She put back, repaired her loss, and reached S. Francisco, leaking and with masts cut. The seven other vessels sustained no damage. Mr. Lühdorf estimates the actual value of imports at £53,000, exclusive, however, of the furs on board the Constantine, and the naval stores brought by the Tsarina. The merchandize imported consisted of colonial and manufactured goods. Further details are not given. We are made acquainted however with the value of the merchandise sent up the Amur from Nikolayevsk, and that received at Nikolayevsk from the Upper Amur.

|  | Imported into Nikolayevsk from the Upper Amur. | | Sent up the Amur from Nikolayevsk. | |
|---|---|---|---|---|
| Sables . . . . | 2868 pieces | £3,494 | 6418 pieces | £8,507 |
| Fox Skin . . . | 53 „ | 7 | 1070 „ | 783 |
| Manufactures . . | — | 2,367 | — | 4,039 |
| Arms . . . . . | — | 2½ | — | 159 |
| Copper and Iron . | — | 154 | — | 83 |
| Crockery Ware . | — | 125 | — | 75 |
| Millinery, etc.. . | — | 1,480 | — | — |
| Clothing . . . | — | 272 | — | — |
| Hides . . . . | 25½ pieces | 20 | — | — |
| Drugs . . . . | — | 296 | — | 219 |
| Tea . . . . . | 1020 lbs. | 300 | 952 lbs. | 278 |
| Loaf Sugar . . . | — | — | 5,992 „ | 285 |
| Ground Sugar . | — | — | 7,094 „ | 434 |
| Wines . . . . | 40 bottles | 23 | 10,908 bottles | 1,630½ |
| Victuals . . . . | — | 574 | — | 102 |
| Cattle . . . . | 144 head | 1,463 | — | — |
| Horses . . . . | 42 „ | 494 | — | — |
| Tobacco . . . . | 15,224 lbs. | 334½ | 397 lbs. | 18 |
| Cigars . . . . | — | — | 794,200 ps. | 1,438½ |
|  |  | £11,406 |  | £18,051 |

An analyzation of this table justifies Mr. Lühdorf in the large reduction he has made in the value of imports, as stated by government. Tea is estimated at 5s. 11d. and 5s. 10d. the pound respectively, being only one penny in the pound in favour of that imported by sea. Loaf-sugar is 11½d. the pound, ground-sugar, 1s. 2½d. the pound; a bottle of wine received by sea is charged 3s., and the wine sent down the Amur, 11s. The tobacco sent down the Amur is valued at 5¼d., and that imported by sea at 11d. a pound. A horse costs £11 15s., and a bullock, £10 3s. Corn, which must have been imported from the Upper Amur in considerable quantities, is not mentioned at all unless included under "victuals." Owing to the irregular supply from the interior as well as from abroad, prices at Nikolayevsk vary considerably. In 1860, a pound of fresh meat cost 5$d$. to 8$d$. a pound of rye-flour, 1$d$., a pound of wheaten flour, 1$s$. 3$d$., an egg, 2½$d$., a bottle of brandy, 4$s$. 6$d$. During winter, fresh meat is scarcely to be procured. The dried and salt meat sent down the Amur is hardly fit for human food, and coarse rye-bread and oatmeal are almost the only other articles to be obtained during that season.

The export trade during 1859, was on a much more restricted scale than the import. Vessels bringing goods are obliged to leave in ballast, there being no articles of export. They would of course be glad to take on board a cargo of timber; but this the prescience of the Russian Government forbids. An export trade, in fact, scarcely exists at all. In 1856 a specimen of salt meat was taken by a foreigner and a large quantity was ordered for the summer of 1857. The specimen however on arriving at Hong Kong was found worthless, and the order was countermanded. Another merchant at Hong Kong wrote for hams, but the barrels on being opened were found to contain nothing but bones. In 1859 the value of the articles exported from Nikolayevsk was £2,967, and they included

| | | | |
|---|---|---|---|
| 83,000 pounds of wool | £1,500 | or | 4½$d$. a pound. |
| 3,646 ,,   ,, tallow | 61 | ,, | 4$d$.   ,, |
| 100 hides | 52½ | ,, | 10$s$. 6$d$. each. |
| 975 pounds of salt meat | 18 | ,, | 4¼$d$. a pound. |
| 361 ,,   ,, dried meat | 5½ | ,, | 2¼$d$.   ,, |
| 740 sables | 1321 | ,, | 36$s$. each. |
| 398 squirrel-skins | 9 | ,, | 5½$d$.   ,, |

All these articles must shortly become staples of export, in addition to the productions of the mineral kingdom, and the forests.

In 1860, there was, if anything, a falling off in the exports, but it is satisfactory to be able to state, that up to the 14th of October not a single disaster had happened at sea. The following vessels arrived at Nikolayevsk:—

The Hamburg brig " Greta," from Hong Kong.
„ „ bark " S. Francisco," from Hamburg.
„ Hawai brig " Hero," from Honolulu.
„ American schooner " Alert," from S. Francisco.
„ „ „ brig " Orbit," „ „
„ „ bark " Bering," from Boston.
„ „. „ " Starking," „ „

The Hamburg brig ",Steinwärder," from Hamburg, was lightered in Castries Bay, and the Hamburg schooners " Franz " and " Louise " were expected.

# APPENDIX.

## HISTORICAL AUTHORITIES.

THE following works by F. G. Müller have laid the foundation for the early history of the Amur, and his successors have frequently availed themselves of his researches, often without acknowledgment.

Sammlung Russischer Geschichte, von. F. G. Müller.
    I. 1732. Albazin and the disputes about it.
    II. 1736. History of the Amur under the Dominion of Russia.

Büsching's Magazin für Historie und Geographie.
    II. 1768. Information about the Amur, by Müller, written 1741.

* Monthly News, Instructive and Entertaining.
    1757. On the regions of the Amur, by Müller.

Additional information on several points is derived from
    Witsen, Noord en Oost Tartarijen. 2 vols. Amsterdam 1692.
    Du Halde, Description de la Chine, vol. iv. The Hague, 1736.
    Eb. Fischer, Sibirische Geschichte. 2 vols. St. Petersburg.
    St. Petersburgen Zeitschrift von Oldecop, 1822.
        Vol. iv. Khaborof's Adventures.
        Vol. v. Albazin.

The following papers are based more or less upon the labours of Müller.
    Scherer, Nordische Nebenstunden.
        I. 1776. Description of the Amur.

---

* Denotes that we were not able to procure the works named.

* Monthly Papers (Ephemiestyachnia Sochinenya).
    1756. History of the Amur under the Dominion of Russia.
    1755. Paper on the frontier of, 1689.
* New Monthly Papers.
    1795. Description of the Amur.
* The Siberian Messenger (Viestnik) by Grigory Spasky.
    1824. Historical and Statistical information on the Amur.
* The Son of the Fatherland (Sin Otechestva).
    1848. Conquest of the Amur in the 17th Century, by Shchukin.
* Journal for the Cadets of the Imperial Military Schools, 1840—49.
    27. Khabarof's adventures.
    29. Albazin destroyed by the Chinese.
    38. Nerchinsk Expedition to the Amur.
    77. The Russians on the Amur in the 17th century, from Documents in the Archives of Irkutsk and Nerchinsk.

The Documents which Müller consulted have lately been published.

    Historical Documents (Akti Istoricheskskie) collected and published by the Archæological Commission of the Russian Academy, vol. iv. 1842.
    Supplements, vol iii., 1848.
    The Muscovite.
        1843. Historical Documents on the Amur (Milovanof), etc.
* The Son of the Fatherland.
    1840. Documents on Khabarof's Expedition, also published by the Archæological Commission.
* The Moscow Telegraph. Edited by Polevoi.
    1833. Documents from the Yakutsk Archives.
* The Russian Library. Edited by Polevoi. Moscow, 1833.
    Documents from the Albazin Archives.
    Viestnik of the Russian Geographical Society, 1853.
        Two Documents. Edited by Spassky.

The following works also contain frequent references to the Amur.

Broughton; a Voyage of Discovery. London, 1795.

APPENDIX.

Krusenstern; Voyage round the World. London, 1802—6, 1813.
Lisiansky; Voyage round the World. London, 1813.
Timkovsky, Travels. London 1827.
E. Ysbrant Ides, Driejaarige Reize naar China. Amsterdam, 1704.
J. F. G. de la Pérouse; A Voyage round the World. London, 1798.
Golovin, Japan and the Japanese. London, 1852.
Lange's Travels to Peking, 1715, 1719, 1727 and 1736, in the "Jetziger Staat von Russland II.," and "Pallas Neue Nordische Beiträge II."
J. Bell of Autermony. Travels to divers parts of Asia. Glasgow, 1763.
A. Brand. Neue Beschreibung seiner Chinesischen Reise. Amsterdam, 1699,
J. H. Plath. Die Völker der Mandschurei. Göttingen, 1830.
Siebold, Nippon, Archiv. zur Beschreibung von Japan. Leyden, 1832, etc.
Siebold, Geschichte der Entdeckungen im Gebiete von Japan. Leyden, 1853.
Siebold, Elucidations to the discoveries of M. G. Vries. Amsterdam, 1858.
Stuckenberg's Hydrographie des Russischen Reiches, vol. iv., contains a good deal of historical information.

Recent Russian travellers have contributed by their discoveries to elucidate the early history of the Amur, and Middendorf especially, gives detailed information on the Russo-Chinese frontier.

Middendorf, Siberische Ruise, vol. iv.
Bulitschef, Reise in Ost Siberien, vol. i. Leipzig, 1859.

Maack describes the ruin of Albazin and of an ancient fort near the Usuri; Romanof those of Kodogorsky; Collins, Albazin and ruins near the Sungari, etc.

The information about the Roman-Catholic Missions is derived from the "Annales de la Propagation de la Foi." We are not quite certain about the position of some of the stations; our enquiries at Paris were without result.

The recent history of the Amur has been derived from a great variety of sources. The Russian scientific travellers are generally averse to giving political information; but personal intercourse with Russian officers and others personally acquainted with the Amur regions, enabled us to test the information of Russian, German, French and English newspapers, and to fill up many gaps. The Revue des deux Mondes, vols. 16 and 18, contains the account of "Une Campagne dans l'Ocean Pacifique, par E. du Hailly." The works of Whittingham and Tronson contain information about the movements of the Allied squadron.

## HISTORICAL SKETCH OF RECENT GEOGRAPHICAL EXPLORATIONS.

We propose, in this chapter, to give a historical sketch of recent geographical explorations on the Amur, in order to enable the reader to judge in some degree of the knowledge we possess at present with regard to these regions. This chapter at the same time will enable us to name the authorities whom we have consulted in the compilation of the geographical portion of this volume.

We may fitly date recent explorations from the journey of Middendorf[a] across the tributaries of the Amur in 1844, a journey undertaken upon his own responsibility, and which has undoubtedly aided in again drawing the attention of Russian statesmen to these regions. In our geographical part we shall speak at length of this journey. A few years subsequently the same region was traversed by the astronomer L. A. Schwarz, a member of the Expedition charged to explore the Transbaikal province between the years 1849 and 1852. Schwarz determined a number of astronomical positions[b] from which we are enabled to lay down Middendorf's route with a greater degree of accuracy. Väganof's unfortunate expedition in 1848 we have already mentioned. But neither the labours of Schwarz nor those of Middendorf extended to the Amur itself, and it was reserved for Muravief's first voyage in 1854, to supply us with the first account of that river. Most of the gentlemen attached to this expedition have published their observations.[c]

[a] A. Th. Middendorf, Sibirische Reise, vol. iv. Preliminary Reports in the "Bulletin de l'Academie de St. Petersbourg, Classe Phys. et Mathem." vols. ii. to vi. Bär and Helmersen, Beitr. z. Kenntn. d. Russ. Reiches, 1855.

[b] Zeitschrift für Erdkunde, 1856.

[c] Permikin, Description of the Amur, in Memoirs of the Siberian branch of

We may at once mention here Admiral Putiatin's journey up the Amur in 1855, during which Lieutenant Peshchurof made astronomical observations.[d] In the same year Shenurin, Raebsky and Chikachef travelled by land from Nikolayevsk to Udsk or Ayan, and thence to Yakutsk.[e]

In 1857, Leopold von Schrenck and Carl Maximowicz arrived at the mouth of the river, the former deputed by the Imperial Academy, the latter by the Botanical Garden of St. Petersburg. Schrenck, on reaching Nikolayevsk, 18th August, 1854, immediately set about building a small house, and employed his leisure hours in making botanical excursions into the neighbouring forests. On the approach of winter he made preparations for a journey to Sakhalin, and on the 8th February, 1855, he started with three dog-sledges, each drawn by twelve dogs. Following the coasts of the river and Liman he came to Cape Lazaref, and on the 13th crossed the narrow strait to Sakhalin Island. On the 15th February he arrived at the Gilyak village Tyk, where his reception was inhospitable, if not hostile. Snow-storms detained him here for three days, and only by threats and heavy payments could he procure shelter and food for the dogs. We may however mention in extenuation of the conduct of the Gilyaks, that their fishing season had yielded a very poor return; provisions were short, and some of them had even gone inland to the Tymy river, where the fisheries had been more productive. Without provisions a continuation of the journey was not to be thought of, and Schrenck resolved to postpone the exploration of the island to a more favourable period. He returned to Cape Lazaref, and crossed the country between the sea and the Amur by following the Tymy river in the direction of Pul. This route generally offers no difficulty, but owing to the heavy snow-storms the tracks of

---

the Russian Geogr. Society. ii.; Anosof, Geological Sketch of the Amur, id. vol. i.; Sverbéef, Account of the Governor-General's voyage down the Amur, id. vol. iii.; Permikin and Anosof, Description of the River Amur; Viestnik, Russ. Geogr. Society, 1855. Translations in extract in the Journal of the R. Geogr. Society, vol. xxviii.; and Permikin's account in Petermann's Mittheilungen, 1857, and Malte-Brun's Nouv. Annales des Voyages, 1859. Also in the "Extraits des publications de la Société Impériale Geographique de Russie en 1856 et 1857."

[d] Petermann's Mitth. 1856 and 1857. Morskoi Svornik, 1857.

[e] Morskoi Svornik, 1857; Memoirs of the Siberian Branch of the Russ. Geogr. Soc., vol. iii.

the native sledges had been obliterated, and it took Schrenck four days to reach Pul, whence he ascended the Amur to Mariinsk. After a short stay the journey up the river was continued. On the 16th he came to the mouth of the Gorin, ascended that river to Ngagha, the first village of the Kile, and on the 25th had returned to its mouth. The journey down the Amur proved rather troublesome on account of thaws and occasional rains, and advantage was taken of the night for travelling. But having once passed Mariinsk the signs of approaching spring were wanting altogether, and at Nikolayevsk, on the 9th April, winter still reigned supreme, the temperature, even at noon, scarcely rose above freezing-point, and deep snow still lay in the forests. During Schrenck's absence meteorological observations were continued by Mr. Polivanof, the draughtsman, and the apothecary, Mr. Lentz, promised to continue them during the summer. On the 25th May, 1855, the earliest date at which the river became partially free of ice, Schrenck ascended with two Gilyak boats to Mariinsk, where he arrived on the 4th June. After a rest of two days he ascended the Amur, but met General Muravief at Pulyesa, and was ordered by him to repair to Castries Bay, where it was intended to make a settlement. This mission fulfilled, Schrenck obtained the desired authorization to ascend the Amur, and on the 6th July he departed in company with Maximowicz. On the 11th of August, our travellers arrived at the mouth of the Usuri, where the Manchu official received them in a very friendly manner, even offering guides and provisions, of course on payment. Having ascended the Usuri to the mouth of the Nor (24th August), want of cotton-stuffs to pay the guides, and the sickness of some of the rowers made a return imperative, and on the 1st September, our travellers found themselves once more at the mouth of the Usuri. On the 16th Sept. they came to Mariinsk, where Maximowicz remained; Schrenck proceeded to Nikolayevsk, and prepared for a winter-journey to Sakhalin. He was absent on that journey from the 11th February, 1856, to the 24th March. We have published in another part of this volume a full account of this journey. On the 21st May the river became partly free of ice, and Schrenck started on his return to Europe, which he made by way of the Amur, ascending that river up to Ust Strelka. As the news of the peace of Paris had just arrived, a detachment of Cossacks who were ordered to go back to their ordinary stations were placed at Schrenck's disposal. His party numbered forty men in all, with a canoe, three barges carrying his own collection, and a boat carrying that made by Mr. Maximowicz. Mariinsk was left on the 27th June; the wind proved favourable, and exactly one month after, the flotilla arrived at the Russian station opposite the Sungari. It was however on entering the narrows of the Bureya that the real hardships began. In consequence of heavy falls of rain, the waters of the Amur had risen considerably, and the current was more rapid even than usual. Towing the boats was out of the question, the precipitous banks affording no space to walk along the shore. Progress had then to be made by the aid of oars alone, in a broiling sun, and this severe labour soon exhausted many of the people, some of whom had moreover suffered from scurvy when staying at the mouth of the river. At the Khingansk post (Pashkof) fresh provisions were procured, and after reposing a day and a half they started afresh. At Khormoldin (21st August) a Chinese official, deputed by the governor of Aigun, met the expedition and accompanied it to Aigun (23rd August), admission to which was however refused. The Cossack station at Komarsk was passed on the 3rd September, and on the 6th October Schrenck arrived at Ust Strelka. He ascended the Argun, in preference to the more rapid Shilka, until the 21st Oct., when the formation of ice put a stop to his further progress at the village Mulachta. The remainder of the journey was made by land.[f]

Carl Joh. Maximowicz had been ordered in 1853 to accompany the Diana as botanist on a voyage round the world. She reached Castries Bay on the 23rd July, and owing to the outbreak of war, Maximowicz landed here, and subsequently continued his journey to Nikolayevsk in company with L. von Schrenck. Having explored the summer flora in the vicinity of that post, he proceeded on the 18th September to Mariinsk, arrived there on the 3rd October, and between the 21st October and 4th November made an excursion to

---

[f] Reports on Schrenck's journeys have been published in the Bulletin de l' Acad. de St. Petersburg, Classe Physico-Mathém., vols. xii. to xv.; the Mélanges Physiques et Chimiques, ii.; Petermann's Mitth., 1856; the Bulletin de la Soc. des Naturalistes de Moscow, 1859 (Catalogue of Insects, by Mochulsky). Of his larger work, Reisen u. Forschungen im Amurlande, part i., containing the Mammals, has been published in 1859, and part ii., containing the birds, in 1860; 4to., 570 pp., 16 plates and a map by Lieut. Samokhvalof.

Castries Bay to explore the marine flora. On the breaking up of the ice, 10th May, 1855, Maximowicz in two boats ascended the Amur, but here, like Schrenck, met the Governor of Eastern Siberia, and was ordered back to Mariinsk. The journey to the Usuri, July to September, 1855, Maximowicz and Schrenck undertook together. Whilst waiting for rowers to take him up the river, in the spring of 1856, Maximowicz made an excursion to Kidzi lake and the river Yai. At length, on the 20th July, he left Mariinsk, and hastening his journey arrived at Ust Strelka on the 20th Oct. On the 29th March, 1857, he was again at St. Petersburg.

Maximowicz has incorporated into his work on the Flora of the Amur[g] the labours of other travellers, including those of Maack, Schrenck; of Karl von Ditmar, the explorer of Kamchatka, who early in 1856 ascended the Amur; of Dr. Weyrich of the Vostok, who in 1853 and 1854 gathered a few plants on the west coast of Sakhalin. The works of Maximowicz and Schrenck are most extensively used by us in our description of the Fauna and Flora of the Amur.

The next expedition to be mentioned is that sent in 1855 to the Amur, under the auspices of the Siberian branch of the Russian Geographical Society. Mr. Solovief presented half a pud of gold for that purpose, and also undertook, the publication of the account. Richard Maack, favourably known by his exploration of the Vilui, was put at the head of it, and was accompanied by G. Gerstfeldt and Canditat Kochetof as naturalists, Fuhrmann, the companion of Middendorf, to prepare specimens of natural history, and Lieut. Sondhagen of the Topographical Corps. On the 18th April the expedition left Irkutsk, and on the 16th May, at Chita, they were ordered to join the third of the military expeditions sent that year down the river. Maack started a few days before, and was thus enabled to examine more at leisure the ruins of Albazin; but the remainder of the distance, as far as the lower end of the Bureya Mountains, which was made in the company of his military friends, was traversed very rapidly. On the 20th August he arrived at Mariinsk, and after a stay of six days entered upon his return voyage, escorted by twenty Cossacks. Kochetof and Sondhagen

[g] Maximowicz, Primitiæ Floræ Amurensis. Versuch einer Flora des Amur Landes. St. Petersburg, 1859, 4to., 504 pp., 10 plates and a map, 17 shillings. Preliminary Accounts in Bulletin de l'Academie, vol. xv. Erman's Archiv. 1858, and Mélanges biologiques, ii.

remained behind at Mariinsk. On the 12th October, Maack arrived at Aigun, and solicited permission to proceed through Manchuria to Tsurukhaitu on the Argun. This was refused, and he continued his voyage on barges, but was stopped by the ice on the 15th Oct. A Cossack was despatched to Aigun to ask for assistance, and Maack was glad when he was invited to return to the town, where he was lodged within the enclosure containing the government buildings. His request to proceed through Manchuria was forwarded to Peking, but negatived, and it was proposed to him that he should remain at Aigun during the winter, and return to Mariinsk in the ensuing spring. The governor however placed no obstacles in the way of his departure for Transbaikal, and even supplied him with seventeen horses and provisions. On the 24th November Maack left the town, and after surmounting considerable difficulties on the road, arrived at Ust Strelka on the 1st January, 1857. The account of this expedition was published in 1859, and is accompanied by a route-map of the Amur from the surveys of Lieut. Sondhagen, a geological map, plans of Albazin and Aigun, and numerous lithographs, beautifully executed. In addition to a diary of the progress of the expedition, we find in it a geological report, a description of animals and plants, and Tunguzian vocabuaries.[h]

In the same year that Maack was staying on the Amur, the labours of the East Siberian Expedition[i] were extended to it. The first proposition to send an expedition to Eastern Siberia was made to the Russian Geographical Society in 1850, when two gentlemen, Mr. P. W. Golubkof and E. K. Hutten-Czapsky, presented for that object £4,680 and £4,220 respectively. As Transbaikal was at that time being explored by the local authorities, it was resolved

[h] Richard Maack's Expedition to the Amur, St. Petersburg, 1859, 4to., 610 pp., 35 plates, 4 maps, £6. An excellent *resumée* of this work has been published by C. de Sabir, in Malte Brun's Annales des Voyages, 1861, vol. i. See also a Paper on the Manègres (Manyargs), by the same author, Bulletin of the French Geogr. Society, January, 1861.—(C. de Sabir has also published, for private distribution, a work entitled Le Fleuve Amour, 150 pp. illustrated and map. Only 150 copies have been printed, and we have not hitherto seen a copy.) Also Gerstfeldt, Ueber einige neue Arten von Platoden, Ameliden Myriapoden u. Crustaceen Sibiriens, in Mem. pres. à l'Acad. Imp. par divers Savants, viii., St. Petersburg, 1859. The same, on the natives of the Amur Viestnik, 1857, Erman's Archiv. xvii., xviii; On the Future Prospects of the Amur, Petermann's Mitth., 1860.

[i] Compte-Rendu of the Russ. Geogr. Soc., 1857-60, Zeitschr. für Erdk., 1857, ii. iii. Viestnik, 1857.

to confine this expedition to Kamchatka, the Kuriles and Russian America. The original plan was however abrogated, and it was resolved to explore the territories between Irkutsk, the Lena, Witim and part of Transbaikal. L. A. Schwarz, the astronomer, was placed at the head of the expedition, and attached to him were Lieutenants Roshkof, Smirägin and Usultzof, Mr. A. Radde, of Danzig, as naturalist, and Mr. E. E. Meyer as artist. On their arrival at Irkutsk, in spring, 1855, General Muravief, on the recommendation of Schwarz, divided the expedition into three sections. The first was to explore the Lower and Middle Amur; the second Transbaikal and the Vitim; and the third Southern Transbaikal and the Upper Amur.

At the same time he still further increased the staff of the expedition by adding to it Lieutenant Orlof, of the Topographical Corps. In accordance with its programme, the labours of the expedition were confined chiefly to Transbaikal and the government of Irkutsk. We only notice here those journeys which have reference to the Amur.

Lieutenant Roshkof, in 1855, descended it. As far as the Bureya mountains, he travelled in company with the government expedition, and thence to Mariinsk in that of Mr. Maack. He wintered that year at Nikolayevsk. In 1856, he was engaged taking astronomical observations along the Amur below the mouth of the Usuri, and in March, 1857, visited Sakhalin, and in the summer again returned to Transbaikal by way of the Amur.[k] The artist Meyer descended the Amur in 1855, a month later than Roshkof, and was then recalled. Lieutenant Orlof, in 1856, traversed the territories of the Oronchons from Gorbitza to the Aldan and Olekma.[l] Lieutenant Usultzof, in 1856, travelled along the southern slope of the Stanovoi mountains to the Gilui and Dzeya, which latter he descended on a raft.[m] In 1858, he traversed the country between the Dzeya and Silimji. Radde, the naturalist in 1857, examined the banks of the Middle Amur, from the mouth of the Bureya to that of the Usuri. He wintered in the Bureya mountains, and in spring and summer, 1858, explored the neighbourhood of the mountains, and

[k] Astronomical positions, see Compte-Rendu, of the Russ. Geogr. Soc., 1856-7.
[l] The Oronchons, Viestnik, Russ. Geogr. Soc. 1858; Zeitsch. f. Erdkunde, 1858.
[m] Viestnik, 1858. Erman's Archiv, vol. xviii. Journal Royal Geogr. Soc. vol. xxviii. Zeitsch. f. Erdk. 1858, v.

APPENDIX. 441

returned at the close of the season to Transbaikal and Irkutsk, with a rich collection of objects of natural history.[n]

Of other government expeditions we may mention the survey of the country between Castries Bay and the Amur by Captain Romanof, with a view to the construction of a railway or canal (1858).[o] Mr. Maximowicz returned to the Amur in 1859, but failed in ascending the Sungari, owing to the hostile attitude assumed by the Chinese population near Sansin. In August he ascended the Usuri as far as the Ima, in company with Mr. Arthur Nordmann, son of the Professor at St. Petersburg. Maximowicz had intended to proceed to Japan by way of Nikolayevsk, but the lateness of the season frustrated this plan, and, instead, he ascended the Amur and Usuri during the winter, and in the spring crossed the coast-range to Olga Bay, whence he continued to d'Anville Gulf.

In 1859, the geologist, F. Schmidt, despatched by the Russian Geographical Society, arrived at Nerchinsk. On the 18th of August he passed Ust Strelka, and on the 4th October, arrived at Khabarovka; he then returned to Blagovesh'chensk, and during the winter made meteorological observations, in conjunction with Dr. Holtermann. He had also occasion to meet there Anosof and Basin, two mining engineers, and Maack, who were able to supply him with valuable information. In the spring of last year, Dr. Schmidt, with his companions Dr. Glehn and Brylkin, proceeded to Sakhalin.[p] D. G. Meynier and Louis von Eichthal started for the Amur in the spring of this year, the expenses of their journey being borne by the Association for the Acclimatisation of Plants and Animals, at Paris.

The first exploration of the Usuri took place in 1858, as a preliminary step to the occupation of that river. In that year, Lieutenant Veniukof ascended the Usuri nearly to its source, and thence crossed the coast range, coming upon the channel of Tartary, a short distance north of Port Vladimir. A detailed account of this

---

[n] Radde, Viestnik, 1858 and 1859; Bulletin Physico-Mathématique, 1859; Journal Royal Geogr. Soc. xxviii.; Zeitsch. f. Erdk. 1859, vi.; Lectures held before the Russian Academy, in Petermann's Mittheilungen, 1860, translated from the "Russkoe Slovo." A large work by Mr. Radde is in preparation.

[o] Topographical sketch of the country between Castries Bay and the Amur, Viestnik, 1859; Erman's Archiv. xix.

[p] Compte-Rendu of the Russ. Geogr. Society, 1860.

journey has been given before. A more exact survey of the whole region extending between the Usuri and the sea, and south to the frontiers of Korea, was made in 1859, in pursuance of Article 9, of the treaty of Tientsin (see ante p. 142). Colonel Budogorsky directed this surveying expedition, which worked in three sections, each composed of an officer and nine assistants. A map shewing the results of these surveys has been published by the Russian Topographical Office. Usultsof determined seven astronomical positions (east of the Usuri?) The Cossack officer, Dariyitarof explored the Suifun, and its tributary the Huptu; and Captain Gamof, of the Topographical Corps, specially detached on that service from St. Petersburg, furnished nine astronomical positions along the Amur, and twenty along the Usuri and its tributaries up to Lake Kingka. He also ascertained barometrically the altitude of several mountains, and made a valuable collection of plants and animals.

In the same year, R. Maack returned to the Amur, and having been joined by Brylkin, descended the Amur to the mouth of the Usuri, where he arrived in the beginning of June. Maack ascended the Usuri and Sungachan, and partly explored the Kingka lake. On the 25th September, he was again at Khabarovka, near the mouth of the Usuri, embarked on the steamer Kazakevich, and on 6th October, arrived at Blagovesh'chensk.

Besides these official travellers, the Amur has been visited by a number of gentlemen led thither by business. Of these the first rank is due to Perry McDonough Collins a citizen of the United States belonging to California, who, appreciating the importance of the Amur regions as a trading mart, induced his government to appoint him commercial agent; rightly judging that in this official capacity greater facilities would be afforded him for gaining a knowledge of the country. On the 7th January, 1857, he arrived at Irkutsk, having traversed the whole of Russia and Siberia. During the winter he made excursions to Kiakhta and some of the Daurian mines, conceived a project of building a railway to connect the Amur with Kiakhta and Irkutsk, and on the breaking up of the ice, descended the Amur. From Chita to Nikolayevsk he spent fifty-two days on the way, and in August left the Amur to return to S. Francisco.[q]

[q] A voyage down the Amoor, New York, 1859. Explorations of Amoor River, 35 Congr. 1 Session, Ex. Doc. No. 98.

Mr. Pargachevsky, a Russian merchant, has given us an account of his journey up the Amur in the winter 1856-7. Leaving Nikolayevsk on the 16th November, he arrived on the 25th of February, at Ust Strelka, thus passing ninety-eight days on the journey, of which seventy-one were of actual travel. The journey, as far as the Sungari, had been performed with dog-sledges, and the remainder with horses.

In 1857, Mr. Otto Esche and Henry Jacoby, two German merchants established at S. Francisco, arrived at Nikolayevsk, where Mr. Jacoby wintered, and in August ascended the Amur on his return to Europe.[s] We understand that one of the clerks of Mr. Esche is about publishing a *Chronique Scandaleuse* of Nikolayevsk, in which the administration of the Russian authorities at that place will be rather roughly handled. Another German merchant, Fr. A. Lühdorf, author of a work on Japan, at present established at Nikolayevsk, has published an account of commercial activity there.[t] In Russia, several statements were published which represented the affairs on the Amur as being in the most flourishing condition, the foreign commerce of great importance, and the importation of foreign merchandise such as to influence considerably the prices, not only in Transbaikal, but even at the fair of Irbit.[u] Mr. Dmitri Savalakhin, in a letter addressed to the Morskoi Svornik, and dated Chita, 2nd July, 1858, was the first to protest against these exaggerated, and in many instances, mendacious accounts.[v] Finally, we would refer to the China Telegraph, a paper published in London, and supplied with information from Russia, and occasionally from correspondents on the Amur, with the latest news regarding Russian enterprise in Eastern Asia.

We have already mentioned in our last chapter, the expeditions undertaken for exploring the sea-coast, but will here recapitulate. First as to the Russians. An "Amur expedition" was organised in 1848, when Captain Nevilskoi, of the Baikal, left Kronstadt in order

---

[r] Viestnik, 1857; see also Le Tour du Monde, 1860, No. 7, where there is however a great confusion of dates. The illustrations are not authentic.

[s] Zeitsch. f. Erdk. 1858, iv.; Erman's Archiv. vol. xvii.

[t] Petermann's Mittheilungen, 1858.

[u] See for instance, Nazimof, On the Navigation of the Amur in 1857, Morskoi Svornik and Erman's Archiv. vol. xvii.

[v] The truth about the Amur, Morskoi Svornik, and Erman's Archiv. vol. xviii. with remarks by Mr. Henry Jacoby.

to explore the mouth of the Amur. Several other ships were placed under his command, and the surveys were carried on in 1849, 1850, and 1851. Captain Boshnak discovered Port Imperial in 1852.

The Vostok, Captain Rimsky-Korsakof, continued the surveys in 1853-4. The Pallas, Admiral Putiatin and Captain Unkovsky, made a survey of the coast of Korea in 1854. The outbreak of the war however put a stop to Russian explorations and surveys, which were resumed in 1857. In that year Putiatin, in the America, discovered Port Vladimir. In 1859, Port Nakhodka and Voyevod island were discovered. Detailed accounts of these surveys are to be found in the Russian Naval Magazine (Morskoi Svornok).[w]

Of equal importance with the labours of the Russians in these quarters are those of the English, called forth chiefly by the late war. In 1855, surveys were made of the coast of Manchuria, from the frontiers of Korea to about 43° north latitude; and a number of bays, including that of Victoria and Port Sir Michael Seymour, were discovered. The results obtained are to be found in the Admiralty charts, from the surveys of H. Hill, S. W. K. Freeman, May, Wilder, Johnson, and Jones, and the "Chinese Pilot," compiled by John W. King, Master, R.N., and published in 1861. Valuable descriptions of the countries visited by the allied squadrons, are to be found in the works of Whittingham and Tronson.[x] In 1859, the Actæon and Dove were surveying on the coasts of Manchuria and Sakhalin. Mr. Arthur Tilley visited Nikolayevsk on board the corvette "Rinda,"[y]

The French, under Admiral Guérin, of the Sibylle, made some trifling observations in Victoria Bay.[z] The United States' North Pacific exploring expedition approached the Amur from the north.[a]

We may also mention here an account of the Liman of the

---

[w] For instance, Rimsky Korsakof, cruize of the Vostok, 1853-4; Morskoi Svornik, 1858; Putiatin, Cruise of the America in 1857. (See also Erman's Archiv. vol. xvii.) Chart of the Channel of Tartary, id. 1858.

[x] Bernard Whittingham, Notes on the late expedition against the Russian settlements in Eastern Siberia. London, 1856. J. M. Tronson, Personal Narrative of a Voyage, etc., in H.M.S. Barracouta. London, 1859.

[y] The Amoor, Japan and the Pacific, London, 1861.

[z] Renseignements Hydrographiques, etc., per M. Le Gras, Capitaine de Frégate. 2nd Edition, 1860. Furet's "Lettres sur les Iles Japonais," etc. Paris, 1861.

[a] Habersham, the North Pacific Exploring Expedition, Philadelphia, 1857.

Amur, published by the Hamburg Captain George Krell (China Telegraph, vol. i. p. 151). Another account has been communicated to us by Captain Prütz, and we have added it to this work as an appendix.

In conclusion, we will mention Mr. Thomas Witlam Atkinson's beautiful works, "Western and Oriental Siberia," and "Travels on the Upper and Lower Amoor,"[b] containing a great deal of information, and conveying a vivid idea of regions hitherto scarcely trodden by the foot of a European. From the route-map appended to the first of these works, it appears that the furthest point in the East reached by Mr. Atkinson was the north-eastern extremity of Baikal Lake, at a distance of upwards of four hundred miles from the Amur. The rather ambiguous wording of the title of the second of these works has led most reviewers to consider the latter part of the volume to be based upon personal experience. Mr. Atkinson however never was on the Amur, and his descriptions have been derived from Maack's Travels on the Amur, published at St. Petersburg in 1859.[c]

### REMARKS ON THE NAVIGATION OF THE CHANNEL OF TATARY, CASTRIES BAY AND THE GULF OF THE AMUR.

*By Captain L. Prütz, of the Arkhangel brig Orus.*

I left London on the 30th March, 1859, with a cargo bound for Nikolayevsk on the Amur, and lost my ship there in the ice. On the 28th July, 1860, I returned to Europe in a Hamburg ship, by way of St. Francisco. In what follows, I have set down my remarks on the navigation of the above waters, and on the resources available in case of necessity.

[b] The complete titles of Mr. Atkinson's works are:—Oriental and Western Siberia; a Narrative of Seven Years' Exploration and Adventures (1847—1853(?) no dates are given in the book), in Siberia, Mongolia, the Kirghis Steppes, Chinese Tartary, and part of Central Asia. London, 1859. And Travels in the Regions of the Upper and Lower Amoor, and the Russian Acquisitions on the confines of India and China, with adventures among the mountain Kirghis and Manjours (Manchu ?), Manyargs, Toungouz (Tunguzians), Touzemtz (see Appendix) Goldi and Gelayaks (Gilyaks), the hunting and pastoral tribes. London, 1860.

[c] See our illustrations, Nos. 7, 8, 20, 25, 29, 41, 54, and Plate 2, Beiton and Long-tor in the Appendix.

*The Channel of Tatary.*—The land on both sides is high, and offers no striking land-marks to the navigator. The depth varies, and is often most considerable near the land, a circumstance rather dangerous to vessels going up and down Channel, as thick fogs occur frequently. Northerly winds and a clear sky are said to predominate from August to April, and southerly winds and fogs from May to the end of July, but I found in September strong south-south-east or south-east winds, with a clear sky, and in August 1860 we had a fresh breeze from the south-west and west-south-west with thick fogs, and in the course of six or seven days the sky was clear for scarcely twelve hours in all. If the Channel were not free from shallows, many disasters must happen. The currents mainly depend upon the wind.

*Castries Bay.*—It lies about thirty-five miles south of the entrance to the Gulf or Liman, and foreign vessels call here to take up a pilot. Large ships discharge their cargoes here, for vessels drawing more than twelve feet cannot enter the Amur. The bay is safe, but has two dangerous places. One is the sandbank Vostok in the middle of its entrance, having but three feet of water over it. Wooden staves with brooms have been erected in 1860 on its north and south ends. Vessels can pass on either side of this bank, according to the direction of the wind, but generally they keep to the south. The second danger is a reef running out for the distance of a mile from Oyster Island. It also has been marked by staves. There are three islands in the bay—Oyster, Observatory and Basalt Islands. The best anchoring ground for large vessels is west, per compass, of Observatory Island, in five fathoms. The bottom is mud, and the anchorage safe, but in autumn the ships are exposed to violent westerly winds, blowing down the ravines of the bay. Further in, the bottom is said to be strong, and not safe.

The southern extremity of the bay is a good land-mark to vessels about to enter. Seal Rock lies at about four cables' length from the mainland; it very much resembles a lighthouse. Vessels cannot pass between it and the mainland. On the summit of the Klosterkamp Peninsula, a lighthouse is being built, and a light is expected to be exhibited here in the summer of 1861. Cape d'Assas is the most prominent point of the northern side of the bay. On the shore of the bay there are only five or six wooden houses, and this settlement is called Alexandrovsk. A harbour master and about twenty soldiers live here.

The navigation from Castries Bay to Cape Catharine, where the Gulf or Liman of the Amur commences, presents no difficulties, and full reliance may be placed upon the lead. Only two navigable channels lead through the Liman, the eastern to the sea of Okhotsk and the western between Capes Catharine and Pronge to the mouth of the Amur. The latter is about sixty-five miles long. It is frequently very narrow, and many places are altogether impassable for ships drawing more than twelve feet of water. Buoys were laid down in 1860 to mark the dangerous places between Capes Catharine and Jaore. The beacon-buoys with flags, indicated on the map, can be passed on either side. Between Capes Jaore and Pronge, conspicuous beacons constructed of wood, have been erected on the shore, besides the floating buoys.

The best anchoring places along this Channel are, about five miles north of Cape Catharine; near Cape Lazaref; near the Chagmut Island; north of the Khazelif or Seven Islands; and near Cape Pronge.

The lead is not to be implicitly trusted, for the depth of the water varies suddenly, and often differs considerably from starboard to larboard.

Between Cape Pronge and Nikolayevsk, a distance of twenty-six miles, there is one very difficult place, marked also with buoys and beacons. The anchorage opposite the town is safe.

The winds during spring and as late as August are southerly; from August to the end of October they are north-west. Navigation is interrupted as early as the beginning of November, but the ice does not become fixed before January or February, owing to the strength of the current at that season of the year, and it does not break up before the end of May or beginning of June. The disruption is accompanied generally with a violent thunderstorm and rain. The cold during 1859 and 1860 was as much as 30° R., and the ice was six or seven feet thick. The snow in most places was from twelve to fourteen feet deep. The breaking up of the ice is not dangerous, for it is mostly sunk by the large quantities of snow lying upon it. The tide is inconsiderable, being only from one and a half to two feet at Nikolayevsk, and is much influenced by the direction of the wind.

Help and supplies are not easily procured at Nikolayevsk. Everything must be obtained from government, who are fully occupied with their own ships. In case of the most ordinary accident,—such as damage to a keel, loss of sails, ropes or rudder,—the vessel can undergo no repairs, or if at all, at immense loss and trouble. Even provisions are wanting still. The river is rich in fish; and the forests surrounding the town contain plenty of timber of first-rate quality, but no one is permitted to fell wood there for exportation.

*London, October,* 1860.

## ADDENDA AND ERRATA.

Page 73. The Russian Clerical Mission at Peking. According to late advices the Archimandrite Gury has been raised to the dignity of bishop. The connection of the Mission with the descendants of the ancient Albazinians is to be restored, and several of them are expected at Irkutsk, where they are to undergo a course of religious instruction, preparatory to their being re-admitted into the bosom of the Greek Orthodox church by baptism.

Page 117, last line. Instead of Shilinsk, *read* Shilkinsk.

Page 132, line 13 from top. Instead of Sybille, *read* Sibylle.

Page 136. One melancholy event in connection with the war, and with which we were not acquainted at the time these pages passed through the press, has been communicated to us by a friend residing at Nikolayevsk in the following terms:—" It is unfortunately true that about 400 infantry were sent at the close of 1855 from Castries Bay to Kiakhta, of whom eleven only attained the end of their journey. With an insufficient supply of provisions, these miserable men, late in the season, left Castries Bay to ascend the Amur in barges. At that time the banks of the river had not been colonised, and when winter overtook the party some 1200 versts below Shilkinsk, they died from hunger, exposure to the cold and exhaustion. The eleven survivors subsisted upon the flesh of their fallen comrades. Government hushed up the affair, and those responsible for the disaster, at whose head is Major-General Busse, who neglected to supply the battalion with suitable provisions, though ordered to do so, went without punishment. The surviving soldiers were sent away, and a Junker (ensign) amongst them was silenced by being promoted. Some years subsequently, the affair became known. It is true in its most revolting details." Major-General Busse has been promoted Governor of the Amur province !

Page 141, line 13 from bottom. The vessels despatched in 1857 to the Amur, were the "Askold" frigate, the screw corvettes "Novick," "Voyevod" and "Boyarin;" and the screw gunboats "Jigit," "Plastun" and "Strelok."

Page 146, line 18 from top. Instead of Griden 14, Rinda 10, and other vessels, *read* Griden 14, Rinda 10, and Oprichnik 2.

Page 148. The Ukase respecting the free exploration of mineral treasures is to take force in 1865, as far as the banks of the Amur are concerned; but along the coast they may be explored at once, on condition of the workmen and provisions being brought from beyond sea.

Page 148, line 13 from bottom. The object of Count Muravief's journey to Japan was to bring about a cession of the southern portion of Sakhalin. In this he did not succeed.

Page 150, line 13 from bottom. Instead of Bries, *read* Vries. The Government has made a grant of land to Captain Vries, but German colonists from San Francisco have not arrived yet. They could only be induced to go there by large privileges being conceded to them.

Page 152. In accordance with Article 3, of the Treaty of Peking, Admiral Kazakevich came to Khabarovka on the 16th May, 1861, in expectation of finding there the Chinese Boundary Commissioners. They had not however arrived, but let the Admiral know that they would meet him in June, at the Kingka Lake. Kazakevich accordingly proceeded there, on the steamer "Mechanic," accompanied by Colonel Budogorsky and forty-five Cossacks. On the 30th, he met the Chinese Commissioners,—the maps of the country were compared, the boundaries laid down upon them, and certified copies exchanged on the 10th July. A London morning paper speaks of this arrangement as a fresh cession of territory to

Russia; whilst in reality it merely carries out one of the articles of the Treaty of Peking.

Page 189. The number of stations between the Usuri and Sofyevsk has lately been increased to thirty, distinguished by consecutive numbers.

Page 199. The present population of Nikolayevsk is estimated at 4,000; the increase being due mainly to the arrival of 1,000 convicts in 1859.

Page 200. Recent researches show that volcanic rocks do not exist on the Lower Amur.

Page 225. The batteries at Castries Bay were dismantled in 1857.

Page 227. The names of some of the bays along the coast of Manchuria have lately been changed by the Russians. Bullock Bay they call Jigit Bay; Sybille, Plastun Bay; Shelter Bay, Oprichnik Bay; Hornet Bay, America Bay; Napoleon Gulf, Usuri Bay; Guérin Gulf, Amur Bay. The Channel of Tatary is called Nevilskoi Channel!

Page 231, line 5 from top. Instead of Nakhimof, *read* Nakhodka.

Page 232. The Russian station Novgorod, we believe, is situated in Posyet Bay.

Page 234. The whole course of the Usuri, and the shores of Kinka Lake, are now occupied by Cossack stations.

Page 280. CLIMATE ON THE USURI.—Mr. Maximowicz has made some meteorological observations on the Upper Usuri, at Busseva, six miles below the Sungachan, of which the following is a *resumé*:— The minimum thermometer indicated, on the 23rd March, $-6°$ F. In the sun it thawed, however, from the middle of March, and the snow disappeared in many parts; but only on the 20th of that month did the minimum thermometer rise above freezing point in the shade. During the night severe frosts occurred until the 12th of April. The river opened on the 15th April, and the last frost observed during the night, occurred on the 9th May. On the other hand, the temperature at noon was occasionally very high. On the

30th March, for instance, 56° F., on the 17th April, 74°, and on the 13th May, above 80° in the shade. The last snow fell on the 4th May, the first rain on the 28th April.

At its mouth the Usuri became covered with ice on the 15th November, 1858, and opened on the 20th April, 1859.

Page 286. Gold has also been discovered on the Modolane, a tributary of the Oldoi, Upper Amur; 3,600 pounds of sand yield 66 grains of gold.

Page 316. To the names of Mammals must be added, Felis minuta, Mustela flavigula, Bodd. and the Mole.

# GLOSSARY AND INDEX.

*The approximate latitudes and longitudes of all places mentioned in the volume will be found in the Index.*

ABBREVIATIONS.—R., *river*; Sta., *station*; Trib., *tributary*; Vill., *village*.

### A.

ABAGAITU, 49¼°N. 118°E.

Abuera, R., 47°N. 135°E. 242.

Achani, a native tribe mentioned by Khabarof; the same as Poyarkof's Natki, and the Negda or Negedals of the present day? 53°N. 137°E. 19.

AchanskoiGorod. Position uncertain, but probably about 50°N. 137°E. 19, 184.

Adams, Russ. Acad., 68.

Agaric, 311.

Agutha, 6.

Ai or Yai, R., 51½°N. 140¼°E. 191.

Aigun, Treaty of, 263.

Aigun, Sakhalin-ula-hotun. The old town stood on the left bank of the Amur, 50¼°N. 127¾°E. 42, 48, 176, 295.

Ailagir Tunguzians, 41.

Aimkan, tributary, of Gilui, 54°N. 127°E. 211.

Aishin, Sushin or Niuchzen-Gin Dynasty, 6.

Aishin Gioro, 7.

Aki, Mangun vill. (51°N. 138°E.) 104.

Akul, head-river of Imma, 46°N. 136°E. 246.

Albaza, Daurian prince. His village was occupied in 1651 by the Cossacks, but again evacuated in 1658. In 1662, Chernigovsky built upon the site Albazin, 18.

Albazin=Yaksa of the Chinese, 53¼°N. 124½°E. 18, 24, 27, 36. Chernigovsky there, 38. First Siege, 46. Abandoned, 64. Geogr., 167, 277.

Albazinians at Peking, 73, 448.

Albazikha, Emur or Emuri, rivulet, opposite Albazin. 168.

Albert Peninsula, 43¦°N. 132¼E. 231.

Alexandrovsk, 51½°N. 141°E. 116, 225.

Aldan, river, 58°N. 130°E. 9, 23.

Alder=Alnus incana, 306.

Alnaster fruticosus, syn. Alnobetula fruticosa, 306.

Amazar, Great, or Lower Gorbitza, 53½°N. 122¼°E. 166.

Amba Sakhalin, vill. 50¾°N. 127½°E. 173.

Amcho, vill., 49°N. 136½°E. 186.

Amgun river, corrupted into Khamun, 53°N. 138°E. 46, 193, 203.

Amgun mountains, 52¾°N. 140°E. 189.

Amumish, Numisha, trib. of Dzeya, 54¾°N. 128°E. 41.
Amur Province, 74, 145.
―― Company, 146, 158, 421.
Anadir, Goelette, 127.
Andrushkina, vill., 53°N. 125½°E. 40, 169.
Angan, rivulet, 52½°N. 126¼°E. 170.
Aniva Bay, 46½°N. 143°E. 113, 117, 200, 284.
Anosof, 118, 436.
Antelope, 322.
d'Anville, Gulf, 42¾N. 130¾°E. 232.
Aom, trib. Usuri, 47¼N. 135°E. 241.
Apaokhin, 6.
Apple trees, 298, 303.
Arbod, mount., *see* Castries Bay, 225.
Argun, river, 50°N. 119°E. 27, 62, 161, 163.
Argunskoi Ostrog, 51½°N. 120°E. 64.
Arsenic, 286.
Arshinski, Daniel, 37.
Ash=Fraxinus Manchurica, 303.
Asheho, a town believed to be identical with Alchuka. Such does not however appear to be the case, as Asheho is mentioned as "a newly-founded town," whilst Alchuka is found already on the Jesuit maps. Its approximate position is 45°N. 128°E. ? 78.
Aspen=Populus tremula, 304.
d'Assas, Cape, *see* Castries Bay.
Asses, 319.
Atkinson, W. Th., 445.

Atychan Khrebet or mount, 55½°N. 125⅜°E. 215.
Avvakum, 139.
Ayan, town, 56°N. 139°E. 129, 134.
―― brig, captured, 128.

B.

Badger, 322.
Bagatirief, Lieut., 56.
Baldachin, native vill., five days above mouth of Dzeya, 12.
Balkash Lake, 53°N. 108°E. 152.
Banbulai, Daur. prince. His village, 52°N. 126½°E. 16, 22.
Barnaul, town, 53°N. 83½°E. 276.
Barracouta Bay, Port Imperial, Haji Bay, 49¼°N. 140¾°E. 116, 126.
Barr, Mr. 197.
Bashnak, Lieut., now Capt., 116, 433.
Bear, 320, 380, 395.
Beiton* (Afanaei), 47, 49, 50, 52, 64.
Beketof, 32, 34.
Belen-ho or Tur, river, tributary of Kingka Lake, 151.
Bernizet Peak or Mount Spenberg, 47½N. 142¼E. 267.
Biankina, town, 52°N. 116¾°E.
Bibikof, Lieut., now Capt., 118.
―――― Cape, Longtor or Daoshe-khada, 51½°N. 126¾°E. (*See* also Longtor.) 171.
Bieluga=Accipenser huso, 334.
Bijan, river, 48°N. 132½°E. 286.
Bikin, trib., Usuri, 47°N. 135°E. 243.

---

* Mr. Atkinson (Travels on the Amoor, pp. 421 and 437), states that Beiton was an Englishman, whose real name was Beaton or Beatson. But though Mr. Atkinson affirms this upon the "very best authority" we cannot subscribe to his supposition. The old Russian documents tell us that Beiton was a Prussian or German nobleman in the service of Poland, who was taken prisoner, and exiled to Siberia. Any one at all acquainted with the Russian method of transcribing foreign names, must feel convinced that Beiton resembles the sound of the German name Beuthen much more nearly than that of Beaton. The latter, in fact, would be written *Biton* in Russian. There are several villages named Beuthen, and the younger son of one of the possessors of the barony of Beuthen in Silesia used to write his name Peitum. In Polish the name of that place is Bithom. Another Beuthen in Silesia is called Biton by the Poles. We believe, therefore, that unless proofs superseding the old Russian documents are produced, the assertion that Beiton was a Devonshire man must fall to the ground.

## GLOSSARY AND INDEX. 455

Birches. Betula alba, white birch — Betula fruticosa, shrubby birch—Betula daurica, Daurian birch — Betula costata, ribbed birch, 305, 306.

Bird-cherry=Prunus Padus, 298.

Birars, a tribe, 30°N. 130°E. 341, 342.

Blagovesh'chensk, 50½N. 137⅝°E. 143, 174, 279.

Bobac, 322, 355.

Bogdanovich, Russ. Academ., 68.

Bogorodskoi, vill., 52¼°N. 140¼°E. 126, 192.

Bokhai or Phuhai, empire, 5.

Bokhi mounts., 50°N. 137°E. 187.

Boland Lake, 49¾N. 136¼E. 187.

Borboi Khan=Bogdoi. Corruption from Bokhai (?), a title applied to the Governor of Manchuria and Emperor of China. 11, 16.

Boshnak, Lieut., now Capt., 166, 444.

Boshniak island, 51⅜°N. 140⅝°E. 190.

Boyarin, Russian title of nobility, equivalent to Lord or Baron.

Boyar Zin, son of a Boyarin.

Boyets, rock in the Ingoda, 152°N. 113°E. 165.

Bratskoi Ostrog, 56°N. 103°E. 34.

Brianda, rivulet, 55°N. 127°E. 10, 42.

Bries, *see* Vries.

Bruce, Admiral, 124, 127.

De la Brunière, 78, 306.

Brusyænoi Kamen, 53⅓°N. 123½°E. 39.

Brylkin, Mr., 441.

Buckthorn, Rhamnus daurica, 301.

Bugodorsky, Colonel, 148, 442, 449.

Bullock Bay, 45°N. 136¾°E. 227.

Burdock, 310.

Bureinsk, 50¾N. 132¾°E.

Bureya, river,=Bystraya? 50°N. 131°E. 43, 177, 203, 205.

Bureya mounts., frequently called Khingan, 50°N. 132°E. 19, 179, 261, 279.

Buri, vill., Usuri mouth, now Khabarovka, 48½°N. 135½°E. 185

Burling, Mr., 158.

Burunda, river, 53¼°N. 125¼°E. 169.

—— or Tolbuzin, Russ.sta. 169.

Burukan, 53°N. 136°E. 203.

Busse, Major-General, 117, 145, 448.

—— Port in Aniva Bay, 266.

### C.

Cangue, a Chinese mode of punishment consisting in wearing a heavy wooden collar.

Capitan rock, in the Ingoda, 52°N. 113°E. 165.

Castries Bay, 51¼°N. 141¼°E. 126, 129, 136, 144, 155, 191, 224, 281, 415.

Catharine, Cape, 52°N. 141½°E. 436.

Cats, 319.

Cattle, 319.

Cembra Pine=Pinus Cembra, 178.

Chado, vill., 46¼°N. 130°E. 263.

Chagmut island, 52¼°N. 141¼°E.

Changa Khan, a title of the Emperor of Russia=White Lord, 55.

Cha-she, village mentioned by de la Brunière. Perhaps Khakhe, opposite Khungari mouth, 50°N. 111.

Chechigin, T. Y. 22, 27.

Chechwiski Volok, 26.

Chernigovsky, 38.

Chetvert, measure of capacity, 10=7·21 bushels.

Chikachef, Capt., 139, 435.

Chinskoi Volok, on the Lena, 28, 38.

Chipin Ostrog, near Albazin, 24.

Chirikof, 113.

Chisholm, Lieut., 136.

Chita, 52°N. 113¼°E. 164, 497.

Chkharbakh, vill., 53°N. 141°E. 273.

Chlia, lake, 53¼°N. 140¼°E. 193.

Chogal, lake, 52¼°N. 140°E. 190.

Chokondo, mount., 50°N. 108°E. 163.

Chotzial mounts., 50°N. 136½°E. 187.
Churinof, Russ. Sta., 51°N. 138°E. 189.
Coal, 178, 286.
Collins, P. McD., 139, 442.
Crillon, Cape, 46°N. 142°E.
Cross Peaks, 51½°N. 140°E.
Cork tree = Phellodendron Amurense, 301.
Cyril or Kirile Cape, 50°N. 137°E. 187.

D.

Dabuka, Lake, 45°N. 133⅓°E. 237.
Dabukyt, tributary of the Gilui, 54½°N. 126°E. 210.
Dalai Nor, lake, 49°N. 117°E. 163.
Dariyitarof, Lieut., 442.
Daurians, a native tribe, 48°N. 125°E. 10, 11, 15, 173.
Daraul, Daurian prince. His village stood about 52°N. 126½°E. 16, 17.
Deception, Obman or Baikal Bay, 53⅔°N. 142½°E. 269.
Delangle Bay, 48°N. 142°E. 269.
Delisle de la Croyère, Cape, 51°N. 143¾°E. 267.
Dere, Deren, vill., 51¼°N. 138⅔°E.
Deshnef, Russ. Sta., 47⅔°N. 132 °E. 182.
Destitution Bay, 49¾°N. 140½°E. 226.
Ditmar, Karl von, 438.
Dobro, Russ. Sta., 47½°N. 131½°E. 182.
Dobikhan or Khue-bir, river, 45°N. 134¼°E. 234, 251, 286.
Dogs, 317.
Dolonskoi Ostrog, 51½°N. 128½°E. 41, 46.
Dondon or Mucheng, vill., 49½°N. 136½°E. 82, 186.
Dosh'chanik, a barge.
Dotzili-oforo, plateau near Usuri, about 46°N. 247.
Dozi, Tung. chief, 11.
Ducheri, tribe, about 48°N. 132°E. 19, 31, 54.
Dui, vill., 50¾°N. 142⅓°E. 156, 269, 286.
Duka or Dukika, tributary Amgun, 53°N. 138°E. 43.
Dukda, river, 53°N. 130°E. 209.
Dye stuffs, 313.
Dyrki, vill., 48°N. 133⅔°E. 182.
Dzeya (Zeya) = Je-üraekh of Yakutes, Ji-onikan of Tunguzians, Chekira-ula of Manchu, 9, 173, 203, 279, 210, 217, 407.

E.

Eichthal, L. von, 441.
Ekaterin-Nikolskaya, Russ. Sta., 48°N. 131°E. 161.
Elizabeth, Cape, 54½°N. 142¾°E. 268.
Elizevskaya, Russ. Sta., 51½°N. 139½°E. 189.
Elk, 323, 354.
Elle-iao-tze, red-haired people, the Orochi?
Elliot, Commodore, 130, 136.
Elms, 305.
Emmero, vill., 49½°N. 136½°E. 187.
Equus Hemionis, is not found in the prairies of the Amur, but confined to the steppes of Central Asia.
Ermine, 321.
Esche, Otto, 443.
Estaing Bay, 49°N. 142°E.
Etu, vill., 48°N. 134°E. 182.
Eugénie Archipelago, 43°N. 132°E. 231.

F.

Fafarof, Ivan, 54.
Febvrier Despointes, Admiral, 124.
Fedorovsk, Sta., 51⅔°N. 141°E. 191.
Feodorovskaya, Russ. Sta., 51½°N. 139⅓°E. 189.
Fin-fish, Balaenoptera longimana.
Firs, Abies Sibirica, Siberian fir or pitch; Pinus sylvestris; Scotch pine or fir, 307.

GLOSSARY AND INDEX. 457

Fox, 321.
Fournichon, Admiral, 124.
Freiburg, Mr., 134.
Freeman, S. W. K., 434
Frolof, Gavrilo, 43.
Fudza, river, 44¾°N. 135°E. 254.
Fuhrmann, 438.
Furruhelm, Capt., 139.

G.

Gamof, Capt., 442.
Gantimur, 35.
Gavrilof, Lieut., 116.
Geong Mountains, 187.
Gerbillon, 57.
Gersfeldt. The name of this traveller has been erroneously transcribed from the Russian as Hertsfeld, a mistake partly accounted for by the Russian letter Г representing both our H and G., 118,438.
Genquen, identical with old Aigun? 55.
Gibson, Captain Sir R., 133.
———— Lieut., 134.
Gilbert or Avvakum River, *see* Olga Bay.
Gilui river, 55°N. 126°E., 10, 41, 209, 214.
Gilyaks, 13, 23, 270.
Gin, dynasty, 6, 252.
Ginseng, Jinseng, Panax G., 91, 253, 309.
Girin, 43¾°N. 126¾°E. 4, 74, 261, 283.
Gishigin, 60°N. 150°E. 145, 154.
Glehn, Dr., 441.
Glutton, 322.
Gogul Kurga, trib. Upper Dzeya, 55°N. 130°E. 12.
Goguli, tribe, about Bureya mounts., 19.
Gold, 286, 452.
Goldi, 84, 92, 239, 244, 263., etc.
Golovachef, Cape, 53½°N. 142°E.
Golovin, Fed. A. Count, 56, etc.

Golovin, Peter Petro., Voivod of Yakutsk, 10.
———— Mission to China, 74.
———— Russ. Sta., 133½°E. 48¼°N. 184.
Golubkof, 439.
Gonoma, Konam, river, 57°N. 130°E. 10.
Gorbitza, Great, or Amazar, 53½°N. 122¼°E. 66, 113.
———— Little, 53°N. 119°E. 66.
———— Village, 53°N. 119°E. 165.
Gorin R., 51°N. 137°E. 187, 203.
Gorinskaya, 50¾°N. 138°E. 189.
Gorod, town.
Goshkevich, 134.
Grabof, Col., 56.
Greta, brig, 134.
Guérin, Admiral, 434.
Gugudar, Daurian prince, his village, 52½°N. 126°E. 17.
Guilder, a florin, 1s. 8d.

H.

Habersham, 134, 434.
Hai-tsing-yu-kiang, 103.
Haji Bay, *see* Imperial, Port.
Hamilton, Port, 34°N. 127¼°E. 140.
Hares, 322.
Hawthorn, Crataegus sanguinea, 303.
Hemp, 312.
Heng-kong-ta, vill., on Lower Amur, position not known, 111.
Hermogenes, *see* Yermoghen.
Hianphu, 6.
Hieromonakh, a Russian priest bound to celibacy.
Hill, 434.
Hodseng, a tribe of Goldi at Usuri mouth, 267.
Holtermann, Dr. 421.
Horner, Cape, 54°N. 142¼°E. 268.
Horolag, Khorolag R., 48¼°N. 134¼°E. 183.
Horses, 318, 343.
Hunchun, town, 42¾°N. 130¼°E. 232, 253.

Hunchun, river, at the town, 152.

Huptu river, 44°N. 132°E. 151.

Hurka, Khulkha or Mutwan, river, 45°N. 130°E. 262.

Hutong, vill., on Lower Amur. M. Brunière was murdered here, 106.

Hutten-Czapsky, exact position not known, but supposed to be 52⅔°N. 439.

## I.

Iarakhan heights, 53°N. 132°E. 209.

Ides, E. I., 71.

Ignatief, General, 142, 151.

Ilkhuri Alin, 49°N. 128°E. 176.

Ilikan, river, 54½°N. 127°E. 216.

Ilimsk, 57°N. 105°E. 26, 35, 38.

Iluam-yu, a large fish.

Imma, Niman or Ema, river, 46°N. 137½°E. 245.

——— Chinese post opposite its mouth, 101, 246.

Imperial, Port — Barracouta Bay, 49°N. 140⅓°E. 155, 226.

Ingoda, river, 51½°N. 115°E. 35, 164.

Inkan or Inkansk, 53°N. 132°E. 207.

Inokentievsky, Russ. Sta., 48°N. 132°E. 179.

Irgen Lake and Irgenskoi on its shore, 52°N. 112°E. 34, 37.

Irkutsk, 52½°N. 104⅓°E. 276, 406.

Irkutskoi, Russ. Colony, 52¼°N. 140¼°E. 126.

Iron, 286.

Issyk-kul, lake, 43°N. 79°E. 152.

Ivanof, 24.

Izenei, 21.

## J.

Jacoby, 443.

Jacha, Joada, vill., 48°N. 134¼°E. 238.

Jaer river, 52¾°N. 135⅓°E. 205.

Jai, village, now Sofyevsk, 51½°N. 140°E. 144, 189.

Jaltula, tributy. of Gilui, 55°N. 126°E. 216.

Jaore, Cape, 52⅔°N. 141⅓°E.

Jare, vill., 49½°N. 136½°E. 187.

Jepko, tributy. of Bureya, 51⅓°N. 133⅔°E. 206.

Jesuits, 76.

Johnson, 444.

Jones, 444.

Jonquière Bay, 51°N. 142⅓°E. 129, 269.

## K.

Kada, lake, 52°N. 140½°E. 189.

Kaja, vill., 50½°N. 127⅔°E. Dzeya mouth.

Kallgan, 41°N. 114°E. 73, 152.

Kaluga, Accipenser orientalis, 334.

Kamara, Komar, Humar, river, 52°N. 134°E. 22.

Kamarskoi, Ostrog, at mouth of Kamara, 51½°N. 126¾°E. 25, 29, 33.

Kamchatka, 144.

Kanghi, 8, 39.

Kandagan, there is a village "Kandagan" on Samokhvalof's map, 49½°N. 129°E. 55.

Kasatkina, Russ. Sta., 49°N. 130½°E. 179.

Kashenitz, 28.

Kashgar, 40°N. 75°E. 152.

Kazakevich, Admiral, 139, 145, 416, 449.

——— Promontory, 52°N. 126½°E. 171.

——— Russ. Sta., 48⅓°N. 135¼°E. 186.

Kentei Khan, or Great Khingan, 50°N. 110°E. 163.

Kenka, *see* Kingka.

Kerak, tributary of the Ur, 53½°N. 126°E. 211.

Kerbeli, river, 51½°N. 132°E. 207.

Kerbi, river, 52½°N. 136°E. 205.

Kerbechi, near Shorna—the Great Gorbitza, 53½°N. 122¼°E. 62.

Kerlon, 49°N. 117°E. 161, 163.

Kerlon, of Amur, 51°N. 127°E. 172.

Khabarof, 14, 16, 27.
Khabarova, vill., 59°N. 110°E. 28.
Khabarovka, town, 48¾°N. 155 °E 144, 186.
Khamykan, 52¾°N. 135¾°E. On Nemilen, 204.
Khai-zi, district in Manchuria, 7.
Khazeliv or Seven Islands, 52½°N. 141⅓°E. 423.
Khankuli rivulet, 46⅔°N. 134⅔°E. 243.
Khilok, river, 51°N. 108°E. 35.
Khingan, Little, the Bureya mounts. —Great Khingan, the Kentei-Khan—Khingan mounts. in Manchuria, 50°N. 120°E. 259.
Khinganskoi Piket, now Pashkof, 49°N. 130⅔°E. 138, 179.
Khingka, *see* Kingka.
Khoekhtsi mountains, 48½°N. 137°E. 184, 236.
Khoicha village, 48°N. 134°E. 238.
Khoil river, 51½°N. 140⅓°E. 191.
Khormoldin, 49⅔°N. 128¼°E. 427.
Khoro or Kholo river, 48°N. 135°E. 238.
Khorolog or Horolog, 48¼°N. 134½°E. 183.
Khrebet, mountains.
Khula village, 49°N. 136¼°E. 186.
Khungar or Khyddi river, 50°N. 138°E. 186.
Khungari village, 48°N. 134¼°E. 238.
Kiakhta, 50½°N. 106½°E. 71, 144, 153, 410.
Kidans, 5.
Kidzi Lake, 51⅔°N. 140⅓°E. 189.
——Village, 51⅔°N. 140⅓°E. 126,192.
Kile, a tribe on the Gorin, allied to the Goldi, also called Samagers.
Kileng, according to Maack a tribe about the Gorin mouth, identical with the Kile or Samagers, 367, 426.
Kimai-Kim, 261.
Kinneli, 48¼°N. 134¼°E. 182.
Kingka lake, 45°N. 133½°E. 231, 249.
King, John, 434.
Kinneli, 41¼°N. 134¼°E. 182.
Kirile Cape, 50°N. 137°E. 187.
Kirensk, 58°N. 108°E. 38.
Klosterkamp, Clostercamp Peninsula, *see* Castries Bay.
Kochetof, 438.
Kochulyu, tributary of Kerbeli, 51½°N. 132½°E. 208.
Kokorei, Daurian prince; his village stood opposite the Dzeya mouth, 18, 24.
Kokhan, tributy. Gilui, 55°N. 126°E. 210.
Kolpa, 11.
Komar, Kamara, Khamar, river, 52°N. 135°E. 171.
Komarsk, 51½°N. 127°E. 138, 171.
Konstantinof, Russ.Sta., 50°N. 128°E. 179.
Konstantinovsk, Port Imperial, 49¼°N. 140¼°E. 116, 226.
Konuni, tributy. Tugur, 53⅓°N. 136°E. 203.
Korchin, a district, 44°N. 124°E. 259.
Korea, Kingdom, 42°N. 130°E. 5.
Kornilof, 113.
Kornitzki, 5, 56.
Korovin, 56.
Korsakof, Major-General, 138, 141.
————Promontory, 51⅔°N. 126¾°E. 171.
———— Post, 48½°N. 135⅓°E. 172, 186.
Kossogorski, 51⅔°N. 140⅓°E. 31, 192.
Krell, Capt., 445.
Kruchina, vill. on Ingoda, 164.
Krusenstern, 113.
Kuang-cheng-tzay, in Mongolia, position not known to us; our inquiries at the office of the "Propagation de la Foi" in Paris were unsuccessful. 98.
Kuburkhan river, 45½°N. 135°E. 249.
Kuduli river, 55°N. 126°E. 215.
Kulja, town, 44°N. 82°E. 410.
Kuprianof, Russ. Sta., 49½°N. 129°E. 179.

Kurga river=Hurka ? 32.
Kurile Islands, extending between Yeso and Kamchatka, 154.
Kusnetzof, Admiral, 126, 141.
Kusunai, 48½°N. 142°E. 157, 269.
Kutskoi Saltworks on the Lena, 57°N. 106°E. 126, 141.
Kutomand or Sverbéef, Russ. Sta., 53¼°N. 124°E. 167.
Kvasinino, Russ. Sta., 47¾°N. 132°E. 182.
Ky river, 48¼°N. 156°E. 238.
Kyoekh-kaya mounts., 540°N.,130°E. 209.
Kyrma, Cape, 48½°N. 134¼°E. 184.

## L.

Ladyshinsky, 68.
Langusof, 71.
Larch, Larix daurica, 307.
Lavkai, Daurian prince ; his village, 53½°N. 122½°E. 10, 14, 167.
Lazaref, Cape, 52¼°N. 141½°E. 201, 426.
Lentz, 436.
Lesseps, Cape, 49¾°N. 140½°E.
Li, a Chinese, 8.
Li, a Chinese mile=608 yards.
Liao or Kidans, 5.
Lifule river, Tadukhu of Orochi, 44¼°N. 135¾°E. 257.
Liman or Gulf of the Amur, 53°N. 141½°E. 283, 436.
Limes, Tilia cordata et Manchurica, 300.

Litvintzof, Russ. Sta.,51¼°N. 138⅞°E. 189.
Lobanof Rostovskoi, 26.
Loginof, 56.
Longtor,* a promontory opposite the Komar mouth, 172.
Lotodin, 17.
Löwenstern, Cape, 54°N. 143¼°E. 268.
Lugof, Russ. Sta., 48½°N. 135°E. 184.
Lühdorf, 443.
Lynx, 320.

## M.

Maack, Rich., 20, 438.
Maackia, 302.
Magiri Tungusians, on the Dzeya, 41.
Malaya Nadeshda, rock,53°N.125½°E. 169.
Mamia Rinso, Japanese astronomer, was sent in 1808 on an expedition to Sakhalin and the Amur, in consequence of Russian encroachments upon that island and the Kuriles. His maps and reports are to be found in Siebold's "Nippon."
Mamia Strait, discovered by Mamia, 52°N. 141½°E. 265.
Manyargs, Manegers, Monyagers, 65, 166, 170, 173, 218, etc.
Manchu, 5, 18,21, 30, 173, 175, 248, 263.
Maples, Acer, 300.
Marble, 286.

---

* Atkinson states (p. 438), that "Beaton was here on the 12th March 1682, and it is probable that he remained some time in the fort which Khabaroff had built, standing directly opposite this singular rocky mass. He may have thought that it resembled some of the rocky cliffs in his own land, designated by the word 'Tor,' not uncommon in Derbyshire, and thus, as a remembrance of his native home he may have called it 'Long-tor,' on account of its extent." Beaton or Beatson, as Mr. Atkinson writes Beiton's name, actually did stay for twelve days opposite Long-tor (see p. 50), but no unbiassed person could conclude from this that it was he who named the promontory in question. Maack's work furnishes ample evidence that there is scarcely a locality on the Amur, without some native name. Besides, there are numbers of words in other European languages similar to "Tor," rock (torris, tour, tower, thurm, torre, etc.), and "long" is equally universal (longue, lang, longa, etc.) But also among the Manyargs, the native tribe dwelling around this promontory, we find a word similar in sound, viz. "turi," which according to Maack's vocabulary means earth or land, and we consider it likely that "tor" is identical with it.

## GLOSSARY AND INDEX. 461

Maria, Cape, 54¼°N. 142½°E. 268.
Mariinsk, 51⅞°N. 140⅜°E. 116, 125, 157, 192, 281.
Marten, 321.
May, 444.
Maximof, 34.
Maximowicz, 120, 263, 435, 441.
Mergen, 49¼°N. 124⅞°E. 74, 262.
Meyer, 440.
Meynier, Dr., 441.
Middendorf, 69, 144, 203, 434.
Mikael Semenof or Mikhailo Semenovskaya, Russ. Sta., 48°N. 133°E. 182, 263.
Mikhailof, Mikhailovskoi, New and Old, 52¾°N 140¼°E. 126, 192.
Milovanof, 41, 39.
Ming, 7.
Mogami Toknai, a Japanese, visited Sakhalin in 1786, and repeatedly afterwards, and advanced to 52°N. on the west coast.
Moho, 56.
Mokcha rivulet, 53¼°N. 127°E. 218.
Monastir, site of Russian Convent, 53¼°N. 124°E. 166.
Mongalia river, 53¼°N. 122°E. 213.
Mongols, 7.
Mordvinof Bay, 46¾°N. 143¼°E. 269.
Moscow, 26.
Moskvitin, 9.
Mosquitos, 81.
Muchem Dondon, 49½°N. 136½°E. 82, 103.
Mukden, capital of Leaotong, 74.
Mules, 319.
Müller, 68, 113.
Mungu-Nongo or Chotziel mounts., 50°N. 136⅞°E. 187.
Muravief, Count, 114, 117, 125, 139, 142, 148, 434.
Muravief, Russian settlement, Aniva Bay, 157, 266.
Muren river, 45¾°N. 134°E. 247.
Musk-deer, 323.
Musibo, landing place, north of Castries Bay, 51⅞°N. 141°E. 191.

Myetlin, 113.
Mylnikof, 45.

### N.

Nadeshda Steamer, 169.
Nadimmi, capital of Manchuria, position uncertain, 20.
Nagiba, 22.
Nagiba, Nagibovskaya, Russ. Sta., 47⅞°N. 131¼°E. 182.
Naikhe, vill., 49½°N. 136½°E. 186.
Naize, vill., 46½°N. 134½°E. 243.
Nakhodka harbour, 42¾°N. 133½°E. 231.
Nangtara river, enters Sea of Okhotsk, 23.
Nara river, 53°N. 130°E. 207.
Narantzum, Russ. Sta., 51°N. 127°E. 174.
Natkani, tribe, 9.
Natki, tribe, identical probably with the Natkani, the Negda of the present day, 13.
Nemilen river, 53°N. 130°E. 204.
Neludskoi Ostrog, opposite Nerchinsk, 35.
Nelly river, see Castries Bay.
Nerchinsk, 52°N. 116½°E. 35, 55, 276, 278, 414.
Nerchinsk Zavod, 51⅓°N. 119½°E. 276, 278.
Nettle, 312.
Nevelsky, Capt., 116, 443.
———— Bay, 47¼°N. 142°E. 209.
Ngagha, vill., 51°N. 136½°E.
Nigidals or Negda, 53°N. 137°E. 204.
Nikolayevsk, 53¼°N. 140¾°E. 116, 126, 157, 197, 276, 281, 425.
Nimakan, and Niman, rivers, 53°N. 133°E. 206.
Ninagir, tribe of Oronchons, 344.
Ninguta, Niulgut, 44½°N. 149½°E. 21, 262, 282.
Nintu river, 45°N. 135°E. 253.
Nishan river, 46½°N. 134½°E. 244.
Nismenaya, Russ. Sta., 50½°N. 127⅞°E. 179.

Nonni, Nonki, river, 48°N. 124°E. 16, 162, 262.
Nor river, 47°N. 134°E. 242, 426.
Nordmann, 441.
Novgorod, 42½°N. 130½°E. 156.
Novo Zeisk, *see* Zeiskoi.
Nurkhatsi, 7.
Nyi Bay, 52°N. 143½°E. 273.
Nyungya village, 48½°N. 134¾°E. 184, 367.

O.

Oak, Quercus Mongolica, 303.
Odoli, 43½°N. 128°E. 7.
Ojal mountains, 50°N. 137°E. 187, 286.
Okhotsk, 59°N. 143°E. 9.
Okelnichi=Official of olden times having the superintendence of boundaries and settlement of boundary disputes.
Okolkof, 39.
Oldoi, Oldekon, 53¼°N. 123½°E. 166, 211, 213.
Olga Bay, 43¾°N. 135½°E. 156, 230, 284.
Olekma river, 60½°N. 121°E.
Olekminsk, at mouth of Olekma, 27.
Oldekon, *see* Oldoi.
Olgamza, 17.
Omutei, 18.
Onon, 50°N. 115°E. 164.
Onon of Amur, 52¼°N. 126½°E. 170.
Oou river, 48¾°N. 130¾°E. 179.
Orlof, 116, 440.
Orel Lake, 53½°N. 140½°E. 193.
Orochons, Oronchons, tribe, 54°N. 132°E. 166, 211, 213, etc.
Orochi, tribe, 48°N. 138°E. 366.
Oroki, or Orotskos, tribe, 50°N. 144°E. 399.
Ostafeva, 41.
Ostrog, a place within an enclosure of palisades.
Otter, 321.

P.

Panova, village fifty versts above Albazin, at Oldekon mouth, 40.
Panther, Felis Irbis, 320, 383.
Panza, Cape, 53⅗°N. 141½°E. Amur mouth, 200.
Pargachevsky, Mr., 443.
Parker, Capt., 124.
Pashkof, Gov., 32, 35.
———— Russ. Sta., 49°N. 131°E. 179.
Patience, Gulf of, 49¼°N. 143½°E. 267.
Peking, Russian Missions to, Ides 71, Golovkin 68, Langusof 71, Golovin 72, Perovsky 73, Petrillovskoi 22, Milovanof 39, Spafarik 40, Venukof and Fafarof 54, Loginof 56, Korovin 56, Golovnin 113, Perovsky 73, Ignatief 143, 157.
Perm, 58°N. 56°E. 408.
Permikin, 118, 434.
Perovsky, Counc. of State, 73.
Perfirief, Max, 9.
Pereyra, Jesuit, 57.
Pesh'churof, Capt., 435.
Peter the Great, Bay of,=Victoria Bay, 42°N. 132°E. 153.
Petrillovskoi, A. Ph., 22.
Petrof, Yushkof, 11.
Petropavlovsk, 53°N. 159°E. 122, 125, 128.
Petrovskaya, Russ. Sta., 48½°N. 134½°E. 184.
Petrovskoi, 116.
Petrovsk or Petrovskoi Zavod in Transbaikal, 51°N. 110°E. 409.
Petun, 45¼°N. 125°E. 74.
Phuhai or Bokhai, empire, 5.
Picea, *see* Pitch and Spruce.
Pigs, 319.
Pilavo, Piliuvo, 50¼N. 142¼E. 270.
Pines. Pinus Cembra=Siberian or Cembra Pine, P. Manchurica= Manchu Pine or Cedar; P. sylvestris=Scotch fir, 308.
Pique Bay, 44⅜N. 136½E. 228.
Pisina, Russ. Sta., 48°N. 131°E. 181.

Pitch=Picea Ayanensis, 307.
Pogobi, Cape, 52¼N. 141½E. 201.
Pokrovskaya Sloboda, near Albazin, 40.
Polecat, 321.
Polikarpoyevskaya, Russian post, 48¼°N. 131°E. 181.
Polivanof, 436.
Polyaekof, 24.
Pompeyevskaya, Russ. Sta., 48½N. 131°E. 181.
Poplars, 305.
Poplonski, Capt., 116.
Popof, Lieut., 118.
Potapof, 33, 36.
Poyarkof, Vasilei, 10.
——— Russ. post, 49⅓°N. 128¼°E. 179.
Price, Admiral, 123.
Prokopief, Nikita, 24.
Promyshleniks, adventurers who go to Siberia to seek their fortunes, but generally lead miserable lives as huntsmen.
Pronge, Cape, 52¾°N. 141¼°E. 436, 200.
Prunes, 302.
Prütz, Capt., 147, 445.
Pshangar, mounts., or Vakaz, 52°N. 143°E. 273.
Pud=36·106 English pounds.
Pul or Pulo, vill., 52½°N. 140¼°E. 75, 105, 193, 420.
Pulyesa, village, above Sofyevsk, 424.
Pushkin, Lieut., 134.
Pushchin, 67.
Pustoi Island, 51⅔N. 140½E. 190.]
Putiatin, Admiral, 116, 120, 131, 139, 435, 444.

R

Racoon dog, 322.
Radde, Russ. Sta., 48⅔°N. 130⅓°E. 179.
Radde, Naturalist, 440.
Raebsky, Lieut., 435.
Ragusinsky, Count Sava Vladislavich, 68, 72.
Rakovia Harbour, Kamchatka, 128.
Rats, 323.
Reindeer, 318, 339, 398.
Rhododendron, 310.
Rimsky-Korsakof, Capt., 117, 444.
Rinso, *see* Mamia.
Roe, 322, 354, 356.
Romanof, Capt., 144, 441.
Rosemary, wild=Ledum palustre.
Roshkof, 440.
Rusinof, 69.
Rybenskoi, 56.
Russo-American Company, 424.

S.

Sable, 321.
Salmon-trout Bay, *see* Aniva Bay.
——— R., *see* Castries Bay.
Sakhalin-ula-hotun=Aigun.
Sakhalin island, 75, 265, 343.
Samalga river, 48°N. 139½°E. 239.
Sansin, Ilan-hala of Manchu, 46⅓°N. 129⅔°E. 79, 82, 88, 263, 296.
Sargu Lake, 49¾°N. 137°E. 187.
Savalàkhin, 443.
Savin, Lieut., 116.
Schelling, Baron, 134.
Schmidt, F., 441.
Schrenck, L. v., 120, 268, 435.
Schwarz, 424, 440.
Seals, 323.
Sedge-grass, Calamagrostis purpurea, 313.
Selenginsk, 51°N. 107°E. 56, 414.
Selimda = Silimji.
Selimbrinskoi Ostrog, 52°N. 129°E. 41, 46.
Senotrussof, 43.
Serkof, 69.
Service-tree, Sorbus Aucuparia, 299, 303.
Shakhmati, Russ Sta., 51½°N. 139°E. 189.

Shaman, a Tunguzian word meaning exorciser of spirits, 364, 384, 392.
Sham-mao-tze = Long-haired people (the Manguns?).
Shan-alin = white mountains, 43°N. 128°E. 4, 259.
Shelekhof, Russ. Sta., 51°N. 138½°E.
Shelesin, 67.
Shelter Bay, 44½°N. 136°E. 229.
Shemelin, 114.
Shenurin, 435.
Shetilof, 68.
Shelgenei, Daurian prince, 18.
Shilka river, 52°N. 117°E. 8, 9, 33, 165.
Shilkinskoi, 52¼°N. 118⅔°E. 165, 406.
Shivili river, 53½°N. 136°E. 209.
Shobelzin, 68.
——— Russ. Sta., 49½°N. 129°E. 179.
Shologon, tribe of Oronchons, 344.
Shorna, 53°N. 119°E. 66.
——— Ur or Urka, 53½°N. 122½°E. 62, 66.
Shunchi, Emperor of China, 8, 17.
Shygoey or Shevei, 5.
Sibku, river and vill., 47°N. 134°E. 242.
Sihote-alin, the Coast Range, 470°N. 137°E. 232.
Silimja, Silimda or Selimba, river, 52°N. 130°E. 208, 219.
Silver, 286.
Silvi, vill., 48°N. 133°E. 377.
Sim, river, 48°N. 135½E. 239.
Simoniof, 26, 32, 36.
Sin boyarskoi = son of a boyar or nobleman.
Sinyavin, 56.
Sira-muren, river, 43°N. 123°E. 259.
Siranusi, Japanese Settlement, 46°N. 142°E. 267.
Sisan = Sakhalin.
Sitka, brig, 127.
Situkhu, Little, river, d'Anville's Carma, 45½°N. 135°E. 256.
Situkhu, Great, river, d'Anville's Kuzumé, 45¾°N. 135°E. 251.
Siza, vill., 48½°N. 135°E. 185.
Skripitzin, Ivan, 164.
Skripizin, Col. Feder, 56.
Sloboda, large vill., having one street
Smalenberg, A. v., 56.
Smerenkur, tribe of Gilyaks on Sakhalin, 389.
Smirägin, Lieut., 440.
Sofyvesk, town, 51½°N. 140°E. 144, 189.
Sokha, a primitive kind of plough used in Siberia, hook-plough.
Sole river, 49°N. 138°E. 186.
Solomon's Seal, Polygonatum, 311.
Soldatovo, settlement opposite Albazin, 53°N. 124½°E. 40.
Solons, tribe, 357.
Solovief, 428, 438.
Sol Vuichegodsk, village in the government of Volagda, 14.
Sondhagen, Lieut., 438.
Sorok = 40 skins.
Song, river, 49½°N. 128°E.
Spafarik, 40.
Spaskaye, Russ. Sta., 48½°N. 138½°E. 184.
Spruce, Picea obovata.
Squirrels, 322, 350.
Stag, 322.
Stanovoi mountains, including the Olekma and Dzeya mts., 56, 202.
Stepanof, 27, 33, 36.
——— Russ. Sta., 48°N. 133¼°E. 182.
Stirling, Admiral, 133.
Stolnik = "Carver" to the Tsar, a dignity now extinct.
Stretyinsk, 52⅓°N. 118°E. 144, 163, 407.
Stuiver, a Dutch coin, value about 1*d*.
Suchi, Cossack vill., 51⅔°N. 140⅓°E. 192.
Suffren Bay, 47¼°N. 139°E. 227.
Sungachan river, 45°N. 134°E. 234, 247.

Sungari, Shingal, river, 46°N. 128°E. 12, 22, 28, 32, 161, 182, 259.
Sungarskoi Piket, 48°N. 133°E. 138.
Susu, vill., 47°N. 130¾°E. 84, 264.
Sverbéef, Capt., 118, 435.
——— promontory, 49°N. 130¾°E.
Sybille Bay, 44°N. 136¼°E. 228.

T.

Taba Tabamatsi, river, 51¾°N. 141°E. 191.
Tabakh Cape, 53°N. 141°E. 200.
Tamara, a large fish, sturgeon.
Tanda, 55°N. 125°E. 214.
Targachins, tribe dwelling about Mergen, 50, 365.
Tatar monuments, 53°N. 140°E. 191.
Tatary, channel of, 50°N. 141°E. 283, 435.
Tendi river, tributy. of Ur, 53¾°N. 125¼°E. 211.
Tebakh, Cape, 53°N. 141¼E. 200.
Ternai Bay, 45¼°N. 137¼°E. 224.
Thui-tsu, 7.
Tiger, 320, 382.
Tilley, Arthur, 444.
Tobacco, 311.
Tokose, 310.
Tolbuzin, Larion, 37,
——— Alexi, 46, 49, 52.
Tolga, Daurian prince; his village, 50¼°N. 127¾°E. 18.
Tomi, river, 51¼°N. 128¼°E. 221.
Tomsk, 56½°N. 85°E. 9.
Toro rivulet, 52¾°N. 126¼°E. 170.
Tousemtz, or rather Tuzemtz, the Russian for Native. Maack describes the Tuzemtz at the Sungari mouth; and Atkinson was thus led to suppose the name applied to some particular tribe.
Transbaikal, the province beyond Lake Baikal, 404.
Treaties, Nerchinsk 54, Kiakhta 72, Aigun 144, Tientsin 73, Peking 151, 449.
Tro Gilyaks, on Sakhalin, 389.
Troitsk Monastery, on the Lena, 38.
Tronson, 229, 434.
Tsagayan, Cape, 52°N. 126⅓°E. 170.
Tsichevskaya, Russ. Sta., 49¾°N. 128°E 179.
Tsifaku, river, 46½°N. 134½°E. 243.
Tsitsikar, town, 47½°N. 123¾°E. 74.
Tsurukhaitu, 50⅓°N. 119°E. 71, 163.
Tsyan-chzu, district of Manchuria, 7.
Tugur, river, 53½°N. 136°E. 23, 203.
Tugursk, old Russian fort on the Tugur, 23.
Tugir or Tungir, river, 55°N. 121°E. 38.
Tugirsk, old fort on Tugir, 14, 22, 28.
Tukorindo glacier, 54°N. 127½°E. 217.
Tumen river, 43°N. 130°E. 152, 232.
Tunguzians, 4, 55, 339, etc.
Tundra, a mossy and swampy tract, resting upon a frozen subsoil.
Turczaninow, 64.
Turme, vill., 48½°N. 135°E. 184, 238.
Turuncha, 18.
Twan-moa-tze, people who shave the head.
Tyan-min, Nurkhatzi or Tai-tzu, 8.
Ty, Neva or Boronai.
Tyk, vill., 51¾°N. 141¾°E. 270, 425.
Tymy, on Sakhalin, 51¾°N. 143½°E. 270.
——— Mainland, 52½°N. 140°E. 425.
Tyr, vill., 53°N. 140°E. 154, 193.

U.

Uchalda, river, identical with the Ud, 9, 23.
Uchur river, 58°N. 132°E. 10.
Uchurva, 20.
Ud river, 54°N. 125°E. 9, 62.
Udinsk, 52°N. 107°E. 56, 414.
Udskoi, 54½°N. 134½°E. 145.
Udal or Chogal Lake, 52½°N. 139¾°E. 190, 193.
Ukakyt, 53°N. 136°E 204.

Ukhtr, Uktu, vill., opposite Bogorodskoi, 52°N. 140¼°E. 105.
Uksumi, vill., 49°N., 136½°E. 286.
Ula grass, 313.
Uligari Tribe, 41.
Ulu biri, Manchu Station, mouth of Oou, 48⅔°N. 130⅔°E. 179.
Ulusu Modon, Manchu Sta., 51⅓°N. 127°E. 172.
Ulya river, 59°N. 142°E. 9, 13.
Umaltin river, 51°N. 133°E. 206.
Umlekan river, 52⅓°N. 127⅔°E. 11, 218.
Unkovsky, Capt., 444.
Ur; Shilova of old Cossacks, 54°N. 125°E. 10, 211.
Urga, town, 48°N. 106°E. 152.
Urka, Uruchi, river, 53⅓°N. 122½°E. 10, 14, 24, 28.
Uryupina, vill., 52⅓°N. 120°E. 164.
Urup, island, 46⅔°N.150°E. 116, 135.
Ushakof, Col., 139.
Usur and Usourdur, tributs. of the Silimji, 53°N. 131⅓°E. 209.
Usuri, river, 47°N. 135°E. 89, 234, 250, 280, 450.
Usultzof, Lieut., 213, 440.
Ust, mouth.
Ust Dukikanskoi, 53°N. 138°E. 43, 46.
Ust Kut or Ust Kutskoi Saltworks, 57°N. 106°E. 28, 38.
Ust Strelka, 53½°N. 121¾°E. 163, 166, 212.
Ust Zeisk, 50½°N. 127⅔°E. 138, 222.
Uvarof, 23.

### V.

Vaganof, 114, 434.
Vanda, mounts., 49½°N. 134°E. 186.
Vasilief, 69.
Vazilief, 24.
Venault, 100.
Veniukof, 100, 441.
Venukof (Nikifor).

Verkhne Udinsk, Old Udinsk, 52°N. 107°E. ?,414.
Verolles, 78.
Victoria Bay, 43°N. 132°E. 231.
Vitim river, 54°N. 116°E. 10.
Vladimir Bay, 43¼°N. 135½°E. 140, 229, 284.
Vladivostok, Port May, 43¼°N. 132°E. 156, 231.
Vlassof, Ivan, 49, 58.
—— Ivan Zin, 56.
Voikof, Fedor, D., 41.
—— Andrei, 43.
Voilochnikof, 46.
Voivod=Duke.
Voken river, 46¼°N. 130°E. 242.
Vongo river, 45°N. 134¼°E. 234, 253.
Vorovskaya Pad, vill. on Ingoda, 51½°N. 115°E. 165.
Voskresenskaya, Russ. Sta., 48°N. 133°E. 182.
Vosnesenskaya, Russ. Sta., 48¼°N. 133½°E. 184.
Vries, Capt., 150.

### W.

Walnut, Juglans Manchurica, 302.
Wanda or Uandy Cape, 51½°N. 142°E. 269.
Weasel, 321.
Wei-tze-keu, vill. ten leagues East of Sansin, 101.
Werkholinsk, 55N°. 105°E. 27.
Weyrich, Dr., 438.
White Whale, Delphinapterus Leucas, 313.
Whittingham, 434.
Wilder, 434.
Willows, 304.
Wolf, 321.
Woodsia ilvensis, rock woodsia, 310.

### Y.

Yablonoi Khrebet, Apple mountains, 58°N. 115°E. 163.

# GLOSSARY AND INDEX. 467

Yaksa=Albazin.
Yakutes, tribe of Siberia, 204, 208.
Yakutsk, 62°N. 130°E. 9, 14, 16, 22, 24, 31, 40.
Yang-koan, vill. Leaotong province, 98.
Yashnoi Simovie, Winter-habitation where the tribute is collected.
Yassak, tribute in furs.
Yekaterino Nikolskoi, Russ. Sta., 48°N. 131°E. 262.
Yeniseisk, 58°N. 97°E. 9.
Yerebtzof, Russ. Sta., 51°N. 138½°E. 189.
Yermoghen, Hermogenes, 38, 47.
Yeshen, district of Manchuria, 7.
Yew, Taxus baccata, 307.
Yome Lake.
Yupitatze, Fish-skin people (the Goldi).
Yuen, dynasty, 7.

## Z.

Zavod, manufactory, smelting works.
Zeiskoi Ostrog, 54°N. 127¼°E. 41, 46.
Zeya, *see* Dzeya.
Zorok, forty skins.
Zorokin, 27, 36.
Zimovie, wintering-place.

www.ingramcontent.com/pod-product-compliance
Lightning Source LLC
Chambersburg PA
CBHW021420300426
44114CB00010B/570